# The Story of England

*By the same author*

In Search of the Dark Ages
In Search of the Trojan War
The Smile of Murugan: A South Indian Journey
In the Footsteps of Alexander the Great
Legacy: The First Civilizations
Domesday
In Search of England
The Story of India

# The Story of England

MICHAEL WOOD

VIKING

*an imprint of*

PENGUIN BOOKS

VIKING

Published by the Penguin Group

Penguin Books Ltd, 80 Strand, London WC2R ORL, England

Penguin Group (USA) Inc., 375 Hudson Street, New York, New York 10014, USA

Penguin Group (Canada), 90 Eglinton Avenue East, Suite 700, Toronto, Ontario, Canada M4P 2Y3
(a division of Pearson Penguin Canada Inc.)

Penguin Ireland, 25 St Stephen's Green, Dublin 2, Ireland (a division of Penguin Books Ltd)

Penguin Group (Australia), 250 Camberwell Road, Camberwell, Victoria 3124, Australia
(a division of Pearson Australia Group Pty Ltd)

Penguin Books India Pvt Ltd, 11 Community Centre, Panchsheel Park, New Delhi – 110 017, India

Penguin Group (NZ), 67 Apollo Drive, Rosedale, North Shore 0632, New Zealand
(a division of Pearson New Zealand Ltd)

Penguin Books (South Africa) (Pty) Ltd, 24 Sturdee Avenue, Rosebank, Johannesburg 2196, South Africa

Penguin Books Ltd, Registered Offices: 80 Strand, London WC2R ORL, England

www.penguin.com

First published 2010

1

Copyright © Michael Wood, 2010

The moral right of the author has been asserted

Set in 12/14.75 Bembo Book MT Std
Typeset by TexTech International
Printed in Great Britain by Clays Ltd, St Ives plc

A CIP catalogue record for this book is available from the British Library

ISBN: 978-0-670-91903-1

www.greenpenguin.co.uk

# Contents

## *Contents*

# List of Illustrations

# List of Maps

# Acknowledgements

A project like this involving book and films is a team effort in the best sense of the word. The last year we have spent great deal of time in Kibworth, and this book could not have been written, nor the films it accompanies made, without the help of the people of Kibworth Harcourt, Kibworth Beauchamp and Smeeton Westerby; to them my heartfelt thanks for their hospitality, generosity and friendship. What Leslie Clarke wrote about their predecessors in 1944 (see p. 402) is still true. Warm thanks are also due to the Warden and Fellows of Merton College, Oxford, and the staff of the Leicestershire and Rutland Record Office at Wigston; we have made many visits to these institutions, whose members have been incredibly generous with their time and access to their wonderful archives; to both not only thanks but our deep appreciation of their role in promoting the humanities today. Julia Walworth, Librarian of Merton College, and Julian Reid, the college archivist, were unfailingly generous with their time and their expertise: it was a true privilege to have access to one of the most extraordinary libraries in the world. Thanks, too, to Robin Jenkins at the Wigston Record Office for his tremendous help, good humour and knowledge, and his generosity in bringing his precious documents out to the places where they were written: at a time of cuts to the humanities such a welcoming and accessible institution shows exactly why history matters to all of us. A very special thanks is also due to the 'onlie begetter' of this project, Cicely Howell, who from across the other side of the world, amid all her other commitments, most generously fired off advice and suggestions, and between trips to the outback for her present work in conservation, scanned transcripts of medieval documents and supplied maps from her old Kibworth researches. Thanks as well to George and Pamela Weston, Philip Porter and the members of the Kibworth History Society: founts of knowledge on the story of the village and unstinting in answering our frequent requests for help and advice; to Professor Chris Dyer, who generously gave his time and anchored us in the real lives of our medieval ancestors; likewise to Peter Liddle of Leicester County Council, who offered his unfailing generosity and many memorable insights; to Dr Carenza Lewis and Cat Ranson, who set the ball rolling with a fantastic weekend on the Big Dig and helped us afterwards as the impact of the finds sank home, aided and abetted by Paul Blinkhorn, with his irrepressible verve and great expertise. Thanks also to Charles Phythian-Adams, the staff of the Jewry Wall Museum, Leicester, the National Archives at Kew, the British Library, the Women's Library, the Harborough Museum and the Bodleian Library in Oxford.

In Kibworth I would especially like to thank everybody who participated in the Kibworth Big Dig and in the History Day, the pupils and staff at Kibworth High School, Martin Brown, Bill Pringle, Clare Edgeworth, John Mulholland, John Sharman, Kibworth Parish Council and Kibworth Cricket Club. I would also like to thank the following individuals: Stephen Butt of BBC Radio Leicester, who helped it all happen on the ground, Abraham Smith and family, Andrew and Bev Southerden, Andy Cooper, Angela Edwards, Anita Harrison at the Leicester Guildhall, Simon Jones, Benjamin Nicholas and the Choir of Merton College, Betty Ward, Wayne Coleman and family, Rose Holyoak, Bryan Porteous, Celia Ponting of the Hallaton Field Work Group, Charles and Pam Tear, Chris Standish, Professor David Carpenter, David McGrory, Dr David Cox, Robert Howard, David and Amanda Churchill, Nick and Janet Davis and family, Debbie Miles-Williams, Pauline Carroll, Deborah Sawday, the staff of the Bewicke Arms in Hallaton, the Mercers' Company, Edward Garnier MP, Eileen Bromley, Elaine Robb-Murphy, Emma Boyd, Eric Moss, Alison Foster, Fiona Ure of Leicester County Museums, Frank Hargrave, Gareth Owen and the Sealed Knot Society, Glyn Hatfield, West Stow Anglo-Saxon Village, Gordon Arthur, Dr Graham Jones, Jim and Helen French, Hilary Surridge, Iris Pinkstone, Isobel Cullum, Jamie Whitcomb of the Relay for Life Kibworth, Kibworth Methodist Church, Jane Pudsey from Coventry Archives, Jane May at the New Walk Museum, Janet Briggs of Windmill Farm, Bob and Janet Connelly, Jean Clarke and the Great

Bowden Archaeological Heritage Group, Jeremy Taylor of the University of Leicester, Jess Jenkins at the Record Office in Wigston for her great generosity in allowing me to use her unpublished researches, Joan Croxford of the Manor House at Kibworth Beauchamp, Joan Fillingham, John Capps and John and Christine Brammall of the Hallaton Field Group, Judith Bayes (the daughter of Bert Aggas), Professor Judith Jesch of the Nottingham University Centre for Viking Studies, Julian Barker, Julia Aalen at Weald and Downland, Ken and Hazel Wallace of the Hallaton Field Group, Dr Kevin Feltham of the Kibworth Harcourt Conservation Society, Laura Hadland of Leicester City Museums, Lesley Gill of Kibworth Harcourt Parish Council, Linda Butt at De Montfort University, who most generously allowed the great texts of Nichols and Burton to be taken on location, Liz Lacon at Lewes District Council, Liz Mayne at De Montfort University, Liz Doull at Coventry History Centre, Ludger and Ruth Fremmer of St Wilfrid's church in Kibworth for their tremendous hospitality, thoughtfulness and willingness to support this project in their very busy lives, Lynne Beasley-Reynolds of Kibworth Parish Council, Marcus Lynch at St Mary's Guildhall, Margaret Bonney at the Wigston Record Office, Mark and Deborah Parr of Priory Farm, Mark and Vanessa Stanbridge of Beauchamp Grange Farm, Martin Featherstone at Anglia Battlefield Tours for a truly memorable trip with the High School to the Somme, Beaumanor Hall, Mary Ireland of Priory Farm, Fred Hartley, Matty Holmes, Maureen Bullows, Dr Maureen Jurkowski of the English Monastic Archives Project at UCL, who was so generous in sharing her exciting research on the Lollards and suggesting new leads, Michael Hawkes, Michael Kilgarriff, who splendidly oversaw the re-creation of the 1880s Penny Concerts, everyone at the Kibworth Last Minute Theatre Company for their sterling work in performing the concerts and other moments from the theatrical past of the village, Michael and Liz Vicars at Newstead Farm, Neil Christie of the School of Archaeology & Ancient History (at the University of Leicester), Neil Finn at ULAS, Oliver Creighton, Martin Carver, Neil and Jane Beasley, Professor Nicholas Orme for coming to Wigston to explore early education in the village, Nicolas Bennett at

Lincoln Cathedral, Nicky and Bob Tully, Norman Harrison of Kibworth History Society, Pat Grundy at the Wigston Record Office for her great support and assistance and her transcripts of many of the documents, especially the Tudor wills from Kibworth, Jeanette Ovendon, Patrick Rooke, Paul Stone of Kibworth CE Primary School, Paul Carter at the National Archives for his advice and help and a memorable day on the Poor Law documents, Peter Clowes at the Wigston Framework Knitters Museum, Peter and Eunice Hayes at St Wilfrid's church, Philippa Britten, Richard Clark of Leicestershire County Council, Dr Richard Jones, Richard Moore, Richard Pollard of Leicestershire County Council, Richard and Mary Green of the Last Minute Theatre Company, Richard and Julia White, Robert and Vanessa Lawson and Susie Purling and Richard Clowes for their many kindnesses, Dr Robert Peberdy of the Victoria County History, Robin Hollick, Roger Bland of the Portable Antiquities Scheme, Dr Roger Highfield of Merton, Roger Whiteway, Rosemary Culkin of the Great Bowden Archaeological Heritage Group, Rosemary and Ian Williamson of Manor Farm, Sally McDonald, Sarah and Lino Poli at the Boboli restaurant, Simon Clarkson, Stephanie and Neil Paull of the Vikings Reenactment Group, Stephen Poyzer and Anne Robinson and all at the *Kibworth Chronicle*, Steve Pollington for his memorable readings of Old English, Dr Sarah Salih, Stuart Rose, Robert Haigh, Roy Hendell, Colin Cree and all the farmers of Laxton – what a pleasure to film with them again after so long – John Stevens, Wendy Scott and Lyn Sturgess for their help at the History Roadshow, John Wadland, Paul Thompson, Arthur Hazilrigg, Charles Stops, Alan Axon, John Billings, the Simons family, Sherry Nesbitt, John and Penny March, James Ryan, Stuart and Emma Kendall, Terry and Alison Iliffe, Tim Porter, Tim Allen at English Heritage, Chris Baldwin, Bob Holman, Kathy Flower-Bond and all at Weald and Downland, Jean Robinson and Anne Whykes at West Stow Anglo-Saxon Village, Benedict Coffin, Sandra Orchard and all at the Viking Society, Bill Sykes and Gareth Owen and all at Sealed Knot, the Simon De Montfort Society in Evesham, William Jacob of St Giles-in-the-Fields, Dr Turi King at the Department of Genetics, University of Leicester, Ted Smith and the Kibworth Brass Band, the Kibworth bellringers, Debbie at The Bookshop, Kibworth, the staff of the King's Head in Smeeton, Ash at Raitha's Restaurant, Mary at the Deli, Robin and Emily at the Old Swan, the staff at the Coach and Horses, and everyone who has helped make this project happen: my apologies if I have inadvertently omitted anyone. Working together on this project has been a pure pleasure: to all, my heartfelt thanks.

On the book, I must thank Tony Lacey and Ellie Smith and everyone at Penguin who had faith in this idea and who saw this book through in record time; to Mark Handsley and Pru Cave, who edited a very difficult text so well; and a special thanks to James Evans, who researched the later films in the series and stepped into the breech as film and book deadlines collided to draft my Civil War, eighteenth-century and Victorian chapters – without his help this book would never have been finished in time, or so well.

Finally the members of the crew who made the films of *The Story of England* were, at Mayavision, Jasmine Allodi, Gerry Branigan, Callum Bulmer, Stephen Butt, John Cranmer, Matt Currington, Howard Davidson, Ben Davis, Wayne Derrick, Mick Duffield, Freya Eden-Ellis, James Evans, Peter Harvey, Elizabeth Herrick, Lauren Jacobs, Aleksandar Nikolic, Tamsin Ranger, Kevin Rowan, Andrew Smith, Sally Thomas, Jon Wood and Aaron Young; and, at Envy, Marc Corrance, Bob Jackson, Jannine Martin and Vicki Matich. Martin Davidson and Janice Hadlow at the BBC backed this project from the start, and Richard Klein and Cassian Harrison saw it through. To have achieved this complex series in just over a year has been little short of miraculous: thanks to one and all.

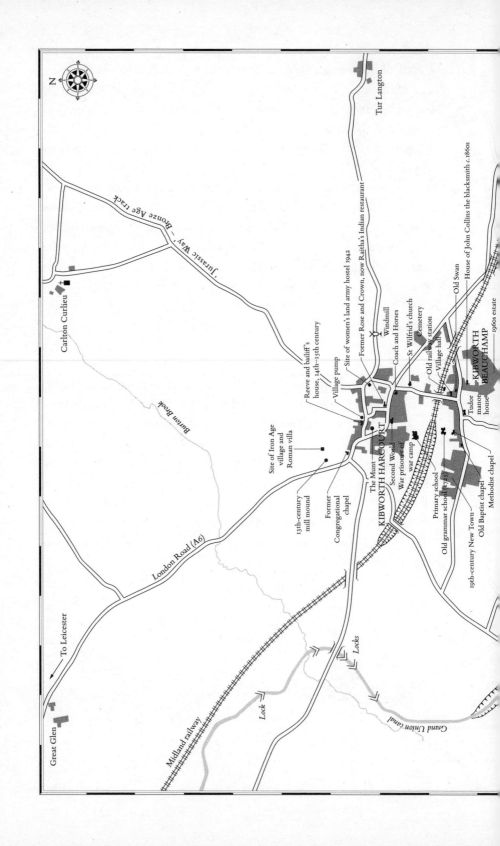

N

Great Glen

To Leicester

Midland railway

London Road (A6)

Lock

Locks

Grand Union canal

Carlton Curlieu

'Jurassic Way' – Bronze Age track

Burton Brook

Site of Iron Age
village and
Roman villa

13th-century
mill mound

Former
Congregational
chapel

The Munt

Second World
War prisoner of
war camp

KIBWORTH HARCOURT

Primary school

Old grammar school (1725)

19th-century New Town

Old Baptist chapel

Methodist chapel

Reeve and bailiff's
house, 14th–15th century

Village pump

Site of women's land army hostel 1942

Former Rose and Crown, now Raitha's Indian restaurant

Windmill

Coach and Horses

St Wilfrid's church

Cemetery

Old railway station

Village hall

Tudor
manor
house

KIBWORTH
BEAUCHAMP

Old Swan

House of John Collins the blacksmith c.1860s

1960s estate

Tur Langton

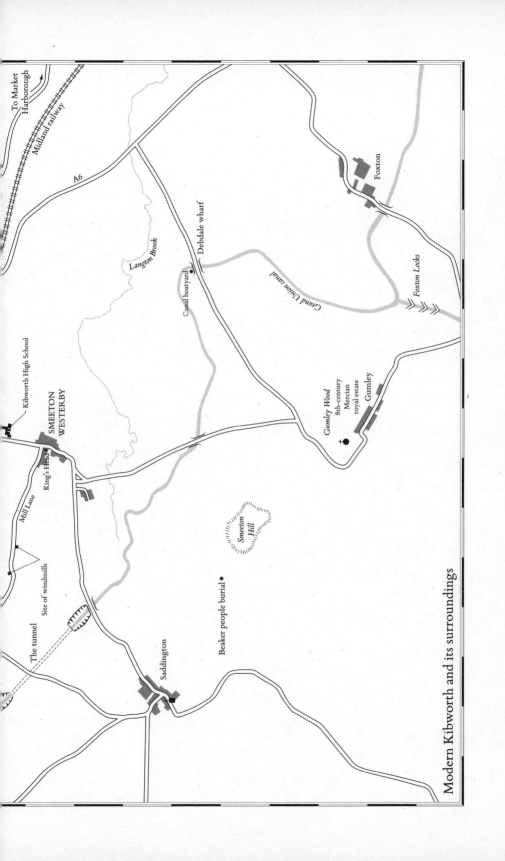

Modern Kibworth and its surroundings

# Introduction

It is easy to generalize, as William Blake remarked, but 'to Particularize is the Alone Distinction of Merit'. Historians needless to say are not quite the same kind of animal as poets, but, inspired by Blake's advice, this book contains a very simple particularizing idea. It tells the story of one place through the whole of English history. Alternatively, it could be said that it tries to tell the story of England through the eyes of one place. It is a narrative in which as far as possible the subject is the people, not the rulers. Of course, rulers play their part in the story, but the important action takes place not in the palaces of the rich and powerful, but in the houses and fields – and in the minds – of the ordinary people. And ordinary lives are often no less dramatic, as I hope will become apparent in the tales that follow, from the Vikings to the Somme, and from the Lollards to the Suffragettes.

The village I have chosen lies in the centre of England, and is remarkable for its ordinariness. It is not Ambridge, nor does it look like a Hovis advert; but that is what I like about Kibworth. It was not exactly chosen at random – the astonishing treasure trove of manorial documents from the village in Merton College, Oxford, had already opened up the possibility of telling real people's lives in the medieval past, of tracing peasant family trees for a dozen generations, of hearing the voices of peasants involved in political revolution, religious radicalism and educational betterment. All that gives the would-be storyteller a fighting chance. But the truth is that such are the records of England that almost any place could have done; indeed, there are hundreds of villages where to a greater or lesser degree such records exist. Over the years I have spent much time mulling over quite a few of them: rich Anglo-Saxon charters from Hampshire, Worcestershire and Oxfordshire; the astounding manorial documents for the villages of northern Suffolk and the Northumbrian mining towns that define people's material lives in the Middle Ages;

churchwardens' accounts from Devon hill villages that chart the inner lives of English people over the great psychological rupture of the Reformation. But the Kibworth manorial documents, on which the historian Cicely Howell had already done a fascinating study of tenure and inheritance, are particularly rich and informative, especially as they come from a place that lies on a linguistic and cultural divide in English history.

What clinched the choice though was the industrial history of Kibworth Beauchamp, the other side of the track from the Merton manor, with its framework-knitters, factories, canals and railways. Many English rural villages have fascinating documents, but their history falls away at the end of the old agricultural world with the eighteenth-century enclosures; and now many have simply become commuter villages. But with its housing estates, new schools, Indian and Chinese takeaways, on the fringe of the multiracial city of Leicester, Kibworth is emphatically England in miniature: it is where most of us live today, and even allowing for the many regional and local differences in England, its history is the story of us all.

So with the medieval history of Kibworth Harcourt and the industrial story of Kibworth Beauchamp to rely on, there was the bedrock of a narrative. But it still could not have been foreseen precisely how things would turn out, how rich one place – chosen as I have said almost at random – would turn out to be. For example, we started off with nothing before 1066 except a few archaeological finds recorded by Georgian antiquarians and Victorian local historians. Given that, the reader may feel some surprise at the length of my narrative before 1066, but the hope that intense on-the-ground scrutiny might bring results was startlingly fulfilled when in the summer of 2009 the villagers began this project with a dig across Kibworth. Some fifty-five test pits yielded evidence of prehistoric Beaker people and Romans; remarkable pottery from the early and late Anglo-Saxon period and all the way through the Middle Ages; debris from Georgian coaching inns, frame-knitters' workshops and railway navvies' camps; and even in one pit household throwouts from the Swinging 1960s. Even before we had taken stock of this unforeseen wealth of new evidence a magnetometry survey by our friends in the

Hallaton group came up with Iron Age houses and a complete Roman villa. All of which makes me think that, as the historian William Hoskins suggested long ago, the national story can indeed be told from almost anywhere. The details of the story will be different in each place, but it is the same story: the growth of an English community in one place over time, and the interaction of the local with the national narrative.

The process of gathering material and developing the story I see as a kind of crystallization (to use a term from Stendhal) in which disparate fragments and impressions, moments in time, shards of memory, gradually come together to form a picture, but of course one only given the warmth of life by our imaginations. This idea it seems to me is particularly apposite to the task of historians. Starting with no documents and a few chance archaeological finds, imagination above all is what is needed to try to construct the beginnings of a narrative without any real sources. Then when documents come in, the process of crystallization begins as a community grows, and changes, and its relations become more complex. Finally, when the documents become richer and more revealing about people's lives, we hear them speak for themselves rather than through texts produced for their lords.

In the speculative beginnings of this narrative, as is the case in most places in England, the clues – and the voices – are few indeed; but I have tried to be ruled by the documents where they exist. Indeed, I have not been able to resist giving plentiful detail of some of the documents from the village story: so in these pages the reader will find the survey of the village from Domesday Book in 1086, the first full account from the 1280s, medieval poll taxes, the list of Black Death victims from the village court book, important sixteenth-century wills, and many later examples of the raw data of social history, including letters from a local suffragette sent from Holloway prison.

However I have not allowed myself to stray too far into imagined events, despite what was often a great temptation to do so. It is true that we cannot prove that the peasant John Wodard was with Simon de Montfort in the army of Kent in 1264 (though the lord of Kibworth did indeed intervene on Wodard's behalf in Kent that October).

No document says that Harry the Hayward consulted his almanac as I picture him in the North Field in the first winter of the Great Famine; nor is there evidence that the vicar Hulman dined with Wycliffe in Lutterworth on his journey to Kibworth in February 1380; still less is it known that the woman whose remains were found at Glen Parva was one of a band of settlers who came from the Welland to Kibworth in the fifth century. But I hope the reader will treat such speculations with indulgence. Only in one case have I tried to create a lost text, Cybba's charter in the 730s; but fortunately we do have precisely such a document from that time. If, as is likely, he had one, then it would have been like this.

A word is in order too on my title. The theme is England, not Britain. The narratives of Scotland and Wales have attracted much attention from historians in recent years as the nature of the union has increasingly been questioned. Their own rich histories, of course (along with those of our Irish neighbours north and south of the border), have very different trajectories, even though their destinies have long been bound together within what Bede called 'the beautiful and fecund island of Britain'. Just the same kind of project might be attempted in their lands too. But this is about England, and there need be no apology for that. It is often forgotten these days, but England is the core state in the British Isles, and its role in history is large. For a small country on the far western shore of the Eurasian land mass, its influence on the world in literature, language, politics, law and ideas of freedom has been out of all proportion to its size. Why that should have been is an interesting question in itself.

Going back to William Blake: the grand-sweep narrative has many merits and offers many insights, and a number of historians have produced weighty and stylish accounts of the history of Britain in the last ten years alone. But the grand sweep is only one perspective; it cannot easily give a sense of the slow organic process by which all of our communities have grown, and still continue to grow. This was a process due in great measure to the imaginations, sensibilities and sense of communality of the people themselves — a process which I hope is vividly conveyed in this story of one English village over time.

# 1. Searching for England

Near the centre of England, not far from the crossing of the Fosse Way and Watling Street, where rolling hills stretch south to Rutland, the walker comes upon an ancient trackway that can be followed for miles along hawthorn hedges past occasional clumps of oak and gaunt stagheads of elm and ash. An offshoot of the Jurassic Way, this prehistoric path runs from the Wash all the way down to the south-west. Fording the River Wreake at Melton Mowbray, it skirts the great Iron Age fort of Burrough Hill, then winds south by Robin a' Tiptoe Hill through the heart of the Midlands, across the Avon watershed and on to the great prehistoric sacred circle at Avebury and the creation mound and springs at Silbury Hill. But here on the south Leicestershire upland, the road runs along a saddle which divides the Trent and the Welland, passing through pretty villages, Tilton and Illston on the Hill, and down into a lovely valley beyond Carlton Curlieu. Here for several miles the road is followed by the parish boundaries – a sure hint of its great age. On either side the green pasture is etched by the curving ridge and furrow of the medieval plough teams, faint gores and headlands, the deep bone structure of their world.

Near this route Beaker people left their burials 4,000 years ago accompanied by their distinctive upright pottery with its pitted rims and chequered patterns. But the origin of this track probably lies in the Middle Bronze Age, roughly between 1500 and 1000 BC, a time which saw the beginnings of organized societies in Britain, and with them for the first time long-distance trade. Along it over the last two or three centuries there have been stray finds of Bronze Age tools: a chisel and a flanged axe at Kibworth; at Husbands Bosworth a merchant's hoard of bronze implements – nine socketed axes, gauges and chisels, two long spearheads and a sturdy ferrule for a spear stock. These are the first hints of a human story, conjuring up the image of a buskined Bronze Age brogger striding out under wide Midland skies clutching his precious pedlar's pack of tools which he had made and hoped to sell or barter somewhere along the route. A pointer too to individual human initiative and enterprise, which will be the running thread of this narrative.

Much later, but still before the Norman Conquest, the track was used by English peasant levies in their grim struggles against the Vikings. Then the Anglo-Saxons called it a 'herepath', an 'army path', and in the Middle Ages it was still remembered locally as 'le ferdgate', combining the French direct article and the Old English word for army ( *fyrd* ) with the Scandinavian word for road – *gata* – in the speech of the Viking settlers who came here in the late ninth century.

At a weathered cast-iron signpost marked 'Gartree Road' the old track crosses the Roman Via Devana. For many hundreds of years the Gartree Bush or 'Council Tree' stood here, where a cluster of gnarled elms made a ring round an old grey thorn on an ancient tumulus. This was the local moot place known as *methelou* (the 'meeting' or 'speech' mound). From Old English times right down to the Georgians it was the gathering place of the members of the hundred, the old English unit of local administration which lies at the root of the English representative system. This is where the Domesday jurors from Kibworth and surrounding villages met William the Conqueror's assessors in spring 1086 to describe their lands and communities, and to grudgingly declare their wealth; where for centuries the local court deliberated, and as an aged eyewitness remembered in the 1790s, 'the impanneling of the jury, and the paying of the chief rents and many other things used to be performed.' (It is easy to forget it now, but English freeholders were long accustomed to vote in the open air like their Anglo-Saxon ancestors, even in some places as late as the nineteenth century.) From the site of the Gartree thorn the track continues through Tur Langton, past the Bull's Head (the jurors' traditional watering hole, now boarded up and awaiting a saviour), until the white sails of Kibworth windmill can be seen peeping over the trees on the left-hand side. Half an hour's brisk walk takes the traveller down into the little white-painted lanes of workers' cottages at the back end of Kibworth Harcourt.

Kibworth now is almost a small town: in miniature it's the kind of place most Britons live in today. It straddles a main arterial road, the A6, and is easily passed by without a second thought; at rush hour the commuter traffic roars through in ruthless disregard of the pedestrian. Behind the trees there are new housing estates and concrete and glass infill, but the older core is of handsome timber-framed houses made of warm red Leicestershire brick. By the Jubilee gardens, there is a late-seventeenth-century grandee's house, with high chimneys, scrolled pediments and stucco pilasters (in the eighteenth century the dissenting 'academy' which was sited in the building had a curriculum unrivalled in Britain). Across the road by the village pump is the old 'slang', once the cart track to the open fields, now gated and thick with fallen branches and leaf mulch, and a much older farmhouse of red brick on an ironstone base with Victorian diamond diaper work on the garden wall. By the gate a weathered terracotta plaque marks successive rebuildings in 1475, 1695 and 1860 (though now tree ring dating gives us another new build in 1385 and one even back before the Black Death, in the 1320s after the Great Famine). Harcourt's seven Georgian coaching inns are gone: the old Rose and Crown is now Raitha's Indian restaurant and the Lord Nelson is the Boboli pizzeria; only the Coach and Horses is still a pub, with carriage wheels and a painted inn sign depicting the London mail. (This curiously enough was the place where a young Thomas Cook stood at the side of the road waiting for the stagecoach and dreamed up the idea of modern tourism.)

Walking away from the main road, the visitor comes to the medieval church of St Wilfrid in golden ironstone surrounded by old yew trees in a grassy churchyard full of fine tombstones in local slate, with a monument to the men of Kibworth who died in the Great War. Further on, the road descends to the now disused railway station, which was closed in 1968 after the Beeching reform. This is Kibworth Beauchamp, which in contrast to Kibworth Harcourt was a workers' place during the Industrial Revolution; then it was known in some quarters, somewhat disparagingly, as 'radical' or 'stockeners' Kibworth. Beauchamp still has many three-storey weavers' cottages with their typical tall workshop windows on the top floors, and

behind the houses by the traffic island is the big range of a derelict
framework knitting factory which served as the telephone exchange
during the Second World War. Beauchamp, like Harcourt, is a medieval settlement, but virtually all that survives from that period is an
early-Tudor manor house opposite the off licence, with whitewashed
stables and a pretty cupola topped by a clock and a weather vane.
Here in the centre of the village there's a busy Co-op, and a tiny
bookshop which runs children's evenings and a women's reading
group; there's the Swan Inn, the Firenze Italian restaurant, Indian
and Chinese takeaways, a new secondary school, a sports complex
and a cricket field (Kibworth's cricketers were in 2008 the national
village cricket champions). At the end of the village is the 'New
Town', with rows of Victorian terraces built a century and a half ago,
when the population here expanded three or four times in a few generations, as did that of England as a whole. But human beings have
lived in this landscape for a very long time, starting after the settlement of lowland Britain following the end of the last Ice Age. By
about 8000 BC, there is evidence of nomadic hunter-gatherers, whose
flint tools and arrowheads have been picked up in village closes.
Beyond the back gardens of the Kibworth Fish Bar and the Moka
Coffee Shop, up on Smeeton Hill (whose brooding outline borders
the parish towards the west), Beaker people left their burials, and
nearby metal detectorists have picked up gold and silver coins of the
Corieltauvi, one of the tribes and kingdoms which underlie our oldest regional identities, what historians now recognize as the different
'pays' of England.

From the highest point of the village, looking to the north-west,
there are wide views across central England to Leicester Forest and
Charnwood. These are the 'champain' lands described by the travellers
John Leland and Celia Fiennes: what local farmers still describe as the
'best fattening land in England'. And on the horizon eight or nine
miles away is Leicester itself. Like all our urban conurbations which
have grown apace since the nineteenth century, this once small Tudor
town has spread its suburbs in every direction, swallowing the thriving medieval villages of Wigston, Oadby and Blaby, welcoming
newcomers from all over the world. Indeed, Leicester intends to be

the first city in the world to declare all its ethnic communities minorities, even the so-called 'white English': when that happens it will be the first truly multiracial place on earth.

Unlikely as it may seem, then, unpromising as today's landscapes perhaps appear at first sight, the earlier pasts are still here, in the streets and fields, and they exist in the place names too. Linguists specializing in the prehistory of British speech tell us that this area was 'the Land of Rivers'. The Roman name of the city, Ratae, didn't survive their departure, but the pre-Roman name did; for Leicester derives from Ligoracester in Anglo-Saxon, which means the fortified town of the Ligore, an ancient river name used to describe themselves by the early Celtic folk who settled here. The name was still current in the twelfth century when William of Malmesbury described the Legra 'flowing past the town'. And indeed the name is still with us. Though today the river down to its confluence with the Trent is called Soar, in old maps and documents it changes its name somewhere under the Victorian railway arches of Leicester and becomes the Leir, one of whose tributaries rises ten miles to the south, near Watling Street and the Warwickshire border near the tiny village of Leire. This very ancient name comes from the same pre-English word Legra – which with delightful synchronicity is identical to the Roman name for the Loire – a pleasing thought for Midlanders!

So in a place where it might be thought that all trace of the deep past had been erased by the early twenty-first century, the encoded memories which have taken millennia to build up are still in places retrievable, even though so much has been rubbed away since industrialization and the ensuing boom in population from 8 million in 1800 to almost 70 million today. In England the landscape has always been more than the sum of its parts: the English have always mythologized every corner. In every small locality it is possible to see part of the whole story. Which is perhaps why the local history of every county, parish and village has been more intensively cultivated here than anywhere in the world: in the belief that every place is its own version of the grand narrative, that every place is also part of the national story.

## *Corieltauvi: the Hallaton treasure*

So our village grew up in a prehistoric 'Land of Rivers', whose ancient names though largely unnoticed still grace our modern maps. The first inhabitants here after the Ice Age were pre-Celtic Meso- lithic people who came into Britain from about 8000 BC onwards, and to whom today's British owe much of their DNA. Around Kib- worth they left their hand-worked flints and arrowheads. Then came the Celts in the late Iron Age who lived in permanent settlements with circular huts, cattle corrals and fields. They made pottery and bronze tools and traded widely, importing ceramics, metalwork and luxury products from Roman Gaul. The Celtic tribe in the region were long known to us (from a passage in the geographer Ptolemy) as the Coritani but from recent finds we now know their name was in fact Corieltauvi. They spoke a dialect of a language ancestral to mod- ern Welsh, akin to that preserved in the earliest Welsh poetry. As we shall see, there are still faint traces of their speech to be found in field names and topographical features in the landscape around Kibworth and its neighbouring villages. They occupied the lands east of the Trent around the Soar, the Welland and the Nene (Celtic or pre- Celtic names all). The tribe had two or three centres and perhaps two or three 'kings' ruling at any one time from hubs in Leicestershire and Lincolnshire. Only recently the sensational discovery made at Hallaton near Kibworth of a hoard of well over 5,000 gold and cop- per Corieltauvian coins – the largest Iron Age hoard ever found in Britain – has given a glittering picture of the wealth of these local communities on the eve of the Roman invasion. On a wooded hill inside a ditched sacred enclosure the treasure was deposited with thousands of pig bones, the leftovers of sacrificial rituals; with them were silver ingots, bowls, plaques and jewellery, and even a Roman parade helmet. The hoard perhaps was in some sense a tribal treasure. On the coins are the resonant names of shadowy Corieltauvian kings, including some previously unknown: Volisios, Dumnocoveros, Dumnvellaunus, Cartivelos and 'Vepo the son of Cor'. New finds at Kibworth Harcourt of a magnificent gold stater and a silver coin of the Corieltauvi hint too at a settled society with a money economy which under its kings seems relatively seamlessly to have become Roman – a process that would be repeated in these parts over the intervening centuries with succeeding invasions, settlements and migrations, right down to today.

That's the historical setting for the village which is the subject of this story. We will call it Kibworth. But in reality, as locals will tell the visitor, there is no such place. For as we have seen already, the old parish contains two Kibworths divided now by the railway track. Both bear the names of their twelfth-century Norman landlords: Kibworth Harcourt and Kibworth Beauchamp, originally perhaps 'Upper' and 'Lower', which lingered on in local speech until this century as 'Top' and 'Bottom' 'Kibburth'. Their stories have been proverbially different – Harcourt is said to be a posh, country, horse and hounds, agricultural kind of place; Beauchamp on the other hand was said to be a poorer village with an industrial history and a reputation for non-conformism and dissent. Edmund Knox, the redoubtable vicar during the 1880s, tells an amusing tale that the two communities even argued in the parish hall about sharing a common sewerage system, the Harcourt gentry being reluctant to contemplate their effluent being 'contaminated' with that of the mere 'stockeners'. (A testimony when all is said and done to how the serendipity of history can divide even the very closest of neighbours!)

The Kibworths with their contrasting histories form the core of this story, but we should also mention the other component of the old parish, the hamlet of Smeeton Westerby on the southern edge of Kibworth, with its farms and smithy, its tall weavers' cottages, its crowded allotment gardens and its pub, the King's Arms – a real old-fashioned alehouse with tap room and snug. Today a place which keeps to itself, behind red brick walls, no bigger than it was in the 1880s, Smeeton is a small farming hamlet whose families have always intermarried with those of the Kibworths but it is a place with its own distinctive history going back into Anglo-Saxon times, when, as its name suggests, it was a settlement of metalworkers, the 'smiths' tun'.

Kibworth is a plain place then with no frills, and it might be thought with nothing special to recommend it, nothing out of the ordinary. It is Middle England, geographically and historically. In its history one might think it is no different from thousands of other places. But here as everywhere the tides of history have left their mark on the lives of the ordinary people: sometimes in the most extraordinary way, from the Black Death to the Civil War and the Industrial Revolution, with turnpikes, canals and railways, highwaymen, suffragettes and soldiers on the Somme. As with most villages in England solid documentary evidence for this history only begins in the eleventh century with William the Conqueror's Domesday survey, and then manorial rentals, court rolls, poll taxes, Tudor wills and all the obsessive recording, accounting and measuring of the medieval rentiers. But long before that it had a community, with field systems, customs and dues, forms of authority and justice, one of thousands of places from which the national story grew and crystallized. And it is the growth of that community which is the story told in this book.

The focus where possible is on the lives of the ordinary people. History from the bottom up is not so fashionable these days as the lives of kings and queens and of the nobility, but it offers great insights. Of course, only through examining the source material for working people can we see the lives of the bulk of the people of England through their history. But such sources can also be strikingly revealing about the national story and how it impinged on, and how it was shaped by, the local community. It is also true to say that though local history has often been dismissed as a lesser branch of historical studies, it is only through close examination of local conditions that real historical change can be observed. A case in point is the great change in society from the feudal order to a capitalist and industrial society. In a place like Kibworth, where the documents are so rich almost year by year from the late thirteenth century to the turn of the eighteenth, it is possible to see close up the economic and social forces which led to the breakdown of the medieval structures of lordship and exploitation and the rise of individualism and capitalism. In other words, the big picture can be generalized, but it can only be particularized at the level of the communities who themselves lived through such changes.

But to take the lives of the people back beyond the period of parish registers and hearth taxes and to try to touch the experience and even the voice of the English back in the time when many of their key institutions and ideas were still being shaped – all this presents some knotty problems for the historian. For most places in England it is simply not possible to do so before the sixteenth century. So to begin to construct our historical narrative the first task is a necessarily allusive one; namely to try to get some sense of the history of the community *before* the documents, when our only clues come from sifting fragments: coins, sherds, bone combs, bronze pins and brooches, the good gifts of archaeology. And with that search, as a kind of prologue, our story begins.

## *The early searchers: a chorography of England*

By a pleasing coincidence, at the very moment when Edward Blunt was proofreading the first sheets of Shakespeare's First Folio in the Jaggards' printing shop in the autumn of 1622, another work was going through his press which is the first marker in our story: indeed, after a licensing snag over *Troilus and Cressida*, Blunt held up printing the Folio to see it through. While not of such earth-shaking significance in the history of literature, William Burton's *Description of Leicestershire* deserves its more limited fame as one of the early pioneers in English local history. Burton devoted twenty-five years' work to his project. It was based on detailed local research and written with a critical eye: he recorded the Roman inscriptions of Leicestershire and even went to the trouble of issuing a carefully corrected copy of Saxton's pioneering map of the shire. Burton had also studied the earlier travellers: William of Worcester, who wrote about England in the middle of the fifteenth century, and above all Henry VIII's antiquary, John Leland, the troubled and driven genius who journeyed round England in the 1540s, and whose itinerary is the raw and unmediated forerunner of all topographical accounts of England – an unrivalled description of the country, though not destined to be published till modern times. Burton was responsible for saving some of Leland's manuscripts, which he gifted to the Bodleian in Oxford. Also there are copies of his own notebooks, among them densely scribbled transcripts of now lost Leicester sections of Edward I's 1279 Hundred Rolls Survey, an even more detailed account of England than William the Conqueror's Domesday – including accounts of the Kibworths and Smeeton Westerby which have never been published. Obsessive as perhaps all the best local antiquarians are, Burton revised his book through his later life, constantly gathering information for planned future editions. He also contemplated three different parish histories – perhaps the first of their kind – of his native Lindley, of Dadlington and of Theddingworth near Kibworth. None of these ever saw the light of day though their notes would be invaluable to all later searchers.

Burton's work was not in fact the first. Strictly speaking county history began with William Lambarde's *Perambulation of Kent*, a work Burton generously recognized as 'hard to overpraise'. Lambarde began writing in 1570, the year in which as far as we know the first British cartographer, Christopher Saxton, commenced work on his great atlas of the English counties – the first national atlas. Lambarde's *Kent* was published in 1576 and with it detailed exploration of England began. Though in recent times there has been much argument about the extent and significance of Romanization of the country, the point of view of these early researchers was to see English and British history as an organic whole and Roman civilization as one of the roots of England. This was especially the theme of William Camden's *Britannia*, a study of Britain and Ireland county by county which was first published in Latin in 1586. Camden said his aim was 'to restore antiquity to Britain and Britain to its antiquity' and he did so with the help of a network of correspondents without which any true antiquarian scholarship finds it hard to flower. Though printed in Latin, Camden's book proved very popular, going through seven editions by 1607 (a remarkable testimony to the literacy and scholarship of his early-Stuart readership), and an English-language edition was published in 1610, spurring a wider range of readers.

Camden had called his work 'chorography' – the word derived

from the Greek *choros* – 'place' – and Camden got it from the ancient geographer Ptolemy, who distinguished between geography as the study of the physical makeup of the whole world, or of large parts of it, and chorography, which looked at smaller parts, particular landscapes or places: 'province, region, city or port' as Ptolemy had put it. For Camden topography, geography, historical texts and monuments show how what we might call the givenness of the past is still discernible in the landscape and he inspired generations of on-the-ground searchers who combined antiquarianism and travel, a peculiarly English genre. He also attempted a first overview of the antiquities of Roman Britain. From then on England's past from the prehistoric to the present would be seen as a continuum.

Camden then was the template for what followed: Carew's *Cornwall*, Westcote's *View of Devonshire* and then Burton's *Leicestershire* in 1622. The focus of these and all later works was the English shire or, to use its Norman name, the county. The shire was an ancient Anglo-Saxon unit of organization, with its subdivisions into hundreds, manors, villages and parishes, and the English obsession with the shire is worth a moment's pause. The shire has provoked intense loyalty in England, and still does, and it is not just a matter of cricket teams, still less of county councils and local administration. It is to do with the ways one defines oneself. For someone to say he or she is a Yorkshireman or Yorkshirewoman is to convey pride in a particular regional and cultural identity. The shire is still felt to be a real not an imaginary entity. Even now among the older generation in England the shire boundary – an obscure landmark it may be, an ancient ridgeway perhaps, a Roman road, or a Dark Age earthwork, a sunken lane with its towering hedgerows – also represents a frontier on a mental map beyond which things are done differently. The furious reaction to Edward Heath's abolition of Rutland in 1974 showed the level of feeling about such local identities. Rutland was the smallest shire and the one perhaps with the least-evident markers of ancient identity, but it was Anglo-Saxon nonetheless (and for all we know very much earlier, perhaps of the Iron Age). The roots of England's shires are often as old: back in the Viking Age the Anglo-Saxon Chronicle speaks of the 'men of Devon' or the 'men of Hereford' marching out to defend their land and support their king. Some shires overlie pre-Roman Iron Age tribal divisions and almost all were in existence by the tenth century. Along with the boroughs they were the essential unit of local administration, with their functions in justice, crime and punishment, and defence, and because they were the focus for local representation, over time they created intense loyalties. Even now, though the hundred lost its last judicial functions in the 1850s, the shires are often still the unit of local government, and still give their names to sports teams, societies and clubs. They are a focus of local sensibility. Never so diverse as the regions of France, nonetheless the deep identity of the 'pays' of England in custom, food, farming and dialect often reaches back into prehistory. Village, parish and shire underlie the country, and the shire came first.

The golden age of English chorography was between the late seventeenth and late eighteenth centuries, when learned antiquarian societies were formed and some of the great county histories were published. The greatest of all was John Nichols's *History and Antiquities of the County of Leicester*. Nichols was a London printer who collaborated with Abraham Farley on his landmark 1783 printing of Domesday Book, which he rightly called 'the most invaluable as well as the most *antient* Record in this or any other kingdom'. Nichols devised the typeface to render as closely as possible the script and marginalia and abbreviations of the Great Domesday manuscript. This contribution was a source of lasting pride to him; he would later say 'on the correctness and the beauty of this important Work I am content to stake my typographical credit.' Farley and Nichols's Domesday has been justly called the greatest publishing venture in British history, and is also one of the most beautiful books ever printed. But at the same time Nichols was gathering materials for the most ambitious of all county histories. In four huge volumes (published in eight parts) he described Leicestershire parish by parish, drawing on a vast network of informants at parish level, on personal autopsy, on Burton's unpublished notes and transcripts, and on a mass of historical manuscripts and antiquarian literature. Nichols included finely engraved illustrations of churches and monuments, coins and sculptures, Roman mosaics and inscriptions, and even (a first, this) the contents of Anglo-Saxon pagan graves: belt buckles, sword blades and cruciform brooches – all engraved with forensic precision. In Kibworth he illustrated the church and its monuments, and even reproduced the Roman gold coin of the Emperor Julian found in 1723. Another path-breaking achievement for its time, his prefatory volume summarized what was then known about the Romans, and laid before his readership the full text of the Domesday folios for the shire which Nichols had prepared with Farley. Paid for by public subscription this vast undertaking amounted to 5,600 folio pages – 5 million words – and would surely be unthinkable today. It has many errors of course, but its vast assemblage of material, though uneven in its scholarship by today's standards, was an indispensable tool for the searcher after the history of Middle England. He taught them, and us, where, and how, to look.

As Nichols was publishing his early volumes in the 1790s another great source of knowledge was rapidly developing in the study of English antiquity, namely, maps. The mapping of England had started with Saxton's pioneering maps in the 1570s, and along with tithe maps, estate plans and enclosure awards maps are an unrivalled source of local detail where they survive. Much of the detailed place name evidence in this story is derived from the wonderful estate maps of Kibworth Harcourt, starting in 1609, which are kept today in Merton College, Oxford, along with the tithe maps of Kibworth Beauchamp and Smeeton now held in the archives in Leicester and Lincoln. These often preserve precious details of Viking, Saxon and even pre-Roman Celtic field names passed down in local speech by the villagers. Nichols had produced finely drawn and coloured maps for each of the county's hundreds, but cartographically speaking everything was changed by the creation of the Ordnance Survey, which began work in 1791, and published its first one-inch map (of Kent) in 1801. By the 1830s the whole of England had been mapped, and by the 1840s also in the scale of six inches to the mile. Later still, in the 1860s, a twenty-inch scale series followed, among the most beautiful and informative maps ever made. No searcher after the villages parishes and shires of England can do without them, and given the massive changes in the English landscape over the last seventy years, even the old cloth-backed one-inch tourist maps of the 1920s and 1930s have now become valuable – even haunting – historical sources in conveying the pattern of the countryside before the full onset of urbanization, motorways and industrialized agriculture in our own time.

Such topographical and textual explorations led to the founding of learned societies, beginning in 1717 with the London Society of Antiquaries, at whose early meetings some of the finds at Kibworth were first discussed and examined. During the nineteenth century local historical societies were founded in practically every county (an honourable mention here is due to the solitary forerunner, the Spalding Gentlemen's Society of 1710), a veritable explosion of county and town history societies who met regularly to discuss and publish finds in their annual journals. It was as if social change in the Victorian age was now so visible and so sweeping, with urban society expanding everywhere, that the investigation of antiquity had suddenly grown urgent and intensive in response; as if in an age of irrevocable change – as their past began to recede from them at an ever faster rate – the English were gripped by the impulse to explore and examine themselves. Supplemented by gazetteers, by parish and village histories, Murray's Handbooks, and the massive and still ongoing Victoria County History in 1899 – the greatest single publishing venture in English local history – and taken up by moderns like Arthur Mee, Nikolaus Pevsner and W. G. Hoskins, the flood shows no sign of stopping.

Finally a further crucial development in our understanding of the local past should be mentioned here: the founding of the English Place Name Society after the First World War. This great project, which is still under way, aimed to provide scholarly accounts of the history and derivation of all place names in every shire, parish, village and hamlet, even recording field names from tithe maps. Often recorded in different forms over many centuries, place names carry a special wealth of information. A subject till then (and still sometimes even now) plagued by false etymologies, amateur scholarship and local patriotism was able to achieve clarity and accuracy. Leicestershire is lucky here in that it is the subject of some of the society's most recent and authoritative publications, incorporating the very latest onomastic and philological knowledge. The pages of the Leicester volumes are a treasure trove of fascinating and even at times astounding information, from medieval sacred wells, canal wharves and bargemen's pubs to ancient field names, and, as it must for any town or village in England, the study of place names underpins the whole of the early part of this narrative.

## The first finds

Such then are the tools for the seeker after local history. In Kibworth the first clues emerged in the early eighteenth century and were recorded by the assiduous Nichols. In 1723 a beautiful gold coin of the emperor Julian (who died in 363) was turned up in the street in Kibworth Beauchamp (one of only two that have been found in Britain). Then in 1730 a Roman stone inscription in Latin was found in the village (but since tantalizingly lost without ever being recorded). Around the same time a hoard of Roman coins was excavated, though Nichols reports 'since gone out of the county' (perhaps this was the fourth-century hoard reported in the minutes of the London Society of Antiquaries from 'near Leicester', comprising 600 bronze coins of Diocletian, Maximian, Maxentius and Constantine the Great). In 1788 building labourers having demolished the old rectory were digging new foundations in the vicar's garden south of the church when 'about a yard below the surface they discovered several pieces of Roman pottery in perfect preservation.' What subsequently happened to these urns or jars is not known – they do not appear to have survived or been illustrated – but it sounds very much as if the workers had unearthed part of a Roman cemetery. From these finds the first hints had emerged that though the village is first recorded in 1086 in Domesday Book, and is unknown to the Roman geographers and itineraries, like so many places in England, it had a much longer prehistory.

## The excavation of 1863

In Kibworth that history came vividly to life in 1863 when a remarkable excavation took place in the village. The story was reported in
the newspapers and in the minutes of the new county historical society, but has been curiously ignored since and is still surrounded by
mystery. The various accounts are a little confused, but several clear
facts emerge from which a tentative picture may be drawn. The dig
evidently took place at two separate locations. First was a low burial
mound of the Bronze or Iron Age out on the Leicester road: a circular tumulus surrounded by a ditch, on which a post windmill had
been erected in the thirteenth century. At the same time inside Kibworth Harcourt, behind the gardens and inns on Main Street,
excavators cut a massive trench into a much bigger mound known
locally as the Munt. There are many village stories about the Munt.
It has been variously described as Iron Age, Roman, Viking and Norman, and one nineteenth-century villager claimed that it was the
grave of a legendary Celtic king called Cibbaeus who had 'come to
the village from Wales'. (Intriguing as this story might appear, it is
probably no more than a nineteenth-century antiquarians' tale. The
eponymous Cybba who gave his name to the village was as we shall
see evidently Anglo-Saxon.)

The Munt is now tucked behind a row of eighteenth-century cottages and a former coaching inn, the Admiral Nelson, which is now
converted into the Boboli pizza restaurant. A big eroded grassy
mound spread over a few hundred square yards where sheep graze in
the summer and children play in the winter with their toboggans in
the snow, it has seen many events in the village story, including a
memorable scene in 1936 when Ellen Wilkinson addressed the Jarrow
marchers and a crowd from both 'radical' and 'county' Kibworth. It
is likely that in its final phase the Munt was the motte of an earth and
timber Norman castle erected in the immediate aftermath of the
Norman Conquest when there was severe fighting in this part of
Leicestershire. But the Victorian excavation suggested that the
mound had a more ancient and complex history. It had first been

opened in 1810, when the London–Harborough road was rerouted on a new by-pass round the village to save mail coaches hitting the corner house on the tight bend on Main Street. The road was driven through open ground close to the motte and removed much of what must have been an outer bailey. In the 1840s further finds which are now lost were exhibited in Leicester. But in 1863 the Munt was dug again when the newly formed county Historical Society picnicked on the spot and were treated to a learned lecture on the finds. This time the dig was a more scientific affair, though by modern standards it was still swift and brutal; but the finds caused something of a sensation in local antiquarian circles.

In the summer of 1863 a deep trench was cut through one side of the Munt and reached undisturbed black soil some nine feet below the surface. At the bottom was a cist grave, whose sides were lined with paving stones, containing burnt materials including bones, teeth, a bone bodkin and a decayed iron candelabrum. Fragments of Samian ware pottery were recognized as Roman, and perhaps date the grave to the late first or second century AD. The presence of some kind of lamp stand or oil lamp holder is especially interesting as such artefacts are depicted in fine wall paintings recovered more recently from a Roman house in Leicester; as a holder for Roman clay oil lamps this piece of ironwork then might have been hung on a chain, or stood on a tripod in the burial chamber.

Scrutinizing the 1863 accounts, for all their vagueness of description, modern archaeologists think they describe a Romano-British burial, and evidently of someone of importance in the colonial period, perhaps a member of the aristocracy of the Corieltauvi: a local potentate, then, or a prince. (In Roman Britain, as elsewhere in the empire, the main colonial landowning class in the countryside would usually be made up of descendants of the late-Iron Age native aristocracy.) Most likely then a British chief of the Corieltauvi tribe had been buried under the mound at Kibworth. Could the village have been the centre of an Iron Age 'royal' estate? Would this account for the recent metal detector finds of gold and silver staters of the Corieltauvi? The Munt clearly deserves proper excavation with modern techniques, but even through the 1863 discoveries an unexpected window opens up, however indistinctly, on local British society under Roman rule – and of course on the beginnings of the village story.

## Further clues

In the late twentieth century further clues began to emerge. Over the last few decades Roman finds have turned up in a number of places in the village. Most intriguing is the discovery at the windmill mound by the A6 of a bronze coin of Constantine, along with Roman pottery, wall plaster chunks with keying, and fragments of Roman roofing tile, one still bearing the paw print of a dog. These were excavated by an indefatigable local engineer and archaeologist called Bert Aggas, who was painstaking and accurate in recording his finds. He even questioned villagers in the hope of gathering more information on chance finds that might shed some light on their past. Aggas found more sherds of Samian (the fine burnished orange-brown posh tableware dating from the first to second century). But he also found little square stone tesserae from a mosaic floor, and battered and broken chunks of several hand-querns: strong hints that a substantial Roman farm building lay somewhere nearby. The Roman pottery was scattered across the site underneath the grassed-over ridges, but not in the furrows, of the medieval field, which had evidently never fallen out of use till it was enclosed by Act of Parliament in 1789. Had the village fields then been continuously farmed since Roman times?

On the basis of these finds the area round the windmill mound field was targeted in the summer of 2009 with field-walking by villagers and archaeologists and scanned using magnetometry by the Hallaton group who had discovered the Hallaton treasure. On the first morning the Roman villa was located close to the windmill mound and by the close of the weekend the group had recovered its complete ground plan a hundred yards square. Built perhaps in the late first or second century, the Kibworth villa had been nothing palatial like the huge villas of the Cotswolds or the south coast,

Fishbourne, say, or Chedworth. It was a simple working farm with an entrance gateway and central courtyard flanked by ancillary buildings, probably at first in indigenous-style mud brick and timber-framed halls with courtyard verandas, barns and animal sheds. Later it was probably rebuilt in stone, with floor mosaics composed of stone and pot tesserae, and perhaps bath houses for the owner and the workers (the spring or well that fed the villa is now lost but survives in the field name Banwell – Bana is an Anglo-Saxon male personal name). Around the villa the magnetometry survey also found evidence for the indigenous population: a late-Iron Age community of round huts, with rectangular animal enclosures. Still more recently metal detector finds have added further detail to this picture: a few hundred yards from the villa site coins of the Corieltauvi have been found, including magnificent gold and silver staters from the first century BC or early first century AD – just before the Roman Conquest. These coins are similar to ones found in the Hallaton treasure, whose links with other parts of Britain (including coins of Cunobelinus of Colchester) and Gaul show that even before the Roman Conquest the people of the Kibworth area had wider contacts, and perhaps even traded with the empire.

All this proved that there was already a community here when the Romans came. Along with the grand burial mound, the gold and silver coins might also hint at the presence of British persons of high status after the Conquest. The finds showed too that the place continued as a thriving estate whose people cultivated the land and used coins until the very end of the Roman period. (Recent metal detector finds, along with several Roman dress brooches, include copper coins from the second century in Kibworth Beauchamp, and three fourth-century coins from Kibworth Harcourt.) The latest pottery finds now include fine black wheel-made ware from the back yards of the 'City' (a cluster of workers' cottages from the Industrial Revolution) and abraided Samian from the garden of one of the Victorian villas near the church. Bearing in mind the likely cemetery in the rectory garden, these discoveries suggest an area of Roman settlement about a kilometre and a half across – pretty much defining the land where human settlement has clustered ever since.

## Topography of the village

So by chance – and much of it in the last year or two – traces of an older history have appeared, and although a blank for so long, a picture of the place long before 1066 has begun to emerge. Here ancient Britons, Romans, Saxons and Vikings with a continuity of society dwelt for at least 2,000 years. This story of course can be paralleled in many English villages, each one reflecting the national story, but each one unique in its own particular local detail. In all of them the first facts of village history are soil and water. From prehistory till now human settlement has been determined by the local environment out of which people have made a living, and fed, housed and clothed themselves and their families. Humans first settled in Kibworth because of the good grazing land and the spring line along the Jurassic Way. In Merton College the tithe map of 1609 marks no fewer than seventeen wells within the village of Kibworth Harcourt alone. These springs (so locals say) have never dried up, and they still flow today. The municipal piped water supply only came after the Second World War, and the last local to accept the new-fangled innovation of taps did not do so until 1976. Most of the old wells are still to be found behind the houses. In Kibworth Beauchamp the Tudor manor house still has a pump in its kitchen and in Harcourt the village pump (though its handle no longer works) still stands on the street by the wall at the Jubilee gardens. Older villagers remember that in the 1920s and 1930s each farmhouse had its own well. Betty Ward for example, who was born in 1921 in Priory Farm (an early-Tudor farmhouse), recalls: 'Ours was a deep well at the farm, very deep and very dangerous. We used to pump the water from that well and it never let us down.'

These springs are the reason for the placing of the villages. The settlements at Kibworth and Smeeton lie on boulder clay soils and (in the case of Harcourt) partly on a sandy gravel bed dotted with springs. They lie between the shallow valleys of two important stream systems in central England – to the north the Soar and its tributaries, which flow into the Trent, and to the south the Welland, which flows east into the Wash. The low rise (it is scarcely a ridge) on which

Kibworth stands forms a watershed between these two systems. From Kibworth two streams flow down to the Welland. One is called Langton Brook and rises in the Kibworth village springs; the other is near an ancient junction of country tracks north of Kibworth called Three Gates. It is unnamed on today's Ordnance map but appears on earlier estate maps as Langton Caudle – in Anglo-Saxon the 'cold well' or 'cold spring'. But in medieval documents, according to the Tudor traveller John Leland, and till recently in local speech, it was the Lipping. There is no other Lipping today in England, but the name is still found on the other side of the North Sea in Schleswig, in the ancestral lands of the Anglo-Saxon settlers who came here after the fall of Rome, in the district of Angeln, the place which gave its name to the Angles and to England. Unnoticed by the traffic that speeds south towards Northampton, there is a connection with the early-English migration into these parts in the fifth or sixth century.

On the northern side of the parish another stream, the Burton Brook, flows into the valley of the River Sence, which skirts the edge of Wistow and Kibworth parishes and joins the Soar south of Leicester. This river the Celts called the Glen. This name may derive from the Welsh word for valley; but the early forms of the name make it more likely that it comes from the Welsh word *glano*, meaning 'sweet or good-flowing water'. This is what Sence means in Anglo-Saxon: the Anglo-Saxon immigrants in the Dark Ages then simply translated the local Welsh river name into their own speech as Sence: which in Old English has the connotation of 'holy' or 'clean' water (the word could even be used in the sense of a cup or draught of pure water). So the Anglo-Saxon word replaced the Welsh; but the British name has survived in today's village names of Great Glen and Glen Parva, at opposite ends of the same stream. Glen indeed may conceivably have been the name of the whole Roman estate covering our village, as remembered still in the ninth century when the King of the Mercians held his court next door to Kibworth *aet Glenne*.

So though this early in the tale we cannot yet piece together a coherent 'chorographical' narrative, let alone the tale of individual lives, with these disparate fragments the story begins to take shape and an ancient landscape begins to come to life. The pre-Roman river names spoken by the Iron Age tribe here, the Corieltauvi, survived and came down to us; names from the deep past which are still spoken though their significance is forgotten. Though modern genetic studies show the lowest percentage of the ancient British DNA occurs in a band across from East Anglia into this part of the East Midlands, reflecting perhaps the track of the most intensive Anglo-Saxon migrations after the fall of Rome, yet it still represents two thirds of the lowland British population as a whole. This can only be at best a rough guess, but it is an indicator. It is very likely that in the main the ancient British population survived here too, underneath the overlay of Germanic newcomers who were fairly rapidly assimilated. Today the people speak modern English, which is derived from Anglo-Saxon, the incomers' speech; Anglo-Saxon and Viking place names dominate in the village fields and lanes; but behind it all lie the ancient Britons, and sometimes even here there are names of Celtic origin. For example, in one of the great open fields in Kibworth Beauchamp one big furlong was known to Kibworth farmers as the Gric or Grig. In local speech one spoke of going as far as 'the Gric Meare' (or boundary), or of going 'up on Grig' or 'along Grig'. This word comes from *creig*, meaning 'hill' in primitive and modern Welsh, and was perhaps left by British-speaking people whose coins are still found in Kibworth fields and whose language must have still been spoken here in the early Anglo-Saxon period. Such indigenous names for landmarks and fields were part of the mixed speech of the Dark Ages (when it was still possible even in the early eighth century to hear Welsh spoken not far away in the fens on the edge of Northamptonshire.) In the story of England this layering of culture, language and custom on to much older, and often unseen, identities will be a recurring theme in our account: part of the mysterious crystallization which shapes the life of every community over time.

# 2. The Roots of a Community

The village of Kibworth emerges into the light of history in the first century AD. The Romans invaded these islands in AD 43, and Britain became a province of the Roman Empire: its name, Britannia, simply Romanizes the Prydein of its native speakers (as it still is in Welsh; its meaning is 'land of the painted people'). Their conquest of lowland Britain seems to have been swift here, and even perhaps without fighting. Rapidly extending their power north and west, the Romans engineered great military roads, Watling Street, Fosse Way, Ermine Street and the Via Devana, all of which cross in Leicestershire in the very centre of the island. There they laid out a new capital which they called Ratae Corieltauvorum – 'The Ramparts of the Corieltauvi' – at the junction of Fosse Way and the Via Devana, where a small Iron Age settlement already existed on a low gravel terrace by a ford of the River Soar. The early Roman fortress has yet to be detected by modern archaeologists below the grand remains of the later *civitas*, but it seems likely that the legions present in the area were the Ninth or Fourteenth.

Soon the short-lived military cantonment became a well-heeled tribal capital in the province of Britannia Secunda, its administrative functions replacing the Iron Age fort at Burrough on the Hill and the tribal mint at Old Sleaford. From the late third century, after an imperial reorganization, the province received a more grandiose title honouring the empress: Flavia Caesariensis. By then the town was walled with a forum and basilica, a huge bath house and even a small gladiatorial arena. Beyond the city a network of farms – villas – spread out across the countryside providing the food surplus for the army and the bureaucracy, and wool for export. So the Celtic 'Land of Rivers' became a prosperous Roman colony in the British province of Flavia Caesariensis.

To the Romans, Britain was always an *alter orbis*, another world (that is, situated outside the traditional tripartite division of Europe, Africa and Asia) 'set at an angle' to the European landmass. The island was one of the last to be annexed to the imperium and remained a peripheral place, though valuable for its raw materials: its tin, silver, gold and lead, its grain and above all its wool (which would be a staple of the economy throughout the Anglo-Saxon and medieval periods). But though on the edge of the civilized world and in some sense 'underdeveloped' as we would say, the province took on the air of a land of milk and honey in some colonial literature: 'How lucky you are, Britain,' gushed one Roman panegyricist in AD 310:

more blessed than any other land, endowed by Nature with every benefit of soil and climate. Your winters not too cold, your summers not too hot; your cornfields so productive, your herds numberless, your dairy herds overflowing with milk, your sheep flocks heavy with wool: and to make life even sweeter, your days are long and your nights short, so while to us the sun may appear to go down, in Britain it merely seems to go past!

He might have been writing about the villa estates around Kibworth and Medbourne, 'the best grazing land in Britain – if not the world', as Kibworth farmers still describe it today.

The people of Britain thus became part of a bigger world. Even here in Leicestershire imports came from the farthest corners: a Hellenistic Greek box with fine ivory decorations showing the Egyptian god of the dead, for example. The jackal-headed Anubis found its way to Leicestershire on the same sea routes that brought pilgrim flasks from early-Christian Alexandria. The people of the Roman villa estate at Kibworth found themselves part of what the Romans called an *oikoumene*, a single world; and at this moment a citizen could travel from the Atlas Mountains to Hadrian's Wall or from Syria to York (as the world traveller Demetrius of Tarsus did) and still be part of the imperium. A Greek-speaking British doctor, Hermogenes, raised his altar here in Greek to the 'Mighty Saviour Gods' of the mysterious oak-clad island of Samothraki in the Aegean Sea. Likewise

Roman émigrés erected shrines to their ancestral deities by Celtic streams and sacred woods, like the one near Leicester at the spring of Willoughby on the Wolds which they called Vernemetum, using the old Celtic word for a sacred grove. In the 'Land of Rivers' water shrines were naturally especially popular among locals and colonists. No fewer than seven sacred springs have survived around Kibworth and the Langtons, where the Celtic goddess Anu is still honoured today at her ancient spring, though now in the guise of a holy well dedicated to the Christian St Anne. At Hallaton, St Helen, the mother of Constantine, has taken the place of Elena, the Celtic deity of the waters. In the thirteenth century the customary pilgrimage of the Kibworth people was to an ancient chapel above the Welland by a still more ancient sacred spring.

All this was the residue of the ancient pantheism of the Celts. Such indigenous cults were easily assimilated to the Mediterranean classical pantheon. In this part of Leicestershire figurines of Venus have been found, and clay lamps bearing her figure binding her hair. The three-horned bull deity of the Celts, Tarvas Trigaranos, was happily accepted here by the Roman colonists. The Celtic cock became a symbol of Mercury. Hercules too found his local avatar here in Leicestershire. The world before monotheism was naturally and easily ecumenical. A civic-minded Roman Briton, Aponius Rogatianus, commemorating his parents and ancestors, endowed his local *mithraeum* with an altar to 'Mithras of Persia, the Greek Apollo, Anicetus of the Celts and Sol of Rome', in his mind all names for the same god. Such syncretisms were typical of the time. The Leicester citizen who treasured his Egyptian ivory Anubis, the food dealer on Hadrian's Wall, the merchant in Colchester or the soap maker in Aleppo, the scribe in the baking square of Timgad or the flax maker by the breezy beaches of Amorgos whose crimson-dyed cloths were exported as far as Britain along with the fine Samian found all over Kibworth, all could say, 'Cives Romanus sum.'

## *Life in the villa*

Roman Britain at its height was a populous land. One of the surprising recent developments in our knowledge of Roman Britain has been the enormous increase in rural settlements discovered by modern surveying techniques, by field archaeology and aerial photography. This means that old estimates of the population of Roman Britain at 2 million maximum are probably way off the mark. By the third century the population was more than 3 million – maybe even 4 million at the height of the empire, before military disasters and social conflict in the late fourth century were followed by climate change, and a series of pandemics, famines and natural catastrophes between the middle of the sixth century and the late seventh. It is an extraordinary thought that Roman Britain may have had a larger population than England at the accession of Elizabeth I in 1558.

The towns were the essential transmitters of *Romanitas*. Civilization after all means life in cities. The people of the Kibworth villa and its peasants and slaves, like all such places across Britain, were dependent on their local provincial capital with its market and its amenities. The *civitas* of Ratae was ruled by leading members of the community, probably in this part of the world descendants of the tribal aristocracy of the Corieltauvi. If our villa owner belonged to an important clan with wide estates it is possible that he was a member of the council of the *colonia*, a citizen of Rome but proud of his Celtic lineage and tribal identity. (Celtic royal names from such people – Maporix, for example – have turned up in graffiti in Leicester.) Such men were expected to provide for many civic amenities from their own pockets, a duty at first willingly accepted but later enforced as the economy was progressively squeezed. In the second and third centuries towns all over Britain were provided with civic buildings and other amenities. But the urban population was sustained by the countryside, by the villas. Food production was the major occupation of the population. And wool was a major part of the surplus of any landowner. So with the exception of a small mercantile class, wealth was dependent on land ownership. The economy of our villa would have been mostly in arable, and also in sheep whose fleeces might have been carted off by road to the imperial weaving mill in Winchester before being exported as 'British woollens'. Some of the great villas were almost what we would recognize in the eighteenth century as wool mills.

The boulder clay lands of Kibworth, Glen and the Langtons were a valuable source of income to their owners back in Roman times, just as they were after 1066 to landlords like the Norman Hugh Grandmesnil, the Harcourts and Beauchamps in the Middle Ages, or Merton College, all of whom organized, regulated and exploited the labour of their workforce in much the same way. Even in Roman times it appears that a proportion of the population were free farmers. But the Roman Empire organized farming in Britain on a large scale for the first time, increasing food production to feed the army and the bureaucracy. And with a fast-growing population, the countryside was increasingly opened up to farming, as is revealed locally by the pottery scatter found in the fields around the villa site at Kibworth, and by the frequent finds of pieces of stone querns or hand-mills which were used to grind flour. From now on until the Industrial Revolution Kibworth would be a farming community.

As for the ordinary people, circular huts appear on the magnetometry surveys, where seven or eight houses can be distinguished, but no doubt more lie underneath the present village and adjacent fields. The inhabitants were of British descent (of largely the same DNA shared by Irish, Welsh, Scots and most lowland English even today). As we have seen, they were British-speaking; though perhaps with a sprinkling of people of foreign descent who spoke the Latin language too. During the empire most of the peasants lived in timber-framed houses with mud walls and thatch – the indigenous style of peasant housing till recently in south Leicestershire (in the 1860s Kibworth still had nearly twenty of these 'mud houses').

As for the villa itself, modern excavations of villas and town houses in the region have given us a sense of how the owners and the workforce lived. Such houses were in reality just big working farms with barns, stables and accommodation blocks for the slaves and other staff.

Inside they were sparsely furnished, as farming places still tend to be. They had plastered or tiled floors, wooden furniture with simple decoration. Little bronze dolphins as table brackets (such as have been found locally) might be the only hint of city style; a locked box decorated with bone inlay to contain valuables; tripod lamp stands for the clay oil lights which were used everywhere after nightfall. In the second century, along with cheap local pottery or wooden tableware for everyday use, the Kibworth villa owner used fine orange-red Samian tableware for special occasions. In the corners of the main living room were little incense burners – tazzas – used in the ceremonies of the house, such as family commemorations and anniversaries. For domestic cults there was a shrine room with a little stone altar to the gods of springs and waters. These spirits and deities as we have seen had a very tenacious life around Kibworth and in the little valleys down to Hallaton and the Welland. And though our villa was an ordinary place, later in its existence it had a mosaic floor and plastered walls with wall paintings. In the local capital house murals have been excavated which are among the best found in Britain and which give an idea of what provincial firms of painters could achieve. In luminous colours they show shaded verandas hung with garlands and lamps, peacocks and yellow singing birds, musical instruments and the theatrical masks of comedy and tragedy. The pigments range from deep red ochre, cinnabar and lime, blue frit, terre verte, soot and charcoal, to still intense yellow ochre. They are a haunting suggestion of the good life that spread out even to the villas along the Glen and Langton Brook.

## Farming

Farming was the key activity and food production the most important job in the empire. Traces of Roman farming at Kibworth may still be detected on the ground. In Kibworth Harcourt aerial photographs and old maps reveal traces of huge ancient furlongs such as are found in other parts of Celtic Britain. The crucial evidence comes from two quarters, the first being a dig by the local archaeologist Bert Aggas, who has already figured in this tale. Aggas never published his finds but left a set of detailed notes with hand-drawn maps and plans. Just outside the village at the town end on the Leicester road, as we have seen, he excavated a prehistoric burial tumulus which had been used as a windmill mound in the thirteenth century. In the same field he also found scattered fragments of Roman pottery left by 'manuring' (when broken pottery mixed up with the manure in the farmyard is taken out and dumped on the fields). Field-walking by villagers in 2009 picked up more sherds in a neighbouring ploughed field.

We know then that the windmill field and its neighbours were under cultivation during Roman rule. Running away from the windmill mound across today's pasture there is still a prominent rise in the ground which from tithe maps can be identified as the former edge of a huge ancient field whose hedge has long since been grubbed out. The old field divisions here have mainly gone since the last strips of the medieval open fields were broken up after enclosure in 1789; but the ridge and furrow still visible on the ground show the older pattern. With the seventeenth-century estate maps in Merton College we can see what was once here. In an arc round the northern edge of the village was a large field more than a kilometre long and known as the Banwell Furlong. The prehistoric windmill mound was at its western end, the newly discovered villa close by. Then on the other side of the A6 (which was evidently already a track in prehistory) there was another huge curving furlong precisely lined up with the Banwell. This furlong was of the same dimensions – a thousand yards long – and was also ploughed in strips across its width. In the Middle Ages this second great field was called Peasehill or Peas Sik Furlong (an Old English word, 'peas' is first recorded in the eighth century – its meaning was wider than modern 'pea', covering a variety of green legumes and describing one of the staple crops of the Dark Ages and of the medieval three-field system). The Roman pottery sherds under the plough ridges indicate that these furlongs were cleared in Roman times or earlier, and that they had never gone out of cultivation for any long period of time between the later fourth century and the high Middle Ages in the heyday of the open-field system.

Banwell Furlong then and its companion Peasehill are perhaps fields from the late Iron Age or the time of the Roman villa. The peasants grew grain and legumes in these fields, which they ploughed with the improved Roman heavy plough. They kept pigs and cattle. On the streams they grew osier beds, in the meadow flax for clothing, dye plants, woad and madder in their cottage gardens. Their basic food in addition to meat consisted of the vegetables which have been the staple diet in Britain ever since: peas, beans, onions, garlic, white carrots and cabbage. Beyond the big fields they opened up grazing land on the clays for the sheep flocks that must have provided the commercial wealth of the estate. With the villa then, the pattern of the manorial economy, which would last until the eighteenth century, or even later, was set.

### Kibworth in the late-Roman world

With such scattered evidence – field finds, surveys, metal detectors, chance coin finds – we can build our first tentative picture of the village. It was a classic Romano-Celtic tribal settlement of huts and farm protected by an outer ditch and hedge. We can imagine a few hundred acres of arable, some woodland, sheep pasture and several ox teams kept in the villa barns. The workforce would have been mainly dependent peasants, *coloni*, and their families, with some hired labour and some slaves, *servi*, who lived in a workers' block among the farm buildings. But there were also free tenants farming their own fields with their own oxen and their own flocks.

That is as far as we can go in building up a picture from the fragmentary finds in the soil. To endow the early people of the village with the warmth of life we must turn to the fragmentary inscriptional material from Leicestershire (including vivid curse graffiti scratched on pot-sherds), supplemented by Roman texts discovered in recent years elsewhere in Britain. Fragments of letters from elsewhere in second-century Roman Britain are from garrison communities but vividly convey a flavour of the civic life of the provinces: grouses about deferred promotion, birthday invitations, grocers' orders, the weather and for some émigrés, Romans like Marcus Novantico for example, the irritatingly provincial customs of the natives – the Brittunculi, 'the little Brits'.

Some texts were written by native British-speakers whose day-to-day speech was Celtic and whose Latin was plainly tentative (as might be expected in a countryside only lightly Romanized), but the letters reveal the everyday life of real people whose concerns were no different in many ways from those of today: news, shopping, charitable donations, family connections, the mess, the club, ordering luxuries from London – Massic wine for birthday parties and festivals of the goddess, 'Celtic beer' for daily consumption (British drinking habits have not changed). Virilis the vet writing to his academy chums ends with a flourish: *vale Londini*, 'farewell, deliver this at London'. In Leicester there is Primus, the tile maker, the women Atica and Martina; and one of the more delightful couples from anywhere in Roman Britain, Lucius the gladiator and his actress lover Verecunda, his scratched love token telling of a match surely made for the Roman tabloids: in short, the stuff of civic life of any time.

Such letters and the supplies they describe, with news of the outside world, came from the city to the villa by horse or ox-drawn carts past milestones set by the deified Hadrian with their comforting sense of measure and order and permanence. And with them a last glimpse of late-Roman Kibworth. In the veranda round the villa courtyard the stores are unloaded from the wagon; as the lamps are lit the *coloni* are bringing the oxen in, while slaves scurry about their tasks. For the dinner party fairy lights are strung out into the open air. The kitchen is busy. Tonight there will be food on the tables, Samian wine, Italian fish paste and Colchester oysters. In the corner of the shrine room terracotta tazzas spiral incense in front of the altar to Mercury as the owner and his family pour a libation to the ancestors, around them even here, as a classical poet said, the 'soft breeze of wealth'. The luxuries bought by civilization. For the elites at least, the gifts of *Romanitas*.

## 'The awful revolution'

From the late third century the Roman world was rocked by a series of crises that would lead eventually to the fall of the empire in the

West and the collapse of civic order and the disappearance of Roman power from Britain. This 'awful revolution' was played out against a background of social uprisings and class war, the internecine rivalries of usurpers and warlords, and bitter religious divisions which helped undermine the ethos, the group feeling, which had underwritten the idea of *Romanitas*. But the biggest factor in these changes was the migration of impoverished immigrants from outside the empire who would turn lowland Britain into a world of pagan Germanic tribes – and then eventually into a Christian Anglo-Saxon kingdom of England. All these changes are marked in the story of the village, at first almost imperceptibly, later in vivid detail as the life of the people unfolds in their landscape.

In the 330s in York the restored empire of Constantine the Great was formally proclaimed Christian, but in the village life seems to have gone on as usual. There is no trace of Christianity yet in the area, though the coins the people carried in their purses as they went to market in Leicester or Medbourne carried Christian emblems now along with the emperor's head. As yet decline and revolution were only a shadow on the horizon, and Christianity was not yet the future but merely, perhaps it seemed to the old families of the Corieltauvi in the hills between the Glen and the Welland, a faint damp stain rising up the wall of their traditional culture; and it was one whose spreading spores would eventually disintegrate not just the old image but the mansion itself. However, the first serious anxieties which arose for the people of the late-Roman village came in the form of a very real physical threat: the barbarians.

Around the year 400 the peasants were still farming their strips of arable on the Banwell Furlong, giving their surplus to a local British lord. They still used coin to buy and sell in the neighbouring towns. One clue may be illusory, but a tiny find made at Kibworth may hint at the coming change. It was made near the windmill mound, fifty yards from the villa site, by the side of the local track which became the A6, just where it crosses the Jurassic Way. There, a late-Roman belt buckle plate or strap end turned up, decorated with a dragon-like figure. The buckle is identical to a bronze belt buckle of the late fourth or fifth century found in the ruins of the Jewry Wall bath house in Leicester. These items of late-Roman military gear are often associated with army units drawn from Germanic peoples beyond the imperial frontiers. Could this be a hint of a late-Roman army in Kibworth in a time of growing anxiety? Could it even have belonged to a Germanic mercenary, one of the *laeti* or *foederati* which late-Roman civic communities employed for their defence? Such an isolated find would not be worth interrogating did we not know elsewhere of the presence of such people, and it could be a faint pointer to the growing militarization of society even in the countryside. Did warfare or disorder spread down the Via Devana towards 400? On such tiny hints it would be unwise to build much. The buckle could after all have been lost by a soldier home on leave. But nonetheless in the wider world the times were changing.

Before Constantine the empire had already been rocked by disasters; the third century had been a time of civil wars and military juntas. In the 330s the new order of Constantine adopted Christianity and for a while deployed its forces with renewed energy and muscular conviction. But later in the century there were more rebellions and regional secessions. The coin finds recorded by John Nichols in the eighteenth century and those found since show Kibworth was still an active late-Roman community through the fourth century; indeed, the villa itself may have survived. Archaeological explorations in the wider region show villas still working after 400 close by in Rutland and the Welland Valley and new metal detector finds show the circulation of coinage well into the fifth century. The Kibworth settlement then still functioned in a world of trade and markets through the fourth century and into the fifth, maybe even still with connections to a wider world. But towards the end of the fourth century the military threats seem to have grown which would eventually lead to the Romans abandoning Britain.

As glimpsed in our fragmentary sources, and from finds in the soil, the fall of Roman Britain is as yet imperfectly understood. But the tale in Britain superficially resembles decolonization struggles in the modern world, or the factional fighting that happens in the post-colonial aftermath, as say in Angola and Darfur, with suppressed regional and tribal identities reasserting themselves as they did in the late-twentieth-century Balkans. The reasons for the breakdown of the Roman Empire in its different regions were similarly complex. Economy and climate, a widening gulf between social classes, structural and bureaucratic failure in the army and civil service, ethnic rivalries and an increasing dependence on brought-in military aid as complacency took over self-help: all played their part. The pervasive sense was of 'the Other World against This World', coupled with that indefinable loss of 'group feeling' that leads to failure of nerve in a civilization.

The fall of Rome then involved complex processes, as great changes in history always do, out of which our modern identities and communities emerged. For the Kibworth settlement life went on as it had through the late fourth century, its local markets still functioning at Leicester and the little town at Medbourne. Only after 400 does the impression grow of a coming Dark Age. The clues are again provided by recent coin finds. The last large shipment of Roman coins to pay the army began to arrive in Britain in AD 402. After around 407 no new coinage is in use. Finds from buried hoards suggest the last currency to circulate in the region between Kibworth and the Welland were of the usurper Magnus Maximus (383–8), Arcadius (Eastern emperor 383–408) and Honorius (Western emperor 393–423). All these are also represented in new finds by local metal detectorists around Kibworth. Coins of Honorius found nearby in Rutland surprisingly suggest the circulation of money well into the fifth century, and with that a functioning economy. But the coins are not the whole picture. In the late fourth century our narrative sources from the centre show that the administrative coherence of the Roman world was beginning to break down, and at the same time there are the first hints of the presence of large numbers of Germanic migrants from outside Britain.

## Barbarians

In the late fourth century the growing disorder had begun to present pressing problems for the civic authorities in Britannia. The Romans had never conquered Ireland or what is now Scotland, and there were now constant raids from these quarters. There were also raids from Angles, Saxons and Frisians along the North Sea coasts, a mere two or three days' sailing from Jutland and Saxony. Writing before the crisis, in the 380s, the Byzantine historian Eutropius says the north-western seaboard was already infested by Franks and Saxons all the way down to Brittany. This was the result of a longstanding tension between those inside and those outside the imperial frontiers. Back in the third century the Romans had studded the coast on both sides of the Channel with forts extending from Brittany to Frisia, and from the Solent to the Wash. For almost two centuries now the British author-ities had also employed federates, mercenaries and economic migrants, planting them in colonies outside their cities, to defend not only against seaborne invaders but also against other tribes and kingdoms around their borders inside Britain. There had always been this kind of policy of recruitment in empire. Inscriptions on Hadrian's Wall show Frisians and Germans employed there as early as AD 212. In 278 the emperor brought Germans living beyond the Oder to Britain to quell a revolt; in 306 Constantius Chlorus brought in Alemanni. More recent Rhineland pottery found on Hadrian's Wall is from German forces used in the reorganization of northern defences in 369. Britain then was already changing.

The process of deliberate settlement by the government was con-tinuous and long term. Many of these troops married local women and remained in Britain. It is possible even that the belt buckle found in Kibworth belonged to such a person. The Roman authorities in Britain also bred German *laeti*, subsidizing their families to live on estates as agricultural workers and peasant soldiers – farming the lands attached to the forts of the 'Saxon shore' and owing military service. Though sparsely mentioned in Roman accounts such people reappear

in the early Anglo-Saxon law codes under that name. In the coastal
zone especially, along the 'Saxon shore' on the eastern seaboard, Germanic languages were already spoken, and the first signs were on the
way of a mixed British–Germanic society.

## The fall of Rome

In the last years of the fourth century and the first years of the fifth,
the empire was rocked by tremendous events. A series of revolts took
place in Britain, where tyrants used the province's military resources
to fight continental wars. The reverberations created in the Kibworth
area are revealed in the burial of moveable wealth, among these the
Whitwell Hoard of 870 silver siliquae, one of many buried at this
time. On the last day of December 406 a huge confederation of barbarian tribes crossed the Roman defence works along the Rhine and
eventually settled permanently inside the empire. Within months, in
early 407, a British soldier proclaimed himself Western emperor and
stripped Britain of its troops to fight a savage civil war lasting four
years before it ended with the usurper's death. Almost inevitably in
the midst of this perfect storm – with Goths marching in Italy, Vandals camped on the Rhine, and usurpers fighting each other's legions
in Gaul – the Roman government chose to sever connections with
the province 'at the outermost edge of the known world'.

In 410 the empire was already split between East and West with
emperors in Rome and Byzantium. In the eastern Mediterranean
heartland, on the edge of Europe and Asia, Constantinople was secure
behind the vast new Theodosian land walls, its empire more urbanized, populous and wealthy, with standing armies and a powerful
fleet, the bastion of a Greek civilization that still ruled to the Euphra-
tes and Aswan. In the Latin West the Emperor Honorius had moved
his court from Rome to Ravenna to be nearer the Alpine passes, the
military axis of empire, but also behind the coastal saltings, malarial
marshes and winding waterways of Ravenna, to be better protected
from barbarian attacks which were now threatening Rome itself.

Our information about the ensuing events in Britain comes from the historian and civil servant Zosimus, who worked for the imperial treasury in Constantinople. It was in 410 in Ravenna, Zosimus tells us, that the Emperor Honorius, in response to a British petition for military aid against Saxon barbarians threatening their shores, wrote his famous letter to the twenty-four *civitates*, the city councils of Britain, 'ordering' or 'exhorting' or 'counselling' them to provide for their own defence. This critical moment in British history Zosimus records in a laconic parenthesis with a frustrating lack of detail:

Thus happened this revolt or defection of Britain and the Celtic nations, when Constantine usurped the empire, by whose negligent government the barbarians were emboldened to commit such devastations . . . [then] Honorius, having sent letters to the cities of Britain, counselling them to look after their own security . . .

On 24 August 410, the city of Rome fell to Alaric and the Visigoths, 800 years after it had last been entered by a foreign army. The Eternal City was not destroyed, its people not massacred, though they endured three days of looting. But as a symbolic moment it has few peers. The mausoleums of Augustus and Hadrian and the graves of other emperors were ransacked and their ashes cast into the Tiber. Bronze portrait busts, gilded peacocks and funerary furniture tumbled into a rubbish heap.

The dreadful symbolism of the moment was recognized at the time and cast reverberations far and wide. Far away in North Africa in the sleepy provincial town of Hippo Regius (now Annaba in Algeria), the former pagan, ex-professor of rhetoric in the schools of Milan and now a Christian bishop Augustine was inspired to conceive the idea of his magnum opus. With Rome sacked and Huns, Goths and Vandals breaking the frontiers of the imperium, he would write about the End of History, and a new city that would rise – the City of God, a Christian world to usher in the end of time, in which history was redemptive, purposive and leading to an appointed end. It was an interpretation which barbarian successors in the northern reaches of the empire would embrace wholeheartedly and never quite abandon; a book whose ideas defined the mentalities of the

Dark Age West, of the barbarians who built their new kingdoms on the ruins of Rome and who in time would become the new Romans.

## On the ground in Britain

Now we enter the period where our evidence simply gives out, both for the village and for lowland Britain as a whole. On the ground even the scatter of archaeological finds dies out and we are reliant on a few tantalizing hints in written sources, the most important being from a civil servant far away in Constantinople who perceived these distant events through a glass darkly. Zosimus's disappointingly brief account has had a transfixing power in the narrative of British history. He was a bureaucrat in Constantinople with a greater tale to tell than the fate of a remote underdeveloped province far away from the powerhouses of civilization in Constantinople, Antioch and Alexandria. But we can supplement it (cautiously) with the earliest narrative source for British history, the priest Gildas in his book *The Fall of Britain*. Gildas was writing in the 540s, well over a century after these events. But he wrote in a still literate zone (the Cumbrian region), in a learned culture with its own living Latin tradition, and he had access to both oral stories and written records. His is the only near-eyewitness account and he had a good general grasp of what had actually happened in the cities of lowland Britain in the decades before his birth, and in the villa societies in the regions of the Welland, the Weald and the Cotswolds. His main goal was not historical accuracy but a raging polemic against the failings of contemporary British rulers, and some of the more lurid parts of his text describing blood and thunder, fire from sea to sea and the violent destruction of cities, with the dead left unburied in the streets, have found no confirmation in archaeology. But Gildas was clearly well-informed on these events, some of which he alludes to in passing as if they are still common knowledge looking back over the previous century and a half.

As Gildas tells it, the turning point came in 383, when the country was stripped of troops by the Roman general Maximus. From then

Britain, 'despoiled of her whole army', reeled under growing instability with attacks from Irish raiders in the north-west and Picts in the north. Gildas seems to refer to the same events as Zosimus but with more detail: 'As a result of their terrible and ruinous onslaughts, Britain sent envoys with a letter to Rome desperately requesting a military force to protect them and vowing wholehearted and undiminished loyalty to the Roman Empire so long as their enemies were kept at a distance.'

Gildas tells of the despatch of a well-equipped legion by sea from Gaul, the defeat of northern enemies and the refurbishment of a turf wall in the north. But after reinforcements were withdrawn, more invaders came by sea. Then 'for a second time envoys set out with their petition.' Gildas tells the tale (apparently from an oral tradition) of how one arrived in Rome, 'so it is said', and rent his clothes and cast dust on his hair in the ancient gesture of supplication. 'The Romans were as distressed as is humanly possible by the story of such a tragedy' and again sent military aid and won some spectacular victories with their 'surge'. But such an enemy – like the Taliban today – is notoriously prone to vanish – and then return.

The Romans again responded. Further reinforcements were sent, the wall in the north was refurbished and victories were won, but with new crises on the continent once again legions were withdrawn, leaving Britain open to 'annual plundering expeditions that took heaps of loot overseas'. Finally the aid dried up, and here Gildas seems to give us the gist of the contents of the letter sent to the city authorities in Britain mentioned by Zosimus; we may imagine the town council of Ratae among the twenty-four *colonia* of Roman Britain receiving this fateful missive: 'The Romans informed our country (*patria*) that they could no longer be taken up with such energy-sapping expeditions.' The huge military resources 'of so great and splendid an army' could not be committed by land and sea for the sake of battle with mobile enemies, thieves and bandits who would not engage in conventional warfare, and had no taste for face-to-face, hand-to-hand combat.

These are words we have heard often with insurgencies in our own time. All the more difficult because the Romans had no means of seeking the enemy out in their own bases, which lay far beyond the frontier of *Romanitas*. One imagines the assembled citizens bracing themselves:

Rather (from now on) the people of Britain should stand alone, get themselves accustomed to arms, fight bravely, and defend with all their powers their land, property, wives, children and more important their life and liberty. Their enemies were no stronger than they unless the Britons chose to relax in laziness and torpor. This was the Romans' advice.

Even then, Gildas adds, there was still a final injection of public money. There were last-minute military construction projects from public and private funds and new military constructions, defensive walls, and 'the citizens were left instruction manuals on weapons training.' Also, to combat the growing threat from another quarter, Anglian and Saxon sea raiders from the continent, the Romans 'left towers overlooking the sea at intervals on the South Coast where they kept their ships: for now they were afraid of the barbarian beasts attacking on that front too' (this is apparently a reference to the refurbishment of forts on 'the Saxon shore', actually erected during the previous century but restored at this time). And then, finally, says Gildas, 'et valedicunt tamquam ultra non reverturi' – 'then they said goodbye, meaning never to return'.

## Epilogue

Of these tumultuous events locals in the valleys of the Glen and the Welland must have had knowledge through their provincial and civic authorities in Leicester, and through long-distance hauliers, merchants and travellers who were always a source of news. But, of course, in the villas to the south, at Great Glen, Langton and Kibworth, the world did not change that year; nor perhaps for the next few decades. In some places in the Welland valley in the early fifth century villas were refurbished, new extensions built, new mosaic floors laid; so not only did town councils and rural landlords continue to function but even travelling firms of mosaic craftsmen were still able to find work. But what of those last-ditch injections of military funds, and the defence instruction manuals mentioned by Gildas? Is the belt buckle found near the Kibworth villa after all a clue to the increasing frequency of raids from the sea? Were the local nobility of the Corieltauvi concerned enough to employ their own *laeti*, importing paramilitaries to their towns and farms? For them, for their peasant tenants and their slaves, the revolutions of the fifth century were as yet only a shadow on the horizon. But in the years after 410 they must have been fully occupied with the events described by Zosimus from afar in Constantinople: 'then the British set about organizing their own defence and freed their cities from the barbarian attacks . . . and went on living on their own without obedience to Roman laws . . .'

The next forty years are among the most critical in British history but are among the least understood. The situation on the ground was evidently radically different between western Britain, where Roman British society survived with cities and tribal 'kings', and the east, where a mixed British and Germanic society was already developing. But the Roman world didn't disappear into a void: civil society still existed. Even close to London in 429 Verulamium was a still functioning city, where the former Roman official Germanus of Auxerre, who came from Gaul to visit the shrine of Alban the protomartyr, could be received by civic authorities and find pilgrim hostels and the wherewithal to receive visitors. Indeed some cities – Bath, Cirencester and Gloucester among them – survived as centres into the late sixth century. But, according to a Gallic chronicle, in the late 440s 'Britain fell under the control of Saxons.'

Gildas's account also points to the same decade: he says that in 446 attacks by Anglo-Saxon raiders had become so severe that British authorities made a further last-ditch but fruitless appeal for military aid in a letter to the Roman consul Aetius. By then, if later traditions are to be believed, disorder had spread across southern Britain and civil wars had broken out between regional warlords, with mercenary revolts and counter-marches by predatory armies. Gildas gives us graphic images of the breakdown of civic order: demolished buildings and overturned altars, unburied dead in town squares. Where this took place is not known, for no archaeological evidence of wholesale devastation has so far been detected, and it may be that Gildas is reporting a localized disaster. But there is one significant detail where his sweeping account has been amply confirmed. In lowland Britain this was a period of progressive abandonment of cities by local authorities and of retreat to the old Iron Age hill forts. Over forty of them have yielded archaeological evidence of this shift, among them Cadbury Castle in Somerset and the magnificent fort at Burrough Walls on the Jurassic escarpment over the Wreake valley near Leicester – the old tribal centre of the Corieltauvi. There is no doubt then that by the middle of the fifth century important social change was in the offing. *Romanitas* was on the wane and in lowland Britain, still populous, and in places still well-off, a return to older modes of society was under way.

And in Kibworth, our scanty sources, such as they are, now run out. The villa is abandoned, its wall paintings crumbled, the floor tesserae scattered and its coins are out of use. The local community is left to fend for itself under a Welsh-speaking chief (though perhaps still owing allegiance to a civic authority in Leicester), while to the east the news is of a growing number of Anglian and Frisian settlements, in some places tribes and clans settled under their chiefs around towns, bearing weapons in exchange for land, speaking a language very different from that of the Britons. *Romanitas* with all its benefits is over now, and its technology, its level of material wealth – and its order – for many would not be regained till the eighteenth century. Locally and nationally the narrative now moves into the hands of the newcomers.

# 3. Angles and Saxons

Some time towards the end of the fifth century, perhaps around the year 475, a band of people picked their way up a little stream which flows down between low hills west of the River Welland. Heading towards the Kibworth ridge, their track led past British villages and ruined Roman villas by Langton Brook and on Glooston Hill. Men, women and children, horses carrying packs, tents, poles and cooking pots; we might guess a couple of hundred people in all. Their war gear was not Roman – their wooden circular shields were studded with leather with iron bosses, they had dragon-patterned belt buckles, fleece-lined wooden scabbards and enamelled sword hilts. Their spears had long wide flanged blades, their horses' harnesses had crude linked-iron bridle bits. Though there were echoes of Roman war gear in the leaders' helmets hanging on leather straps from their saddles, these were mutated copies of Roman cavalry helmets with neck flaps and cheek pieces, but with boar's head nasal pieces inlaid with garnets, and tinned plaques with serpents and wolves' heads.

Among them was a striking young woman. She was of medium height – 5 foot 6 inches, well-built and strong. She was young, around twenty years – it is easy to forget that most of the new migrants must have been young. She wore a linen tube dress with a wool undergarment held by two bronze cruciform shoulder brooches with elongated horses' heads. Her jewellery included animal bone amulets, rings and, at her waist, girdle hangers, softly tinkling, delicately punched with dotted lines of decoration: imitations of a Roman chatelaine's keys – not real keys but symbols of her position as woman of the house, the *hlafdig*. Round her neck hung a bear claw amulet and a large orange fluted Roman melon bead. As for her ethnicity, that is another matter. We speak of the newcomers as Anglo-Saxons and refer to the 'Coming of the English' as a definable historical event; but the fact is that the population of Britain remained largely the same. The same people who were there in the Iron Age and under Rome emerge again at the end of the Dark Ages speaking Anglo-Saxon. As we cannot hear her speak we cannot tell whether she was British or of mixed race. Her dress and ornaments might indicate that she was what we call Anglo-Saxon – except the fluted Roman bead: perhaps an heirloom from her British grandmother? On such matters archaeology is silent.

They were then, we must imagine, typical of the migrants of the day, an amalgam of native Britons and older settlers – Frisians, Angles, Saxons and Danes – plus new migrants from Frisia, Jutland, Denmark and Belgium in the later fifth century. It would have been a two- to three-day journey across the wide seas – 'ofer brad brimu' – in long curving ships propelled with oars like the fourth-century Nydam ship from Denmark. There were clearly some Frisian-speakers. Place names such as Rothwell and Rothley contain the Frisian word *roth* ('clearing') and in two places south of the Welland migrants buried their dead with pottery from the same Frisian workshop as examples found at Saint-Gilles-les-Termonde in eastern Flanders, revealing a remarkably precise example of connections between the continent and this part of the East Midlands in around 500.

But the majority of the settlers in East Anglia and the Midlands were speakers of the Germanic dialect we call Anglian, which takes its name from a region of Schleswig still called Angeln – on a promontory projecting into the Bay of Kiel on the Baltic side of Jutland. This is where the name England comes from, as Bede writing in 721 says in his famous summary of the origin of the *gens Anglorum*:

From the Angles, that is, the country which is called Anglia, and which is said, from that time, to remain desert to this day, between the provinces of the Jutes and the Saxons, are descended the East Angles, the Middle Angles, the Mercians, and all the race of the Northumbrians, that is, of those nations that dwell on the north side of the river Humber, and the other nations of the English.

Though the ethnic mix of early England was predominantly Celtic, the basic story of a sizeable Anglian migration from Jutland must be true. It is likely that the ancestors of many of the band who settled in Kibworth and its region had been in East Anglia for a couple of generations or more, some maybe since the end of Roman rule. Others were recent migrants come over to join their kinsmen and kinswomen. They may have had a paramount leader for whom they used the word *cyning*, 'guardian of the kin', from which comes our word 'king'. According to an ancient Midland tradition he was a man called Icil, son of Eomer, grandson of Angeltheow and ancestor of the Mercian royal pedigree. Long afterwards this family tree was remembered by a descendant, the holy man Guthlac, who was born around 673 and whose family tree dated back to the late fifth century, counting 'step by step' over 200 years, the 'oldest and noblest family in Mercia back to Icil with whom it began in days of old'.

In today's parlance they were economic migrants as much as warbands, hoping to find a livelihood in new lands in lowland Britain. They had made their way into the East Midlands through the Welland valley, leaving as their markers cemeteries with distinctive knobbed pots; their war gear and brooches; and also their place names – as always, silent markers. The earliest stratum of place names left by Germanic migrants consists of names ending in 'ham', the Old English for a 'village or collection of dwellings'. This very common English place name (West Ham, Tottenham and Fulham for example) is a marker for the early Anglo-Saxon expansion across lowland Britain from the east. It is especially associated with Roman sites, towns, villas and the roads by which they travelled in the decayed but still populous former province of Britain. These 'ham' names have their greatest concentration in the east, the earliest area of settlement. There are large numbers in Lincolnshire, seventy in Suffolk, nearly eighty in Norfolk and a small sprinkling in the East Midlands: six each in Rutland and Northamptonshire, a dozen in Leicestershire. This spread is indicative of the Anglian expansion out of East Anglia from around 500. The Welland, their route into Leicestershire, is not a big river (it is only navigable as far as Spalding) but it is a very old cultural boundary between zones. Its valley for example appears to have been a border zone between the Corieltauvi and the Catuvellauni. Surrounded as it is by fine farming country, it is one of the earliest settlement areas in the Midlands.

Beyond the Roman town of Medbourne, where an Anglian community had already settled, 'marvellous goodly meadows' stretch between Welham Hill and the Langtons, as noted by the Tudor traveller John Leland. In the area is a cluster of early Anglo-Saxon cemeteries, one of them on the river at Welham. It was from there perhaps in the late fifth century that a new wave of Anglian settlers moved into the lands that would become the homeland of the Middle Angles and eventually part of Mercia. From Welham, the shallow valleys of two streams fed by springs on the Kibworth ridge naturally led the migrants northwards and both are marked by early-Anglian cemeteries.

Heading on foot up towards Kibworth the traveller crosses one of the streams, the Lipping, by an ancient ford at Stonton Wyville which is still twenty yards wide in wet weather, the water deep enough to cover a car. Small but fast flowing in winter, when it can still flood neighbouring fields in the bottom of the valley, the stream is a perennial source of good water. Beyond the ford the walker passes under 'Knaves Hill', its name derived from the Old English *cnafa*, meaning 'boy', 'youth' or 'young warrior' – it is the site of an early-Anglo-Saxon cremation cemetery. The newcomers seem to have moved along the stream and over rising country to the low ridge on which Kibworth stands today.

There on the ridge where the Roman villa stood, a Welsh-speaking community still lived, cultivating the fields by the abandoned buildings. Here perhaps one of the lesser migrant leaders and his clan stayed while another group moved into the neighbouring valley of the river the Celts called Glen. Here they settled, leaving rich warrior graves and the burial of the woman described at the top of this chapter. Close by was the former *civitas* of Leicester, with its Roman walls still standing, where the old British population continued to live, perhaps under a civic authority, a *praefectus civitatis*; maybe even with a Christian church. Big Anglo-Saxon cemeteries outside the city at Thurcaston and Humberstone are further signs of the newcomers' presence. By now civic amenities had declined and although the Roman aqueduct still functioned, the grand civic buildings were no longer in use. From early Anglo-Saxon poetry it is easy to imagine the migrants' response to the huge and now derelict bath house, one of the most dramatic surviving Roman buildings in Britain, now falling into ruin. 'Wreatlic is thaes wealstan, wyrde gebraecon . . .' – 'Wondrous wallstones, broken by fate . . . the courtyard pavements smashed, the work of giants, their roofs fallen, the cement on their gates split by frost . . . the bright painted murals in the town . . . many the bath houses.'

The earliest English settlement at Kibworth dates from this time, around 500. Its presence was completely unsuspected till the summer of 2009, when a stratified fragment of an incised patterned early-Anglo-Saxon bone comb was found with pottery and metalworking slag under the car park of the Coach and Horses pub on the A6. These were not chance drops. The slag was perhaps from making tools or iron swords; or brooches and pins for women's and men's clothes, like the pair of cruciform brooches found recently by metal detectorists, which probably came from the grave of an early settler; the first traces of the 'English' inhabitants of the village.

## From Angeln to England

So into this fragmented late-Roman world, still perhaps with its run-down but partially functioning cities and its populous countryside, the migrants came, and out of it the earliest English tribes and kingdoms emerged. They were led by kings who were able to establish dynasties and dominate their region with their armed followings, whom they rewarded with treasure, weapons, war gear, slaves, women and land. The first Anglian immigrants in the area may be dated to around 475–500, later than in East Anglia, and the first 'kings' arose perhaps in the sixth century. Our settlers who had journeyed over-land from their core area of power in Suffolk were augmented by new migrants from across the North Sea who had come in increasing numbers into eastern Britain after the early 400s. That said, historians are still in the dark as to exactly how things happened on the ground and about the beginnings of that imperceptible process in society, language and custom by which the Roman Britons became English.

How such people got their land in the Glen valley and the Kibworth hills, how they appropriated the villa sites along the Langton Brook, is not known – whether for example it was by negotiation or even treaty, through deals between Anglian *cyninges* and a surviving civic authority – a *praepositus* or *praefectus civitatis* in Leicester (as there was still in Lincoln in the 620s); whether it was by peaceful assimilation or by ethnic cleansing, killing the men and enslaving the women and children. Depending on local circumstances, no doubt both were the case.

Later written sources for these events are to say the least patchy. Bede wrote his great account of the origin and conversion of the Anglo-Saxon kingdoms in the 720s at Jarrow in Northumbria on the Tyne using largely Northumbrian and Kentish sources and inform-ants; the Anglo-Saxon Chronicle, compiled from earlier material in Wessex in the 890s, inevitably has a southern viewpoint. But the annals of Mercia are lost. Our only account of these momentous events from a Midland perspective appears in much later chronicles of the thirteenth century, and is piecemeal, confused, unverifi-able and hence of dubious value (because it is possible that it is simply an imaginary reconstruction.) It describes an invasion from East Anglia into the East Midlands, the lands of Middle Angles, towards 500, and the formation of an early Mercian kingdom in the Trent valley in the 570s or 580s. This account does at least match what is known from DNA and archaeology. In reality though it was perhaps not a single datable event but a long process by which British tribal groupings in the old area of the Corieltauvi were overcome by Anglian-speaking chieftains from eastern Britain with their ethni-cally mixed warbands. A key idea though is the tradition that just like the Goths, Vandals and Huns in their wanderings in Europe, the Anglo-Saxons came to Britain with what the Germanic tradition called *cyninges* – kings.

Post-Roman Kibworth then comprised both Anglian and British communities. The Anglian chief's wooden hall was of a kind exca-vated at West Stow village in Suffolk (dating from the 420s to 650), a simple timber frame on a raised wooden platform set inside a fenced enclosure to keep the animals safe from rustlers and wolves. Around it were other huts, a threshing floor, a clay bread oven, a small mud and thatch horse mill, weaving sheds and a smithy working metal. Most Anglo-Saxon villages of any size would have had these. Initially we must conjecture the native and Anglian communities lived alongside each other but separately (as for example is implied by the place name Walton, north of Kibworth: the 'tun of the Welsh'). The area the Anglo-Saxon migrants chose for their first settlement was a few hundred yards away from the Iron Age fields of the Britons, on rising ground near the site of the Roman cemetery, suggesting that at first they deliberately put down roots away from the huts of Britons. The find of slag, pottery and a bone comb fragment places the early centre at the present Coach and Horses pub, on the ancient track which in time would become 'the King's highway' and then Main Street and finally the A6: the core of today's village of Kibworth.

This first century of 'English' history is shrouded in darkness. During this time the tale of the migration was shaped into a narrative in the courts of various early kings of Angles and Saxons. In modern times a number of royal and noble burials have given insight into the early culture of the Anglo-Saxons, such as the ship burials at Sutton Hoo and Snape and most recently the rich East Saxon princely grave uncovered at Prittlewell by Southend. But despite the almost incredible riches of the seventh-century Staffordshire treasure, archaeologists have not yet found the grave of any early chief of Mercia. But there is one key area of evidence. We know these early Mercian kings were commemorated in song, that their pedigrees were handed down in poems that hark back to the migration period, like *Beowulf*, which was originally composed in an Anglian-speaking region perhaps on the edge of the Fens. Memories and traditions of the migration-era kings were turned into heroic narratives which were recited and sung by bards before the hearth in the king's hall. 'Since we first came over the wide waves, seeking Britain, to overcome the Welsh and win ourselves a kingdom' as a later poem put it. In Anglo-Saxon culture this foundation myth was told and retold for centuries; rather as in the USA immigrants from Ireland and Italy maintain a tenacious loyalty to the idea of their places of origin.

The voice of the Anglian migrants themselves can be faintly heard in their earliest poems, like *Widsith, Deor* and *Beowulf,* which though composed much later contain oral traditions harking back to real people and events in the late fifth century. Of course, no written texts exist from the English themselves from this time. Except for a few runic inscriptions, writing only starts among them when their rulers adopted Christianity, starting in Kent in 597. But in their oral stories the Mercians and later English preserved dynastic pedigrees and heroic tales of their ancestors before they came to England. The possibility of a historical kernel to such material has often been rejected by modern historians, but oral traditions can have great tenacity – after the migrations of Indo-European speakers into late-Bronze Age India poems were preserved with uncanny linguistic accuracy for two millennia before they were committed to writing.

The early Old English poems were all composed in the Anglian dialect and some contain very archaic survivals in verse forms, metre, language, images and stories. For example, one of the earliest Old English poems about a bard called Widsith contains fragments of royal deeds and genealogies from before the migration: stories about kings' deeds, their generosity, gift-giving and success in war. These were the kind of songs sung in the royal and noble halls of the Middle Angles around Kibworth in the Dark Ages. One in particular long remembered in Mercia was the tale of a continental chief called Offa of Angeln (after whom the famous eighth-century king of Mercia was named). This Offa may have lived in the fourth century AD and around him in later times legends gathered among the Anglian peoples in Britain which were put into writing in eighth- and ninth-century Mercia, and were still available as traditions in the later Middle Ages in the great cult centre at St Albans, where they had particular reason to remember the generosity of the Mercian royal family. In these legends the ancient Offa lived on the continent three generations after Woden, but more realistically was the father of Angeltheow, grandfather of Eomer and great-great-grandfather of Icil, who was viewed as the founder of the Mercian dynasty in Britain and was perhaps the chief who led the migration into the Midlands. This first Offa also appears in *Beowulf* – 'famed for his fighting and giving by men worldwide; spear-bold warrior he ruled wisely with wisdom over his inheritance . . .'

These poems give us a sense of the heroic culture which the Anglian warbands brought with them into the Midlands of Britain around 500, within living memory of the migrations. Traditions partly invented no doubt, but partly commemorating real ancestors of the kings who would rule in the English Midlands in the seventh to eighth centuries and create the first kingdom of what they called the '*patria* of all the English'. Even if all the stages were not accurately remembered such poetic genealogies contain the kind of real pedigrees found in pre-industrial societies across the world, where the descent of kings and heroes is always best recorded, from the Rig Veda to Homer and the Irish epics. It is likely then that Angeltheow and Eomer were real chiefs in Europe, that Icil was the man who either brought his kin group to Britain or who founded a kingly line in Britain at some date between the late fifth century and the 510s or 520s: 'the famous and most noble kin among the Angles, descended from the royal line of Icil'. If anyone, it was this man who led his clan and his warband from East Anglia into the land of the Middle Angles around 500.

## Change and continuity

By the mid-500s the British-speaking societies of the eastern part of Britain had fallen under the domination of the newcomers. The news by then had travelled to the other end of the Mediterranean. In a report that must have sounded rather like a tale from another planet, in the 540s in Constantinople the historian Procopius spoke through a Latin interpreter to an Angle travelling with a Frankish embassy who told him that Britain was no longer 'Roman' but now divided between the indigenous Britons, Angles and Frisians. Later Midland traditions indeed refer to a push west in the middle of the sixth century, and to wars in the Midlands in which the Angles were victorious and the Britons driven into flight. Modern geneticists have speculated that there was ethnic cleansing in some areas of the East Midlands with the massacre of male populations and the enslaving of the women, but as yet this is only speculation. By the middle of the sixth century the Angles were the dominant element in the population. But how they gained their land here – by fighting; by occupying empty land where they began to plough and raise stock; whether they even negotiated with a still surviving local British aristocracy – whether in fact the Corieltauvi in some sense became the Middle Angles – cannot be known. It may be that in some places the new-comers drove out or killed the menfolk and took British women as their wives. In others they clearly settled alongside the indigenous population, opening up new land in marginal areas. In the Kibworth area one or two field names have survived from Welsh speech; the most important being the open field name Cric or Gric in Kibworth Beauchamp, a tiny hint, could it be, that Beauchamp began as a settle-ment of dependent Welsh serfs?

But none of this is firm enough to build on. All we know for sure in the Kibworth area is given us by the buried woman described at the beginning of this chapter, the warrior graves found near her, the two women's brooches picked up by metal detectors at Kibworth, and the bone comb, slag and pottery under the Coach and Horses car park. That is as far as it goes for the first century of the 'English'. The newcomers lived alongside the native British-speakers, who still farmed their big furlongs and tended their flocks of sheep, perhaps trading their surplus with an Anglian lord. But stratified among the finds under the Coach and Horses, the smelting slag and pottery show they had come to stay.

## The catastrophic sixth century

By the middle of the sixth century Anglians and Frisians had settled under their lords in the lands between Glen and the Welland where Kibworth now lies, and around them lived the indigenous British population with whom over time they intermarried and merged identities. All perhaps owed allegiance to a 'king' who ruled in the old Roman city of Leicester. In time the patchwork of tribes occupying the fens and wolds between East Anglia and Leicestershire became known as Middle Angles, their ethnic roots of diverse origins, Celtic and Danish, Germanic and Frisian. The genetic makeup of the early Anglo-Saxons then was particularly mixed. But out of them the English would emerge.

The first century of this new society was particularly hard. Anyone who was lucky enough to survive and live to an old age on the low ridge above the Glen where Kibworth now stands, who lived through the century after the fall of Rome, would have seen far-reaching changes. Between the third and seventh centuries the archaeological record of settlements has suggested that the population of lowland Britain fell to less than a million, fewer people than a millennium before in the Iron Age. Climatologists tell us that the early Anglo-Saxons suffered from colder and wetter climate conditions between the fourth and ninth centuries, culminating in a mini-Ice Age in the early tenth. One of the biggest and most wide-ranging events was a catastrophic volcanic dust storm followed by pestilence in the 540s. The great plagues of the 540s and 680s and the natural catastrophes such as the so-called narrow tree ring event of 536 have attracted a lot of attention from historians recently. Ice cores reveal an extensive acidic dust layer. The health and growth of trees (as seen in annual growth rings for a fifteen-year period) were greatly diminished across the northern hemisphere. Annals from Ireland in the west and as far as China in the east describe the impact: prolonged dry fog, crop failure and acute bread shortages. The historian Procopius, who was alive then, says that during 536 'a most dreadful portent took place: the sun gave forth its light without brightness, and it seemed very like the sun in eclipse for the beams it sent forth had no brightness.' The contemporary Byzantine administrator and antiquarian John Lydus speaks of a full year of half-light which killed all the crops. A later chronicler, Michael Syrian, says the sun was dimmed for eighteen months: 'each day it shone only for four hours and even then its light was but a feeble shadow, so that the fruits did not ripen.' The statesman and scholar Cassiodorus writing in Constantinople is our most vivid eyewitness: 'we were astonished to see no shadow of ourselves at noon, to feel the mighty strength of the sun enfeebled and the phenomena that accompany an eclipse prolonged for almost a whole year. We have had a summer without heat, the crops have been chilled, blasted by north winds, and rain denied.'

This is what the people in the villages of Britain experienced too. Tree rings cut from bog oaks excavated in Ireland show the British Isles were as severely affected. Though long ignored or underestimated, these were great events, their effects more widespread than those of any battle or change of dynasty, the most protracted short-term cooling in the northern hemisphere known over the last 2,000 years. Tree ring specialists think the fifteen-year period after the initial impact in 536 was catastrophic, and it is probably no coincidence that in the middle of that period plague swept across the Eurasian landmass as far as Britain. The cause is generally identified as a huge eruption on the scale of Tambora in 1815 (the biggest since the last Ice Age) or the 1883 eruption of Krakatoa. Though its extent has been disputed, when we see the effect of a minor eruption in Iceland in 2010 it can be seen that environmental damage could have been tremendous and an almost unbearable strain on subsistence farmers who worked the fields under their lords in the Britain of the Dark Ages. As with the aftermath of 1815, in what was known as the 'year without a summer', most deaths were due to starvation and disease as the fallout ruined agriculture. Even in Western Europe, failed harvests brought famine and typhus: newspapers in 1815 told of hill farmers' families in Wales travelling the roads of England begging for food. Harvests also failed and livestock died in large areas of the northern hemisphere. Such events though thinly recorded perhaps help account for the decline in population and the depression of society visible in the archaeological records across Western Europe.

This natural disaster of 536 was followed by the great plague of 541–2: 'a universal plague through the world which killed the noblest third of the human race' as Procopius described it. Pestilence continued to return to the Mediterranean basin through the sixth century and into the seventh, ending with the great plague of 682. The mortality figures are unknown but the Black Death in the fourteenth century killed a third of the population, maybe more (as we shall see, two thirds of the tenants in Kibworth died). The later plague changed everything: work patterns, labour law, freedom itself, but we have no idea how the sixth-century disasters unfolded: whether for example the deprived peasantry who survived won economic freedoms in a contracted agricultural economy. No one knows. But a comparable catastrophe in the sixth century may be the single most important reason for the steep drop in population from its height in the late-Roman world (some think 4–5 million) down to 2 million in the eleventh century. Though largely unknown in the historical record, it may be then that the biggest event of the late-Roman world and the Dark Ages was the plague. It contributed to the collapse of society back to subsistence conditions in many places; and in Britain the technological level of the fourth century was perhaps not regained till the seventeenth or even the eighteenth century.

## *The village: 500–700*

So the first English settlement grew up at Kibworth in very harsh times, emerging in the sixth century in poverty and hardship out of the older Roman British world: its population a Roman-British core (particularly of women) with a smaller Anglian elite. Kibworth was not yet a village, or at least not as we imagine the English village, as a concentrated mythic image of the eternal unchanging English landscape. The origins of the English village are comparatively recent, nucleated from the tenth century onwards by powerful lords in a swathe from Devon to Northumberland. Older patterns continued (and still continue) in the hill country of the west and south-west, where a landscape of isolated Iron Age farms still remains; but the open-field landscape of the English Midlands with its nucleated villages, of which Kibworth is a classic example, only developed after the Viking Age.

Throughout the sixth century the settlement at Kibworth (and thousands like it) was just a fenced enclosure containing the farmstead of the Anglo-Saxon lord and his extended kin, the scattered houses of the peasants and serfs, a cattle barn, a bread oven, a well, a threshing floor and a cattle corral of hurdles and thorn brakes, with perhaps an outer enclosure of brushwood to keep out wolves and bandits. The people lived in platform huts roofed in reed thatch or wooden shingles, and the craftsmen and craftswomen worked in weaving sheds and woodsmen's workshops with one end sunk below ground, like those excavated at Stow in Suffolk (dating from AD 420–650). Such sunken huts were still used into the twentieth century by the wood turners of Bucklebury in Berkshire, the last of whom as late as the Second World War made wooden bowls on a pole lathe as his ancestors in the Dark Ages had done. (This wooden tableware, which was used by most ordinary people until the early modern world, is called in English dialect 'treen', an Old English word signifying 'made of tree'.) Compared with the Roman world this was a subsistence existence but it was the life of most ordinary people in England until comparatively recently, even in some places well beyond the Industrial Revolution.

In the wooden hall of the lord there may have been some imported luxuries. A description of a local nobleman's house in the seventh century hints at possessions: 'a dwelling house furnished with an abundance of goods of all kinds in the district of the Middle Angles'. There the lord gave hospitality to his warband, as in traditional Germanic society, the women (as in *Beowulf*) 'offering the joy of the hall', serving mead and greeting guests, 'carrying the flagon, filling the cups the warriors held out'. The headman was the *hlaford* (our word 'lord', literally the 'bread giver'); his wife, the *hlafdig* (the 'bread kneader' – the lady). Soon the Angles were intermarrying with the locals and in the village over time the language and customs of the Angles would replace those of the Welsh. Welsh was still spoken in the region in the early eighth century, but in the landscape the Britons left few things save river names.

## In the runes: words and thoughts

Kibworth in the Dark Ages was a subsistence place whose horizons had closed down. Hardly any finds from between 500 and 900 were found in the village dig in 2009. One sherd of eighth-century pottery suggests that they used clay and wooden tableware, wooden spades and rakes, even wooden ploughs – though it would be hard to plough the heavy clays around Kibworth without iron. But there is scanty evidence to bring the people to life. They have not yet got names; nor has the place. Its British name is yet to be discovered; its medieval and modern name, which means the enclosure of a man called Cybba – Kibworth – will come later.

The people of Kibworth were illiterate and it is very unlikely anyone in the village came into close contact with literacy at this time. But the small class of priests and seers among the pagan Anglo-Saxons used a system of writing before the Latin script was reintroduced into lowland Britain by missionaries from the Church of Rome. Starting in the fifth century in Frisia, the continental Angles, Saxons and Frisians used a system of writing which they brought over with them from the continent to Britain. They called it 'futhorc' – we call it runes – and it was the script of priests and seers, the ritual specialists. Incised or marked on bones, pottery, ivory combs, it was a system of twenty-six signs, later expanded to thirty-three. Each magical sign had a phonetic value but also a meaning in itself, and as we search for a way into the thought-world of our early ancestors, clues perhaps lie in these magical symbols.

One cluster of signs denotes aspects of material life – wealth, need, distress, gift, cup, torch, joy. A further group describes the weather – sun, hail, ice – and another trees – oak, ash, birch, yew, thorn. Animals named include horses and aurochs. Some allude loosely to time – day, year, harvest – and to nature – stone, land and lake. Weapons of course figure in the futhorc signs – spear and bow – and the masculine world – warrior, estate, ride, hero. Finally, death and the hereafter are found in the signs for grave and god. 'God', like 'soul', it is as well to remember, is a pre-Christian Anglo-Saxon word. The pagans too believed in such things.

To the modern reader these mysterious glyphs – scratched or incised on disc brooches, burial urns, weapons, bone tools and combs – appear fantastically allusive precursors to what will become the English language. It reveals a world-view and images that will run through Anglo-Saxon poetry with its down-to-earth fatalistic and ruminative streak. In them perhaps we can glimpse the bedrock of the speech, thought and values of the early villagers. Few such early texts exist (only with Christianity and Latin script do we get full-length texts) and only as grave inscriptions and commemorations on the continent. In England about thirty fragmentary runic inscriptions have been deciphered on bone combs, sword hilts and sherds: brief signifiers or prayers for auspiciousness. Some are men's and women's names. A recent find near Leicester was of a runic inscription on a pair of disc-headed pins representing the name of a woman, Ceolburg. Among the few longer inscriptions that have enough characters to be read is one from the East Midlands that recalls our dead twenty-year-old at the start of this chapter. It reads, 'the grave of Sithaebaed the maid . . .'

## Religion

The people of the village like most of the early English were pagans, worshipping their ancestral gods from Jutland – Thor, Woden, Thunor – and the auspicious deities of forest, river and spring of their British neighbours. They made offerings at trees, rocks and rivers, performed animal sacrifices, and did bloodlettings to propitiate spirits and avert the inauspicious hour, mixing blood or semen in their food for magical protection, fertility or potency.

The narrative of English history from the seventh century is portrayed in our histories as Christian. But in truth, as always, the reality was more complex. The conversion took many centuries and was perhaps never quite fully accomplished, at least in the terms in which the Church saw it. The early villagers had come with their ancestral gods from the continent: gods of storm and thunder, gods of fertility and auspiciousness. Faint traces of less salubrious demons (in the old English language) survived in the landscape near Kibworth until early modern times – Thyrspit in Nevill Holt and Shuggborowe in Burton Overy, where demons lurked; Tommor in Great Easton (a hobgoblin) – and Grendels (the name of the water demon in *Beowulf*) were ubiquitous denizens of ponds, meres and water-filled pits. That such names have survived at all is testimony to the lingering power of these folk beliefs – a world of fairies and demons which declined only after the sixteenth-century Reformation. One particularly strong aspect of this, which was inherited by the early English from the Roman and Celtic past, is the ancient sacred wells that were mainly adopted by the Church in the Middle Ages but still survive all over England. Also noteworthy is the persistence of the belief in sacred trees, mentioned disparagingly by Bede in the eighth century. The meeting place of the jurors of the local hundred right up to the eighteenth century, as we have seen, was at the 'Gartree', a landmark tree on an ancient burial mound.

And close to Kibworth one sacred tree had a very long afterlife. In the woods at Great Easton a place called Holyoak Lodge marks the site of a pagan Anglo-Saxon shrine to the god of thunder, Thunor, which seems to have been worshipped long after the arrival of Christianity. As late as the twelfth century a little Christian hermitage – the Mirabel – was built close by to combat the continuing superstition of the locals. And on the gravestones in Kibworth for the last three centuries can be seen the names of the Holyoak family, who still flourish in Kibworth today. The thought-world of Old English paganism is by and large lost to us, but its sensibility underlies the later culture and language – and religion – of the English people.

# 4. The Beginnings of Kibworth

In the seventh and eighth centuries, like many villages in England, Kibworth emerges as a defined place and perhaps as a community: very likely this is when it got its name. The difficulty for the historian is that, as for most places in England at this time, any narrative still has to be composed from a virtually total lack of evidence, though the village dig in 2009 furnished a few significant clues. This period of the village story represents a horizon of change in which societies and economies in the West begin to pick up after the breakdown of the Roman world. The popular view is that the Dark Ages were a very hard time for ordinary people, most of whom were engaged in a lifelong battle against want, working first to feed their betters and then themselves, with the ever-present threat of famine, plague and war. This, one suspects, is by and large true. But brutal times are often also, out of sheer necessity, times of creation. And the roots of many rural and urban communities in England grew in this period.

The slow signs of recovery in the seventh and eighth centuries were brought about by that great institution of the Dark Ages: kingship. Chronicles and poems may sometimes give the impression that kings spent their time fighting battles, raiding, exacting tribute, hunting and feasting in the royal hall while bards sang their praises. But the law codes – one of the distinctive creations of the Barbarian West – tell another story. English law codes of the seventh century show that as soon as they came under the influence of the Church, Anglo-Saxon kings were expected to adapt the heroic warrior ethos of their ancestral Germanic tradition to the Christian moral universe. A king should not only be a 'plunder lord' and 'ring giver' but also look after the people, protect them against violence and want, and promote Christian religion. These ideals did not always sit easily with traditional Germanic kingship – winning battles, exacting tribute and gaining 'everlasting glory', as the poets of the Dark Ages put it. But there were many advantages to a king in joining in a Christian order with fellow kings and from the late seventh century the first signs of improvement in material life are shown by widespread evidence of trade, with the movement of pottery and coins. In the 2009 dig the first sherds were found in the village of high-status Ipswich ware pottery and of the tiny coins known as sceattas. Minted in their millions from the late 600s these coins are a clear sign of the growth of trade routes from the rich eastern seaboard, and from established royal trading ports or wics, such as Ipswich and London (Lundenwic). Another important emporium was 'Saltwich', the former Roman salt-making centre at Droitwich, what the Mercian charters called the *vico emptorio salis* with its coveted salt houses and furnaces spread over twenty or thirty outlying villages. Producing one of the essentials of life, this was one industrial centre from the Roman Empire (and it cannot have been the only one) which may have continued to function uninterrupted through the Dark Ages. In the eighth century salt ways spread out from it across southern England, including one that passes on the old 'Jurassic' track through Kibworth and Tur Langton.

But it is likely that life lived in the eighth century was nasty, brutish and short. The annals of the time are dotted with disasters: plague, cattle murrains, smallpox, even hurricanes. In the village the dry summer of 719 was followed by torrential rains and floods in 720. The period of drought and famine from the late 730s and early 740s culminated in 741, when 'the land bore no fruit.' The wet year of 759 inaugurated two years of pestilence and sickness, which caused havoc among the poor – especially in a virulent outbreak of enteric dysentery. The heat wave of summer 783 presaged more weather disruption with heavy snows later in the decade. All these phenomena were devastating to pre-industrial societies.

## Hard times: Kibworth in winter 762

The event which stayed sharpest in the memory of most people in the eighth century was the severe winter of 762–3, which is recorded in annals across Britain and Ireland. There had been great snowfalls in

each of the previous three winters, starting in 760: a pattern which
had already precipitated famines. Now 'there was a truly immense
snowfall, and the thick snow hardened into ice, such as no one
had ever seen before.' According to Northumbrian annals 'the snowfall oppressed the land from the beginning of winter' (religious
calendars generally note this as starting on 21 November with 'the
start of freezing frosts', but perhaps a later date is meant), 'almost till
the middle of spring'. Irish observers agree that the 'great snow'
stayed on the ground for three months creating 'great scarcity and
famine'. The cold was so severe that 'many trees and plants withered,
and even many marine animals were found cast up dead on frozen
estuaries.'

In response to the big freeze people struggled as best they could to
keep warm, and that same winter 'towns, monasteries and villages in
various districts and kingdoms were all at once devastated by fire,'
says a Northumbrian annalist, 'for instance the calamity struck *Stret-
burg*, Winchester, Southampton, London, York, Doncaster and many
other places.' The result of people lighting fires in the extreme cold
to keep warm, this is a vivid indicator of the bitter conditions of winter in the early Middle Ages. And, as with the mini-Ice Age of the
1310s, extreme winters were followed the next summer by scarcity,
famine and an abnormally severe drought. Bread shortages are widely
reported across Britain and Ireland. Such disasters in a subsistence
society hit the peasantry hardest and the aftermath – in starvation,
infant mortality, poor health and failed crops – must have been prolonged. For the scattered thatched mud huts along the low ridge
where the village now stands, it was mostly a simple matter of survival. Sunset was early on those winter nights above the valley. In the
law codes' brief glimpses of the peasants' existence, the villages shone
as tiny pinpricks of light in a surrounding sea of darkness. There
were wolves in the forests and the lonely horn of a traveller out late
must alert the villagers to where he is for fear of being attacked as an
intruder. Inside the houses lit by guttering oil lamps, those long cold
dark nights were perhaps a time for songs, stories and poetry and for
news of a wider world from a trader or returning pilgrim. And then
early to bed. Another night in eighth-century England.

## The beginnings of Kibworth

How then did the scattered early-Anglian settlement above the valley of the Welland become an English village called Kibworth? The village story now takes us into the days of the kings of Mercia, who were the first to call themselves kings of all the English. And, as for any English village, along with the topography the place name contains a first vital clue to the history. The name Kibworth means the 'enclosure' – *worthig* in Old English – of a man called Cybba. Who was this Cybba? This Anglian name appears nowhere else though there are related forms in the Midlands such as Cubbel. But it resonates suggestively with names in the Mercian royal family, particularly the alliterating 'P' names and 'C' names in two branches of the royal pedigrees, such as Pybba, Penda, Peada, Peaga, Crida and Cnebba. Like Pybba, or the royal holy woman Tibba, Cybba is bisyllabic and hypocoristic, a shortened diminutive as a nickname or term of endearment. The name evokes what an eighth-century writer called the 'noblest line of the Middle Angles', which could be counted back 'step by step' to Icil in the migration era. People had long memories in the Dark Ages and many Mercian nobles by the eighth century could trace their royal descent, however distant. Perhaps then Cybba belonged to a minor branch of the royal tree: a man who in the heyday of the Mercians in the eighth century was gifted his own estate by the king himself.

The second part of the name, 'worth', common as it is in England today, may also be surprisingly significant. Settlements' names involving 'worth', though frequent in Old English charters, only start to appear from about 730. And some early ones in Mercia are of high status, like Brixworth with its magnificent royal church, the royal estate of Bosworth, or Northworthy, the old name of Derby, the 'capital' of the North Mercians. At an early stage the word seems to have developed a meaning akin to burh, 'a fortified place'. Tamworth, the royal 'capital' and ancient centre of the South Mercians, changed its name from Tomtun ('the tun of the dwellers on the River Tame') in the early eighth century to Tomeworthig, when Mercian

kings encircled it with a defensive enclosure, which has been excavated by modern archaeologists. Whether Anglo-Saxon Kibworth
was just a ditched demesne farm or whether it actually had a defensive enclosure is not known, though a village ditch survives at
Harcourt enclosing an area comparable to the Tamworth defences. In
seventeenth-century maps the village still nestles inside this circuit,
with its houses, tofts and gardens, the boundary defined by a hedge
and ditch and a line of medieval fishponds.

Though no document has survived to tell us about the history of
Mercian Kibworth, and though topography and archaeology are
all we have on which to build our picture, we may guess an eighth-
century date for 'the enclosure of Cybba'. This would have been the
lord's residence, but attached to it just to the south may have been a
village of dependent serfs which in time would become Kibworth
Beauchamp. The crafts and artisanal skills which went with such a
noble estate in the Dark Ages were provided by the village of metalworkers at the 'smiths' tun', Smeeton, perhaps servicing both Cybba's
estate and the royal residence at Gumley, 'Godmund's wood', a mile
to the south. In the later Anglo-Saxon period the king himself
retained part of Smeeton, and another royal hall lay on the River
Glen two miles to the west. These royal centres were visited by the
kings on their itineraries and must have loomed large in the lives of
the Kibworth peasants who provided food supplies not only for their
lord, but also for the royal feasts when huge numbers of royal courtiers
and guests had to be fed.

As for Cybba himself, if the land was formally given to him as
with other royal land leases of the eighth century, then we need only
a little imagination to picture this founding moment. The scene is the
royal hall at the *vicus regius* and hunting lodge of Gumley on the south
border of Kibworth parish, where the Mercian kings Offa and Aethelbald held court several times at the height of their empire between
the 740s and 780s. It is still a closed village today and thick woods still
cover the hill where the Mercian kings hunted with hawks and
hounds and speared wild boar. The king now is Aethelbald, a griz-
zled veteran, masterful and violent like most Dark Age kings, who
owes his power to coming out on top in internecine feuds (and indeed

he was eventually assassinated by his own bodyguard). Aethelbald may well be the king depicted in full powers on the recently discovered Repton stone sitting on a prancing warhorse with its docked tail, carrying a short shield, a flat bladed sword and a *seax* – the Anglo-Saxon short dagger – his stern face with big moustaches the very image of a Germanic king of the Dark Ages, 'plunder lord, deed doer, ring giver, leader of men'.

In the hall are assembled kinsmen, sub-kings, the bishops of Lichfield and Worcester, some of the ealdormen of the tribes of the Middle Angles, and the thegns and companions, some of whose names we know: Peada, Ofa and Cusa. Present too are noble hostages from other kingdoms for that is how kings ruled outside their stemland: through military force, the exaction of tribute, the taking of hostages. The king himself was very likely illiterate, but his royal clerk impersonates him with high-flown titles, in Latin:

I Aethelbald by God's gift king not only of the Mercians but also of all the provinces which go by the name of 'South English'; for the good of my soul and the remission of my sins, freely grant to my faithful companion or minister, Cybba, a certain piece of land, namely twenty-five hides in the province called by men of old 'Middle Angles', by the river called *aet Glenne* with all perquisites belonging to it, fields, woods and meadow . . . and if anyone try to violate this gift let him know he will make reckoning to God on the great day of judgement. This charter is written in the year of our Lord 736 in the royal vill of Gumley in the province of the Middle Angles. I Aethelbald king of Britain confirm my own donation with the sign of the cross . . .

To this the scribe would have added a note on whether Cybba was free to bequeath his estate to any of his kin, and specifying the customary burdens on the estate: whether for example it was free of all secular dues except the customary road repairs and bridge and fortress construction, or military service. Perhaps the land of the lord (known as the inland) was farmed by unfree peasants for the lord's own profit; and the free peasants (on what was known as warland) could sell their surplus but were liable for taxes and military service. As for the population of Kibworth in the eighth century, its tax assessment in later times (without Smeeton) was twenty-five hides: the hide of 120 acres being traditionally land enough to support one family. In reality the land had to support far more people in later Anglo-Saxon times, but if the assessment bears any relation to reality, then that might indicate that between a hundred and 150 people could have lived there in Cybba's day.

In return for this gift of land Cybba might have had to pay the king annual rent. This could have been in silver coin, or war gear, or in horses and tack, the things a king constantly needed to replenish in order to reward and expand his armed following. But as important royal estates lay next door to Kibworth at Gumley and Glen, the rents are more likely to have been in kind, to feed the court with the surplus produced by the Kibworth peasants. A contemporary text gives us details of the food rent for a ten-hide estate:

10 vats of honey, 300 loaves, 12 ambers of Welsh ale, 30 of clear ale, full grown cows or 10 wethers, 10 geese, 20 hens, 10 cheeses, an amber full of butter, 5 salmon, 20 pounds of fodder [= about 500 bushels]and 100 eels.

As well as feeding and sustaining their lord Cybba, then, the unfree Kibworth peasants would have had to provide food supplies for the king when he was in residence with his court next door.

Cybba's charter would also have briefly delineated the bounds of the land given and the rights to pasturage and timber. No early charters survive in this part of the East Midlands, but if all Kibworth was originally one estate (it had broken into several manors by the eleventh century) then the bounds would have been recorded in this way (some of these ancient boundaries survive in tithe maps of the eighteenth century, still using the old Anglo-Saxon word 'mere' for boundary): 'These are the bounds of the estate at Cybba's worth: first at the boundary of the ceorls' tun [Carlton] along the Burton Brook by the boundary of the people of Glen to the wood at Godmund's wood [Gumley] then from the boundary tree to the ford of the stream and then along the boundary of the people of Langton back to the brook at Carlton.'

Once this had been read out in the hall, the royal gift would be sealed with solemn oaths, with a symbolic piece of turf from the land placed on an open Gospel book. The charter was then copied twice on a sheet of vellum which was cut in two as a 'chirograph', the join in a sawtooth shape that could be fitted together to prove its authenticity. One half went to the king's 'halidom', his relic box and treasury, which his Mass priests lodged in the cathedral archive at Lichfield; the other half went to Cybba himself to keep in his chest in his hall in Kibworth: to hold as the title to his 'bookland', lord of the settlement which from then on will bear his name.

With Cybba comes the beginning of a continuity of lordship: the association of Kibworth with lords who from the eleventh century can be named all the way through the later history of the village. The late-Saxon landlords Aelfric, Edwin and Aelfmaer, then the Normans, William the Conqueror himself, Hugh Grandmesnil and Roger of Busli who fought with him at Hastings, and after them the Harcourts and the Beauchamps who gave their names to the two halves of the village. Later still there were the Earls of Warwick, the Plantagenets, the Dudleys and even briefly Elizabeth I herself, along with Merton College, Oxford, which still rents out the fields in Kibworth Harcourt today as it has since 1270. As with so many places in England, then, Cybba was the Anglo-Saxon owner who started the pattern of lordship, the tale of exploitation of the poor by the rich that has lasted until modern times. An important part of the narrative of English history is the story of how the rulers asserted and enforced their claim to the labour and surplus of the working people, and how the people fought to establish their own freedoms under the law. In Kibworth, thanks to the astonishing documentary record from the 1200s, that story can be told in detail over the centuries through the rent strikes of the early fourteenth century which loosed the bonds of feudal tenure, to the rise of the Tudor yeoman farming class, down to the Enclosure Act of 1789. In this way the English polity developed in a constant negotiation between rulers and ruled, workers and landlords: a negotiation which of course still continues today.

## Tribes and kingdoms

For three centuries the lives of the people of the village were bound up with the politics and economy of the kingdom of the Mercians. In the eighth century their kings rose to be rulers of all the southern English, on their coins and charters claiming to be 'Kings of the English', and even lords of Britain. The Mercians ruled from the Welsh border to the Fens, and from the Humber to the Thames. Other 'nations' beyond their boundaries – the East Angles, West Saxons, Northumbrians and people of Kent – paid them tribute and acknowledged their overlordship. The centre of Mercian power was the Trent valley and their main royal centre at Tamworth ('the enclosure on the Tame') was the place where their kings gathered their *fideles*, their ealdormen and thegns, to celebrate the chief Christian feast days. Their name means the 'border people', referring most likely to the western frontier with the Welsh kingdoms: it was not an ethnic title; nor were they at all a homogeneous ethnic group. There were some thirty Mercian tribes speaking different dialects and languages, including Welsh. Their kings though called themselves Angles, and it is after them that England is called by that name today. One of the great problems in the early history of England is that contemporary sources are mediated by the West Saxons, the ultimate makers of England; but on the origins and hegemony of Mercia we are less well-informed. The Mercians were the most successful of the early English kingdoms; but because they lost out in the end to the kings of Wessex, a great part of their story was forgotten and is only now being recovered through manuscripts, coins, sculpture and recent finds, including the extraordinary late-seventh-century Staffordshire treasure.

The peoples between Leicester and the River Welland, including the villagers of Kibworth, were part of the loose confederation of tribes known as Middle Angles who lived in the Fens and the eastern Midlands between the East Angles and the Mercians proper ('original Mercia' as they said – who were notionally the 'West Angles'). This huge region had fallen under Mercian lordship in the early seventh century in the course of extended conflicts between Mercians and the East Angles. No more than the Mercians were the Middle Angles of one ethnic identity: a grouping of many tribes and clans, they came to be viewed as a distinct regional grouping with their own borders and their own leaders – perhaps a distinct branch of the royal descendents of Icil. The process which brought them together is not known. The Middle Anglian tribes are evidently part of an older and now largely lost pattern of early English society but they probably emerged along the Fen edge between the East Angles and the Mercians of the Trent valley after the migration period. A mysterious tax assessment document known as the Tribal Hidage lists various tribes, including small peoples down the Welland in Northamptonshire as far as the Fens. Some of these were certainly within the Middle Angles but unfortunately the key tribal groupings in the East Midlands, Leicestershire and Rutland are still not identified.

There is one last thought as we consider Mercian origins and the foundation myths of the early English. The cultural contours of the Middle Angles with their mixed British and Anglian population seem to bear a close relation to the earlier Roman-British kingdom of the Corieltauvi. The Corieltauvi also appear to have been a loose federation of tribes with several rulers, and there is an apparent correspondence between the spread of coin and pottery finds of the Corieltauvi, and the distinctive Middle Anglian granitic-tempered pottery found between the Trent and the Welland in the Anglo-Saxon period. It would be fascinating to know whether the mix of indigenous people and an immigrant elite which developed in this region represents the continuance of an older regional identity – whether indeed the Middle Angles were actually in some sense a successor state of the Corieltauvi. But what such an observation might mean, it is as yet difficult to be sure.

## The coming of Christ

The culture of the pagan Germanic tribes who had migrated to Britain in the Dark Ages was transformed by Christianity. By the time of Cybba in the eighth century, his region had been nominally Christian for two or three generations. Celtic Christianity had survived the fall of Rome in Ireland and Western Britain, and after Gregory the Great sent his mission from Rome to Kent in 597 under St Augustine Christianity began its triumphal progress among the elites of the early Anglo-Saxon kingdoms. According to Bede's famous story, the Gregorian mission of 597 began in a slave market in Italy where Gregory saw captive Angles waiting to be sold (vivid proof by the way of how easily violence and enslavement crossed frontiers at that time). So touched was the Pope by their fair looks that he remarked: 'These are not Angles but angels.' Immortalized by Bede, the story was loved by the English ever after – it made them almost a chosen people – and though there were many Anglo-Saxon tribes and language groups, thanks to Bede it was the Angles who gave England and the English their name.

The first rulers to convert were those of Kent in 597, then the East Angles in the 620s, the Northumbrians in 627, the West Saxons in 634 and finally the Mercians from the 650s onwards. These of course are the dates of the conversion of the royal families and their elites, not the mass of people, which took a lot longer. The narrative of this process was created by Bede in his *History of the English Church and People* completed in 731. His was an idealized and teleological narrative, but in practice in the remoter regions conversion was certainly not finished by the eleventh century – if indeed not later still. Bede's own letters offer eye-opening insights into the conditions in the countryside of his own day, where what he calls 'demon-worship' was everywhere, sacred rocks and trees were widely worshipped and 'there are many places that have not seen a bishop from one year to the next.' The early Old English law codes show pagan beliefs were widespread in the countryside along with customs which we must assume were common to the villagers of Kibworth in the seventh century and indeed much later: pin sticking, voodoo, magical charms, bloodletting and animal sacrifice. The tariffs drawn up by the Church in the penitential manuals sent with missionaries into the field show such practices were found all the way through society from freemen to slaves: 'If a husband sacrifice to devils . . . if a slave sacrifice to devils.' Some of the folk cures for impotence and childbirth against which the orthodox railed – mixing blood or semen with food, for example – are still found in wilder parts of the globe today wherever traditional cultures have escaped the globalization of the mind.

This was the kind of thing the Church warred against for centuries but it was part of a deep matrix of belief in propitiation and auspiciousness which even now has never quite gone away. Though the narrative which has come down to us has been almost completely controlled and articulated by churchmen, such hints in the sources are a warning against accepting at their face value 'official' narratives which (as we shall see again in the Reformation) represent sweeping historical change simply as the consensual acceptance of a new thought-world by the ordinary people. In reality there is a wide gulf between learned theological belief on the one hand and popular religious practice on the other. What people actually do – their rituals of auspiciousness, their responses to childbirth, death, disease and suffering – these things are not always conditioned by theological belief, and they can take centuries to change.

Under the early Mercian kings the people of Kibworth were pagans who sacrificed to pagan gods and 'revered stones and trees' as Bede says. At the root of their religious practice was an animism similar to many polytheistic religions still in the world today. Near to Kibworth they had a sanctuary in a sacred wood or grove (*leah*) of the thunder god Thunor whose 'Holy Oak' is revealed in Domesday Book and in the much later place name Thunor's Leah. The many local sacred wells and springs in the area were also adopted by the Christian Church when Christianity came to the Mercians after the death of the pagan Penda in battle in 655. The key figure in this was Penda's son, King Wulfhere, 'a man of proud mind and insatiable will' who was long remembered as an ardent supporter of the Church. Under his aegis a small band of missionaries borrowed from Northumbria fanned out among the Middle Angles. In a wild countryside whose population was still largely pagan they founded wooden churches thatched with reeds 'in the Irish fashion', but at that point there were only three bishops for the whole of the *gens Anglorum* – a measure of the progress of conversion. It necessarily began on a small scale: the first missionaries were St Chad and three companions. A diminutive man, Chad favoured barefoot evangelizing like the early fathers, and he and his missionary monks established centres where they laboured like common men, ploughing and sowing as well as preaching, exemplars of the holy life. Later when the tough old Greek Archbishop Theodore of Tarsus travelled across England to draw up a progress report, not surprisingly he thought Chad's admirably ascetic bent too slow, and he is said to have physically lifted the tiny and unassertive Chad on to a horse and told him brusquely to get on with it. Already seventy years old, Theodore was a man in a hurry: he had the *gens Anglorum* to convert.

## St Wilfrid

It was perhaps at a wooden preaching cross in Kibworth in the late seventh century that Christianity was first preached to the ancestors of our villagers, on the low hill where the church of St Wilfrid was later built. But by whom precisely? The dedication of the church itself raises the interesting question as to whether the key figure who brought Christianity to the village was St Wilfrid himself. A very different character to the unassuming Chad, Wilfrid was a fractious Northumbrian monk who exploited his friendship and influence with the Mercian kings to the full – and not just for spiritual gain. Wilfrid's special relationship with Wulfhere began in the late 660s when he was invited by the king to come down to Mercia where the king needed a bishop who could organize and get things done. In return Wulfhere rewarded Wilfrid with 'many tracts of land', on which Wilfrid according to his biographer 'soon established minsters for the servants of God'. Later in the 690s Wilfrid worked as bishop among the Middle Angles perhaps in the old Roman city of Leicester. From here he sponsored missionary activity both in Mercia and abroad among the Angles' continental cousins, the Frisians. Ambitious and worldly, a dedicated missionary, Wilfrid was a man who made enemies easily and endured more than one exile, but he was the dominant personality in the missionary activity among the Middle Angles in the late 690s and the first decade of the eighth century. Could this be why the church in Kibworth is dedicated to him?

Traces of Wilfrid's presence have been detected north of the Humber in church dedications where tradition says he actually preached. In the East Midlands too there is an interesting cluster of Wilfrid dedications on the Trent near Newark, at pre-Conquest churches at Kirkby-in-Ashfield and Calverton, and at the Anglo-Saxon royal estate of Screveton just off Fosse Way. Not all are certainly early dedications but it is possible that some of these early churches mark places where Wilfrid preached and founded minsters at the behest of King Wulfhere. There are some faint hints that Kibworth church once had high status, and the Anglo-Saxon kings held land in part of the old parish. None of this adds up to more than speculation, but a Roman cemetery site and a sixth-century Anglian settlement at least offer the possibility that though Kibworth church is first recorded in the thirteenth century, it could have existed much earlier – and even that Wilfrid himself could have preached here to the Middle Angles.

The Christian narrative is so wedded to the English story, to English culture and, till only recently, to the English sense of identity that we have tended to think it was both inevitable and a good thing. That narrative has been composed by Christian scholars in monasteries and schoolrooms, from Bede in the eighth century to Winston Churchill in the twentieth. And of course some saw it that way, though others like King Penda no doubt agreed with the pagan Frisian king who at the last moment stepped away from the baptismal font saying he would rather spend the next life with his brave pagan ancestors, even though in hell, than with the pallid Christians in their heaven. The truth is that these were long-contested legacies, and Christianity brought by no means unqualified benefits to kings in the Dark Ages. Likewise the allure of the pagan religion of the ancestors has been underestimated by later writers: especially where it met the needs of auspiciousness, fertility and rites of passage (which Christianity, unable to erase, would absorb right across the world from the Andes to Orissa).

What counted above all for kings in the Dark Ages in a time of chronic instability and random violence was their ability to keep power, to win battles and to attract warriors with food, gifts and treasure. But royal clans were forever split by internecine feuds, kings were deposed and murdered by their own kinsmen as well as by their outside enemies. So what counted too was legitimacy. And as the power of the Church grew among the Germanic barbarians in the West, kingship was reshaped, extended and dignified, especially through the liturgies that conferred kingship as a divinely anointed office. The first great Mercian king, Penda, was a pagan but his sons and daughters were receptive to the new faith and ploughed their dynastic wealth into religion, establishing minsters on royal land and founding the great Mercian monasteries at Repton, Breedon and Peterborough. In later English history, the enormous wealth and resources diverted into the Church would lead to frequent tensions in the state, from the anti-monastic reaction in the tenth century to Henry VIII's Reformation. And there would be tensions too about the Christian message itself and who should control and interpret it: this would be the subject of numerous bitter battles in English culture till the decline of religion in the nineteenth and twentieth centuries. In Kibworth dissenting traditions have been particularly strong from the Lollards in the fourteenth century to Congregationalists, Quakers, Methodists and other radicals right up to our own time. But from the eighth century until the twentieth English history to a greater or lesser degree will be Christian.

## 'The terror of the Arabs'

Seen through the eyes of Bede, Cybba's world looks like a threatening, unstable but undeniably exciting place. At the time Cybba made his enclosure at Kibworth and built his wooden hall, the English were no longer isolated or unaware of the outside world. As they always have been, they were inveterate travellers. Wilfrid himself went from Leicester to Rome simply to pursue a court case. Other intrepid Britons 'versed in diverse far-away places' reached the Holy Land bearing Greek–Latin phrase books and giving the lie to the idea that all English people are hopeless at other languages! In the Wirral evidence of such journeys turned up recently in a seventh-century Egyptian pilgrim flask showing St Menas of Alexandria in the sand on a Dark Age trading shore. Coins minted in the Caliphate came in merchants' packs along with lapis lazuli from Afghanistan which would be ground up to adorn beautiful manuscripts created under the aegis of the Mercian kings.

Such contacts and exchanges were symptomatic of a time of profound historical change. The vacuum left by the collapse of the Roman Empire was filled in northern and Western Europe by the barbarians – Franks, Goths, Angles, Saxons. In the East, in the late seventh and eighth centuries, the Arabs became the great power in the Mediterranean. In Bede's lifetime Muslim Arab armies had advanced into southern France, and up in Jarrow they heard the news: writing the year before the Muslim defeat near Poitiers, Bede spoke of the 'gravissima saracenorum lues', the high-water mark of an astonishing movement which took Islam westwards across North Africa to the shores of the Atlantic, and eastwards to the Indus. In the process, as Bede was well aware, the Arabs had overrun the Christian heartland of Syria and Palestine, with all the biblical holy places. Christianity's intellectual powerhouses had gone too, like Alexandria, Edessa and Antioch – from where Theodore of Tarsus had begun the amazing journey that finally led him out to the wilds of Britain. The wooded countryside of Mercia with its thatched 'Irish-style' churches must have seemed to him a far cry indeed from the soaring dome of the Hagia Sophia in Constantinople or the great basilica of his native Edessa (on whose flora and fauna he lectured his wide-eyed students at Canterbury, pausing to recall the mouth-watering Syrian melons, which he described as 'rather like cucumbers but much bigger – the melons in Edessa are so big that a camel can scarcely carry two of them').

The southern shores of the Mediterranean were now conquered by the Arabs, the Visigothic kingdom of Spain was overthrown and Constantinople manned its defences against Islam and hardened its Eastern orthodoxy against the Latins. No wonder that the popes in Rome, rebuffed by the Greek world, now looked north for help, money and new souls. To the papacy, underdeveloped northern Europe was a new world just as Latin America would be in the sixteenth century. This looking north is a characteristic of the age. It has been seen as a turning away from the Mediterranean world of late

Antiquity, the beginning of a new Europe on the Atlantic seaboard, a shift in gravity from the old classical world round the shores of the Mediterranean 'like frogs around a frog pond' as Plato had put it. And indeed, as an Arab civilization was flowering across the Mediterranean, beyond the Alps, albeit at a much lower level of material achievement, a new northern civilization was beginning to emerge.

## The village in the eighth century

In the eighth century the peasants of Kibworth, free and unfree, found themselves part of that civilization, under a lord protected by a great king, who proclaimed himself 'King of the whole *patria* of all the English'. The Mercian kings were itinerant, constantly travelling their kingdom, always on the move, showing themselves to friends and foes alike, raising their food rents, bribing, rewarding, cajoling and threatening. Such was the reality of Dark Age rule. In documents of the eighth and ninth centuries we can see them staying on the royal estates around Kibworth, receiving ambassadors from Charlemagne who came to negotiate marriage alliances or to buy English woollen cloths woven and dyed in workshops in villages like Kibworth. English needlework and metalwork were also coveted, made in royal workshops like that at Smeeton close to the royal hall at Gumley above Kibworth. There the king was praised by poets for his royal deeds and his famous ancestry back to the legendary Offa of Angeln and the later kings who came across the sea, 'overcame the Welsh' and carved themselves a kingdom in Britain.

But in the background of these splendid feasts were the peasants of the village who provided meat, food and beer for the kings and their guests; who provisioned the kings' huntsmen and their hawks and hunting dogs; and fed his horses and grooms. At Kibworth, chance finds have added colour to this picture: metalworkers' slag, silver sceattas, and the Ipswich ware, which perhaps contained the salt carried on carts from the salt houses and furnaces at Droitwich. These were the first signs that even the peasants of Kibworth were touched by the slow rise of the Dark Ages.

The archaeological finds suggest that the three main villages that make up the old parish of Kibworth already existed before the ninth century. First was the lord's 'worth', which will become Kibworth Harcourt. Inside the enclosure was the lord's hall, his cookhouse and weaving huts, barns, stables, workshops and maybe a wooden chapel. His peasants had several ox teams, kept sheep, pigs and beehives. They had a communal bread oven and perhaps a horse mill as well as later a water mill on Langton stream. For protection from wolves and bandits there was the ditch. Harcourt is still partly surrounded by its early ditch – to the north-west and north-east the housing plots and gardens run away from the main road and end at the village hedge and fishponds. This formed a protection used throughout the Middle Ages, when there were bars on the entrances at night, all the more necessary no doubt in the violent world of the Dark Ages.

A few hundred yards to the south was the village of dependent peasants, unfree serfs and estate workers, which in time would become Kibworth Beauchamp. Surviving field names here suggest at least part of the village may have been owned by the king, in which case these serfs may originally have owed their labour to the royal estate at Gumley. Finally, in the south of the present parish, along a low ridge was the artisanal settlement of smiths and metalworkers at Smeeton. In material terms the life of the ordinary people must have been strikingly similar to the late-Roman and Dark Age estates (except that now Anglian not Welsh was spoken). Pigs, oxen, horses, hens, goats and geese were kept in all the villages. The houses of the better-off were on the rise near the church, while the serfs and cottagers dwelt by the stream where the railway now runs, or in the wet boggy land still called The Marsh whose inhabitants even in the nineteenth century lived in mud houses, their aching bones prone to rheumatism and malaria.

Such then was the beginning of 'Cybba's worth'. Historians can look at the coins and treasure and the illuminated manuscripts of the Mercian kings, and point to their achievements in creating order; the forerunner of the kingdom of England. But at the grass roots the view is very different. In England in the eighth century our community, like the bulk of the population, laboured to feed and sustain their betters, and only then themselves. Privation, disease and (especially in harsh winters like those of the 760s) hardship were their lot. Working with inadequate tools on thick clays our peasants were surrounded by a still wild landscape with great forests. Place names like Wolvey on Watling Street (owned by the last Saxon lord of Kibworth) point for example to the ubiquity of the wolf; the many 'wolf pits' to their lairs or the places where they were trapped. All this was a far cry from the glittering treasures massed in the royal hall, the kind of things described in their poems and discovered to our amazement in the Staffordshire hoard.

The sustainers of that heroic world, the villagers in the seventh and eighth centuries no doubt fell back on the comforts that are left to their like all over the globe: the soothsayer, the wise woman, the *medicus*, the gods of the countryside, the sacred wells, the tree of Thunor hung with prayers too, propitiations at the demons' pit, coins and offerings thrown in Grendel's Mere, prayers too to the saint in his shrine; while the nobles assiduously cultivated the new religion in a half Christian, half pagan world, in a conversion culture. Such times in so many ways are poised on the cusp of history, between the no longer and the not yet. One local nobleman from the 'most distinguished line of the Middle Angles', a man who had spent the last decade of the seventh century as a warrior in the king's hall, turning his eye to the transitory nature of the world and to the end of time, left his family and withdrew to the fens south-east of the Welland where Welsh could still be heard among the eel trappers and basket makers. With Guthlac were his sister Pega and his kinswoman Tibba. Here, driven by the message of the early fathers, he began to 'remake himself' as Origen had said 'in the hope that a better humanity would arise'. On an island in the fens he found his own wilderness, his *pan-eremos*, just as the early Christian hermits had chosen the Egyptian desert, and he lived out the rest of his life in that liminal landscape 'neither land nor water' where he heard demons and saw bears, boar and wild cats. His sister would even go on pilgrimage to find her final rest in Rome. For the peasants, as yet, there were no such choices. But in time – and sooner than might be imagined – they would come.

# 5. Under the Danelaw

In winter the mists sometimes hang like a veil across a mile of flooded fields from the old bridge of the Trent at Willington to the soft emerald green folds of the hills above Repton. The Old English Hrypadun, 'the hill of the Hrype tribe', Repton was a famous royal monastery, the burial place of the Mercian kings. The church, the mausoleum of Kings Aethelbald and Wiglaf and the murdered saint Wistan, stood on a plateau of land a steep twenty feet above the old course of the river which once flowed right under the churchyard. Here in the winter of 873–4 an extraordinary event took place. A Viking army had made its winter camp here and laid out a fortified base inside the precinct of the royal monastery. The place had been chosen not only for its symbolic value but for practical reasons: it was a naturally protected position bounded by river marshes to the west, and to the east by a stream bed coming down from the 'dun'. Inside the monastic grounds the Vikings had thrown up an inner defence work, a ditch and bank with a timber palisade, a curving semi-circle 100 metres across, anchored at both ends on the Trent and centred on the stone nave of the church, now desecrated and perhaps serving as the headquarters of the Viking leaders. Here on that winter's day a sombre ritual took place which would trigger a defining phase in early-medieval English history.

In the old monastic cemetery to the west of the church stood an eighth-century mausoleum, a now roofless, subterranean structure, with a stone floor and walls fifteen feet square. Around it that day was gathered a crowd of perhaps two or three thousand Viking warriors, with their servants and camp followers, including many Anglo-Saxon women and children. Then a group of warriors moved through them bearing a body on a catafalque, down the steps of the mausoleum and through the doorway into the inner tomb chamber, now stripped of its Christian furnishings, its floor laid with a thick layer of marl. In the centre of the chamber was an empty stone coffin, the bones of its former royal occupant summarily thrown out to make it ready for the dead man to receive his final honours.

We can recover more details of this extraordinary scene from the excavators' report. The dead man had been well-built, six feet tall, and about forty years old. By his left side was an iron sword in a fleece-lined wooden scabbard covered with leather, attached to a belt with a decorated copper buckle. By the sword hilt was a folding iron knife and a dagger with a wooden handle, by the scabbard an iron key. Around the man's neck a thong held two glass beads and a silver hammer of Thor. On his legs, mysteriously, was a bag containing the humerus of a jackdaw, and between his thighs the tusk of a wild boar. Perhaps he had been disembowelled and his genitals cut off by those who killed him? His death wound had been a heavy blow to the skull but whilst on the ground he had been finished off with a sword slash that had severed the femoral artery in his upper thigh. As for his identity, it seems that this was none other than the most famous Viking of his era, the son of Ragnar Lothbrok, 'that most cruel pagan king', 'king of all the Norsemen of Ireland and Britain' and founder of the greatest and most long-lasting dynasty of the Viking Age: Ivar, nicknamed 'the Boneless'.

While the dead chief's women began to lament, a young man was brought down to the graveside, aged around twenty, wearing an iron knife at his waist. Perhaps he was the squire or armour bearer to the dead man. Unsteady on his feet from a draught of opiates, he was supported to the edge of the coffin and then killed with a single blow to the right side of his head. Buried in an adjacent grave inside the mortuary chamber he would accompany his lord to the halls of the dead.

Still more extraordinary scenes were to follow. The bones of over 200 men and the remains of forty-nine women – who were believed by the excavators to have been Anglo-Saxons – had been gathered inside the cemetery, the remains of warriors and camp followers who had died of wounds or disease that winter. These were now buried in rows fanning out from the central chamber and neatly stacked around the central coffin. Heavy timber joists were laid on the tops of the cut-down walls to form a roof which was covered with flat slabs and earth. The whole sunken structure was then sealed by a low stone cairn, topped by a mound of pebbles and edged by a kerb of upright stones. All the ritual proprieties of pagan Viking religion seem to have been followed: even the leftovers of the funeral feast were carefully buried in four sunken pits filled with stones.

Finally the tumulus was closed and the last sacrifice took place. Four young captives, perhaps English hostages, were killed and buried in a large pit with a sheep's head at their feet. Then the army raised their shout to Odin the leader of souls, the incarnation of fury and exaltation, the god of battle, death and prophecy. To the army chaplain, the shaman, perhaps fell the duty of speaking the acclamation prayer: 'Gakk i haoll horskr' – 'Welcome to Valhalla, brave one.' Then the whole elaborate funeral monument (surely the most extraordinary royal burial ever found in Britain) was sealed and at its edge a tall marker post was erected, carved and painted with pagan symbols, a mnemonic of the tree of Odin in this graveyard of a revered Christian monastery. Such was the funeral of Ivar the Boneless. As a later saga writer said approvingly, 'He was buried in the true fashion of the old days.'

The Viking army present at Repton that day had already cut a swathe of terror through England, with its allies crushing the kingdoms of the East Angles and the Northumbrians. When it left Repton that spring the army split up, its sights set on new fields of conquest. But these were no longer mere plundering raids. For like the Anglo-Saxons four centuries before, the Danes had come to stay. In the late ninth century their permanent settlement of large tracts of the Midlands north and east of Watling Street, and in East Anglia and Northumbria, would change the culture of England for ever. The people of Kibworth and its neighbouring villages soon found themselves in the border zone between the English and Anglo-Scandinavian worlds in a partitioned country. Like hundreds of similar villages across the Midlands, East Anglia and the north they now owed their allegiance to Viking overlords of the Danelaw. And there a new Anglo-Scandinavian society is about to emerge in which the old aristocracy of the Mercians, those who have survived, are joined as

neighbours and landowners by the leaders and rank and file of the
army of Repton and the many Danes who came into the country in
their wake in secondary migrations.

Remarkably, in the countryside around Kibworth the names of
some of the men in the Viking Great Army of the 870s may still survive in today's village names: men like Slagr 'the Sly', Hrolfr, Iolfr,
Gauti, Aki and Bladr, 'the Blade'. These men take us into the next
phase of the story of England, and of the village, and the next layer
in English identity: the Vikings.

## *The terror of war*

On the eve of the Viking Age the people on the ridge where the village of Kibworth lies today had lived under the rule of the Mercian
kings for two and a half centuries. The villagers as we have seen were
of mixed ancestry, British, Roman, Anglian and Frisian, but by the
ninth century they belonged to the estate named after a nobleman
called Cybba in the kingdom of Mercia. Occasionally great events
had swirled round their lives, as in 849, in the troubled dog days of
the kingdom, when rival claimants in the royal clan came to a meeting on the River Glen by Kibworth, and a young prince of the
Mercians, Wistan, was assassinated at Wistow in the water meadows
below Kibworth. Locals subsequently told of miracles – a pillar of
light had been seen for thirty days in the sky above the murder spot –
and though Wistan was carried to Repton for burial, Wistow
remained a local pilgrimage place until the Reformation. But of the
events of their lives we still have no detail. Then in a few years
between the 860s and 870s the old world they had grown up with was
swept away as the Vikings changed the English political landscape for
all time.

War was endemic in the West in the Dark Ages. Given the preva-
lence of disorder, violence and raiding in the northern world, whether
there really is a moment when the Viking Age can be said to have
begun is a moot point. The perceived difference perhaps was the size
and frequency of the attacks, and their coordination. Contemporaries

certainly thought that something new and deeply threatening had begun to unfold towards the end of the eighth century, and related these events with a growing sense of shock and foreboding. In Kent the first sign was thought to be a sacking of Thanet recorded in 753. West Saxon annals first describe a landing at Portland in 787, an attack by three ships – at most, say, 120 heavily armed men, but enough to overpower the royal coastguard and to strike terror. Believing them to be traders the port reeve, the customs officer, came down to question them, but they drew their swords and killed him and his companions. Then in 794 in the Anglo-Saxon Chronicle comes this:

In this year dire portents appeared over Northumbria and deeply terrified the people. They consisted of huge whirlwinds and flashes of lightning and fiery dragons were seen flying in the sky. A great famine immediately followed those signs and a little after that in the same year on 8 June the ravages of the heathen men miserably destroyed God's church on Lindisfarne with plunder and slaughter.

Northumbrian annals tell the tale with more brutal immediacy, perhaps from an eyewitness account of the atrocities:

in the church of Lindisfarne they plundered and trampled the holy places with polluted steps, they dug up the altars and seized all the treasures of the holy shrine. Some of the monks they killed, some they took away in chains; many they drove out naked and loaded with insults; some they drowned in the sea.

The story was greeted with horror across Britain and soon reached friends abroad: 'The news of your tragic sufferings daily brings me sorrow,' wrote the Northumbrian Alcuin in a letter back home. An alumnus of the school of York, now one of Charlemagne's think tank, Alcuin was part of the great chain of scholarly transmission in the West down from Theodore and Bede, and immediately saw the disaster in terms of Christian history: 'The pagans have destroyed God's sanctuary,' he wrote from Aachen; 'But don't be dismayed by this disaster . . . you survive and must stand like men and fight bravely.

Is this the beginning of greater sufferings?' Alcuin's long consolatory
letter to the monks of Jarrow is a little too sententious to our modern
taste, but behind its religious certainties lay a genuine and deep-felt
fear of the fragility of civilization experienced by all early-medieval
thinkers:

The pagans have appeared on your coasts; carefully hold on to the rule. Put
your faith in God, not weapons. Who is not scared by the terrible fate that
befell the church at Lindisfarne? You live by the sea where the danger first
appeared . . . so remember the words of the prophet, 'from the North evil
breaks forth . . . a terrible glory will come from the Lord.'

  Look, the pirate raids have penetrated the north of our island. Let us
grieve for the suffering of our brothers and beware the same does not happen to us . . . Remember the nobility of your predecessors. Look at the
treasures of your library, the beauty of your churches . . . the order of your
religious life . . .

  All well and good perhaps to write such words from an ivory tower
in Europe; the security of Aachen was a long way from the exposed
Northumbrian coast. Alcuin saw the moral in terms of God's will and
the nation's sins, as sermon writers did throughout the whole period.
And the attacks, as Alcuin foresaw, continued. Irish annals pick up
the tale next with stories of raids on Skye, Iona and Alba and the routine
plundering of Irish houses. Through the middle of the ninth century
the threat grew to the whole Christian social order which had been
created out of the chaos at the end of Rome and the wanderings of
the barbarians. The achievements of kingship and the growth of
Western economies, the stored-up merchants' goods and coins in the
nascent towns, the jewelled manuscripts and portable treasures in the
monasteries – all were easy prey. Soon the Viking armies were growing in size and beginning to act in combination with groups of kings
operating together. A mere three ships in 787 became 140 in Ireland
in 849; 120 were wrecked off Swanage in 877; fleets of over 200 were
soon reported in Ireland; then 700 in a vast combined operation at
the siege of Paris in 885. And as they grew in size the armies began to
contemplate permanent settlement. In the winter of 855 a Viking

army wintered in Sheppey; in 860 they sacked Winchester and compelled the people of Kent and the East Angles to make peace and pay tribute. Then in 866 a large combined force wintered in the territory of the East Angles and received tribute, supplies and horses. This was what Old English called the 'micel here': the 'great heathen army'.

The wanderings of the Great Army during the next few years by land and sea through the islands and archipelagos of northern Britain and through all the regions of England need not be followed in detail here, though to read the year by year account of their movements in the Anglo-Saxon Chronicle is to gain a strong sense of the malign threat they represented, their power and the inability of individual English kingdoms to fight against them. All over England the Great Army's depredations were well-known to the peasantry, who suffered most from its ravaging and plundering. A professional army heavily armed and mobile, with large numbers of horses, it was led by three kings: Ivar (Ingwer), Halfdan and Hubba, sons of Ragnar Lothbrok, who had ruled in Denmark and who seems to have been killed in Northumbria in 865. In 867 they crossed from East Anglia into Northumbria across the Humber estuary. There, taking advantage of a local civil war, they killed both the rival kings and installed a puppet who made peace and paid tribute. In 868 they moved into Mercia, to Nottingham, and made winter quarters there. The Mercians now asked for help from their erstwhile enemies the West Saxons and after 'severe fighting' their joint forces made a negotiated peace with the Danes. The mobility of the Great Army, however, made it impossible to restrict them to one theatre of war, or to one peace agreement. They wintered back in Northumbria then rode back into East Anglia. There in November 870 they defeated and killed King Edmund of the East Angles, who according to an early tradition was captured and put to death with particular cruelty, possibly in some kind of pagan sacrifice. Now in their turn the conquered East Angles installed a puppet king and furnished the Danes with tribute and supplies. Then in 871 the Army moved south and fought a costly series of eight battles and skirmishes against tenacious opposition in Wessex, but unable to overcome the West Saxons under their young king, Alfred, they moved back north.

This was the background to the dramatic events at Repton. In 872–3 a combined army moved into Mercia under four kings, who are named in the Anglo-Saxon Chronicle as Halfdan, Guthrum, Anand and Oscytel. A fifth mentioned by Irish sources and later Scandinavian tradition is the legendary Ingwaer, 'Ivar beinluss', the paramount king who was remembered by the chronicler Adam of Bremen as 'the most cruel pagan king who everywhere tortured Christians to death'. In November 872 they wintered on the Trent in Lindsey and to buy time the Mercian king Burgred made peace, in the now usual pattern by providing money and supplies.

The following year, 873, however, they moved across country into the heart of Mercia and made their base at the Mercian royal church of Repton. At this point Burgred seems to have fought them but was defeated and after a reign of twenty-two years resigned his kingship and fled overseas, ending his days in Rome. The whole kingdom of the Mercians now fell under Viking power. In Burgred's place the Mercians elected a nobleman called Ceolwulf – 'a foolish king's thegn' it was said contemptuously in the south, though in fact he was of the royal kin and would issue charters and coins in his own name as king. But Ceolwulf was to be the last king of the Mercians. In what one contemporary called a 'wretched deal' he agreed to cooperate with the invaders and provided them with hostages and supplies. This took place in a formal ceremony of submission in which 'He swore oaths to them that what they desired should be ready for them on whatever day they wanted it and he would be ready himself and with all those who remained with him, at the service of the army.' To us Ceolwulf sounds like a quisling, but in the face of military defeat and remorseless pressure from a hostile and ruthless army composed of heavily armed professionals, it was perhaps the only sensible course for the moment. Against them the surviving Mercian thegns, the lords of estates like Kibworth, were outnumbered and outfought, and the local peasant levies too poorly armed and organized to offer serious resistance.

The fighting which led to Burgred's defeat may have been near to Repton. It is hard to imagine the Mercian king would not have made an attempt to save this royal cult centre and mausoleum. In 1855 a

Viking Age cemetery was found with fifty-nine male burials only two miles away on a rise above the Trent valley. These were cremations burned on boat planking but traces of clothes, possessions and weapons were found with coins datable to the mid-870s. It was perhaps in this warfare that Ingwaer, Ivar, died, whose death is recorded that year in Irish annals as 'the king of the Norsemen of Britain and Ireland'. Hence it is tempting to associate him with the incredible discovery made at Repton described at the head of this chapter, one of the most dramatic archaeological finds in British history and indeed a find without parallel anywhere in Viking Age Europe.

With the burial of Ivar, the long and eventful stay of the Vikings at Repton was over. In spring 874 the Great Army left Repton and split up, part heading down into East Anglia, part up into Northumbria to the Tyne valley. Then comes the first sign of a momentous change in their tactics. In 876, says the Anglo-Saxon Chronicle, 'the army in Northumbria under King Halfdan shared out the land of the Northumbrians and proceeded to plough and support themselves.' In the following year, 877, the southern army rode back into Mercia, and in August, around harvest-time, began to share it out, allotting some to Ceolwulf and some to their own rank and file. So less than a century after the great Offa had dominated England, the old lands of Mercia were partitioned. The East Midlands, between Trent and Welland, the Lincolnshire Wolds and the Leicester uplands, were divided up, and members of a Viking army settled and took land alongside the English landowners and their peasantry and 'began to plough and to provide for themselves'.

Only in Wessex was King Alfred able to hold his own and defeat Guthrum's army at the battle of Edington in 878. But such was the Vikings' military power that in 886 Alfred was forced to acknowledge the true state of affairs by agreeing to a treaty dividing England from the River Lea above London all the way up Watling Street to Tamworth: a partition of England right through what had been the kingdom of Mercia. The age of Scandinavian England had begun. Exactly what this meant for the people in villages like Kibworth — what happened, what were the numbers, whether it was a small elite or a mass migration – has been hotly disputed. Inevitably chroniclers writing in Winchester or Northumbria saw only part of the picture. The full story is only now being slowly recovered from archaeology, place names and even DNA.

## Slagr 'the Sly' and Blath 'the Blade'

The popular image of the Viking invasions from medieval chronicles to Victorian paintings and Hollywood epics is of blood and thunder, rape and pillage. But as with the 'coming of the English' the reality was far more complex and interesting. What did the 'sharing out' of Mercia mean? How was the settlement negotiated between the leaders of the Great Army and the Mercian king and his council? Did the Vikings actually buy land and property? Did they simply seize choice estates, or were they allotted uninhabited or marginal land away from the local English? Answers to some of these questions have started to emerge recently from fascinating new place name evidence from the East Midlands.

The people of Kibworth were in the main region of Danish settlement, which later became known as the Danelaw. Here, the Middle Anglian lords of Leicester were replaced by Viking rulers, kings or chiefs, whose warriors settled across the Leicester uplands to Rutland. At a local level many estates remained under their English lords – around Kibworth in the Gartree Hundred, several places today still retain the name of an Anglo-Saxon lord, Osulf at Owston, Glor at Glooston, or Cybba at Kibworth. But today's villages also preserve the names of Viking newcomers who, out in the landscape, attached Scandinavian words to villages, hamlets and farms, fields, watercourses and many smaller natural features. Even in Kibworth itself where the field names remained predominantly Old English, nearly a fifth of place names are from the Scandinavian language, and the pattern of these names shows us what might have happened after the share-out of land by the Great Army after 877.

The chronology of these settlements is also revealed by the place names. From the first phase after 877 are hybrid names like Grimston which combine a Viking personal name with the English word *tun* (village). Close to Kibworth there are a number of these hybrids, which suggests the appropriation of already existing English estates and settlements by warriors of the Danish Army. Illston on the Hill just north of Kibworth for example is named after a Dane, Iolfr. Nearby Rolleston preserves the name of another Viking, Hrolfr. Others in the vicinity include Slagr, 'the Sly', who took over the English *tun* which is now Slawston; and the tough-sounding Blath, 'the Blade', who was a close neighbour at Blaston. Iolfr, Hrolfr, Slafr and Blath may have been original members of the army disbanded in 877, veterans who settled in the Kibworth area, 'shared the land and began to plough', backed by the armed force of their friends and retinues − a heavily armed elite who carved out a kingdom in England and farmed land in exchange for military service to their paramount lord, presumably in Leicester, who was now Danish.

Second-stage settlements − those of immigrants who perhaps came into England in the next two or three decades − are indicated by another layer of place names. To the north-east of Kibworth a cluster of names on poorer land contain the Viking word for farm, *by*, as in Galby, Goadby and Frisby ('farmstead of Frisians'). These can be connected with a later phase of settlement, one in which more immigrants, family members and women, had come from Denmark and Frisia. But these were not on as good land as the *tun*s. Little Galby, for example, was never a great success − it was finally virtually deserted in the decades after the Black Death; its name means 'poor soil' in Old Norse, and the land is stiff clay and loam. But Galby is surrounded by villages which kept their English names, King's Norton, Stretton, Burton and Houghton, where evidently the local native farmers had not been dislodged. The Vikings in Galby then had to be satisfied with poor marginal land. Around Kibworth there are a number of these names: Bushby as its name says was a 'farm in the scrubland'; Thurnby, 'the farm on thorny land'; Rainby in Goadby parish was 'a borderland farm'. A further group around Kibworth reveals further outlying Viking farmsteads (thorpe), in Thorpe Langton, Hothorpe and Othorpe − where a field name commemorates another Viking settler called Aki. Thorpes, like tofts, seem to have been from a still later phase of Viking settlement when the squeeze on land for new immigrants had become quite tight. Most picturesquely named is Scraptoft – in Old Norse a thin, poor or even miserable covering of grass: a further hint that some settlers moved round the existing English population to open up new poorer land on the margins, even perhaps buying plots from locals. As regards the settlers, some names may indicate their places of origin. Gauti of Goadby may be as his name implies a man from Gautland. Next door to Kibworth in Great Glen parish the Viking who built himself a small farm at 'Northman's toft' may have been a Norwegian.

These faint footprints of real individuals in the Viking Age are intriguing hints of the treaties and negotiations that happened from day to day as the Viking armies attempted to take some of the rich farmland of the Middle Angles for themselves. The indigenous population though was too large to remove or drive out: things had to be negotiated, and in the end they would have to rub along.

The village reeve and everyone in Kibworth and Smeeton would have warily watched these changes happening around them. On the wrong side of the Watling Street frontier, their overlord after 877 was no longer the King of the Mercians, but the Viking lord, the jarl, of the 'Army of Leicester'. To see precisely how these things might have worked out in practice in Kibworth we only need to walk downhill out of Smeeton Westerby on the Gumley Road. Here sherds of St Neots ware and Stamford ware pottery were found in the 2009 village dig, attesting to the growth of a wealthy and populous community in the Viking Age from the late ninth century onwards. At the bottom in the valley is a little stream which snakes through a field undulating with medieval ridge and furrow. Standing in the field and looking back to the ridge on which the village sits, Smeeton to the right was already a tun by the ninth century, and its name is English. But only a few yards along the ridge to the left are the farms and weavers' cottages of Westerby: in Old Norse *Vesterbyr*, the 'West farm' – founded just to the west of Smeeton by Viking settlers at some point perhaps a few years after the disbanding of the army of 877.

In the farmland below the village the field names are a mix of English and Scandinavian. The little stream at the foot of the hill occurs in tithe maps as the Fleet: *fliotr* in Viking; by its banks there's a carr, in Old Norse *kjarr* – a boggy flat covered with brush – and out in the fields there are wongs, slangs, flats, tofts, holms and siks. In some parts of the East Midlands and north these words are all still used in farming speech. Holme, a familiar northern place name, occurs across the parish of Kibworth, as do gates (in northern speech meaning not an opening gate but a street or track) and siks (in Scandinavian speech a watercourse or ditch between fields which in time becomes a grassy division between field strips). These words still exist in farming speech in the surviving open-field village at Laxton in the East Midlands. The survival of such field names is a strong indication that over the generations Scandinavian dialect spread quite widely among English as well as Viking farmers, and probably that Viking speech was spoken for some generations among a minority of the population even in Kibworth. Perhaps the most notable minor field name in Smeeton, last recorded in the 1960s, but found in documents from the Victorian age back to 1636, is Crackley, whose earlier forms in the seventeenth century reveal the Scandinavian word *craca* = *kraka*, the Old Norse 'raven', with the Old English *leah* – a suitably Viking name in an English field, 'Raven's Wood'.

## Numbers: elites or mass migration?

The Viking settlement depicted in such lurid terms by monastic chroniclers was not an act of ethnic cleansing; nor did it involve the driving out of the native population. The population of England was still low after its peak in the late-Roman world, kept in check by plague, disease, war and natural catastrophe. The countryside was far less crowded, and there was plenty of land available for newcomers, especially in the margins which now began to be cleared for cultivation. Anglian-speaking areas, not Saxon, were favoured for settlement – even Essex was not, despite its proximity to Jutland and Frisia – perhaps because of the linguistic closeness of Anglian and Danish. On the numbers of the settlers modern opinion is divided. Recent historiography has argued for a very small elite. But place names and documents are evidence of transformation by sizeable immigration. In terms of the whole population DNA experts have suggested an addition to the English gene pool of 1 per cent Norwegian and 4–5 per cent Danish; a total of over 5.5 per cent of the total population for the newcomers nationally, though in this part of the East Midlands the figure was probably higher, around 10 per cent. In a national population of one million 5.5 per cent would represent over 50,000 immigrants, twice that if the population was 2 million.

So following the Britons, Romans, Angles and Saxons, the Vikings were added to the racial and cultural mix. Again they were a minority, a few tens of thousands in one to two million. But they will bring important changes in the law, language and customs of northern and eastern England. By the eleventh century the countryside will have been opened up to near its full potential so that in late-Saxon Kibworth there was almost as much arable land as there was in the nineteenth century. All this was to meet the demands of population growth after the Viking Age.

## 'A farmer needs a wife'

In the families of Kibworth and many places like it, the Viking settlers left a long-lasting mark. The stories of the families descended from the Great Army and later waves of migrants can be traced into the period after the Norman Conquest when detailed documents emerge for the first time in the history of the village. Many common Midland names – Tookey, Pauley, Chettle, Gamel, Herrick for example – are Viking in origin, and in estate documents and tax rolls from Kibworth and Smeeton starting in the 1200s some of the most common family names are Scandinavian. One or two, like Thurd or Thored, are only found in this region in Kibworth itself. These people constitute a landowning class of small farmers, freemen or 'sokemen', who are prominent at local level in later manorial documents and tenaciously hold their position in the next centuries to become part of the yeoman class in the fifteenth and sixteenth centuries.

In Smeeton for example there are the Astins and Swans: behind these surnames lie the Danish Haesten and Sweyn – modern Sven. By the thirteenth century these families have several distinct branches of the family tree in separate households, and very likely go back to individual settlers in the Viking Age. These men were perhaps second-generation incomers after the share-out of 877 and it is possible that they were the founders of Westerby, the Scandinavian hamlet west of Smeeton village. There, Sven, Haesten and companions opened up new land, cleared brush and woodland and began to plough. 'Always a distinct place' as Nichols wrote of it in the late eighteenth century, though even then Westerby had only eight houses.

Sven and Haesten still owed military service to their Danish over-lord and had to join his 'here' with their horses and war gear for campaigns into the south against Alfred the Great's successors. But essentially now they were farmers. When Sven married and had children, it is possible that he sent for a bride from Denmark, but more likely he married a local Englishwoman, as did even the chief man in Leicester in the 930s, Earl Urm, who gave his daughter an English name. And if Sven set out to court a wife, the daughter of a local Kibworth farmer, Oswin or Godwine for example, then perhaps he bought her a cheap imitation Danish brooch manufactured in the Danelaw, one of the women's fashions from Scandinavia which were now all the rage in England and which are now being picked up by metal detectorists across the East Midlands. If so, Sven's wife was not the only one: as so often in history, within a short time there was very likely plenty of intermarriage between the indigenous people and the newcomers. It has been suggested that Danish men took more care over their looks. The bone combs with which Viking men combed their long hair, Danish-style, are frequently found in archae-ological digs, and it was said (perhaps not entirely in jest) that they washed more often too. The languages of course were similar, espe-cially the Anglian dialect spoken in the Midlands and East Anglia, so they could swiftly learn to make themselves understood. Did Sven's children learn to speak Danish from their father and English from their mother? On such matters of course our sources are silent, but these are the intimate details we would really wish to know.

Perhaps then some of the new immigrants found a warmer welcome than might be gathered from ecclesiastical writers horrified by the aggression (and of course the paganism) of these 'uncouth, barbarous, berserk, stubborn, treacherous foreigners . . .' Sven of Westerby we must assume took a more relaxed view. He wore the silver hammer of Thor round his neck and he took his children to make offerings to Thunor's 'holy oak' on the edge of Rutland. But he was happy to go to church with his English wife wearing the ring of the English St Edmund, martyred by Sven's parents a generation back in 870, his severed head miraculously protected by wolves like a figure from the pagan past, but now a model to both communities as a courageous Christian warrior favoured by God. In time Sven will baptize his daughters and granddaughters and give them English names but his first-born son will keep the name of his forefathers. He will be Magnus son of Sven, and in time his descendants will become the Swans of Smeeton and Westerby. By the eleventh century they could have bought silk and wine in the market at Lincoln and with a bit of money perhaps even gone to Rome on pilgrimage.

So the Anglo-Saxon settlement of Kibworth became an Anglo-Scandinavian village in the Danelaw, a parable of the Viking Age. We can now picture the village divided into the four communities that appear in eleventh-century documents and which exist today: the northern village (later Kibworth Harcourt), site of the Iron Age, Roman and Anglian settlements and Cybba's enclosure; the 'lower' Kibworth (today's Beauchamp), the old Anglo-Saxon service village with its unfree population of villeins and serfs; Smeeton, with its free peasantry, artisans and farmers; and finally little Westerby, the Viking farmstead of the late ninth or early tenth century whose precise boundary is still pointed out at the end of Smeeton's main street, from where one may look out across the 'fleet' to 'Raven's Wood'. In the one parish are the roots of the English story from the Romans to the Vikings.

# 6. The Kingdom of England

Between 900 and 1066 the peasants of Kibworth – English and Viking neighbours – became part of a kingdom of all England. Though described as the *gens Anglorum* (after Bede), this was in fact a mixed-race state with different laws for West Saxons, Mercians and Danes, and more specifically local legislation in bilingual frontier zones. It was a state embracing people speaking British, Welsh, Cumbrian and Scandinavian languages as well as the various English dialects. In the regions there were even different systems of measuring land and counting money. But the idea was that all owed allegiance to the king of the English: the creation of the allegiance was the key. It was, one could say, a typically English form of improvisation, allowing different and even contradictory systems to work in parallel. How this came about at the grass roots is only now being discovered from a very wide range of sources, and in this story what happened along the cultural and linguistic frontier with Viking England was of crucial importance.

But first, a glimpse of the times. The tenth century has had a bad name, and not without cause. Across Western Europe it began with the ever-present threat of civil war and Viking invasion. Warfare was the tenth-century condition; but so too, as Western Europeans perceived it, was the failure of kingship and the breakdown of allegiance. In 906 Regino of Prum expressed his horror at the post-Carolingian malaise, failed states and ignoble dynasties 'creating kings out of their own guts'. A church council in northern France in 909 pronounced gloomily, 'We now live in an Age of Iron.' But ages of iron, times in which people are forced to go back to first principles and build from the bottom, can be no less creative than ages of gold. Out of the tenth-century disorder, English communities, urban and rural, emerge; an English kingship with national law and the beginnings of a sense of an English culture to which all belonged.

Across the British Isles the century began with hugely disruptive weather patterns, torrential rains and failed harvests. The year 900 was remembered as a year of rains followed by 'great scarcity' and cattle murrain. Plague struck in 907 and cattle pest in 909. From 912, the year of Halley's comet, a time of 'rain and darkness' was prolonged for two years with more miserable harvests. Then in 917 came the first signs of a little ice age which would last into the 940s. As an Ulster annalist wrote:

such snow and extreme cold and unnatural ice this year that the chief lakes and rivers of Ireland were passable on foot, and death was brought to cattle, birds and fish. There were horrible portents too: the heavens seemed to glow with comets; and once a mass of fire appeared with thunder in the west beyond Ireland, and it went eastwards over the sea.

Such lurid omens were widely trusted. The Viking threat was no less imminent than it had been in the late ninth century. The collapse of several English kingdoms in the 860s and 870s showed it was not possible for a single regional kingdom to fight the Vikings and win. The alliance of Mercians and West Saxons, however, was able to turn the tide and eventually create the kingdom of all England. Beyond the Watling Street frontier established by Alfred the Great and the Vikings, the centres of Anglo-Scandinavian power were the old cities of York in Northumbria and the Five Boroughs of the East Midlands, Nottingham, Derby, Stamford and the old Roman cities of Lincoln and Leicester. Each was ruled by its own military oligarchy. The old Middle Anglian provincial capital of Leicester was the centre of the 'army of Leicester', ruled by an 'Army Council' which controlled numerous former Mercian royal estates and wide resources, including Leicester Forest, which as late as the twelfth century was known as the Hereswode, the 'Army Forest'. To the Leicester assembly under its paramount Danish chief, or jarl, our Kibworth villagers of both English and Viking descent – men like Sven of Westerby for example – owed allegiance, tax and military service.

But times were changing fast. The first three decades of the century are among the most dramatic and action-packed in British

history, out of which would appear a new social and political landscape (in Scotland and Wales too). To the south of the Thames a
powerful West Saxon kingdom had emerged out of the Viking wars
under Alfred the Great. Alfred's military victories between the late
870s and the early 890s enabled him to push through draconian forms
of lordship. Galvanized by earlier military failures Alfred was determined that English society should become geared to war. As a
contemporary close to Alfred admitted, 'after first trying gentle
instruction, he then cajoled, urged, commanded and in the end forced
his people to do his will', that is, to accept much heavier levels of
military obligation. Reaction was widely hostile: 'Everyone then was
more bothered with his own particular well-being,' says Bishop
Asser, 'rather than the common good.' But the reforms were pushed
through. The result was the widespread loss of freedoms among the
dependent peasantry in southern England, where as Asser admits 'the
poor had few supporters – if any.' In the Danelaw, however, the free
peasantry survived as a large and distinctive landed class especially in
the East Midlands and East Anglia. In some places in the twelfth century this was 30 or 40 per cent of the population, and in some small
pockets it was over 60 per cent, as opposed to something like 15 per
cent of the English population as a whole.

By Alfred's death in 899 southern English society had been reorganized on to a permanent war footing. Wessex was now studded
with a network of fortified places – burhs – supplied, fed and supported from the heavy labour dues imposed on the peasantry. The
king could put into the field a mobile royal army whose core was perhaps 2,000 'armour-bearing thegns' bristling with weaponry, each
with servants and retinue and equipped with horses and expensive
war gear. These were backed up by 27,000 men who garrisoned the
towns and were financially supported and fed by their rural communities. And these figures do not take into account the peasant levies
which could be called up by the shire to defend against local Viking
attacks. This all amounts to an almost unbelievable proportion of a
population of perhaps half a million people south of the Thames. So
along the Watling Street frontier from Tamworth down to the River
Welland, two militarized societies faced each other, with the pagan

Scandinavian kings and their warbands in the cities of the Danelaw and north of the Humber. The situation was set for war, and war duly came.

Alfred the Great died in October 899, at the age of only fifty. His son Edward immediately had to defend his throne from rivals within his own kin. In the south a brutal civil war ended in a bloodbath on the Fen edge at Holme in Huntingdonshire in 904. The next few years were marked by the marching and counter-marching of hostile armies, in the payment of Danegeld, punctuated by devastating Viking raids into southern England. The very future of the nascent kingdom of the Anglo-Saxons created by Alfred was for a time in doubt. A Midland cleric was hardly exaggerating when he wrote that this was 'a time when it is by no means evident that the written word will survive the terrible dangers that imperil us . . .' What this meant for everyday life is revealed in a lease issued to the Bishop of Winchester in 909 for an estate just outside Winchester. The rent was payable in kind (ale, loaves, meat, cheese and other produce) and makes allowance for the situation arising when rent couldn't be paid 'because of the stress caused by [Viking] raids'. And this was only six miles from the 'capital'.

More graphic still is a lease of an estate near Croydon in Surrey in around 908 which conveys a vivid sense of how endemic warfare and freezing winters combined to make life desperate for the peasantry. This letter to King Edward begs remittance of their tax burdens given the desolate situation on the estate: 'When the king our lord rented it to me it was completely without stock, and had been stripped bare by the heathen men [the Vikings].' The bishop had restocked the estate, but at a cost increased by bad weather which had further depleted the estate:

Now of the cattle which survived the severities of the winter we have 9 full grown oxen with 114 full grown pigs and 50 wethers . . . and there are 110 full grown sheep and seven bondsmen [serfs] and twenty flitches [note how the human stock of the estate are lumped in with the animals and the flesh] and there was no more corn there than could be prepared for the bishop's farm: we have ninety sown acres. [The estate was seventy hides, several thousand acres, so they had been able to plough only a tiny portion.]

Then the bishop and the community at Winchester beg in charity for the love of God and for the sake of the holy church that you [the king] desire no more land of them, for it seems to them a very unfair demand.

If the principal bishopric in Wessex found it so difficult to make ends meet, what was it like for small freeholders up and down the country? Many freemen and freewomen no doubt lost their freedoms in this period, forced to put themselves under the protection of powerful lords. And indeed this was a period when lordship inexorably spread in southern England, paving the way for the Norman feudal order that followed in the eleventh century.

## The conquest of the Danelaw

Where the Anglo-Saxon Chronicle provides a detailed narrative for events in Wessex between the 870s and 920s, the situation in most of the rest of England is largely obscure. Viewed from the other side of Watling Street this is especially so. Situated inside the Danelaw only a few miles over Watling Street, Kibworth was almost on the front line of the war between the English and the Vikings. All this time though the village may well have remained under its English local lord. Four fifths of the field names in Kibworth parish are English, and the village didn't change its name to become 'Sven's worth' or 'Haesten's worth', although as we saw in the last chapter it had Viking neighbours, and enough Viking field names survive in the parish to show that the Viking language was widely spoken. This was very likely a genuinely bilingual society under an English lord. But as with their Viking neighbours, the sons and grandsons of Slagr, Iolfr and Hrolfr, the English landowners here were expected to turn out with their horses, armour and weapons to join the followings of their local Danish earls to fight against the 'kings of the South Angles', as in the disastrous campaign down the Severn valley in 910, and the mounted campaigns of 913 and 917 when the Leicester army was in the combined

Danelaw forces which rode southwards to attack the West Saxon King Edward.

As King Edward and his councillors saw it from the south, their aim was to reunite the *gens Anglorum*. This 'reunification' came about through one of the most brilliant and sustained campaigns in the Dark Ages. Even on the continent the news was of 'the bravery of the English who with Christ's grace defend themselves with strong arms and men and when pirate armies invade from the northern parts, drive them out in violent battles'. While Edward drove West Saxon armies into East Anglia and the East Midlands, reducing Viking army bases one by one, his sister Aethelflaed, 'Lady of the Mercians', with a Mercian army consolidated the West Midlands and Welsh Marches. In 917 Edward took the surrender of the Danish armies of Cambridge and Northampton, bringing the English forces to the banks of the Welland only five miles south of Kibworth. Then from across Watling Street Aethelflaed stormed the Danish fortress at Derby, where 'four of the thegns most dear to her were killed right inside the gate.' Faced by this pincer movement the Viking rulers of Leicester resorted to diplomacy. In early 918 their assembly approved the peaceful surrender of the 'Army of Leicester' and 'most' of the territory they controlled, including the Kibworth area. They now swore allegiance to Aethelflaed as ruler of the Mercians. After her death later that year this allegiance passed on to Edward, then to his son Athelstan, a man who was known to the Viking leadership and who may have spoken some Danish. Athelstan came to the throne in 925 ruling over the lands south of the Humber. The King had been brought up in Mercia and, if a later account can be trusted, had spent time in Danish territory and 'adopted some of their customs'. Within months came a real sign of the changing times: in a great meeting at the old Mercian 'capital' of Tamworth came what had been previously unthinkable, the marriage of the king's sister Eadgyth to Sihtric, the Viking king of York: the granddaughter of Alfred and the grandson of the bloodthirsty Ivar the Boneless who had been buried at Repton. On Sihtric's death in 927 Athelstan annexed Northumbria, and a poet in his entourage was able to salute 'this completed England'.

## *Shires and hundreds*

Claiming to be not only 'king of the Anglo-Saxons' but 'king of the Danes', Athelstan could now put in place his vision of an Anglo-Scandinavian kingdom of 'all the English nation'. Inevitably huge administrative changes followed, especially in the villages of the English Midlands. In Kibworth changes took place that were as far-reaching as anything experienced by the village till the Act of Enclosure in 1779. In southern England and English Mercia in order to support the war effort the countryside had been reorganized into new administrative districts, shires and hundreds, with uniform sliding assessments to calculate the size of the garrisons to be provided for the boroughs and the soldiers for the mobile defence forces. At this time the English kings were still waging war against the Scandinavian rulers north of the Humber in York with whom there were almost constant campaigns and battles up till the 950s. To impose administrative control and to fight this war they needed to reorganize the newly captured lands of the Midlands, and the hundred system was imposed there in a much more regular form. Positioned in the centre of the country, Leicester was the key to regional defence. So the West Saxons created a new *scir*, like those south of Watling Street, divided on the continental model into smaller units called 'hundreds'. Dependent on the burh, where the shire courts were held, these would be the key units of local administration, justice and taxation for many centuries, only finally disappearing in the 1880s.

Once every month the chosen 'tithing men' of Kibworth and Smeeton walked or rode a couple of miles or so north-east to a point where an ancient track crosses the Roman Via Devana. There, on a gentle rise with wide views across to Kibworth and the Langtons and over the Welland valley southwards, stood the Gartree. From the tenth century till the early eighteenth this was the meeting place of the local hundred for the elected jurors of Kibworth and the surrounding villages. Located on a prehistoric burial mound, it was very likely the site of an earlier Anglo-Saxon moot place (law codes as early as the seventh century speak of doing justice at an 'assembly or

meeting place' and already assume the existence of local legal experts
called judges or 'arbitrators' before whom 'right' is done). Like many
moot sites, as its name indicates, the meeting place was at a prominent
tree. The name Gartree is still found in Westland in Norway, where
it signifies a distinctive mark or scar on a tree's bark, but here it seems
more likely to come from the Scandinavian word *geir* meaning 'spear'.
An appropriate name for the meeting place of a hundred – in Viking
speech a *wapentake*, referring to the brandishing of weapons with
which the armed freemen of the region showed their assent to the
decisions of the court.

As far back as the seventh century we find references to meetings
of formally convened bodies where serious social conflicts and dis-
agreements were ironed out in public before witnesses. But the
hundreds mark the real beginning of English local government. They
were probably extended over the country between the 920s and 950s.
An important aspect was fiscal: the profits of law for example went
to the lords of the individual hundreds, whether king, Church or
private owners. But a memorandum from the mid-century shows
that their main function was to handle local law and order, and
to contain feuds and violence, fundamental problems for all early-
medieval governments: 'This is the ordinance on how the hundred
meetings shall be held. First they are to assemble every four weeks,
and each man is to do justice to another.'

Among other business handled at the Gartree, local custom was
declared, new passages in the king's laws were read out, titles to property were established and violence condemned if not punished, with
sureties being fixed to keep the peace, especially for persistent trouble-
makers. As for lower-class representation, lesser freemen could be
present as tithing men, and after 1066 even men of villein status
appeared in the juries. Members were usually men though there are
occasionally jurywomen. The courts were customarily held outdoors
and since the shire court met only twice a year, at Easter and Michael-
mas, these monthly hundred courts must have been the main contact
most people had with the 'trickle-down effect' of royal government.

All this may sound almost democratic, and the Victorians were
prepared to believe that it was, seeing in the hundred and shire 'moots'

and the 'national' king's council, the witan, the origin of the British parliamentary system. In practice of course the courts were far from egalitarian. There was one law for the rich and one for the poor as far as judicial proofs went, and the few surviving accounts of assemblies of the shires show they were often swayed by the voices of men of influence, the big local landowners, ealdormen or thegns. The penalties exacted for fighting at a moot show that tempers regularly flared up. But the point is not that the courts were democratic, but that they were consultative. They mark the beginnings in the English state of the means by which the local and the centre could communicate, and through which the local could have a voice. By the 1260s when the 'community of the realm', including the free peasantry, played a real part in the great events of the kingdom, the local community had found a voice it would never lose.

## The beginnings of civic life

As for the transaction of local business, few documents have survived the devastation of the archives of the Danelaw by the Vikings. In the century or so between 850 and 970 we have very little detail on the ground of the huge changes which took place in society: then documents from the old Middle Anglian monastery of Peterborough open a window on life in the East Midlands. From the middle of the tenth century lists of sureties – guarantees made on oath 'before all the *wapentake*' – record the sales of property, woodland, arable, field strips, mills and homesteads on the Welland east of Kibworth. These give a precious glimpse into life in our region in the tenth century. Indeed, if we could only eavesdrop on them we would no doubt be surprised at the level of what one might call 'civic' life. They show us English and Scandinavian neighbours doing deals, buying and selling property, and even resolving their feuds through the local assembly, with serious cases heard in front of 'the whole army' – that is, the shire court. In a relatively small area there are scores of householders and property owners operating in an active land and property market using a plentiful silver coinage and (for big purchases) gold. Here are priests with English and Viking names; women freeholders called Hungifu and Swuste; a widow from Raunds; a painter called Wulfnoth; and even a pilgrim who had made the journey to Rome. Before the age of fixed surnames there is a certain amount of confusion given the limited number of Anglo-Saxon male names – 'blond Godric', 'Godric the beard' and 'the other Godric' appear in one case. Sometimes the lists of sureties reveal what must have been a daunting level of everyday violence and blood feud, but most cases involve land and house purchases. In Kibworth, as here, these would be confirmed by the new owner in Leicester at a meeting of the whole army ('ealles heres gemotes') when 'the whole army stood security on his behalf that the estate was free and unencumbered by any burdens left by previous owner.' These documents show that by the middle of the tenth century there was already a vigorous land and property market, and well-off peasant families were already wheeling and dealing to expand their inheritance.

Of course, this presupposes at least some contact with literacy for the villagers, though how far literacy had really touched Kibworth and other places like it is a big question. In Anglo-Saxon England literacy was probably more widespread than has been thought. So in the England of the tenth century it is unlikely there was not someone literate in each village: the priest, the leading jurors in the shire court, the tithing men involved in administering law and order, in policing and charity, and members of peace guilds. For all of them the sense was now growing of belonging not only to their village and shire, but also, if distantly, to a national community.

## The open fields

Around that time great changes also took place in the village in the organization of the fields and farming practices. These were more significant than any agrarian innovations in Kibworth till the Agricultural Revolution and the Act of Enclosure in 1779; indeed, they are some of the most revolutionary in the history of the English countryside. The circumstances of these changes are hidden from us by the lack of documents – till recently indeed they were largely unsuspected – but they involved the planned introduction of the open-field system of farming. In this system typically three great open fields are communally farmed in rotation leaving one field fallow each year. The adoption of this system cannot be separated from the creation of the network of towns and shires during the Viking wars. To garrison and supply the towns required the reorganization of the countryside. English peasant society was being reshaped by powerful lordship to facilitate social control, to share animals, plough gear and resources and to maximize production and create surplus.

The first signs of the specialized terminology of the open fields start to appear in the tenth century in southern England, with 'intermixed strips' in open unhedged fields which were communally farmed and in which meadow, pasture and arable were all 'common land'. Some of these documents seem to describe open-field strips where there is no boundary between strips, where, as one tenth-century lease puts it, 'lands are farmed in common and not demarcated on any side by clear bounds because to left and right the acres lie combined with each other.' Still more explicitly one tenth-century estate in Wiltshire is described as 'in individual strips [*jugeribus*] dispersed in a mixture through the common land'. To complement this documentary evidence, in recent years in a systematic survey in the East Midlands archaeologists have found evidence in scores of places of such fields being laid out over eighth- and ninth-century settlements. In this light the Peterborough sureties from the 960s referred to above are also illuminating: one mentions a small estate at Maxey divided into twenty-nine 'portions', presumably groups of strips, and another at Oxney describes thirty acres of arable divided into sixty *sticca*, which sound like half-acre strips in the open field.

Partly effected by royal power, partly by local lords, the introduction of open fields brought about a revolution in the pattern of the English countryside and the nature of agrarian society. It seems likely that the great open fields laid out in each of the three villages in Kibworth parish were laid over earlier Iron Age fields. At the same time the settlements were nucleated, bringing freemen and cottagers into the villages with streets and garden plots alongside the lord's manorial

hall and demesne land: the beginning of the classic English village
landscape. Finds of late-Saxon pottery by the village streets in Smeeton and Kibworth Harcourt offer confirmation of this picture. So in
the last phase of Anglo-Saxon history each community of Kibworth
Harcourt, Kibworth Beauchamp and Smeeton had three-field systems and each had growing populations, which made Kibworth one
of the most populous villages in Leicestershire.


## Haywards, woodwards and reeves

'I can only tell you what I know,' says a Midland reeve in a memorandum from the time. 'You see, estate laws vary from place to place.
Nor do all these regulations apply in all districts. I can only speak of
the customs I know. But in life if we learn well, work hard, and
endeavour to understand it better – the more we take delight in the
task at hand.'

We don't know the name of the Anglo-Saxon reeve in Kibworth,
but he was the predecessor of men we will come to know well in the
fourteenth century – men such as Nick Polle, husbanding resources
in the Great Famine, John Church, listing the dead tenants in the
Black Death, or John Chapman, wrapping up the rent strike in 1449.
In the later period the reeve was an important figure in the village.
Elected by the peasants, he was a man of repute, a trustworthy 'swearing man' whose job was to supervise the running of the fields, to
check the animals, stores and tools, and to look after the routine, the
calendar of the year. In the Anglo-Saxon management texts the job
seems no different. The work practices of the open fields, the field
cycle of fallow and seeded and the overseeing of village custom
required village officials who knew it inside out. In the late Saxon
period these village officials now emerge into the light of day, and it
is in this class of peasants that for the first time we begin to hear the
ordinary voice.

On the variety of custom, the reeve continues, warming to his
tale, his is the expertise of an experienced countryman who from
childhood has mastered all the agricultural tasks; a wealth of practical

knowledge, which explains why the job often ran in families in Kibworth – like the Browns, the Sibils and especially the Polles, who provide many generations of reeves and constables between 1300 and 1600. Presumably dictated to the lord's scribe, the Anglo-Saxon text is in amiable but forcefully idiomatic Old English, with an eye-opening range of technical vocabulary describing the wherewithal of late-Saxon farming. The text also gives a lengthy checklist of all the specialized tools and farm gear needed on a working estate : recognizably a precursor of the detail we find in the later medieval accounts for Kibworth. A Midland text, this could be the reeve of Kibworth in the 1060s working for the lord of Harcourt, Aelfric, son of Meriet, or, in Beauchamp, Edwin, son of Aelferth:

Now there are many different common customs and rights in different places. In some districts there are due winter rations, Easter supplies, a harvest feast for the reapers, a drinking feast for the ploughmen and their helpers, a tip for the mowers . . . a meal at the haystack during harvest, a log from the wagon at wood carrying, a rick-cup at corn carrying, and many other things which I can't go into. This is just a memorandum of the basic provisions I've been talking about – of course there is more to it than this . . .

These Old English management texts also tell us about the jobs and grades of society in a village like Kibworth in the century before the Norman Conquest. Below the landlords – the thegns, Aelfric and Edwin – were the freemen and freewomen in Kibworth known as sokemen, who farmed their own land. Then there were lower men: cottagers, semi-free geburs (later called villeins), serfs and bonded slaves. In one management text the men and women with particular jobs are specified: the beekeeper and the swineherd, the bonded swineherd, the servant and the women slaves. Then come the field workers: ploughman, sower, oxherd, cowherd, shepherd and goatherd, along with the forester, the woodward. These are all found in thirteenth-century Kibworth, when detailed records for the village begin. As in later times there will have been a leather worker in the village who made 'slippers and shoes, leggings, leather bottles, reins and trappings, flasks and leather containers, spur straps and halters, bags and purses'. In the village there would also be a female cheese maker and a granary keeper, and in a big village like Kibworth a carpenter, a miller, a smith, a baker, perhaps even a cook, all of whom existed in Kibworth in the thirteenth century. Then there might have been a priest or monk who lived the religious life but did other jobs in the village too. Towards the year 1000, life in Kibworth was not yet so diversified as it was in the thirteenth century, but any traveller in the English countryside would have seen that society was visibly developing from the inward-looking subsistence life of earlier centuries to a diversified economy already with a market element.

## The rise in the standard of living

By the late tenth century the people of the village could look back on two or three generations of relative peace and security under the protection of the English king and his law. Writing in the 980s a member of the royal family speaks of fifty years of 'peace and abundance of all things'. He seems to be telling us of a perceived rise in the standard of living in English society as a whole, and modern archaeologists have corroborated this, discerning a slow improvement in the material life after the Dark Ages which will blossom in the early eleventh century across Europe, as Ralph Glaber describes in his famous passage of millennial optimism, when 'on the threshold of the millennium, it was as though the very world had shaken herself and cast off her old age, and were clothing herself everywhere in a white garment of churches.'

Hints of this increased prosperity in Kibworth have come from finds by metal detectorists. Two coins of Ethelred the Unready from the late 980s and early 990s have been found recently, one minted in Rochester in Kent and one from York. These finds suggest the circulation of national currency in the village for the first time since the Romans. The find of a lovely bronze strap end from the same period points to the kind of people of thegnly rank who could afford beautifully made things. In the tenth century laws limiting the passage of merchants between southern England and the Danelaw were lifted, allowing free access to all across Watling Street. Recent digs in York and Lincoln have revealed evidence of this opening up of trade: well-made timber-framed town houses with posh leather-studded furniture, French wine and bales of imported Byzantine silk. Coin hoards from the Danelaw from this time now frequently contain gold dirhams minted in Central Asia. The growing accessibility of such luxury commodities comes out in a tenth-century 'interview' with a merchant recorded by Aelfric of Eynsham with its casual assumption that in well-off houses people expected to see luxuries on the table: 'goods from overseas brought by ship . . . I buy precious things that are not produced in this country . . . purple cloth and silks, precious jewels and goldwork, unusual clothes and spices, wine and oil, ivory and bronze, copper and tin . . . sulphur and glass and all sorts of things like that.'

These exchanges were far-reaching. They changed aspirations and widened mental horizons; they even changed language, for the dialect spoken here came to be the form of English most of us speak today. Our sentence structure (which is Danish not Anglo-Saxon) developed in this area of the East Midlands on the linguistic divide between Viking and English speech – in response to the interaction of immigrants and the older population in the tenth and eleventh centuries.

## The workers

How far did these changes affect the peasants themselves? As we saw in the earlier period only wealthy people could have a house with possessions and luxuries. This was now changing for the people of England. In the eleventh century wills begin to give an idea of the personal possessions of a middling person, a free peasant of local thegnly rank who farmed a hundred acres. The wife, say, of Edwin of Kibworth was perhaps a woman like the Siflaed who when she went on pilgrimage 'across the sea' to Rome made a small gift of land to her local church, an annual wagonload of wood from her woods:

and Wulfmaer my priest is to sing Masses for my soul, he and his issue so long as they are in holy orders. To the village church five acres and one homestead, two acres of meadow; two wagonloads of wood; and to my tenants their homesteads as their own possessions; my serfs to be set free; to my brother a wagonload of wood; to the others four head of cattle.

We know how such a well-off farmer, freeman or sokeman (or woman) might have lived in Kibworth. He'd have had a wooden bed for himself and his wife, and another for his children; a wooden chest for the bed linen; and clothes consisting of 'a badger skin coat, best dun tunic, and the best cloak and clasp, two wooden cups ornamented with dots'. Edwin's wife might have treasured 'my old filigree brooch, a hall tapestry and three seat coverings . . . and a weaving frame, little spinning chest'. By 1066 a well-off free peasant household might have servants, often their own children or those of neighbouring families.

Below the likes of Edwin and his wife the many gradations of class in society were well-established before 1066. Ten per cent were still slaves and 15 per cent free, but the large majority were bonded or semi-free, unable to move places or jobs without permission of their lord; these were thralls, villeins, boors and ceorls – words still with a pejorative meaning today. They were the majority of the people of England, their lot vividly conveyed by an interview written as a teaching aid by the schoolmaster and homilist Aelfric around the year 1000. 'How would you describe your work?' he asks the ploughman, an unfree labourer on his lord's demesne. The response is the first piece of English literature in which the working class speaks:

'Oh I work very hard, dear lord. I go out at daybreak driving the oxen to the field, and yoke them to the plough. For fear of my lord there is no winter so hard that I dare scive at home. But the oxen having been yoked up, and the share and coulter fastened to the plough, I must plough a full acre or more every day.'

'Have you any companion?'

'Yes, I have my lad driving the oxen with a goad, who is hoarse now because of the cold and all the shouting.'

'What else do you do in a day's work?'

'I do more than that, sure. I have to fill the oxen's bins with hay and water them, and carry their muck outside.'

'My, my, it sounds like hard work then.'

'It's hard work all right, sir, because I am not free.'

## The village in 1066

Kibworth is one of 13,000 villages and towns the Normans will record in their survey of England after the Conquest of 1066 – when for most English communities detailed records begin. For most of these a similar kind of story can be told, even though there are of course great differences in landscape, custom and language between, say, a Devon hill farm, a Durham mining village or one of the archaic English hamlets on the Welsh side of Offa's dyke.

Norman data for 1066 show that the basic map of the village was already complete, the product of several centuries of growth and change. In the north was the old Anglo-Saxon lord's enclosure, which will later become Kibworth Harcourt, a place of freemen and smallholders. A short distance to the south, beyond the church, where a little stream ran across the road, was the lower settlement, which will become Kibworth Beauchamp, a workers' settlement of villeins and serfs perhaps with a communal oven, its water mill, its big barns and yards for the plough teams; then the hamlet of free farmers, smiths and metalworkers to the south at Smeeton. And finally, at the end of the ridge, the tiny Viking settlement at Westerby, little more than an outlying hamlet consisting of maybe only a couple of farmsteads.

Spread over these four settlements, the combined population of the parish of Kibworth on the eve of Conquest we can estimate at around three or four hundred people: a large place by eleventh-century standards when the county town itself had only a couple of thousand.

As is evident from the way the people are described, class divisions were already strongly marked in the communities – and between the communities. All the sokemen, or freemen, lived in Harcourt and Smeeton; but remarkably there were none at all in Beauchamp. It is hard not to think that the roots of such divisions must lie far back in time. Perhaps Beauchamp had begun in the Dark Ages as a vill of dependent peasants: unfree service labour certainly marks its story for centuries. A survey of 1315 astonishingly shows at that time there were forty-four families of serfs and villeins and only three freemen, so the eleventh-century pattern had not changed.

Originating no doubt at some point in the early Middle Ages in differing circumstances of lordship, the contrasting characters of the three hamlets will continue over the next 900 years, and are still remarked on today, when despite the transformations of industry, enclosure and migration, continuities with the old community and the old village families are still not yet quite broken.

## The last days of Anglo-Saxon England

So there is the village story up to 1066. With a little speculation, a little help from archaeological finds, landscape, place names, test pits, and even metal detector finds, a tentative narrative can be essayed of what one might call the prehistory of the village. Inevitably (as with most English villages) the lack of early documentation necessitates guesswork, speculation and a little imagination. By 1066 the people of Kibworth had already known Celtic, Roman, Anglian and Viking lords – their tribal and regional identities and allegiances had transferred from lords of the Corieltauvi to Middle Angles and to Mercians; and then to 'the king of all the English'. They had seen dramatic changes in the pattern and apparent direction of history. They had lived through famine, plague and climate change. They had endured wars, migrations and conquests. There is no evidence over this first thousand years that Kibworth ever ceased to exist, though in the worst times it may have contracted severely. And from the tenth century the villagers had seen their standard of living improve and the insecurity of life lessen under the protection of the king's law – the thread of English history that continues from then till today.

In the late Saxon period the country grew wealthy. One important source of this wealth was wool, as it had been from Roman times.

There were more sheep than people in Anglo-Saxon England, maybe four or five times as many, and fine English cloth was exported to the continent. But at the end of the tenth century the country's wealth encouraged yet new waves of invaders, which led in the end after a long period of war to conquest by the Danes. From the 990s to 1016 England was criss-crossed by armies as the faltering government lost its nerve. For all its sophistication in administration the English state was still reliant on the energy and charisma of the king: on his ceaseless itineraries, on his military leadership, his ability to bully, cajole and punish where needed, but most of all, in such a diverse multiethnic society, to negotiate effectively.

The hapless king at this time was the butt of a pointed contemporary joke: he was Ethelred ('noble council') Unraed ('no council' – 'useless'). Writing in London, a remarkably acute observer of the time expressed profound loyalty to the idea of the kingdom of the English, even though he judged the king in the end a failure. Ethelred's government raised huge sums of silver coin as 'Danegeld' to buy the invaders off: tens of millions of silver pennies. This was a staggering measure of the kingdom's wealth, but a huge burden on the free peasants of Kibworth and elsewhere, as each hundred was required to gather a levy on each village, which from a place like Kibworth might have amounted to its annual taxable value. The passage of armies devastated large tracts of the country and the government's increasingly panicky attitude to Scandinavian settlers in southern England, people living widely after seventy years of free movement, led to them playing the race card against 'the enemy within'. Had the massacres fomented in Oxford, among other places, occurred more widely they might have undone much of the previous generations' work. But 1016, the year of the battles' resolution, came as a kind of relief to a war-weary country. On a lavish royal manuscript the new king, the bearded flaxen-haired young Canute, is depicted giving a gold cross to the royal house of the New Minster, Winchester, his hand firmly on the hilt of his sword.

A Danish dynasty till 1042 brought back political stability, and opened England in general, and the Danelaw in particular, to the Scandinavian world. The line of Alfred was restored in 1042 in the person of the saintly Edward the Confessor, but great energies were needed to hold the kingdom together in the face of feuding magnates: a task that had worn out some of the great kings of the Alfredian dynasty before they reached fifty. Edward even abolished the national tax on military forces. A vivid image from a contemporary encomium portrays Edward's wife Emma embroidering fancy diaphanous clothes for him for ceremonial occasions. This is a far cry from our image of Alfred dealing with a knotty legal case in plain man's language 'while washing his hands in the closet'; or the plain cloak, woollen leggings and tunic worn by Athelstan, who was praised for his willingness to 'throw off the condescension of royalty and rank and mingle with the common man'. Beyond the Humber the Northumbrians still hankered after some kind of home rule; in the Midlands they still perhaps temperamentally preferred one of their own. But in 1055 a near civil war was averted, not by the king or his high-ups, but by the rank and file – men like the Kibworth thegns Aelfric and Edwin – on the grounds that 'there were good Englishmen on both sides.'

## The Norman Conquest

In the New Year of 1066 the old king died and a new man took the throne: Harold Godwinson, a member of a powerful landed family of eleventh-century nouveaux riches. From that point events unfolded with incredible suddenness. Duke William of Normandy announced his claim to the throne and assembled a fleet and army at the mouth of the Somme. The English king summoned a huge levy, 'the biggest ever seen', from the free peasants of England, supplied and paid by their communities, and for forty days waited on the south coast ready to repel the invaders. Through August contrary winds across the Channel kept William at bay, but meanwhile in the north Harald, King of Norway, landed his fleet in Yorkshire, exciting old separatist urges among the northerners. When the earls of Mercia and Northumbria were defeated outside York the English king gambled all on a lightning move north, riding his royal army up to Yorkshire, where he won a savage battle against the Norwegians at

Stamford Bridge. But the gamble failed. Two days later, as Harold licked his wounds in York, the wind changed and William's fleet was wafted over to Pevensey. Harold's response, unwisely perhaps, was instantly to march back down to the south coast, where events came to a tragic denouement at Hastings on 14 October. There, the king, his brothers and 'the flower of the English nation fell.' Among them perhaps thegns of the Midlands including Aelfric, Meriet's son, and Edwin Kibworth, who now disappear from history. Whether freemen from Main Street went with their lord with horse, helmet and spear and did not return, history does not record.

There were, as might be expected, many opinions about the disaster, and no doubt these arguments were aired in the village as all over England. Harold had acted precipitately; his support had dwindled, 'at the end he only had his paid troops with few from the country.' It was said that only half the English army ever assembled, and those present claimed only a third were even in battle order when the battle began, such had been the speed of Harold's advance. More plausibly in some eyes, God had given the Frenchmen victory on account of 'the nation's sins'. So the nation chewed over the reasons for defeat, as they still do. At Berkhamstead, William received the surrender of the English nobles, including the overlord of Kibworth, Edwin, Earl of Mercia. On Christmas Eve, William was crowned at Westminster Abbey. As the result of one battle, the English world was about to change for ever.

That winter of 1066 the Viking and English farmers of Kibworth saw themselves as belonging to an English state ruled by a king of the English. For people old enough to look back on the war of 1013–16 when Sweyn of Denmark's armies devastated their fields, traversing the country in the long disastrous unravelling of Ethelred's government, it must scarcely have been possible to imagine anything worse. By now the community had been formed with its traditions and customs, its work practices and its class divisions, its rich and poor. The great fields existed with their strips, wongs and siks, 'sunnyside' and 'shady side', paced out by the field jury. Their assemblies met every month at the 'spear tree' to enact the common law. In their pockets one coinage of the realm, still as well-minted and as reliable a currency as it had been in the now golden days of Edgar a hundred years before, when, as old people said, 'You could leave a gold arm ring on a bush and no one would pinch it.' But now again, as with Cnut in 1016, the whole kingdom had fallen to an invader. And this time an invader with a different language and very different traditions of government.

In the story of England the next stage is set. What will happen to the community of the village and the community of the realm – this 'rices anweald', this 'londes folc' as they would have put it – over the next centuries? The England which had emerged out of the ancient slave order of Roman Britain is now about to pass into full European feudalism brutally imposed from above and outside. How will it change, and in what way will it remain the same? How will the feudal medieval order fare with its slaves, villeins, burs and churls? How will our modern world emerge out of theirs?

# 7. The Norman Yoke

Night fell with a chill damp air and a smoky mist near the Sussex coast on 14 October 1066. The dead and dying were strewn in heaps on the low ridge at the edge of the Downs. (Marked now by the ruins of Battle Abbey, the place was then known to the English only by a local landmark, 'the old hoar apple tree'.) Among the 'flower of the English' were the thegns who had stuck by the king, perhaps Aelfric, son of Meriet, and Edwin of Kibworth among them. Picking their way through the blood-streaked mud, the dead horses and smashed war gear, a party of Normans with burning torches searched the broken bodies where the standards had stood, looking for the English king's corpse – or what was left of it. At one stroke England had fallen.

In the immediate shock of defeat we all reach for old consolations to explain shattering events and that autumn the English were no different. 'The Normans had possession of the battlefield,' wrote the Anglo-Saxon chronicler with gritted teeth, as God had granted them victory because of 'the nation's sins'. It must have seemed as good an explanation as any of the scarcely credible chain of events in autumn 1066 which had led up to the battle of Hastings. Many other explanations have been offered by historians since that time as to how the richest nation state in Western Europe fell to a small army of Norman knights, mercenaries and adventurers who had chanced their arm on the greatest prize, hitching their star to the fortunes of William of Normandy.

The Conqueror's coronation in Westminster Abbey at Christmas 1066 had been with the consent of the chief nobles. The allegiance of the people was another matter. Over the next three years he set about subduing England to his rule through warfare, a scorched-earth policy and ruthless repression. Siege causeways were pushed into the Fens, mobile towers and battering rams broke the walls of picturesque former Roman cities like Exeter; deliberate devastation of the countryside was the order of the day wherever there was opposition. But despite the completeness of the defeat at Hastings the scale of resistance was surprising, and it provoked fury: 'In those early days,' wrote one Norman later, 'wherever they could the English laid secret ambushes for the hated race of the Normans, and, when opportunity offered, killed them secretly in the woods and in remote places. In revenge the Norman kings and their ministers, devising exquisite kinds of tortures, raged against the English.'

The Norman army spent the first few years marching, fighting and killing, its path marked by columns of smoke and savage reprisals against the English. The battle hardened Norman knights and mercenaries in the north deliberately engineered a humanitarian disaster, which left a desperate peasantry 'eating grass and rats' and even resorting to cannibalism and selling their own children into slavery. In the Midlands the Normans brought devastation to the rich farming lands around Kibworth. Leicester was besieged and stormed by William the Conqueror; the town was sacked and partly burned, and a large portion of the city destroyed. One hundred and twenty houses were levelled to build a castle by the Soar on the southern edge of the Anglo-Danish borough. After the destruction William handed over a huge part of the shire – some sixty estates formerly under the rule of the Earl of Mercia – to a man who had been with him at Hastings, Hugh Grandmesnil.

In his mid-thirties, a formidable horseman and fighter like his master, Hugh was hard-bitten, masterful and inured to war, displaying that mixture of cruelty and ostentatious piety that characterized a medieval nobleman. For his loyalty he received over a hundred English manors from William, the majority around Leicester, his centre of power, where he was now sheriff. As part of the clampdown Grandmesnil built castles in his main strongpoints and on key routes. On the route between Welland and Leicester castles were constructed at Hallaton, and it appears at Kibworth too. On the track which later became the A6, they cleared and levelled the Anglo-Saxon lord's demesne, barns and ox sheds, demolishing a row of peasants' cottages south of 'the king's highway through the village'. To save time and effort the Normans earmarked the Roman burial tumulus at the Munt as the core of their motte, the conical mound with its palisaded platform which formed the strongpoint and last refuge inside a Norman castle. They assembled the village reeves and press-ganged the villagers into the ditch-digging and construction work, organizing carts and oxen for shifting timber and bringing smiths to on-site foundries to manufacture nails. Norman sappers were adept at carrying prefabricated castles with them and knocking them together at speed, but here they probably had the time to commandeer a local labour unit who brought cut timbers by wagon and ox team from Gumley woods. The reeves would provide the tools from the manor store, as listed in their estate memoranda: 'axes, adzes, awls, plane, saw, auger, mattock, crow-bar, spade, shovel', to shape the tree trunks on site before they were positioned to make the palisades and platforms.

That at least is how it may be imagined. No certain proof has yet been found that the Munt was a Norman castle. It has played such a major part in the village story from the Romans to the Jarrow marchers, but it has had no scientific excavation and over the last two centuries has been too badly disturbed for magnetometry to reveal the shadow of any timber buildings under the soil. As we saw in the first chapter, the mound was dug two or three times in the nineteenth century and cut with massive trenches, so its size and shape can only be estimated now from the account of John Nichols in the late eighteenth century. Nonetheless Nichols gives us enough to indicate with a fair degree of certainty that at some point it was reshaped into a motte and bailey castle. He describes a motte about thirty-five metres wide and six high. It is now only four metres in height but in the Middle Ages it was probably twice that; the flat area on top is still about twenty-two metres across. The motte was surrounded by a ditch about eight metres wide and two deep: similar dimensions to known Norman mounds at Hallaton and Gilmorton, and identical to another castle belonging to Hugh Grandmesnil at Ingarsby. The remains of an entrance causeway six metres wide were once visible on the south-west; and Nichols says that on the south side of the motte a further ditch projected for about forty metres with a bank eight metres wide and still nearly a metre high. This was most likely part of the outer bailey.

Traces of the outer bailey have long since disappeared under the widening of the A6 and modern house building, but inside the bailey were a barn, stables, living quarters and, if other excavated castle sites are a guide, an oven, pottery kiln, querns, leather workshop and a smithy. In short, a small military-industrial complex was thrown up right on top of the village, with a view from the tower all the way down Main Street and across to Leicester Forest. The platform on the keep was now the highest point on the Kibworth ridge and could receive fire signals from Leicester to the north and the Welland valley to the south. A visible symbol of oppression, the castle and its earthworks were a raw scar on the landscape that left a deep mark in the English imagination. As a chronicler wrote in 1086, William 'oppressed the poor people of the English everywhere by building castles'.

So the Norman yoke fell on Kibworth, its overlord now Hugh Grandmesnil and his local subtenant who lived on site with his men-at-arms. It was the beginning of a long process of dispossession across the kingdom. Castles were built throughout this part of the Midlands, by Hugh himself in Groby, others in Sapcote, Hallaton, Hinckley, Mountsorrel and Castle Donington. In all these places Normans lived on the spot, an armed foreign presence, and on other castle sites at Gilmorton and Ingarsby. When the Kibworth reeve and his fellow jurymen testified for Domesday at the Gartree in the spring of 1086 they gave their account of the village and its peasants. They noted tight-lipped (if it is possible to read between the lines of such an austerely bureaucratic record) that a new addition to their community was 'one Frenchman'.

## The Domesday Survey: Kibworth in 1086

It took many years of fighting to subdue the country after the invasion. The most brutal kind of military occupation was made worse by the inability of the Normans to communicate with the conquered except through interpreters. There was immense disruption, with the destruction of crops and death everywhere. The murder of unfree villeins was not even a matter to take to court. But with so much confiscation of property, so many disputes over ownership being brought before the law, the time came to draw a line under what had happened and produce a definitive account of the state of the country. To that end, twenty years after the Conquest, the Conqueror met his councillors at Gloucester over Christmas 1085 and had 'deep speech' about England: 'What kind of land it was, and the nature of its people.' Out of this council came the decision to commission a great survey of England, village by village, manor by manor.

Early in spring 1086 William's circuit judges came to the local meeting place at the 'Gartree thorn' to take the sworn testimony of the local juries from the Gartree Hundred. The Saxons Aelfmaer, Aelfric and Edwin of Kibworth may have been killed at Hastings or in the northern battles, though Edwin may have been among those who testified to the landholding, population and livestock at the Kibworths and Smeeton, along with people who have left their names in the local community till now, among them Godwin, Oswin, Swan, Haesten and Thored. Once free, but now 'with a heavy heart', we can hear their voice in their language: 'Shame it is to tell, but he thought it no shame to do,' wrote one disgruntled Englishman; 'not a pig or an ox or a cow was left uncounted.' The result was Domesday Book. No longer one book, it is now kept in temperature-controlled conditions in the National Archives in Kew and is available to all online. It is the starting point of the full history of Kibworth as it is for most of the towns and villages of England.

Kibworth in 1086 was not one village but three separate settlements divided into a number of different holdings or manors. So the account the local jury delivered to the king's circuit judges for the East Midlands is not in one entry but spread over several folios of Domesday Book. In a sense the account is very much of the moment – what was here that spring of 1086, with brief reference to the status quo in 1066. But in another sense the text gives us in shorthand the crystallization of centuries of lordship going back to the Angles and Vikings, with their different customs, languages and local forms of tenure. Kibworth parish as recorded by the Normans had three main villages and no fewer than eight separate manorial lords (it is important to realize that manor and village are not the same: the single village of Smeeton was

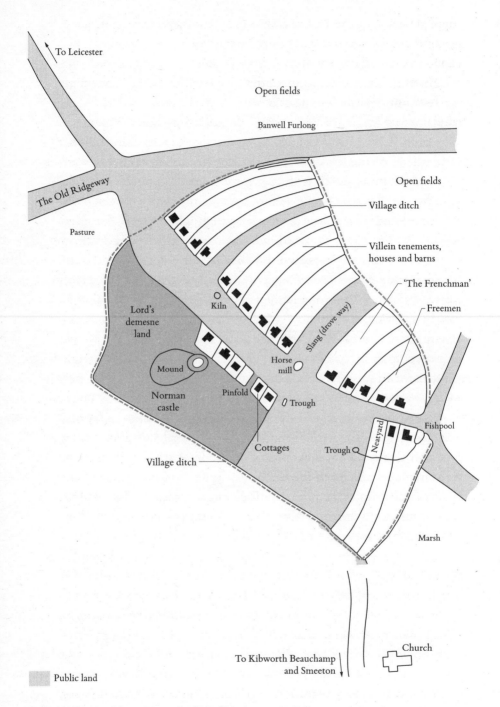

To Leicester

Open fields

Banwell Furlong

The Old Ridgeway

Open fields

Village ditch

Pasture

Villein tenements,
houses and barns

Lord's
demesne
land

'The Frenchman'

Freemen

Kiln

Slang (drove way)

Mound

Horse
mill

Norman
castle

Pinfold

Trough

Cottages

Trough

Neatyard

Fishpool

Village ditch

Marsh

To Kibworth Beauchamp
and Smeeton

Church

Public land

Kibworth Harcourt in 1086, after the Norman conquest

divided between four or five landowners, a process clearly advanced under the Anglo-Saxon kings long before 1066).

Domesday Book was drawn up for practical purposes and was meant to be of practical use, and was indeed consulted for judgements right up to the twentieth century. It is organized by the fundamental unit of English local administration – the shire – but then each shire is divided into the main landholders in Domesday's index page. At the top of each shire every landowner is listed, starting with the king, the chief churches, the great lords, then the smaller landowners. Each of these holdings is then organized and cross-referenced under the rubric of the hundred in which the manor stood, Kibworth being in Gartree Hundred. The Anglo-Saxon landlords were gone by then, some maybe killed at Hastings or in its aftermath. The key men are now Normans – Hugh Grandmesnil, Robert of Vessy, Robert de Bucy and Robert 'Dispensator' (the Bursar) – who fought and won at Hastings. The Domesday account is so important in the history of the English village that we should give it in full; unavoidably it involves some technical terms, and some eleventh-century bureaucratic language, but a lightly annotated Domesday's picture of Kibworth is as follows.

Starting in the northern part of Kibworth parish, today's Kibworth Harcourt (the suffix would come later) was a single manor before the Norman Conquest, as it would be throughout its history. Its land measurements are given in the Danish unit *carucates*, 'ploughlands' (each of 120 acres), and in *bovates* or 'oxgangs' (15 acres). To make the text more clear, these are also given in acres here though they are only an approximation:

Robert (of Veci) holds 12 carucates of land [around 1,400 acres] in Kibworth; before 1066 enough land for 10 ox teams. There are 6 slaves tied to the lord's land. There are 10 villagers [villeins], 6 freemen [sokemen], 6 smallholders [bordars] and one Frenchman. They have 5 plough teams. There are 16 acres of meadow. Value was 40s in 1066, now 60s.

Domesday also names the Anglo-Saxon landowner: 'Aelfric son of Meriet held these lands before 1066 and he was a free man.' This

Aelfric, as we have seen, was an important East Midland thegn with lands in Lincolnshire and also in Warwickshire, at Wolvey on the Leicestershire border. In addition to this information, the Domesday folios for the city of Leicester say that Robert of Vessy 'has three houses that belong to Kibworth Harcourt', an interesting hint of the village's links even before 1066 to the urban life of Leicester, which may have started in an arrangement made by which the countryside contributed to the maintenance of the borough in the tenth century.

Then comes the entry for Kibworth Beauchamp. The village was already split into two manors and listed first are the lands of Robert the Bursar, who had lands next door in Fleckney and Wistow:

In Kibworth [Beauchamp] there are 5 carucates and 6 bovates of land [around 700 acres]. Before 1066 there were 5 plough teams. 8 villagers [villeins] with 6 smallholders have 2 ploughs. There are 12 acres of meadow. Value was 10s per annum in 1066, now 30s. In 1066 Edwin Alferd [i.e. the son of Aelferth] held these lands freely with full jurisdiction.

A second manor in Beauchamp belonged to Robert 'Hostiarius' (a minor royal court official, in English the 'door ward'):

Robert also holds 6 carucates of land [around 720 acres] in Kibworth. Before 1066 there were three plough teams. On the lord's demesne land two and a half ploughs [i.e. teams], 3 slaves. 9 villagers with 2 smallholders have two and a half plough teams. Twelve acres of meadow. Value in 1066 was 30s, now 40s. [Before 1066] Aelmer [=Aelfmaer or Ailmaer] held these lands with full jurisdiction.

So in Kibworth Beauchamp there were around 1,400 acres of arable land and twenty-four acres of meadow. Before 1066 in total there were seventeen villagers (villeins) and their families with eight smallholders and three slaves.

Then comes Smeeton. Here the situation was more complicated. The village and its detached hamlet of Westerby were divided between four or five lords (a medieval estate lawyer's heaven!). One of them was King William himself, an absentee landlord, but a landlord nonetheless. About 160 acres were still known in the eighteenth century as 'the king's share' and in 1086 were farmed by four freemen with thirty acres each. These plots are still clearly visible on the early Ordnance Survey maps.

The main manor in Smeeton was a 500- or 600-acre estate which Hugh Grandmesnil leased to Robert de Bucy with two freemen, one villein and three smallholders. Robert the Bursar held a manor of another 360 acres, probably Westerby, which was farmed by three freemen, two villeins and one smallholder. Four freemen who belonged to a manor four miles away in Bruntingthorpe also farmed here.

In total in Smeeton Westerby there were about 1,100 acres of arable farmed in 1086 by twelve freemen and freewomen and their families along with three villein tenants and four smallholders. There were no slaves. 'There was land enough for seven ox teams,' the account concludes, 'with nine acres of meadow and a wood three furlongs square.' This was the only woodland in the whole parish, which gives an idea of how intensively Kibworth was already being farmed before 1066.

Such was Kibworth in 1086. Like a lot of Domesday the picture is complicated and the detail at first sight off-putting. But some revealing data can be adduced from the entries. First, the arable land under the plough in the parish in the eleventh century was about 4,000 acres, very close to the figure given by Victorian gazetteers. Norman Kibworth had only a small amount of meadow, and a very small amount of woodland, only the three square furlongs in Smeeton. With more than twenty plough teams in 1086 the old parish of Kibworth was already under very highly industrialized farming.

The image that emerges from the dry statistics of the Domesday text then is of an open landscape probably already devoid of hedges, perhaps with a few isolated trees and only one patch of woodland in Smeeton. The three main villages were each defined, nucleated settlements surrounded by their common fields, which were accessed from farm lanes or slangs along which the plough teams were led out from their yards. In Harcourt there was a row of houses and gardens along the 'king's highway', a horse mill, a pond, a chapel, the 'Haagate', and the Slang, from which the field strips of the three great

fields fanned out to the north. The church serving the whole parish
stood on the hill between the 'upper' and the 'lower' village, where
villeins and serfs lived along the road to Smeeton, with great yards
for the barns and ox stalls on the lord's demesne. Further to the south
were the hamlets at Smeeton and Westerby with the largest number
of freemen and freewomen. Each place was at the centre of its
common fields, open and unhedged, worked by rows of plough teams
under the wide Midland skies. This was already industrialized farming
where the majority of society was geared to the production of food.

## Class

What also emerges from Domesday is a vivid picture of the social
classes. In this sense Kibworth is a perfect example of eleventh-
century English society. In the three main settlements – the two
Kibworths and Smeeton Westerby – there were already clearly
defined distinctions in social status. Kibworth Beauchamp was populated by unfree people: seventeen villeins (tied peasants), eight bordars
(cottagers) and three slaves. 'Upper' Kibworth (Harcourt) has ten villeins, six bordars and six slaves, but also six free tenant households.
But in Smeeton, in addition to seven dependent peasant families, the
dominant group are the families of the dozen freemen and freewomen. These are the distinctive class of East Midland sokemen, free
peasants whose descendants we will trace through this story, down to
the yeoman of the Tudor Age, whose class will be an important factor in the rise of English capitalism and in the development of English
ideas about freedom.

So in the eleventh century all the free peasants in Kibworth were
in Harcourt and Smeeton, and none in Beauchamp. This must reflect
older patterns in the late-Saxon village, and maybe even earlier. As
we have seen, Harcourt seems to have been the original centre in the
eighth century, as 'Cybba's worth'. Beauchamp was perhaps a village
of workers and dependent peasants. Smeeton on the other hand was
an artisanal village, even before the ninth century, which later had a
strong preponderance of freemen. The Viking conquest may well

have fossilized these divisions, preserving older forms of freedom lost in the south. Merton College's purchase of Harcourt in the 1270s may have helped fix this too, making Harcourt a 'closed village' and leaving Beauchamp a workers' place, giving the two halves their proverbially distinctive character described in later accounts and still remarked on by older villagers today – and not always in jest.

The total community in 1086 numbered maybe fifteen freemen and freewomen and their families and dependants, thirty villeins, eighteen bordars and nine slaves, men and women; not forgetting the Frenchman! Allowing for five persons per family, this might give a total of between 350 and 400 people all told: a sizeable place when we consider the later population of the parish, which was only 1,200 in 1801 and nearly 2,000 in the 1871 census. So Kibworth was one of the most populous villages in the hundred of Gartree from as far back as the eleventh century – as it is today; with its new housing estates, with over 4,000 people in Beauchamp and 1,000 in Harcourt it is well on the way to becoming a small town.

## Medieval apartheid: life under the Normans

The villagers now lived under the close supervision of their lord's agents, who were backed by armed force. The Norman landlords had bailiffs on site with armed men. It is not certain whether any of the local Anglo-Saxon landlords survived. They may have been killed or not but they were certainly dispossessed, unless like one former freeman recorded in Domesday they now rented their own land from the Normans *graviter et miserabiliter*, 'with a heavy heart and in misery'. The numbers of the Norman occupiers who ruled a nation of 2 million people were probably only ever in the low tens of thousands. Even 50,000 newcomers over the next three decades would amount to a mere 2.5 per cent of the English population – and that is probably a maximum. It had been a classic single-event conquest and it was followed by an unparalleled redistribution of wealth among the alien aristocracy. In 1086 the Domesday folios show that over 50 per cent of landed wealth was now in the hands of 175 lay tenants in chief.

Only two of 1,400 tenants of the thegnly class were Anglo-Saxon, and nearly half of the nation's wealth was held by just eleven men – one of whom was the chief landowner in the village, Hugh Grandmesnil.

Among the lower classes in England as a whole, two thirds of the population were unfree peasants and 10 per cent were slaves. For them life now became harder still. The Norman occupation was remembered as a bitter time for the free peasantry too, who in many parts of the country lost their lands and customary rights. For centuries the English people handed down a myth of the 'Norman Yoke': a folk tradition that 1066 was a brutal and disruptive break in the continuity of English society. This myth was quarried by the radicals in the English Civil War, and has been revived time and again in books and films: 'Norman saw on English oak', as Walter Scott famously put it in *Ivanhoe*: 'On English neck a Norman yoke. Norman spoon in English dish / and England ruled as Normans wish.' But to an extent this is not a myth. 'At first they raged at each other . . . and the Normans took savage measures in response,' wrote Richard FitzNeal a century on from the Conquest, though he believed that by then things had got better: 'But during the time that the English and Normans have now dwelt together, and mutually married and given in marriage, the nations have now become so intermingled that one can hardly tell today who is English and who is Norman.' FitzNeal was speaking only of freemen and admits it was a different matter for the working class, 'the bondmen who are called *villani*', who he suggests were still a race apart as far as the Normans were concerned. But even for the English upper classes it turns out FitzNeal's view was somewhat rose-tinted. New studies of marriage in the Norman period suggest that there was almost no intermarriage for at least three generations. In that first century the villagers lived under a kind of apartheid. Their rulers spoke French, didn't teach English to their children, and viewed the English as an inferior race. Change, however, did come – even in Kibworth – and it came comparatively swiftly from the middle of the twelfth century.

To the Norman overlords the villages of the Midland 'champain' lands were first and foremost profitable real estate. In the early twelfth century the 'upper' village of Kibworth was bought by the Harcourt family (Harcourt is an attractive village in Normandy with a fine castle); and 'lower' Kibworth was taken by the Beauchamps, who were royal butlers, later the Earls of Warwick, from the Grandmesnils. It was these families who gave the villages the suffixes that they still have today. The new lords were Norman and Angevin upper crust, and under them, a century after the Conquest, the social barriers start to break down between conquerors and conquered.

When they do, local East Midland leases begin to give us the stories at grass-roots level. For example Christiana, the daughter of a soke-man, marries a well-to-do local Norman with the blessing of her feudal lord. Though her name is fashionably Norman, her ancestors were of Viking descent for she names her father as Ivo, her grand-father as Swein and her great-grandfather as Magnus (who could have been alive in 1086). Another local girl, with the very Norman name of Asceria, 'the daughter of Joslan', seals a Latin charter with a bequest for the souls of her antecessors – Arngrim, her Viking grandfather, and Wulfgifu, her English great-grandmother.

Similar stories are hinted at by our fragmentary sources for Kib-worth itself. A Kibworth woman, Matilda, in the 1260s and 1270s, was the daughter of Ivo, granddaughter of Heinricus and great-granddaughter of Ivo: all Scandinavian names. Matilda married a local landholder, Richard of Saddington, a member of the local elite, and gave her son a good Norman name, Robert. Such stories are examples of how free peasants could move up in the world – albeit it took Christiana, Asceria and Matilda's families four generations after Hastings to do it.

## The open fields

For all but a few of the villagers, daily life was still devoted to work-ing the land. The whole effort of the community was directed towards producing food. And in the twelfth century this meant open-field farming. This system of communally farmed agriculture spread over much of north-west Europe in the Middle Ages, and was not just an English phenomenon. But it was particularly intensively developed in post-Conquest England, in a great swathe up the middle of lowland Britain from Sussex to the Scottish lowlands. As we saw previously, in England open fields were developed, probably in the tenth century, as a way of organizing town and countryside in an age of war. In some areas pushed through by powerful kings and lords, its adoption must have felt as draconian as the Ministry of Agriculture's 'Dig for Victory' campaign of 1939–45. After the Conquest the system was expanded by local lords as the population grew from maybe 2 million in 1086 to 6–7 million 200 years later. The gradual clearance of new land to feed the rising population can be seen on the ground in Kibworth Beauchamp, where two or three hundred acres of new land were opened up under acute population pressure between the Hundred Rolls survey of 1279 and a village Extent of 1305.

Each of the two Kibworths and Smeeton had three fields; and the holdings of the peasants free and unfree were scattered among the fields so that everyone got a share of good and bad land, light and 'strong' soil. The Kibworth documents in the archive of Merton College give a vivid picture of the complexities of the system. For example, a lease from the 1260s records the gift of one of the Harcourt family to 'Robert son of Richard the Parson' of half a virgate (fifteen acres) in Kibworth held by Robert son of Matilda, and of a further eight acres in Kibworth. Robert's eight acres, scattered through the three great fields, are described in this way by Sylvester, the village clerk (a rood here is a quarter of an acre):

One acre on 'Litlehul' near the land that Roger Wythe held

One and a half roods that lie under Blacklands near the land held by Yvo son of Henry

One and a half roods that lie on Blacklands next to the land held by Reginald 'at the Well'

Half an acre that lies in Crowenersike by the strip held by Alexander son of Robert

One rood upon Reyland next to the land Robert Joye holds

Three roods at 'Walwrtes' next to the land held by Hugh Hurtlebole

One acre lies under Peascrofte

One and a half roods upon Peascrofte near the land held by Robert Joye

One and a half roods under Northul [North hill] near the strip held by Reginald atte Welle

Half an acre on Stalegate near Robert Brun's land

Three roods on Pesilsike near Reginald atte Welle's land

One acre extending into Borettesdale near the land of Roger Wythe

One acre that extends into Pesilsike near the land held by Nicholas son of Simon the reeve.

Describing just eight acres in Harcourt fields, this is the kind of minute accounting in which the village reeves specialized. Remarkably, some of the field names – Blacklands and Peashill sike, for example – can still be traced on the ground through later tithe maps. What astonishes is the sheer (to us) mind-numbing amount of semi-intellectual effort that would be needed to remember it all. A thirty-acre villein holding a spread between the three great fields could have as much as seventy or eighty strips scattered in more than twenty separate blocks across the open lands, and each of the individual furlongs could have its own name! And this document doesn't begin to outline the custom and dues attached to such a smallholding. On which, take this (from the late thirteenth century) for a sample account of the labour dues of a thirty-acre Kibworth villein:

For a full virgate you must do two days ploughing without food ration, bringing your own plough; two days harrowing and hoeing, food provided; two days mowing on the lord's meadow with an extra man whom you provide; gathering and carrying the lord's hay in his cart with no food . . . Six days autumn reaping with extra men as specified; carrying the lord's share of the corn to Leicester market on your own horse and anywhere else but only within the shire; gathering straw for roofing and repairs on the lord's demesne farm. It is the custom for the men of the village to mow the lord's meadow with one shilling and sixpence worth of beer while they do it. The virgate also owes death duty of second-best beast to the lord and the best beast to the Church as mortuary.

(The additional marriage fines, paid when a peasant asked the lord's permission for his daughter to marry, are too faded on the manuscript to read.)

Such was the life of a villein in the thirteenth-century village at the time when the open fields reached their developed form. But even as that farming life emerges into the full light of the documents, it was already changing under the impact of individualism, and indeed of common sense and convenience as a cumbersome system struggled to keep up food production as demand outstripped supply. Already strips were being amalgamated by ambitious peasant proprietors, and freeholders were letting out parts of their holdings to the large number of young people who had no land of their own. But it remained the case that the great fields in each of the villages dominated the working life, custom, language and life cycle of the villagers for the next 500 years.

## The farming year in the open fields

How the whole system worked, with the three-year cycle of rotation of crops, is best seen in Kibworth Harcourt where a mass of early manorial documents survive in the archive of Merton College, which became the landlord in around 1270. Some customs were particular to the area, but the general principles can be applied to all villages of the open-field system from Northumberland to Devon. The operation of the open-field arable was carefully regulated and can be seen in detail in about 300 villages across the country which have surviving sets of manorial rolls. Of these Kibworth has one of the fullest sets.

We know it as the three-field system, but a village could have two fields, four, five, six or even more. The classic type though is three fields. Crops were sown on a three-course rotation. In any year one field would have a winter-sown wheat crop, a second would have a spring-sown crop such as barley or peas, and the third would be left fallow so that 'the land could be rested' allowing nutrients to recover the fertility of the field. Its grass and weeds were left as grazing for sheep.

The rotation of crops on the three fields of Harcourt went over a three-year cycle. In the first year the West or Carr Field had winter-sown wheat; the North Field, the spring-sown crops; and the East or Howe Field would be left fallow. Then in the second year West Field is fallow and North switches to winter-sown wheat, while Howe Field has the spring-sown crops. In the third year West has spring crops, North is fallow and Howe has the winter wheat. The whole system depended on the intense cooperation of the community: 'You don't have to like each other', as a modern strip farmer puts it, 'but you have to work together.'

No detailed account of Kibworth custom has survived. Most of it of course was in the heads of the reeves and the tenants and was passed down orally. But following the farming year from one harvest to the next we can see how it worked in practice. What follows shows the customary use of the one surviving open-field village in the East Midlands, at Laxton, where the strips were still hand-ploughed with horses in the 1940s. From the court books at Kibworth we can see that a calendar like this was followed till the Enclosure Act of 1779. This was all no doubt second nature to Simon the reeve, Harry the Hayward and their neighbours, and there was no reason to write it down:

Midsummer – late June: haymaking; the first hay from the meadowlands is cut and brought into the barns. Midsummer is celebrated by a great bonfire on the eve of John the Baptist (24 June).

6 July: all animals to be cleared from the sykes or siks – the grassy baulks between the ridges.

10 July–1 August: hoeing of the sykes.

1/2 August – Lammas: haymaking in the meadows is completed and the meadows are opened for grazing. Lammas is the celebration of the first wheat harvest – the 'loaf mass', the feast of first fruits. In later times all the women and children in the village customarily helped in haymaking, as can be seen in photographs from the nineteenth and early twentieth centuries.

August: farmers begin the harvest of winter wheat, the field of winter corn in Carr Field.

End of August: with the harvest finished, the winter cornfield is 'broken'. The villagers' stock is allowed to graze the stubbles. The beginning of the harvest of spring corn in North Field.

15 October: the spring cornfield is broken: sheep and other stock are moved from Carr Field to graze on the stubbles.

Mid-October/early November: the farmers move to the fallow field (Howe), which will be next year's wheatfield. This is ploughed, harrowed and sown with winter corn.

1 November (All Souls Day): the meadows are closed for grazing. Festival.

Mid-November: unless very wet, all ploughing and sowing should be completed.

23 November (Laxton custom): all animals to leave the open fields except twenty sheep per freeman/customary tenant on the fallow field. Slaughter of those animals needed for winter.

Late November – Jury Day: twelve jurymen are appointed for the next year's cycle, plus the field foreman. They go out to the new wheatfield (North Field this year), which is inspected on foot and all dykes and individual strip boundaries are checked and if necessary re-staked.

Early December: the Court leet is held, under two officials, the reeve, representing the lord of the manor, and the bailiff. Fines are paid, new tenants sworn in. They appoint various officials, including the hayward and the pinder (who rounds up stray cattle – the Kibworth pinfold was on Main Street near the horse mill at the end of the Slang).

November/December: preparation of the new spring cornfield for planting in the following spring.

21 December – Midwinter: Christmas holiday until Epiphany; the peasants had nearly seven weeks' holiday over the year.

6 January (or the first Monday after): end of the Christmas holiday. Plough Monday was a strong custom in the East Midlands, perhaps of Danelaw origin, when a plough was decorated and taken round by the men in the hope that 'gode spede wel the plow.' This tradition still took place in Kibworth up till the 1930s.

March: the spring cornfield is ploughed and sown.

April: when the young grass has appeared the stock is turned out on to the sykes and closes.

Easter holiday: the celebration of the Resurrection is one of the biggest feasts of the village year.

April: lambing, calving, farrowing of sows, threshing – Kibworth had specialist threshers in the thirteenth century.

Late June: haymaking commences in the meadows. Letting off of the gaits and commons by auction (for the syke grass). With that, from harvest to harvest the cycle of one year is complete. With dancing, singing and a great deal of beer brewed by the village brewsters, the Midsummer bonfire on the eve of John the Baptist.

These tasks of course presuppose many specialist jobs, though all the villagers worked the fields. They elected the field officials from among themselves – the hayward and woodward, the reeves and constables. These were mainly men's jobs though women, as we shall see, could plough and work in the fields helping their menfolk, or even as tenants on their own helped by their children, kinsmen and neighbours, or using seasonal hired labour. Women work as brewsters and traders, and have even been found as reeves and jury members. Specialist jobs in the village are not recorded yet, though a village the size of Kibworth could not have done without a carpenter, a miller, a smith, a cobbler and a baker. This all presupposes literacy too, and in the 1160s we first pick up a village scribe, and one thirteenth-century witness list on a Kibworth document even mentions an *apotecarius*. These are the first signs then that the village was beginning to diversify, a process that begins in the late twelfth century in the English Midlands and which we will find revealed in Kibworth when documents come thick and fast from the 1260s on.

## 'Christ and his saints slept'

These were still very harsh times. A bleak scene recorded by the Anglo-Saxon Chronicle in 1124 serves to remind us. Towards Christmas at Hound Hill, not far north of Kibworth, Ralph Basset (who among his wide estates owned 120 acres in Kibworth Beauchamp) hanged:

forty-six thieves, all at one time, and six of them were blinded and castrated first. And truthful persons said that many of those died very injustly there. But our Lord God Almighty, from whom no secrets are hid, He sees the poor oppressed by every kind of injustice, first deprived of their property, and then of their lives. A very bitter year was this. He who had money had it stolen by violent exactions or corrupt courts; he who had none starved to death.

A letter of the time describes the brutal tactics of William de Beauchamp (who owned part of Kibworth):

He illegally seizes corn, and steals money to pay his retinue. Besides this we have for a long time been forced to give 3s each month for the needs of his servants, and at each season of the year we have been compelled to plough, sow, and then reap sixty acres of his land. And on top of this, our peasants have been burdened with daily services and innumerable works, and he has not ceased to pursue and afflict them to the depths of misery.

1. St Wilfrid's church, Kibworth. The nave and porch are from the fourteenth century, as was the spire, which fell in 1825. The centre of village social life for at least 700 years, it may have had an Anglo-Saxon predecessor.

2. The 'Spear Tree': the site of the Gartree on the Roman road north of Kibworth. On the site of a Bronze Age burial mound, this was the meeting place of local juries from Anglo-Saxon times till the 1720s and gave its name to the local hundred.

3./4./5. Merton College, Oxford: the lords of Kibworth Harcourt from 1270. In the fourteenth-century library is the archive of one English village extending over 750 years.

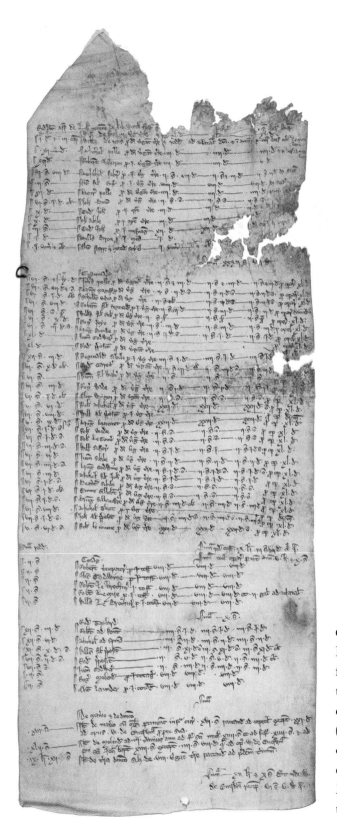

6. Merton's survey of Kibworth Harcourt from around 1280, with the lists of free and customary tenants and (in the fourth section of text) the cottagers, ending on 'Roger the Miller' and 'Alice the Washerwoman'.

7. St Wilfrid's, Kibworth, in the late eighteenth century: with a spire at 160 feet, it was one of the tallest country churches in England. To the right, the 1788 vicarage was built by the site of a Roman cemetery.

8. 'Soldiers turn into reformers': the mood on the eve of the Civil War. The destruction of images, altars and altar rails was the fate of Kibworth church probably between 1547 and 1552. In the 1640s the Puritan vicar John Yaxley joined the soldier iconoclasts and threw out the font.

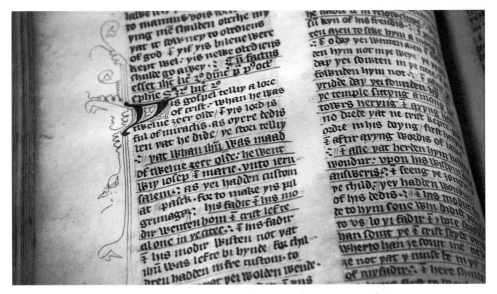

9. A fifteenth-century set of Lollard vernacular sermons from Leicester, perhaps written close to Kibworth. Such English texts were secretly copied and disseminated in the area by the likes of John Barun 'alias Toogood, alias Scrivener', who was among the Kibworth rebels in the rising of 1413–14.

The defcription of the cruell Martyrdome of
fyr Iohn Oldecaftle Lord Cobham.

10. The burning of Sir John Oldcastle at St Giles' Fields in 1417: a number of Kibworth villagers had supported his cause and two, brothers Walter and Nicholas Gilbert, were executed on the same spot.

11. An eight-ox plough team still working in the 1920s in Sussex: the main draft animals from Roman and Anglo-Saxon times until the Middle Ages. Accompanied by his boy with his long goad, the ploughman was the medieval Everyman.

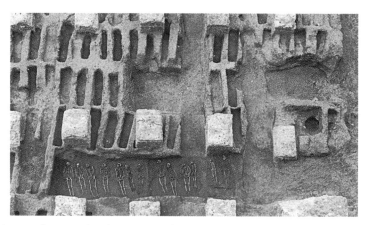

12. Black Death pits: the first scientific excavation in Britain near Tower Hill, London. In Kibworth Harcourt forty-seven tenants – men and women – died in the first outbreak, along with unknown numbers of their family and children: two thirds of the population. Tradition still points out the village death pit on the A6, south-east of the village.

13. Fifteenth- and sixteenth-century housing in Erle Street, Coventry, before the Blitz of 1940 and the ravages of post-war developers: here, Adam Brown of Kibworth's son set up with his new wife in a community of well-off merchants and drapers, some of whom supported the Lollard heresy.

14. Framework-knitters: a family room with the redundant technology of the spinning wheel in the background. With the invention of the frame in the 1590s, knitting spread as a home industry and it became a key East Midlands industry from the eighteenth century, later the main employment in Kibworth Beauchamp.

15. Harold Bromley at a hosiery frame, 1950s: his family have been in the village for over 400 years.

16. The Johnson & Barnes factory in the Victorian 'New Town' in Kibworth Beauchamp: Johnson & Barnes were a major employer, 1901–68.

17. Medieval technology: the post windmill at Kibworth Harcourt, which ceased to be used in the early twentieth century.

18. The bridge at Debdale Wharf on the Grand Union Canal below Kibworth.

DEBDALE

To make matters worse, between the 1130s and 1150s England was racked by Civil War and the Kibworth region suffered further devastations. 'More than we can say,' wrote one contemporary, 'we suffered nineteen winters for our sins when Christ and his saints slept.' Grim times for peasantry. Yet paradoxically this was a time of progressive growth as the centre of gravity of the European economy began to shift to the countries of the western seaboard.

## Boom time

Between 1066 and 1300 England boomed. The population more than doubled in Kibworth and Smeeton from around 300 in 1086 to some 800 two centuries later. It was a time when middling peasant households got more possessions and furniture and there was more variety on a peasant table. New towns were founded across the country in the twelfth century and markets were licensed everywhere. Around this time Market Harborough becomes the alternative local market for Kibworth, as the road we now know as the A6 replaces the old Roman road, the Gartree road, as the main route from Leicester to Harborough and London. Then in 1223 the market came to Kibworth. On 12 March King Henry III granted to 'my faithful and trusted William de Beauchamp a weekly market on Wednesdays so long as it is not a nuisance to the neighbouring merchants'. The market stalls stood around the open space now called the Bank: they sold meat and fish, tools, clothes, leather goods, shoes, cloth and perhaps even luxuries such as spices. The profits from the market in the form of the fees from the stallholders went to the lord, whose family were courtiers and royal butlers.

The arrival of a market suggests that Kibworth was already a village with some crafts – smiths, weavers, dyers and cloth workers – along with the usual service workers found in most villages. And around this time in the Leicester Borough and guild records, we start to pick up members of the village moving away to Leicester to make their fortunes. In those days not everyone could move of course. Villeins needed permission from the lord and were unlikely to get it. Freemen

though, especially if they had a craft or trade, might establish a connection between the village and the town, especially if they had
kinsmen in both. One of the earliest records, of 1 June 1199, involves
a local man, Roger of Kibworth, who along with a parmunter (who
prepared leather for clothing) was entered into the merchants' guild
in Leicester after the coronation of King John. He would be the first
of many.

These gradual changes in peasant society in the twelfth century are
signified by the first record of a village scribe, in the 1160s. He was
needed because even free peasant members of the village community
who owned a few acres were documenting land and property grants
they had made in perpetuity, written by the village clerk, sometimes
even as gifts to the neighbouring church. Peasants are now seen as
competent to found village churches and chapels (there was one in
each of Harcourt, Beauchamp and Smeeton in the Middle Ages) and
peasant families like the Sibils and Polles begin to provide chaplains as
well as reeves and jurymen. Among the peasants found acting as witnesses to grants at this time there are also many women. In one local
grant from around 1160 five freewomen (only one of whom is married) make a grant of land to their church. The long witness list names
priests and landowners but also includes women of the village community, sixteen of whom are variously described as mothers, sisters,
daughters, widows, wives and unmarried girls. A few years later next
door to Kibworth in Carlton Curlieu, Eilieva – the wife of Robert the
cook – sealed a 'cirograph' as her health failed, giving a fur cloak, a
cap, a gold ring, eight pigs, eleven oxen and nineteen sheep to the
women of a nearby nunnery, on condition that 'if she recover from
her illness they will receive her as a nun when she wishes to renounce
the world.' St Guthlac's sister had been a royal woman, Eilieva was
the wife of a cook. Times were changing.

## Englishness rising

By the early 1200s the English people could reflect on the Norman
Conquest with some measure of tranquillity. Even among writers of

mixed descent those events had been 'a terrible havoc of our most dear country'; for Henry of Huntingdon 'the Normans were the last of five plagues sent to Britain, who still hold the English in subjection.' But the feeling did not go away that the English ruling class was an alien and rapacious group still divided by language from their subjects. 'The Normans could speak nothing but their own language,' wrote one thirteenth-century observer:

and they spoke French as they did at home and also taught their children. So that the upper class of the country that is descended from them stick to the language they got from home: therefore unless a person knows French he is little thought of – but the lower class stick to English and their own language even now.

Others, with the passage of time, were able to take a historical perspective on what they saw as the enslavement of the people brought about by William and his followers 'who have held the English in subjection ever since'. Among some of these writers the whole social structure of the feudal system with its gradations of freedom and unfreedom now came to be seen as a consequence of the Conquest: 'For all this thralldom that now on England is through Normans it came, bondage and distress.'

In the thirteenth century the rise of this sensibility will become apparent even at the village level: proletarian, vernacular, nationalist, speaking up for England and the English language, and backed up by a historical view of the English past. All this will feed into the momentous events of the century, from Magna Carta to the rebellion of Simon de Montfort. For trickling down through the shire and hundred assemblies these political ideas will reach the peasantry, who even in a place like Kibworth will play their part in the making of English history.

# 8. The Community of the Realm

In the high summer of 1264, on the days leading up to the full moon on 9 August, pilgrims and merchants coming up from Dover towards Canterbury saw an astonishing sight. Spread over the countryside on the London road under the sails of the 'Black Mill' at Barham Down, just a few miles from the cliffs of Dover, was a vast encampment. There were knights from all over England, with their colourful tabards and flashing escutcheons, their banners streaming, squires exercising their warhorses, armourers busy at their forges. But the mass of those present were peasants, a people's army of England numbering tens of thousands of men. Around the campfires were men of Essex led by their constables, freemen of Norfolk and the Marches under their sheriffs, Leicestershire peasants with their lords, the Bassets, and even a contingent from little Rutland. Looking down towards the sparkling summer horizon over Deal and Walmer, the sea breezes stirring banners and signal flags, the smoke of cooking fires swirling over Barham Hill, it was such an incredible sight that those who were there then were lost for words: 'There was then such a multitude gathered together against the foreigners that you simply would not have believed that so many men armed for war could have existed in the whole of England.'

And there in the crowd, under Saer de Harcourt's standard with its horizontal stripes of red and gold, is John Wodard, freeman of Kibworth. Narrowing his eyes he looks down to the sea (if we may imagine him so) with his horse, spear, helmet and knapsack; on his head below his cap a fresh scar from a recent blow. John came from a peasant family long rooted in Kibworth and Smeeton: his name in Old English means 'wood ward', the keeper of the lord's wood; perhaps it had once been the Wodards' hereditary job to handle infringements of the forest law. The Wodards were a big kin group with several households, one of the most prominent and influential in the village along with the Polles, Swans and Heyneses, some of whom perhaps are with him now among the freemen from Kibworth and Smeeton with their mounts and war gear. They had been summoned here by Simon de Montfort's baronial government, who had overthrown King Henry III and were now ruling in his name. To repel a threatened invasion of 'aliens' from France, Montfort had called for a huge army of peasants from every village, to come with horse, spear and helmet. Around Wodard then were perhaps a dozen of his neighbours from Kibworth and Smeeton, others from Newton Harcourt, Carlton and other places in the hundred of Gartree. All were here for the cause of England.

The atmosphere in those early days was exultant. For the first time peasants from all over England had the opportunity – paid for forty days by their fellow villagers – to meet and talk about the tremendous events which had rocked the nation over the last few years culminating in the defeat of King Henry that May. The deeds of Simon and the barons were already the subject of popular song and poems; and the mood we may imagine was like that during the days of the Armada, or when Napoleon's Grande Armée waited in its barges at Boulogne; or even 1940, with Simon playing the role of Churchill, urging his soldiers that they must 'fight on the beaches and never surrender'. Simon himself was Earl of Leicester (and lord of Smeeton) and his supporters there had come down in force: the Bassets and the Burdetts, the lords of Sapcote, Branston, Huncote, little Galby and Frisby, and Saer de Harcourt, the lord of Kibworth Harcourt. That was perhaps what had led John Wodard here among the freemen from Kibworth when after Lammas he would normally have been about to start harvesting the winter-sown corn on his strips in the open fields.

Behind the peasant involvement in these events lay what might anachronistically be called a working-class view of history. What was in the mind of Wodard and the other Kibworth men in the great army of Kent we can only conjecture from hints in the sources and from popular songs and poetry. But John and his neighbours we must presume shared a vision of 'the gode olde lawes' which had once pertained in England before the Conquest. A common view among the freeborn English too was that the English people had been 'in thrall' since the days of William the Conqueror. As John would have put it, 'sithen he and his have had the lond in heritage that the Inglis haf so laid . . . that thei lyve in servage. He sette the Inglis to be thralle, that or (once) was so free.'

In the folk memory of the later thirteenth century King John in particular had been a monster of venality and partiality (that image goes back far beyond Walter Scott or modern Hollywood epics). Back in their grandfathers' day Magna Carta had largely been concerned with upper-class rights and privileges, but it was nevertheless understood as a stand against autocratic royal rule. But it was felt that the kings since had repeatedly abandoned the charter and that constant struggle and vigilance would be needed to maintain English freedoms. English people too knew that the great charter had been only grudgingly given and confirmed, and that John's successors only half-heartedly observed it: 'feebly kept it was after his day, of King John and the others . . .' who 'granted and confirmed it unwillingly, thinking it to be worth nothing'.

Such ideas lay behind the great cause, the 'community of the realm', which in the thirteenth century swept up even the peasantry of Kibworth and their neighbours. The nub was the law, and the freeborn English peasant's right to use it in court to defend his rights. 'Every king is ruled by the laws that he enacts,' wrote an Angevin lawyer. 'We give first place to the community and we say too that the law takes precedence over the king's dignity.' The rulers were well aware of the feelings of the shire about the common law. In 1219 the justices of the king declared to the king's council that 'we who ought to be judges would become contemptible in the sight of those to whom we have been sent to enact justice . . . we assert most firmly that we have done nothing contrary to the approved custom of the land.' Jurists also acknowledged that 'the custom of the nation is better known to the people of the nation than any foreigner' (England's rulers of course were French-speaking). Asked about the way the system worked, one thirteenth-century legal expert answered: 'Ask the country people, they know best!' South-east Leicestershire's freemen had become a radicalized hotbed in the decades since

Magna Carta. The freemen of places like Kibworth and Peatling Magna, even the villeins of Stoughton, used the courts to defend their status, and when we hear them speak they are not discussing the price of corn but the 'welfare of the community of the realm' on which they believed they could speak in the king's court to the king's justices.

So by the thirteenth century both lawgivers and peasants believed that the law should work for them. During the course of the half-century from Magna Carta to the Barons' Revolt, they found their voice. And that is what had brought John Wodard and his neighbours to Barham Down that summer in 1264 on behalf of 'the community of the realm'.

## Magna Carta

Time heals wounds. Richard FitzNeal, whom we have already met in this story as a member of the government of Henry II in the 1180s writing about Domesday and its aftermath, recounts a casual conversation he had 'in the twenty-third year of the reign of King Henry II, while I was sitting at the window of a tower next to the River Thames', and in doing so lets slip a rare insight into how social change was perceived in England. As he saw it, change in some respects was for the better. Violence, racial hatred and secret killings were on the wane; the reach of justice had improved in most places though the killing of serfs still went unpunished. But 'in most places' the powers that be couldn't get away with killing a villein with impunity, that is, without the murdered man's family having recourse to the law. It is a startling admission of how bad things had been.

FitzNeal was a sophisticated observer and his book is a mine of sharp realistic observations. As he admits, his remarks were not true everywhere, but from the documentary evidence he was broadly right that by 1200 the rapid growth of peasant literacy and access to local courts meant that the issue of rights was perceived as central by both high and low. In the Magna Carta in 1215 King John had acceded to the barons' demands made in response to his wholesale abuses of power. In essence it was a charter for the ruling class but it embodied the crucial principle that the king was bound by the law, that kingship indeed is the creation of the law. Immediately after John's death Magna Carta was reissued in the name of his successor, and there were several versions up to 1225. Since then it has come to be regarded by English people, and by all who have adopted English law, as the chief constitutional defence against arbitrary or unjust rule. Its most famous clauses express some of the English people's most deeply held political beliefs, and pertained to both rich and poor:

No free man shall be seized or imprisoned, or stripped of his rights or possessions, or outlawed or exiled, or deprived of his standing in any other way, nor will we proceed with force against him, or send others to do so, except by the lawful judgement of his equals, or by the law of the land . . . To no one will we sell, to no one deny or delay right or justice.

Later lawyers found here the basis for some fundamental English rights: equality before the law and freedom from arbitrary arrest. To the king, of course, 1215 was a treaty of peace forced on him under duress by barons who had rebelled against the royal authority. But the wheels of change were in motion, and no longer only in the hands of the upper class. The story reached its climax in the Barons' Revolt of 1264–5, under Simon de Montfort, the French-born Earl of Leicester who was married to the king's sister. Simon was a French-speaking aristocrat who despised the ordinary English peasant, but he became a figure of adulation, a hero around whom popular tales, songs and even miracle stories gathered. He was a secular martyr who like Thomas Becket had stood against royal power.

Simon and the barons were determined to maintain the limitations on royal power granted by Magna Carta and to force the king to rule within a framework of custom and common law. Their movement was particularly attentive to the opinions of the shire and of the hundreds, the fundamental units of local rule. In 1258 in the Provisions of Oxford the barons had attempted to reduce Henry III to the status of a constitutional monarch. It has been said that 'no other kingdom in Europe had gone so far towards a republican Constitution.' The name of the movement is most revealing: the barons (who were French-speaking) called themselves the 'community of the realm', *le commun de Engleterre*, translated in the vigorous English version of the Provisions as 'this landes folc'. Claiming to represent the interests of the country as a whole, the barons demanded that elected councillors were to hold a parliament three times a year 'to review the state of the realm and to deal with the common business of the realm and of the king together'. It was bound to end in war. And now not only the barons but the peasants too believed they had a stake in the outcome.

## The people's voice: 'England is free'

Medieval chroniclers were of course interested in personalities, kings and nobles. They themselves tended to be clerics from the upper or middle classes, and the thought of the masses taking political action caused them a shudder of horror. It was of no concern to them whether peasants died, or who they were. But in the revolution of the 1260s the free peasantry of south Leicestershire, Simon's earldom, were widely politicized; they were involved in these events and unnamed freemen must have given their lives for the cause. Some no doubt followed their feudal lord as they were told to do; many though were elected by fellow villagers and supplied with money for subsistence. And some, like Wodard, must have been well-acquainted with events and supported Montfort because they understood the issues having heard them discussed in the manor and at the hundred courts at the Gartree. In the collective memory over the last century or two the rapacious rule of foreigners had left its mark. Now the peasants wanted more say.

In May 1264, though outnumbered heavily in mounted knights, Simon defeated the royal army at Lewes in Sussex. In a brief burst of extreme violence on the downs above the town 3,000 royalists were killed; 1,500 knights and squires were heaped into death pits stripped of their expensive gear, having been slaughtered by exultant peasants. For a moment England stood on the verge of 'Europe's first constitutional revolution' and in the euphoria after Lewes popular songs trumpeted the idea that 'England is now free' and that freeborn Englishmen were 'no longer treated like dogs in their own land'. Big ideas with startling suddenness could now be spoken out loud. 'Every king is ruled by the laws which he enacts. We give first place to the community, we also say that the law rules, and takes precedence over the king's dignity.'

In the aftermath of the battle the king and his son, Prince Edward, were captured and England entered the strange phoney war of Montfort's regency. A brief explosion of anti-royalist violence across the home counties was followed by an uneasy peace as Montfort and his allies attempted to rule through the king. It is in this period that the involvement of John Wodard and the peasants of Kibworth and neighbouring villages began, in that uncertain time when no one knew where the revolution would lead.

## The crime of John Wodard

Back home in Kibworth, four weeks after Lewes, it was the old custom to go on pilgrimage at Pentecost to their mother church of St Mary Arden next to Market Harborough, an ancient Anglo-Saxon minster from where every year their vicar collected the chrism oil. We may imagine the Kibworth people walking from their village in the open air along village tracks in lovely June weather through ripening cornfields. The vicar, Oliver of Sutton, and his chaplains were carrying religious banners, followed by the pilgrims with their emblems and badges. The most important pilgrimages in the village were also Marian, to Walsingham and Lincoln, and pewter pilgrim badges from both shrines have turned up in the village recently, on one of which the Virgin's lilies can still be seen. This Pentecost's journey took them five miles to the River Welland at Harborough, the new trading town founded some eighty years before and already a thriving market with traders, merchants and craftsmen. Today the church of St Mary Arden is a small roofless chapel hidden behind trees on a rounded hill just above the railway station; ignored by almost all visitors to that charming town of coaching inns with its Stuart schoolroom and its magnificent church of St Dionysus. Once much bigger, the church was largely demolished in the seventeenth century, and only the Norman porch survives from that day in 1264.

Below the church the graveyard stretched down the hillside to the Welland, where there was an ancient sacred well known as Lady Well. The pilgrimage probably required prayers at the shrine before its image of Mary, and then bathing and drinking at the sacred well, especially for the sick and infirm, who were borne along by the villagers. The mood we may conjecture was celebratory. Kibworth was a Montfortian village and we might imagine a little touch of victorious football fans arriving in hostile territory with the Montfortian villagers arriving on the royal estate of Great Bowden and insisting on the performance of their ancient customary celebration. But the Bowden people blocked their way, some of them apparently armed. Things grew tense. There was a stand-off at the church door and hotheads began to jostle. What followed was over in a moment, but by one of those miracles of medieval record-taking, the account survives in the National Archives:

When the men of Kybbeworth came to the church of Harborough to make their procession there on Monday in the week of Pentecost in year 48 [9 June 1264], according to what is the custom of the country [*patria*], the foresaid William Kyng came and wished to prevent them from proceeding into the foresaid church, and struck the foresaid Wodard, who came with the foresaid men of Kybbeworth, in the head with an axe, and pursued him, wishing to strike him again and kill him if he could, and the foresaid Wodard, perceiving this, turned round and struck the foresaid William in the head with an axe so that he afterwards died of that blow.

Wodard was accused of murder. By an added piece of good fortune the inquiry by the judge, Gilbert of Preston, into the circumstances in which Wodard killed William King also survives, on a roll recording numerous assizes and inquiries heard by Preston that year. From it we learn that the inquiry was commissioned by the king on 6 October 1264 at Canterbury, which, given the date, means it was commissioned by the Montfortian government when Simon and the king were in Kent directing the English army against the great 'alien' invasion. Very likely it was Saer who obtained the commission on behalf of his man John, appealing for a pardon at the time when the Kibworth troops were outside the city in the great camp on Barham Down. Wodard presumably then was down there in the ranks of Simon's peasant army, loyal to his lord, and perhaps even to his cause.

Preston heard the inquiry the next spring at Rockingham Castle near Market Harborough (the castle is visible from the terrace above the allotments at Westerby) on 11 April 1265. The jurors were all local men who had ridden over from Kibworth and neighbouring villages: William of Gumley, Walter the clerk of Langton and Richard of Saddington (who was married to a Kibworth woman), along with four villagers: Hugh of Kibworth, Richard Fisseburn, Nicholas 'at the Thorn' and John Faukin. With no Bowden men the jury was perhaps loaded in John's favour. They simply had to decide 'whether Wodard of Kybbeworth killed William Kyng of Bowden in self-defence so that otherwise he could not have escaped his own death, or through felony or premeditated malice'.

Weighing up the witnesses, they concluded on oath that King had been the aggressor, had stopped them going into the church and struck Wodard with an axe and had intended to kill him. 'So they say certainly that the foresaid Wodard killed the foresaid William in self-defence and not through felony or premeditated malice.'

With Saer's encouragement, had the fateful Pentecost procession turned into a celebration of the Montfortian victory? This might well have aroused fury at Harborough, which was a royal manor – even William King's name suggests a king's man. Certainly axes at the church door seem hardly the way to welcome pilgrims at Pentecost. King and the locals had evidently come prepared. According to the royal patent rolls Wodard's pardon was finally given at Northampton, on 22 April 1265. The letter patent was issued at the instance of the Lord of Kibworth, Saer de Harcourt, who is specifically called 'a knight of Simon de Montfort, the steward of England'. Thus in the letter which Wodard himself would have taken away and doubtless shown to his fellow villagers, the Kibworth peasant was associated both with Saer, his lord, and with Saer's lord, the Earl of Leicester and guardian of England, the great Montfort himself.

## Alien invasion: 'We will fight on beaches'

Following his capture after the battle at Lewes on 14 May 1264, King Henry was now in the hands of the council of barons under Simon de Montfort. With Prince Edward also under arrest, the royalists grouped for a counter-attack around Henry's French-born queen, Eleanor, and her supporters across the Channel. Eleanor had a deep war chest, and now approached King Louis of France for assistance, gathering allies and mercenaries to form an invasion army. The royalist fleet began to assemble in Boulogne, while back home the barons unleashed a tide of nationalist propaganda picturing the queen's forces as 'a vast horde of aliens thirsting for English blood' who would spare no one if their army got a foothold in Kent. These were the circumstances in which the barons summoned the gigantic army that assembled on Barham Down that August: 'All men capable of bearing arms . . . wherever they live in England, are to join us,' the royal decree runs, 'to protect the country night and day and not to go home without specific orders from us.' Putting words into the captive king's mouth, the royal letters emphasized that 'Peace between ourselves and our barons to the honour of our Lord and for the good of ourselves and of our kingdom is now firmly established thanks be to God.' Simon wrote to the king of France on Henry's behalf: 'We are day by day working on rectifying the problems which have arisen since the time of discord.' At the same time Simon was firing off patriotic letters to the sheriffs in the shires claiming to speak now for all England. The Barons' Proclamation of 7 July said:

We know for a fact that a vast horde of aliens is preparing to invade the land – so let no one plead as an excuse that the harvest is at hand or that some personal cause or private duty calls him. Much better to suffer a little personal loss and be safe than be delivered to a cruel death, with the loss of all your lands and goods at the impious hands of foreigners who are thirsting for your blood.

In late July the transports for the alien army were reported to be assembling at Boulogne, as Hitler and Napoleon were to do later; and beacons were readied along the south coast. The threat of invasion was on everyone's lips, and rumours of a fifth column spread like wildfire, engendering a nasty tide of jingoism against resident aliens. Simon's letters to King Louis of France meanwhile were searching for a diplomatic solution, pointing out that a 'horrendous loss of life in both kingdoms will occur if the invasion takes place'. Meanwhile to meet the 'alien army' the feudal host, summoned in the king's name through the local sheriffs, began to gather. Every magnate and every knight was expected to answer the king's summons. But Montfort also called up a national levy drawn from the freemen of the shires. 'By land and sea . . . capable and trustworthy men are to gather for the defence of the realm.' Watchers were set on the coasts from the Wash to the Solent; in Lincolnshire for example 700 freemen of the shire were put on coast guard with only the poor exempted. The men of London and Greenwich were deployed to defend the estuaries of the Thames and the Medway. The archers of the Kentish Weald camped on the shingle between Romney and Winchelsea – ready literally to 'fight on the beaches'. A circular letter to the shires shows that Midland shires were required to send knights and free tenants, but also 'at the common charge' eight, six or four men from each manor depending on its size. Each man was to be provided by his village with money to cover forty days' supplies.

The atmosphere was at first electric. There may even have been football-style chants though these only survive in French:

> Coment hom le nome? WHAT'S HIS NAME!!
> He's called MON-FORT!!
> He's in the monde and he's big and strong
> He loves what's right and he hates what's wrong
> And he'll always come out on top!!!

Flushed with their first successes the rebels' mood grew ever more anti-alien; they sneered at the king's despised brother Richard ('Thah thou be ever trichard': a deceiver, trickster) and threw metaphorical rotten vegetables at the queen (as indeed Londoners had done for real before the war broke out). But Simon for them was 'brave and true'. Strange for a French-speaking aristocrat not known for his sympathies for the peasantry but now punning on his name, he was 'in the world' – their world – and the commoners were right with him.

The standoff in Kent, however, went on longer than the planned forty days and the army began to suffer as the weeks passed, supplies and money ran out, and the weather began to turn. The call-out had coincided with harvest time and the fieldwork for the autumn. By the end of August there were mounting desertions. One case recorded in detail involves John of Kibworth, a constable and trusted man of Saer. John acted as a messenger for Simon's council in Canterbury. On 29 August Simon wrote 'on the matter of raising funds for expenses for units on the sea coast' to the Sheriff of Rutland: 'We order you without delay to raise further allowances for the aforesaid men until the octave of the coming feast of the Virgin Mary.' Formerly set at 3d a day, the allowance was now put up to 4d. John of Kibworth carried these messages on horseback between the king and the Rutland sheriff. But by 6 September the constables of the Rutland contingent were reporting that 'the men were in want and had exceeded their term and had no lands or tenements from which they could support themselves.' As the muster wore on into the autumn (and one imagines by then sanitary conditions in the camp had become intolerable) the Sheriff of Rutland was eventually forced to ask his villagers to find a hefty 8d a day for each of their men. Only in late October, when the invaders disbanded across the Channel, were the forces finally sent home, just in time to join their neighbours in ploughing last year's fallow field ready for next year's winter corn.

The alien threat had been averted. But the great issue for Simon and the barons once they had power was what to do with it. They had the king in their grasp but they still believed in the office of kingship; they simply wanted to limit its power. Finally the barons began to fall out

among themselves with bitter arguments between erstwhile friends
and allies. Then over in the west, Simon's enemy Roger Mortimer
gathered the Marcher lords against him. When Simon carelessly allowed
Prince Edward to escape and to join Mortimer, he faced disaster. Events
now began to move with all the momentum of a Shakespearean
tragedy. Simon moved his army west to attack Mortimer, only to be
intercepted by Edward, now joined by many magnates opposed to
Simon's overweening behaviour. At the start of August, finding the
Severn crossing at Bridgenorth blocked, Simon forded the river and
made a night march to Evesham hoping to rendezvous with the forces
of his son. Arriving in the town soon after dawn his exhausted army
found itself trapped by superior forces in a loop of the Avon. Realizing
that he was surrounded, Simon is reported to have said: 'God have
mercy on our souls, for our bodies are theirs.'

The battle was over quickly. It was as one contemporary remarked
'the murder of Evesham, for battle it was none'. The recent discovery
of a new eyewitness account conveys with horrible immediacy what
Constable John of Kibworth and John Wodard experienced – if they
were still in the army with their feudal lord (our sources of course
were not interested in the names of the poor rank and file who died
there). Simon marched out of the town and charged his enemy, but
Edward and his generals had appointed a death squad to isolate him
and almost immediately Simon was killed and hacked to pieces. There
it might have ended but hatred and anger among royalists was so great
that they mercilessly hunted their defeated enemies down. Two or
three thousand Welsh foot soldiers were butchered trying to cross the
Avon, 'with the express approval of the king and his ministers'. In the
blood-soaked aftermath even those taking refuge in the abbey down
in the town were slaughtered as altar and shrines ran with blood.
Below the hill many of the fugitives ran into a marshy stretch of
water meadows along the Avon, where they were cut to pieces. Perhaps it was here that Wodard breathed his last breath, or perhaps he
made his way back to the village. John himself disappears from Kibworth documents, though a generation later his kinsman Reginald is
found in a typical village feud in the manor court fighting Nick Polle
for trespass. In the village, life of course went on.

Retribution was inevitable. In the immediate aftermath of Evesham the estates of the Montfortians were pillaged in an irresistible wave, spreading out from the battlefield. And by an incredible chance, in the Court of Pleas records in the National Archives in Kew, what actually happened in the Kibworth area after the revolt is revealed in astonishing detail. Three days after Evesham, on Friday, 7 August, the news of Montfort's defeat and death had already reached the heartland of his powerbase in Leicestershire. Royalists rapidly appeared in the shire with armed forces and the king's marshal, Peter de Nevill and his standard bearer, Eudo de la Zouche. They moved to take control of the villages of south Leicestershire which had been sympathetic to Earl Simon, the estates of lords like Ralph Bassett (who had been killed in the battle) and Saer de Harcourt (who had been captured). Among them were Newton Harcourt and Kibworth Harcourt, and to the west of Kibworth a little place called Peatling Magna.

On Saturday, 8 August, one of Nevill's grooms tried to go through Peatling Magna with a cart of supplies. The villagers objected and 'some foolish men of the village' then sought to arrest him with his cart and horses. In the scuffle the groom was wounded 'in the arm above his hand'. On Wednesday the 12th Peter himself arrived with a large company of armed men to take revenge. Then the villagers confronted the marshal, and, according to Nevill, accused him and his men of sedition and 'other heinous offences' saying that they were 'against the barons and against the welfare of the community of the realm' *(utilitas communitatis regni)*.

Not surprisingly the scene now turned nasty. Nevill threatened to burn the village down unless he got redress and the men took to the church for refuge. Now the women of the village took the lead, led by the wife of one of the peasants. Worried that their houses would be burned, they tried to negotiate a compromise, and according to Nevill promised that a sum of twenty marks should be paid to him as a fine on the following Sunday (a mark was 6s 8d – so twenty was a large sum for a small village).

With the help of the reeve and at the women's prompting – but here the two sides would later strongly disagree over the course of events – five freemen agreed to stand as hostages for the payment of the fine, or perhaps were physically coerced by Nevill into doing so. They were poor freemen, and the rest of the community now clubbed together to provide the hostages with expenses. With that Nevill took the hostages away to prison and waited for the village to toe the line. But that wasn't the end of the story. The community took their complaint about Nevill's high-handed actions to the king's justices of the peace. The upshot was that the peasants took the king's marshal to court. Our surviving manuscript account is the record of this hearing and shows how English villagers now thought they could use the law. The case was brought against Nevill by the reeve and six others 'on behalf of the community of the village' claiming that he had used violence against them and that the five hostages had been taken illegally. Nevill denied force and wrongdoing. He had suffered trespass and violence at the hands of the 'foolish' villagers, who had accused him of heinous crimes 'and beat and wounded and maltreated his men'. Speaking on behalf of the village community, Thomas the reeve and the local priest, who were alleged to have agreed the fine with Nevill, strongly denied that there had ever been any consent: as freemen they had been dragged out of church by force and wronged (in saying this were they perhaps aware of the clause in Magna Carta about arbitrary arrest?). They claimed compensation and the hostages too alleged they had 'lain in prison in wretchedness . . . wherefore they say that as they are free men (*liberi homines*) and of free status, they have been wronged, and have suffered loss of livelihood to the value of a hundred marks.' Thomas the reeve and the freemen of the village insisted that Peter had 'dragged them by force and unwillingly out of the church and the churchyard'. In the end the king's judges decided against them, but the case shines a fascinating light on the political views and class awareness of the peasants during this momentous national crisis. Here for the first time in English politics is the voice of the peasants of England.

## The Hundred Rolls of 1279

The Barons' Revolt had stirred up many questions about legal rights in the body politic. Royal rights had been usurped, ancient rights lost, mortgage documents stolen, debts cancelled by partisans. The peasants who had been down to Kent, who had fought in the armies, and whose villages had suffered at the hands of vengeful partisans knew well now how these things affected them and how some could be contested in law. In the aftermath of the war a flood of legal disputes began between peasants and their lords. Even villeins now went to court to contest their landlord's view of their servile status. In 1275 at Stoughton three miles from Kibworth the landlord's lawyers sneeringly dismissed such aspirations outside the courtroom when they cut short one rights case. They told the 'foolish' peasant litigants they would not be allowed to succeed in their plea, and that if they persevered they would waste a great deal of money; as the defence lawyers would be able to prove them villeins and therefore deny them the right to sue in a higher court. A satirical poem was then penned by a priest on the landlord's side who uses his clever Latin learning to deride the leading peasant agitators and their wives: 'What should a serf do except serve? And his son too? He shall be a serf pure and simple, deprived of freedom. The judgement of the Law, and of the King's court, prove it so!'

From its own side, after such upheavals in politics with widespread confiscation and redistribution of estates, the government was anxious to re-establish clarity over land ownership and rights. Henry III had died in 1272 and was succeeded by his son, Prince Edward. At the time Edward was on crusade in the Holy Land and did not return to England till summer 1274, when he was crowned as King Edward I. Almost immediately Edward undertook a great survey of England, a second, but far more comprehensive Domesday, going into the most minute detail in every community and recording every member of the adult population for legal and tax purposes. Taken in 1274–5 and 1279–80, and known as the Hundred Rolls, these constitute the greatest body of evidence for the social history of England in this period, and the Hundred Rolls of 1279 are the most ambitious survey ever undertaken by an English ruler.

The questionnaire submitted to each of the local hundred juries had no fewer than forty-two questions on tenure, status, income, land holdings, stock and material holdings. Some of the original returns survive in the National Archives in Kew and some in county archives, though more than half are now lost. Had the survey been completed it would have amounted to a comprehensive register and customary of all England down to individual villeins, cottagers and serfs. For any place for which the returns have survived the rolls are a unique resource, some of which such as those from Kent are now available online.

The original returns for Leicestershire, as for most of the country, have not survived. But by a lucky chance the antiquarian William Burton, whom we met at the start of this story preparing his history of Leicestershire, made notes from the now-lost rolls in 1615. A copy of his notes in the Bodleian Library has not yet been fully published, though the antiquarian John Nichols in his first volume published Burton's transcripts of a series of summaries of the 1279 surveys 'made in every one of the individual vills and all the separate places throughout the county of Leicestershire'. But later in Burton's manuscript a set of much fuller transcripts was missed by Nichols and remains unpublished. In them are our first accounts of Smeeton and the Kibworths since Domesday, and they mark another stage in the crystallization of our evidence for the village, as for the first time we are given the names of the families of the ordinary people themselves.

The form was that the local jurymen of Kibworth submitted their information to the jury for the whole of Gartree Hundred, presumably in a meeting in the open air at the Gartree. Armed with the returns for all the twenty-five villages in the hundred, the Gartree jury in their turn reported in person to the King's three commissioners in Leicester. Their evidence was collated, checked and read back to them and they signalled agreement by fixing their seal to it. The names of the 'twelve good men and true' who represented Gartree Hundred are recorded by Burton, including well-to-do freeholders from Smeeton, Foxton and Houghton on the Hill; Thomas Basset, whose family had regained their position after their support for Montfort; and a Walter who may have been the reeve of Kibworth Harcourt. The hearings were held in the Great Hall of Leicester Castle, whose magnificent aisled hall still stands today, the largest and earliest in Europe. There we can imagine – as is vividly recalled by a contemporary chronicler – the hubbub of the jurors gathering from all over the shire, 'the villagers filled the corners of the courtyard and the crossing places in town discussing and conferring together as to what answers they should give. Then when the questions were put to them they made their statements, which were set down by their clerk.'

What the jurymen declared for the two Kibworths and Smeeton is revealed in the Bodleian Library copy of Burton's notebook. The transcript is the first to name the ordinary tenants in the villages, the freeholding families who can be traced sometimes for hundreds of years onwards through the story of the village. First of all is Smeeton. Divided into five or six small manors, Smeeton was a prosperous place, with a dozen free tenants including the Astens, the Alens and Hugh Hasting (all of whom have Scandinavian surnames) and Walter Wodard and his sons Robert and Richard – kinsmen of John Wodard, whom we met in 1264. The Latimers in particular become well-to-do gentry and will play an important role in the Lollard movement in the fifteenth century. By contrast Kibworth Beauchamp, as we suspected from Domesday Book, was a village of unfree workers. Burton's transcript tells us that nearly 500 acres here were held by peasant families in villeinage from the Earl of Warwick. Burton shows that the Hundred Rolls jurors reported that there were only two free tenancies in the entire village of Beauchamp, part of one held by an old village family, that of Will Harm (another Scandinavian name), who had sixty acres. As for the unfree, there were over forty-five families of villeins and serfs farming those 500 acres at Beauchamp, and the acreages indicated by Burton's transcript suggest an expansion of arable by a couple of hundred acres in the previous thirty years as new land was cleared and put under the plough: pushing to the margins of the village to feed the ever-growing population.

In Kibworth Harcourt too the Hundred Rolls give us our first detail on the village families. There are wealthy peasants like Henry Person who had his own *aula*, a small open aisled hall of a kind found for the first time among the peasantry in the late thirteenth century. (A rare if not unique surviving peasants' hall mentioned in the 1279 survey is Ryders Farm at Swavesey in Cambridgeshire.) Then come the free peasant proprietors – Nicholas Faber, William Reynes, Robert Polle, Robert Hering, Richard son of Roger, Matilda daughter of Nicholas Faber, John Boton and John Sibil. These are the key peasant families in the village, some like Hering perhaps descended from Viking settlers.

Let us leave the Gartree Hundred jury in the hubbub of the Great Hall in Leicester. King Edward's commissioners and their scribes are at their long table piled with documents, Henry of Nottingham, Henry of Sheldon and John of Arundel conferring below the towering roof with its huge oak aisle posts. There are the last-minute questions: the status of William Beauchamp's free tenant in Smeeton, Geoffrey of Dalby; the size of the virgates rented by the nine bondmen. And the small print: the pound of peppercorn for Henry Person's hall, the bushel of wheat for benseed and eighteen sheaves of oats for foddercorn, three hens and a cock yearly and five eggs at Easter.

But as the jury set their seal to their account of Kibworth it was clear that a new situation had arisen in Harcourt. In the aftermath of the Barons' Revolt and Montfort's death, Saer de Harcourt's village had been carved up into five separate manors besides the holdings of the main families of free peasants. Four of these were now in the hands of southern aristocrats, from Worthing near Brighton, Portsmouth and Ewell in Surrey: kinsmen and kinswomen of an important grandee who had taken the king's side in the Civil War and now reaped his reward. The fifth and largest part of Kibworth Harcourt, the jurymen had reported, was now under a new lord, 'The House of Scholars of Walter of Merton in Oxford'. How this had come about, and the extraordinary role Merton College will have in the lives of the people of the village, is the subject of the next chapter in our story.

# 9. The Scholars of Merton

Simon de Montfort's bloodied head was sent to Lady Mortimer, his testicles pinned to his nose; his tarred limbs were set above the gates of Gloucester with a placard advertising his treachery. But Montfort was not forgotten. Among the gentry Simon became a heroic figure, around whom popular tales, songs and even miracle stories gathered: he was the priceless flower, *la flur de pris* 'who died unflinchingly (*sauntz feyntise*) like Thomas the martyr of Canterbury', who had also stood bravely against royal power. The recent discovery of a parchment genealogical roll with an account of Simon's deeds scribbled on the back shows the tale was recited in noble houses among sympathizers even seventy years later. His grave and death site almost immediately became places of pilgrimage whose reputation for healing spread as far as Devon and Northumberland, and even France. In 1273, still bruised by his fines, Robert de Vere, Earl of Oxford, a former knight of Simon, made a 300-mile round trip from Essex to the well and the church. There he was 'measured' at Simon's tomb with a length of tallow which was then cut for burning in prayer lamps back home. One of his ancestors, also Robert, had been among the twenty-five 'guardians' of Magna Carta.

But it was not just upper-class supporters who had lost out in the revolt. Memories of the brief flowering of the great enterprise and its articulation of the community of the realm were held even by the peasants in the village. An Evesham Abbey manuscript records nearly 200 miracles in the late 1260s and early 1270s at the Battle Well and these were presumably only a small portion of satisfied customers. They were people of all social ranks: village constables, a carpenter, a miller, tailors, countesses and lords, and even two 'masters of the University of Oxford'. This is a sign of how Montfort had transcended class and status. At his tomb an earl could rub shoulders with a paralysed woman brought in a wheelbarrow on a ten-week trip by her devoted husband. Villagers from the Kibworth area were among those who came here on pilgrimage, keeping vigil at the well, drinking the holy water, washing afflicted limbs in it, and taking it off in bottles for neighbours back in the village. Margery from the neighbouring hamlet of Burton Overy spent the night in hope of a miracle, and, 'by the testimony of the whole village', her eyes were healed. The pond is still there and local tradition remembers that it was still used to bathe eye infections into the twentieth century.

In Kibworth the effects of the failed revolution were especially far-reaching; indeed, in Harcourt they would influence the villagers' lives from that day to this. In Kibworth Beauchamp the landlords were the king's pantlers; but on the other side of the parish Saer de Harcourt as we have seen had been a knight of Simon's retinue. In the immediate aftermath of Evesham the king's men plundered Saer's estates at Newton Harcourt and Kibworth – perhaps, indeed, the Beauchamps were among the king's vengeful partisans. Inevitably, as the bitter fallout of Simon's defeat unfolded, Saer's estates came under close royal scrutiny. Saer's family had run the village for a century and a half or more. They had never been resident, preferring their Oxfordshire estate at Stanton Harcourt with its easy access to the court in London and Windsor, but now having taken the barons' side, Saer (who had survived the disaster) forfeited his lordship and was imprisoned to await trial for treason.

That November while Saer was in prison the king's assessors rode into Kibworth, summoned the village scribe and jurymen, and took an account of the whole village to find out exactly what Saer was worth. In the filing system of the king's archives, now in the National Archives in Kew, is a roll recording this inquisition along with the fines imposed on the king's enemies, including Saer. Saer, it says, was forgiven and conditionally restored by the king, who 'remitting his indignation and rancour of mind, pardons him for all trespasses committed by him during the time when the disturbances took place in the land'. On the back of the manuscript a royal filing clerk has jotted Saer's name to make it easier to locate on a twelve-foot parchment roll. Saer was to be 'mainprized of good behaviour' but still had to face his punishment. He was subject to swingeing fines and like the other pardoned Montfortians was only allowed to redeem his estates for seven times their annual value. Saer's finances were already in a mess – he had considerable debts to Jewish moneylenders – and he was forced to sell up. In the wings now is a new character in our story: Walter of Merton, founder of the 'House of Scholars' of Merton College, Oxford.

## Enter Walter of Merton

A wealthy Surrey grandee, Walter of Merton was a royalist, a former chancellor and 'a man of great liberality and great worldly learning'. Five years or so before, in 1261, Merton had set aside land to found a new 'house of scholars residing at the schools at Oxford'; he was now looking for estates with which to endow his foundation with an income from rents. Once Bishop of Rochester, Walter had been stripped of his office by the barons after Lewes, during the summer of rage of 1264. In that brief heady time Montfort's troops had run amock: their peasant soldiers, John Wodard and his friends perhaps among them, burned barns on Walter's estates at his native village of Merton and at Chessington in Surrey, where manor buildings were looted and fired by the rebels. Walter then had every reason to look on Saer with a vengeful gaze and to view his lands with a calmly covetous eye.

The purchase of Kibworth Harcourt was a long-drawn-out process. Medieval property deals could be no less complicated than today, and there were several leaseholds for Walter to buy up. Saer's bonds to Jewish moneylenders and his debt to a London merchant, on which he had remortgaged part of his property, all needed to be sorted out. The first stage in all this for the people of Kibworth was the king's examination of the holdings of all his enemies. The inquisition of the extent of Saer de Harcourt's lands at Kibworth from November 1265 in the bruising aftermath of Evesham still survives in the National Archives in faded ink on crumpled vellum. The commissioning writ mentions that Saer was then in prison, perhaps as a result of his capture at Evesham. The jurors came not just from Kibworth but also from Newton Harcourt and Glen. Among the Kibworthians are men from what will become well-known village families: 'Robert Aaron of Kybbewrth, William of Reyns of the same, Hugh of the same and William Harin of the same.'

Produced for the king's ministers to assess Saer's entire wealth as preparation for confiscation or valuation, the document needs only a little brushing up to meet the standards of a modern estate agent's brochure. This then is a sketch of the village of Kibworth Harcourt and its people in the aftermath of the Barons' Revolt:

(1) One manor house and nine virgates of land in the lord's demesne. Virgates in Kibworth were thirty acres, so this is around 270 acres altogether. Value £7 12s per annum.

(2) Eighteen and a half virgates of land (=555 acres) held in villeinage, each virgate worth 16s per annum i.e. from the sale of the surplus of the villeins' labour = £14 16s income per annum. With these virgates scattered across the common fields come twenty-nine villeins, who each hold a half-virgate, and four who hold one virgate each. These peasants and their families were tied, coming with the estate, and could not leave without the lord's permission. As terms of villeinage differed from manor to manor, Walter would have been given the full details of services, dues, and any particular local customs and rights.

(3) Rents from eleven free tenants and seven cottagers amounting to 38s 10d per annum. Some of these eleven free tenants must have been the descendants of the six free tenants, the sokemen and sokewomen of Domesday Book in 1086: some of their plots had evidently been subdivided over time. The cottagers did not own land, but held their cottages on the lord's land with specified labour dues.

(4) One mill worth 26s 8d per annum in rents. An innovation of the thirteenth century, the mill was a new post mill built by Saer's family as landlords. It may have been the predecessor

of the one that still stands north-east of the village, rebuilt
in the eighteenth century. Again the terms of use and tenants'
share of repair costs varied between estates, and a prospective
buyer would have been informed of the specific terms under
which tenants had to mill their corn at the lord's mill.

(5) A render of four capons at Christmas worth 6d. Perhaps this
was due from each unfree tenant. A later schedule also mentions one pound of pepper as an annual render.

Kibworth Harcourt at this point was clearly an arable village.
The total extent of the ploughlands may have been about 825 acres. The
total value of the manor was said to be £26 0s 8d per annum. Offers in
the region of ten times the annual income were common in land deals
in the thirteenth century, possibly more, given extras. An offer in the
region of £400 would cover Saer's fine. For a prospective purchaser
Saer's situation was complicated by his debts, but these complications
were surmountable and Walter went ahead with the purchase.

The purchase document survives in Walter's foundation in Oxford,
Merton College, in the thirteenth-century muniments tower. Stone-
built to protect the college's estate archive from the risk of fire, the
archive room is lined with wooden cupboards whose polished drawers are painted with the names of Merton's manors, from Ponteland
up beyond the Tyne in Northumberland, to little Cuxham near
Oxford, and Cheddington, Thorncroft and Ibstone – Walter's old
estates around his native Merton in Surrey. There are three capacious
drawers of Kibworth land documents. The purchase deed is almost
pristine, a small folded pale piece of parchment bearing the wax seal
of Saer de Harcourt. As for the £400 Walter paid: the annual value
of £26 in 1265 is worth more than £13,300 today on the Retail Price
Index; but more than £308,000 using average earnings. The purchase
price in 2010 would be £205,000 on the RPI but getting on for £5m
on the average earnings index. Today *Country Life* gives a good idea of
what Walter was getting – but Kibworth came with its workforce too.

The purchase seems to have gone through (at least on parchment)
in a friendly manner. The Montfortians' aims had been abhorrent to

Walter, but he was too intelligent to be blind to the tensions which had given rise to Saer's espousal of Simon's cause. So despite the fact that his Surrey estates had been plundered by Simon's rebels, Walter's tone was one of relaxed bonhomie between gentlemen, addressing Saer as his *socius* and *amicus*, suggesting a high table 'my dear fellow'. Time to let bygones be bygones.

We have already encountered the Merton archive in this story, and it is now time to introduce it more fully. This amazing treasure trove of English social life is a historian's delight. Among its many holdings it contains rolls for Kibworth from the 1270s to the early 1700s; rentals from the reign of Henry III to 1527; and bailiffs' accounts year by year from 1283 to 1682 (some membranes are even sewn with their original tally sticks labelled 'Cybbeworthe'). In addition there is a rich miscellany of lease books, tithing lists, repair bills, building accounts, letters, family deeds and miscellaneous files and bundles of deeds. The college also holds a series of maps of Kibworth, beginning with two wonderful painted plans of 1609 and 1635 which depict all the village houses with their freeholders and tenants named. The archive even contains a letter from the village butcher, John Pychard, to the fellows of the college in 1447 – it's a real rarity to have a peasant's letter from such an early date. Though the college sold its houses in Kibworth after the Second World War, it still owns fields and one of the farms in the village, and still plays a role in the community, with triennial visits from the Warden and concerts by the Merton choir in Kibworth church.

So from this point in the story, along with the poll taxes and hearth taxes and the surviving court rolls for Beauchamp kept in the National Archives in Kew, for Kibworth Harcourt we have the record of an English village from the thirteenth century till now. In the thirteenth-century muniments tower, the oldest custom-built archive repository in Britain, and in the college library, the oldest continuously working library in the world, one of the most interesting caches of documents in British history gives us the names, houses and jobs of everyone who lived in the village for nearly 750 years. Along with a few score other English medieval manors it is one of the best-documented villages in Britain, if not in the world.

## *The people of Kibworth in 1280*

In the 1270s we can thus finally meet the people of the village by name, describe their jobs, define their relationships and map their houses. We can draw family trees, sometimes over many generations, as with the Polles – fifteen generations down to the 1600s – or the Iliffes and the Colmans – from Tudor times until today. The Merton archive does what cannot be done from the centre or from above: supplemented by new finds from archaeology, wills and dendrochronology, it shines an intimate light on an English community. And on the daily lives of ordinary people throughout history.

Walter of Merton's first act was to draw up a full account of the village, and because of its detail it is one of the most interesting of any thirteenth-century English villages. It was made not long after 1280 (when Walter had initially leased parts of the manor to his three sisters and their husbands – only after a generation or so will the college amalgamate all these holdings). The account is beautifully and clearly written in black ink on a single membrane of vellum, and it begins with the free tenants. These are the lineal (and sometimes no doubt the biological) descendants of the six sokemen and sokewomen numbered in Domesday Book in 1086: inheritors of the free holdings from late-Saxon Kibworth. There are now eleven of them, as we learned from the king's inquisition of 1265 and from the Hundred Rolls of 1279. But now we have their names and holdings, some of them from the oldest families in the village who can be traced sometimes over several centuries. The eleven freemen and two freewomen each hold half a virgate (fifteen acres) or more:

(1) William de Pek, three virgates.

(2) William de Reynes, half a virgate. A well-off freeholder, twenty years later William had a dozen tenants mainly leasing strips and parcels of land from him – one a kinsman, others younger members of well-established village families such as the Swans, Heyneses, Sibils and Peks. William Reynes is

typical of the wheeler-dealing peasant who did well in the boom time of the thirteenth century.

(3) Nicholas Polle, half a virgate. One of the oldest families in the village, the Polles can be followed here until the seventeenth century. They often provided village officials, reeves and bailiffs, constables and ale-tasters in the Middle Ages. Nicholas's father, Robert, had been a freeholder in the 1260s.

(4) Robert Sharon, one virgate.

(5) Nicholas Faber, one virgate. Faber was the village blacksmith. His daughter Matilda had also held one virgate in 1279 but had now married and moved into another village family.

(6) Richard, son of Roger Faber, one virgate.

(7) Henry Polle, half a virgate. Henry belonged to the second branch of the Polles: they had an extensive kin group in the village in the thirteenth century with four separate households and clearly were long-established Kibworth people, perhaps from pre-1066.

(8) Henry Boton, half a virgate plus a quarter. Henry had inherited from his father John, who had been a freeman in 1279.

(9) John Sibil, a quarter-virgate. In addition a tenant, his younger brother Adam, rented five and a half virgates from him. Their father was probably the John who held half a virgate in 1279; but their family name came from a woman who was probably their grandmother, a widowed single parent, whose name was taken by her male descendants and whose story is explored in more detail below. The Sibils are another of the well-recorded peasant families in Kibworth who provide village officials and chaplains over the next century or more. Adam subsequently leased land to nine separate tenants, mainly again the younger children of neighbours, the Peks, Swans, Polles, Heyneses and the chaplain *dominus*, John Godwin.

(10) John Sibil, one messuage (a dwelling house and its plot) held from Henry Person at a rent of 1s 6d plus an annual rent of a pound of pepper, which presumably John bought from a spicer in Leicester or Harborough. (Henry Person had been a freeholder in 1279 but migrated from the village.)

(11) William Brown, one messuage, a housing plot, rent 1d. William, son of Robert Brown, was a freeman with no land, and a tiny holding, though no doubt he rented strips in the open field from one of his neighbours. The Brown family can be traced in Kibworth from the middle of the thirteenth century until Tudor times; one branch became drapers in Coventry and eventually moved to London (see pp. 247–54).

(12) Alice and Matilda Sterre. Very likely these sisters were unmarried or possibly widowed: no children appear later bearing this name and the family disappears from the village.

Those are the free tenants who together held fifteen and a half virgates: eleven holdings and just over 450 acres spread through the three great fields. They and their children were free to move in law, but owed rent to their landlord for their house, garden and allotment, and for their strips in the open fields.

Then the survey lists a further twenty-seven customary tenants or villeins, whose houses probably ran along the north side of Main Street. They include other branches of the Polles, Sibils and Heyneses, along with the Godyers, Godwins and Carters, and Radulf the reeve. The Hugh Harcourt who appears here as a customary tenant could be a man who had taken the name of his lord; or he could be a poor relative left by a lesser branch of the famous family. The name Harcourt is long-lasting as a peasant surname in the village – the religious sisters Mary and Margaret still owned land in Kibworth in the early fifteenth century.

Also among the villeins were other long-lasting families. Hugh Silvester and Emma Gilbert were both people whose descendants will play a dramatic role in the Lollard risings of the fifteenth century. A villein holding half a virgate, Emma was not alone as a woman tenant. Among the villeins was Beatrice Sibil, whose family we have already met, and 'widow Scolate', another matriarch whose sons and descendants will take her name as their family name, and who, as we shall see, left a special mark on the village story.

Finally come the cottagers (twelve in number) who had tied cottages on the lord's land, probably simple mud and thatch tofts along the south of Main Street, for which they paid 2s a year rent. This list is especially interesting because for the first time it gives us specific jobs in the village. There are a skinner and a shepherd. Robert the thresher (*triturator*) is evidently the man who threshed grain for people who couldn't do their own, probably for a small cut of the sack. Like a number of women in the village, Alice Godwine was perhaps a brewster.

Two men, Robert and William, are named as brokers (*brochars*). These might have been wool dealers in a village where sheep were valuable. Though the word can also mean a tapster, in the fourteenth century it is often used as a shopkeeper, middle man or buyer and seller; the poet Langland for example uses it as a metaphor: 'a brochar of backbiting, a buyer and seller of discord'. So perhaps these were dealers who bought commodities at regional markets and sold in Kibworth at a small profit. In the fourteenth century there were several people like that in Kibworth, including men who 'brokered' horses and other livestock at Lutterworth fair, and bought goods at Hallaton and Harborough markets.

Finally at the bottom of the list come Roger the miller; Alice the washerwoman, the woman who washed clothes at the public spring; and, most intriguing, Robert *medico*. In this society disease was an ever-present fact for both humans and animals. Doctors were valued people in the community: they are found in some East Anglian villages in the twelfth century and no doubt existed even in the Anglo-Saxon countryside. Robert was a former bonded serf who had been manumitted a few years before; he was perhaps an expert in country medicine who doubled as the village vet.

## Women in the village

Most women were involved in producing food, and many married women are named as brewsters in the Kibworth court records – ale being an important part of the medieval diet. Isolda Osbern for example had a forty-year career as a brewster from 1320 to 1359. She's notable for being involved in a large number of court cases with her neighbours for unpaid debts, for raising false hue and cry, and on a couple of occasions for wrongfully appropriating other people's goods, especially their grain, which she used in her brewing.

Most married women in Kibworth helped their husbands in the field; single or unmarried women cultivated their own land, perhaps with the help of sons or kinsmen or neighbours. But it was not unusual for women to handle the plough themselves with a small plough team or to lead the team with a goad while the man steered the plough. Along with the free-holding Sterre sisters, the villein's widow Scolate, Beatrice Sibil and Emma Gilbert, three women are named as subtenants of field strips: Alice and Amabil Heynes, and Matilda Bonde, and they presumably worked as farmers alongside the men of the village.

An interesting group of women though emerges in the early documents for Kibworth, two of whom in particular gave their name to very long-lasting kin groups. These were clearly in some way important women in the peasant community, but as they lived just before the horizon of detailed documents, we cannot know precisely why. Most interesting is the kin group in the village which derived its name from a widow called Sibil. She may have been Sibil, the wife of Henry Thurd, who appears in a court case in 1252; but if so it is a solitary appearance and she was dead before the main Merton documents start in the late 1260s. But her name is in the earliest rentals as the by-name of her sons: Ivo 'son of Sybile', a *nativus* (serf) who held half a virgate. In the court roll of 1280, John, a son of Sibil sued Nicholas Polle for assault and battery. By the 1290s the surname had already become hereditary: Ivo is now 'Ivo Sybile' – he was elected one of the chief pledges of the manor of Kibworth Harcourt in 1291 and was appointed an ale-taster round the same time. By then the clan was numerous and extended. One of the tithing lists of this period – a crucial document in the social history of the village – lists over 140 males above the age of twelve in the manor, including Robert Sibile, his sons Roger and William, Ivo Sibile, William Sibile and Alexander Sibile. Robert, who occurs frequently in court rolls between 1280 and 1291, held a virgate in unfree tenure (he is listed in Merton's first survey of Kibworth); he had been village reeve in 1287. Ivo had a daughter, Matilda, who was a brewster between 1281 and 1298 and is most often described as Matilda Sibile, but also as 'Matilda the daughter of Ivo Sibile'.

Such detail drawn from one tiny portion of the Kibworth court rolls shows how one family begins to rise in village society. By the last decade of the thirteenth century the Sibiles have become a powerful influence in the village, led by the Roberts senior and junior. Robert senior was now holding the significant office for the college of *custodies aulae et curiae* and Robert the younger was chief pledge – an important position of trust in the village held by more than one of the clan in the next few decades. Being a pledge meant standing surety for other villagers in a variety of circumstances in the manorial court, whether in cases of debt or trespass or over admissions to new tenancies or as a guarantor of good behaviour. Some of these customary obligations could be quite long term – for example, standing as a pledge for the maintenance of tenements – and, like other unpaid elected offices in the village, pledging has to be seen as an important aspect of reciprocity in the community, as well as a means of gaining status and 'symbolic capital'.

The Sibile kin group continued to thrive in the fourteenth century. Prominent in the rolls in the 1330s and 1340s are a group of women – Constance, Agnes, Emma and Joan Sibil, along with the black sheep of the family, William, son of Alexander Sibil, who was accused of housebreaking in 1349, the year of the Black Death, and for battery in 1352. The most important fourteenth-century member though was Adam, who was active from 1320 to 1348. Adam held a virgate; he was often elected by his fellow villagers as chief pledge and ale-taster in the 1320s and 1330s.

These few details from the family story show how important even unfree peasants could be in the communal functioning of the village. As with other families like the Polles, who also had a large kin network, many of them unfree, the trend towards hereditary naming developed early among the most influential families in the community. If only we knew more about the materfamilias, Sibil, who must have lived in the mid-1200s, and was one of the interesting class of single women – some unmarried, some who had refused marriage, some widowed young, some even divorced. Sibil perhaps was widowed when she was young but by force of character she left her mark on village society.

A second fascinating case study in the Merton court rolls concerns a family whose name again derived from that of a Kibworth widow. Her name appears in many different forms as 'widow Scholas', Scola, Scolate and Scolastica. In a rental of the late thirteenth century she is described as a *nativa*: a bonded unfree peasant tied to the estate. In the account for 1284, 18d is received from Scolastica vidua, while in a rental of 1300 she appears as Scolacia. The court scribe evidently had a great deal of trouble spelling her name. In other rentals and extents and court rolls she is described even more obscurely as Scolasse, Scolac' vidua, Scholace le vediwe and Scolasse vidua. But she is never described by any relationship to a male – except her sons. In her widowhood she was identified simply by her forename, unusual within the community of the village, and by her status as widow, without a reference to a husband. Her sons in the 1290s, named John and Hugh, are called sons of Scolstice or Scolac and her name is found as the family surname through the fourteenth century. Her grandson, Robert, was chief pledge in the 1330s and his younger brother John was executor of Robert's will after he died in the Black Death in 1349. After this the family were well-established tenants: John junior and his wife Agnes appear still as *nativi* in the 1381 poll tax.

Scholastica raises as many intriguing questions as Sibil of Kibworth, especially as she was a *nativa*, a serf. Was her husband an outsider, owning no land in the village, who had died young? Had her tenanted land which she was able to hand on to her sons come down through her father, perhaps because she had no brothers?

Her name, Scholastica, is not uncommon at this time. St Scholastica was the devoted sister of St Benedict of Nursia. Her tale is told in Gregory the Great's Dialogues and was popular in Anglo-Saxon times. She later appears in Caxton's Golden Legend; but her life is told in the South English legendary in Scholastica of Kibworth's own lifetime in around 1270–80. So it was the kind of story well-known to English peasants, people like her parents. The saint's day was 10 February, a widely observed feast day in the thirteenth century. Perhaps it was the Kibworth Scholastica's birthday.

## The peasant landmarket

The Kibworth of Sibil and Scholastica, of Robert the doctor and Alice the washerwoman was not a closed community in the 1290s. Men and women moved widely on pilgrimage and business, to find work, and sometimes even to find love (one young peasant woman followed her lover all the way from Leicestershire up to St Andrews in Fife at this time). Kibworth peasants frequently carried corn by cart on behalf of the college to Leicester and to other places in the county. Tenants might go in person to petition the fellows of Merton or to pay an entry fine to inherit land in the late thirteenth century. For example, John Thored's son Robert anxiously made the journey to Oxford to petition to be admitted to half a virgate of the lord's land; his start in life as an independent farmer.

The treasure trove of documents in Merton also gives us details of commercial life in the village in the 1280s and 1290s which suggest a wide range of personal initiative among the village people. In one case William 'the chapman' testified to the court in Kibworth Harcourt that he had been buying goods for another tenant when he lost 4s 11d and three farthings at Yaxley fair thirty miles away in Huntingdonshire. William was clearly a petty trader making purchases on behalf of the village – perhaps what is described in the Merton documents as a 'broker'. John Walter and his brother also gave money to Chapman, which he spent at Medbourne market seven miles away. Another case in the court book involves the Heynes and Boton families, and concerned a horse that one, Adam, had sold through an agent or middleman (literally an *attornatus*), William Fauconer, a Smeeton freeman, for 10s in the market at Lutterworth. As early as the thirteenth century men in the village apparently worked as merchants or brokers. In a 1290 list of fines for bad brewing, Isobel of Kibworth is described as the wife of Ivo the merchant.

So people travelled. With the huge rise in population between 1100 and 1300 the roads of England were as full as they were in the seventeenth century. By the time Merton bought Harcourt in around 1270 the villagers already had wide connections and Kibworth people were already migrating to the towns. Guild records from Leicester over the next few decades show Kibworth people working in Leicester as curriers, drapers, skinners and slaters. A draper, Richard of Kibworth, who was tallaged in 1359 and entered on the merchant guild roll in 1362, describes himself as of both Kibworth and Leicester. Robert of Kibworth was a boot- and shoemaker who sold his work in the town; and Roger of Kibworth was an ironmonger who rented a shop in Leicester market. All these men brought their skills from the countryside into the town.

Others migrated elsewhere in the countryside for work. This was especially true after the Black Death, but even in the thirteenth century outsiders migrated into Kibworth, and Kibworth people moved away. Some were seeking marriage. When Agnes Man, the daughter of John Man of Kibworth, married Walter Gretham of Shangton and went to live with him, she paid Merton 2s for permission to move out. On the other hand, when Walter Prechour from Wistow married William Polle's daughter Alice, another *nativa*, or tied peasant, he was summoned to Merton's manor court in Kibworth to do fealty to the landlord before he was allowed to move in. John Asteyn of Kibworth Beauchamp, a member of a very old local family, when he married Agnes Smyth of Kibworth Harcourt moved in with her and took on the annual chevage in order to reside there and be treated as a *nativus* on Merton's manor – transferring his unfreedom for love of Agnes! Such was the binding small print of the medieval manorial world.

The marriage horizon for these unions was only two or three miles. Others though moved much further afield. The story of Robert of Kibworth, a Harcourt freeman, does not survive in the Merton archive, but has come down to us because of the accident that the lands he originally owned in the thirteenth century found their way in Tudor times into the possession of the famous Wyggeston Hospital in Leicester, in whose archive the original mortgage documents have been preserved. The story they tell is again one of routine and insignificant daily life, but is revealing nonetheless. Some time in the 1290s 'Robert of Kibworth' migrated from Kibworth to Barkeston (today in the wonderfully named parish of Barkestone, Plungar and Redmile). There he may have married, became a landowner and from 1299 enacted a series of land grants dealing with small parcels of land – a selion here, a strip there, later calling himself Robert 'of Kibworth and Barkeston'. His business dealings in these grants tell us something about Robert's friends and contacts – his links with trustworthy 'swearing men' in other villages. On 21 April 1311 he leased land to a dexter, or dyer, Thomas Dexter of Harborough, his wife Avice and their son Geoffrey. This grant in Barkeston was witnessed by one Richard of Smeeton and Geoffrey the Fleming of Harborough. Market Harborough was one of the many new towns founded in the commercial boom time of the twelfth century and by 1300 was a thriving market and had a small but active commercial life with a couple of dozen craftsmen and artificers, a handful of men described as 'merchants', some victuallers and a pool of servants and labourers. Clues to our Kibworth man's particular line of business lie in his friends' names: the Harborough dyer and the Fleming. Flemings were prominent in the thriving textile industry which had been the subject of recent government legislation in the form of an export tax on wool. Dyers like the Dexter family used madder, woad and the weld plant for the intense reds, blues and yellows that we see depicted in medieval manuscripts. Outside dyers' workshops great bundles of weld were hung up to dry with heaps of orchil, safflower, gall nuts and madder root. Other clothing colours came from more rare commodities such as the scarlet crocus grub or imported purple shellfish from the Mediterranean. All these were imported through specialist dealers.

In November 1311, this time down at Harborough, Robert leased back a life interest in the Barkeston strips in exchange 'for a rose flower given at the Nativity of John the Baptist'. Again Richard of Smeeton was a witness but he was now joined by Adam Andrews of Harborough. Adam's family are later known as spicers, the kind of people who would have imported dyeing herbs and plants, natural dyes. So Robert is now living in the far north of the shire, in the little promontory that sticks into Nottinghamshire. But his web of contacts across the shire included dyers, cloth workers, and dye and spice importers in the south of the shire at Harborough. And among the witnesses was a Smeeton man presumably known to Robert from his early days in Kibworth.

The last grant in the series is dated 25 April 1317. In it Robert grants to one William Grant of Barkby rights in some land held from the Harborough dyer, only calling himself now Robert Lound. (Had he adopted his wife's family as a 'newcomer' or was this a new place of residence? Lound is on the eastern border of the shire north of Stamford.)

Involved with a Fleming, a draper and a dyer, Robert then was very likely in textiles: perhaps a wool dealer or sheep breeder. His field of operations was the whole shire from Barkeston in the north, to Smeeton next to his native Kibworth, and Harborough down south on the Northamptonshire border. A small operator, Robert of Kibworth was typical of a whole class of freemen in the late thirteenth century, migrating, buying, selling and generally wheeler-dealing; he was the tip of the iceberg in a very active peasant initiative in the land market, using the written charter and professional literacy.

Robert's documents are of no great significance in the scheme of things in history – they are the entirely chance survival of a few scraps of the life of a small businessman around 1300. But Robert's story was the stuff of life for many free English people in the thirteenth century. It also offers clues about identity, and the fluidity of names around 1300. This is the time when English people's family names begin to be fixed as surnames, partly because of the government's increasing need to distinguish people more effectively with the exponential growth of documentation; partly no doubt because of the confusing similarity of male names. Surnames in Kibworth don't really begin to appear till the late thirteenth century – a mix of English, Scandinavian and Norman names. Of eighty-five women's Christian names in fourteenth-century poll taxes for the three villages in Kibworth, more than half are called one of four names: Agnes (13 times), Alice (14), Amice (10) and Joan (10). Others though offer an attractively wide range – Emma, Milisent, Matilda, Elen, Lora, Beatrice, Isolda, Dionisia, Juliana, Felicia, Rose, Sarra and Isobel. Far less imagination is shown by parents with boys' names. By now old

English names were becoming unfashionable; with French-speaking rulers and administrators it was best to use Norman names, especially if one wanted to get on in the new craft and trade guilds in Leicester and Coventry. Nearly half the Kibworth men at this time are called John, with Robert, Richard and William coming behind. Men's names in the village have none of the pleasing variety of women's names and by the early 1300s there is little trace of Old English names. Only in a few surnames, pretty much fixed by the 1320s, more or less definitively by the 1370s, do we still glimpse older village histories: the Swans and Asteyns in Beauchamp; the Thords, Godyers and Godwins in Harcourt; the job descriptions in surnames like the Carters, Chapmans and Wodards. Now it is newcomers who catch the eye: men from Naseby and Sibbertoft in Northamptonshire; and even, in Beauchamp in 1381, the cottager Gregory the 'Welshman' and 'Adam Onele'. Could Adam have been Irish? In fourteenth-century Kibworth it would not have been impossible.

## Dark clouds, strange omens

From the Merton documents a picture of Kibworth emerges in its social life and even its physical layout. Documents from the same time also give us the names of the free families in Smeeton (still including the Swans, Astins and Harms whose ancestors we met in the Viking Age) and list the fifty dependent peasants, villeins and serfs who with their families formed the workforce at Beauchamp. Allowing for omissions they suggest a population of well over 250 people in Beauchamp and the best part of 800 people in the whole parish of Kibworth around 1300. This is nearly three times what it was in 1086, and must have greatly increased the pressures on land, housing and employment. The community was thriving and had much more arable under the plough than in Victoria's day. But there were warning signs, including rising prices, inflation and the increased subdividing of plots as free families tried to provide for their children in an increasingly crowded countryside. Court books across the country show that more and more young people were on the move at this time looking for work, seeking a new village under a new lord. Kibworth by then (if we can speak of the whole parish) had a market with a diversified economy and the population of a small town. But in the 1290s a strong run of bad winters and dry summers signalled a longer-term disruptive weather regime. At first a mote in the mind's eye, but now, and perhaps not just in hindsight, a pattern began to emerge which will culminate in a catastrophic sequence of famine and pestilence and the breakdown of the whole system.

These natural phenomena were preceded by signs and omens. This was an age which gave full credence to the supernatural, and these pointers to the inauspicious were taken seriously as the precursors of the dark forces which would threaten the precarious balance of life in the unending battle against want and disorder. In manuscripts around the turn of 1300, along with the first social poetry, political songs and the complaints of the workers against the excesses of the rich, comes a renewed interest in dreams and ancient prophecies. In one manuscript rules for foretelling the weather are coupled with a dark prognostication for the year 1302 by 'Master Meloaus, the Greek'. Addressed 'to all Christians' it speaks of great misfortunes: earthquakes, famines and wars, the division of realms and of peoples, beginning on a specified September day. And at the bottom of the page a note in French assures the reader that 'all these things which were prophesied indeed took place.'

Two hundred years after the Conquest the stage is set for the next phase of history in England and the village, an incredibly dramatic one, which now we can tell through real people's stories, through families like the Polles, the Browns and the Sibils. Their community had gone through the Dark Ages and the age of the Vikings, and had been radically reshaped by the Anglo-Saxon kings of the tenth century. They had endured the Norman occupation and found their own voice in the constitutional rebellion of the 1260s. They had developed consultative institutions from the hundred courts to the field juries, they used charters to buy property and even on occasion went to the king's court to argue their rights. Though villeins everywhere faced discrimination, and serfs and slaves often lived desperate lives on marginal land, still the village was a community with communal rights, obligations and work practices. There were now markets everywhere where they could sell their surplus and even in Kibworth it was possible to buy a piece of silk, or a pound of pepper. As had been the case from the tenth century the law had power over life and death, with a gallows in every manor. But already there are hints in the village of a fundamental shift in British history from a feudal order to capitalism: the shift from labour dues to money rents. As always in history, change was constant, the ongoing process of the growth of society, always in the making, never made.

In the last days of the thirteenth-century boom time the village population (like that of England generally) has expanded to levels it will not reach again until 1800. Marginal land is straining and fertility waning. Crowds of landless men are walking the roads of England seeking security in an increasingly troubled world. And in Harcourt there's a new landlord. What will the lordship of an Oxford college mean to the villagers, the freemen with their timber-framed houses on Main Street, the villeins in their mud and thatch homes, and the serfs, with their wicker hovels and pigs in the forest; the freeborn English with their strips in the common field? And how will they all cope with the catastrophes about to engulf them?

## 10. The Great Famine and the Black Death

Through the autumn of 1314 incessant rains cast a grey curtain over the sodden landscape. The village was not in great shape. The previous year the 'Great Gale' had blown down trees, wrecked fences, and taken roofs off buildings. In the spring hard frosts lasted through into a freezing April, with late flurries of sleet and hailstones, and 'a high mortality of pigeons'. All this was followed by a hot dry summer baking the ground bone-hard, and the Kibworth accounts list extra costs for iron to repair broken ploughshares. And now there were more worrying signs. With the heavy rains the villagers had gathered a poor harvest with great difficulty. Winter ploughing had lasted through October, the ploughmen in their patchwork coats struggling to keep line and length on the furlongs in North Field with their wet clays and steep headlands. So more beer for the ploughmen, more fodder for the oxen and horses, money for new ploughboards. All of this was noted down with concern by the reeve, John Polle, to be entered in spidery brown ink in the court rolls, while the hayward and his dog (Talbot seems to have been the favourite name for haywards' dogs at this time) looked on uneasily as dark thunderheads massed like mountains over Smeeton Hill and Gumley Wood, and the first flecks of snow gusted into their faces. It was going to be a bad winter.

In the village hierarchy the reeve Polle oversaw village custom and practice, exacted fines and negotiated with the landlords, the Merton fellows. From an old villein family, Polle had been elected by the peasants who all knew and trusted him. The hayward's job was more hands-on, to supervise ploughing, mowing and reaping, counting returns on a tally checked with the bailiff. Medieval estate management texts recommended that the hayward be a man 'active and sharp, up early and late', who must have his eyes about him from the crack of dawn. Around his neck he carried a horn to blow for the lunch break and quitting time at the end of day when the villeins and their boys brought the ox teams back from the fields. In his pouch perhaps he carried a little pocket almanac made of folded pieces of stitched parchment, with simple pictures and diagrams: painted zodiacs, eclipses, weather lore, highlighting in red the saints' feasts, the 'red letter days' that betokened auspicious times. The booklet illustrated the dates of the farmers' year with jingles of folk wisdom and even listed bread prices, with different kinds of loaf – maslins, wastels and, the roughest and cheapest, 'horsebread'. But it also gave thunder omens and harvest prophecies with pictures of flattened wheat, its human cultivators stricken by sickness and bedridden. On one page was a sinister image of sodden sheaves of corn and clouds where hooded demonic figures spouted wind and water from their mouths like streams of arrows. And above in doggerel: 'Stormy summers mean wet autumns, and great mortality of young and old.'

Practical busy men with at least a smattering of literacy, the reeve and the hayward were entrusted with the smooth running of the system, the routine of the open fields, and with knowing the weather lore, the harvest predictions and the movements of sun and moon. They were the eyes of the community. At root all their knowledge and expertise, and all the labour of their fellow villagers, was simply to produce food: to feed their betters, and then themselves. And the last page of the almanac depicted their greatest fear, the dire symbol of 'derthe' – a golden knife on an empty table.

Signs of the coming catastrophe had been there in the preceding two decades, starting in the late 1290s with rising grain prices and falling wages, compounded by the demands of landlords and of royal taxes to finance the court and the armies for the king's foreign and domestic wars. Even 7d-a-year villeins found themselves marked down in the national poll tax in 1307. England now was overstretched, an overpopulated land straining under the weight of too many people, 6–7 million, a figure not reached again till the eighteenth century. A husbandman's song from around 1300 tells of too many mouths to feed: 'I heard men upon earth make much moan . . . how he beth tired of here tilyyng . . . good yeres and corn both beth agon' (i.e. have gone away). This was the mood in Kibworth too, bursting at the seams with extra people, *adventitii* – landless newcomers who threw up their hovels on common land and attached themselves to richer peasants to earn a crust and find protection, or simply to survive.

Behind all this was a deeper and much longer-term crisis, born of what we now know as climate change. Disturbing patterns of weather had begun to disrupt the routine of agricultural life, the ploughing, sowing and reaping, on which a largely agricultural society depended. The early fourteenth century was entering a little Ice Age, but whether these signs were read at the time as a long-term phenomenon seems unlikely. Perhaps the pattern is only discernible with hindsight, as we look back over the village records, the thousands of court rolls which have been investigated over the last few decades, those detailed accountings of profit and loss that trammelled the lives of the mass of medieval English people.

From Smeeton Hill the landscape today presents a very different aspect from that of 1314. The arable has almost all gone now: instead, fields of green pasture stretch to the horizon, in places still scored by undulating ridge and furrow left by the medieval ploughmen. Back in 1314 this was all open, bare and brown, with few trees and hardly a fence or a hedgerow: not the green and pleasant land of the English imagination, then, but a highly organized and regulated landscape shaped by the techniques of what we would call industrial agriculture. Below the hill lay the fields of Smeeton and Kibworth Beauchamp, and further to the east the three great Harcourt fields, stretching in a half-circle from north-west to south-east, farmed in rotation each year with one field alternating fallow. Each of the great fields was divided into hundreds of strips, counting, as the Kibworth peasants said in their local speech, 'from sunnyside round to shady side': that is, counting clockwise from the sunrise (in their dialect, *solskift* – a Viking word still found in farming speech in the East Midlands). Across these fields at ploughing time lines of ox teams marched slowly up and down, the boys running ahead with the goad, the men steering behind, 'husbandys with their beasts and ploughs all in a rowe'. Not surprisingly, it then was the now proverbial 'Piers the Ploughman', the English Everyman, who was the hero of the

growing tide of popular song and protest poetry in the early
fourteenth century; for as the ballad makers said, on his shoulders lay
'the mirth of all the land'. 'Gode spede wel the plough' then was both
a proverb and a prayer, for the truth was, the whole community, the
whole country, depended on it.

Walking into Kibworth Harcourt on the eve of the Great Famine,
the visitor – a tinker, say, a horse dealer or a wandering preacher –
saw about sixty houses with yards and long allotment gardens
enclosed by the village hedge and ditch. In the north the ditch ran
along a small stream which was dammed to make fishponds – an
important supplement to the villagers' repetitive diet of meat, bread,
onions and 'caboches'. On the north side of Main Street were the villeins' tenements of typical Leicester mud wall and thatch. Between
some of their gardens and yards was the infill housing of the last forty
years when tenements had been divided and subdivided during the
population boom. Walking further on down the street, the ground
sloped towards the marketplace, past larger stone-based houses which
belonged to wealthier peasants – a class on the rise in the fourteenth
century, people who could afford a hall, a solar and kitchen, cattle
barns and pig yards.

Beyond the bailiff's house the village marketplace opened out at
the junction of Main Street, Hog Lane and the Slang – the big droveway from the village to the open fields. Here on the line of springs
that had first drawn settlers here in the Iron Age was the village's
main source of water: a well which was never known to run dry until
it ceased to be used after the Second World War with the coming of
a piped municipal water supply. Here in the marketplace was the
communal kiln and the horse mill, a rough thatched mud-brick house
sheltering the grindstones. Every Thursday the market stalls sold
cloth, leather goods and shoes, iron locks, tools and farm gear. There
were sea fish brought up the Welland from Spalding, sticks of eels
from the Fens and salted herrings, 'stockfish' from the Arctic Circle
imported through the Humber. There were luxuries too: saffron and
raisins, pepper and cloves from Andrews the 'spicer' in Harborough,
to be used at sheep shearings and harvest feasts. The small village
chapel was close by in Hog Lane; the parish church of St Wilfrid stood

alone on the ridge between Harcourt and Beauchamp. The village had two windmills, one on the hill to the north on the track to Carlton, the other on a Roman mound north-west of the village. All the peasants had an obligation to pay to grind their corn at one or the other of the mills. A new technology then, these were post mills, with a brick base or 'tower' supporting a two-storey 'buck' or mill house with grinding gear and sails; this was turned manually by moving the wooden tiller into the direction to catch the winds that blew over the open-field country.

In Harcourt there were now eleven families on free tenements, some of them descendants of freemen, the *liberi homines* of Domesday Book. Among them were the Peks, the Reynes, the Sibils, the Browns and the Polles. Some of these people were wealthy enough to employ servants and labourers, drawn from the increasingly poverty-stricken landless proletariat who lived at the margins of fourteenth-century society. The bulk of the village community though was nearly thirty customary tenants, villein families like the Godwins, the Carters, the Bondes and the Wades, the reeve John Polle, Roger Joye and Emma Gilbert.

Last in the Merton rent-book were half a dozen cottagers, smallholders saddled as they put it ruefully 'with counte and cot' – that is, with paying tax and keeping a small cottage but with no land. As we have seen, it is among this class of people that the first job descriptions appear in the village in the years before the famine: the miller, the baker, the carter, the threshers and 'brokers', and even the painter (John le Payntour). There was Alice, the village washerwoman, who did her work at the washing place by the marsh, laying out her washing to dry on the meadow. Even an apothecary appears as a witness to one document: he was perhaps the village pharmacist, who procured, mixed and sold herbal medicines, and who may be connected with Robert *medicus* – the 'doctor'.

It would be a mistake to think such people were not familiar with literacy. Even Harry the Hayward had to read and count, as a moderate ability with reading and writing seems to have gone with the job; indeed, the path to literacy in this troubled century would be one of the paths to personal freedom. Numeracy too was essential in the running of the village, though the cumbersome Roman numbering had not yet been replaced by the Arabic system (Harry himself used an ingenious system of finger tallying). With its childlike pictures and rhyming doggerel the hayward's almanac is typical of the shadowy line between illiteracy and literacy in the fourteenth century. The reeves, however, were often more accomplished. John Polle's teenage son, Roger, who followed his father's career path, was certainly able to read and maybe to write. His complaint to the fellows of Merton questioning his expenses suggests a local man of self-belief who could stand up for himself. Roger would be reeve for twenty years between the Famine and the Black Death and the account rolls produced in the 1330s and 1340s under his supervision are unorthodox in layout and expression, terse but masterly in their brevity, and perhaps even from his own hand.

So the Kibworth peasants were used to the written word and they knew the law was meant to work for them too. As their neighbours in Peatling Magna had angrily protested before the king's court, defence of their rights was part of the 'welfare of community of the realm'. They understood the implications for themselves of Magna Carta, the Forest Laws and the Provisions of Oxford (the first edict since the Conquest to be issued in English and to speak in their own speech to 'this landes folc'). Simon de Montfort was still the subject of nostalgic poems and recitals in the noble families that had supported him, and perhaps in the villages too. The flood of popular songs and stories composed in English in the late thirteenth and early fourteenth centuries, England's first 'radical' or 'protest' literature, above all put the peasants' point of view – the perspective of 'Piers the Ploughman'. So in the fourteenth century, radicalized by the peasants' movement over the previous four generations, everything was up for negotiation. Perhaps this helps to explain why the massive blows of climate change, recession, famine and plague would eventually break down the old order.

King Edward and his ministers were not oblivious to this political wind; the rising political involvement of the rural proletariat and popular unrest were a major worry to the court and nobility. But the burgeoning economic and social crisis of 1314 the king did not foresee. In spring 1314 Edward assembled a great expedition to subdue the Scots, marching his army up the Great North Road with a host of 3,000 mounted knights and 16,000 men at arms. With them was a vast baggage train transporting the lavish tents, furniture, bedding and kitchen equipment that would be needed for his triumph. At midsummer, though, the campaign ended in humiliation at Bannockburn with the virtual annihilation of the English infantry force. In high summer as the stragglers fled south and the bedraggled king took ship from Dunbar, the rains that spelled the start of England's plunge into disaster began to fall.

In Kibworth the news of catastrophic defeat in the north was followed by the rain-damaged harvest. The winter ploughing done as well as they could manage, the peasants then settled down to weather the coming storm as best they could. The heavy autumn rain, 'almost continuous' now, burst river banks, and broke dykes and embankments, and soon, inevitably, the chroniclers, like modern headline writers, were likening the weather to 'Noah's Fludde' itself. After the rains came the big freeze and then in the New Year a thick blanket of snow, one fall lasting for three weeks when it was 'scarce possible to get out of the house'. Spring 1315 brought no respite. Around Pentecost the rains started again and soon the pattern of catastrophe had set in across northern Europe as a whole as far as the Baltic Sea and the borders of Poland, where the Teutonic knights waged their interminable war on the Slavs. With grain overnight become gilt-edged, merchants from Tournai to Bodmin bought up any surplus they could lay their hands on, like share dealers before a crash. As the rains carried on into August, the court rolls for England note a large increase in felonies and runaways, and particularly in the petty theft of food, grain and animals. Because of this, on 1 August the Earl of Warwick took the unusual step of writing to John Polle and 'the free tenants of Kibworth and others' charging them to be 'intendent to, and to render their services to the warden and fellows of Merton College as fully as they have done hitherto' (perhaps this was at the request of the fellows – a copy of the letter is preserved among their muniments). The system was beginning to shake.

The Merton fellows' own concern is revealed in their accounts bills that autumn as the famine began to bite and their villagers fell under increasing distress. Crime figures in the village were continuing to rise as the desperate poor stole food from the rich. In the Merton accounts the expenses survive from their agents' journeys up to Kibworth: notes for travel subsistence, horse fodder, food and lodging from inns in Daventry and Northampton. Their trusted 'man', Robert of Gaddesden, made no fewer than thirteen visits in the first year of famine, twelve in the second. And very soon the fellows realized that gathering their customary rents was becoming impossible.

When Robert rode into Kibworth from Oxford in November 1315 he saw a sorry sight: torrential rains had again devastated the harvest and this late in the year plough teams were still out on the Banwell Furlong along the steep baulks by the Leicester road. In the barns behind the houses he found widespread sheep rot; the pigs had 'leprosy and scab' and on one farm the cows had produced no calves. Each deluge swilled a brown tide down Main Street, the 'King's road', gathering in the muddy morass at the bottom in what the peasants called 'the marsh'. Among the village people there was also the 'flux', perhaps typhoid, and many were bedridden in their soaking houses. The images in Harry the Hayward's almanac were beginning to come to life.

On 28 November 1315 the villagers watched in apprehension as a comet left its icy trail across the southern sky, an omen seen across Britain as heralding the worst. That winter famine settled on Britain like a chill blanket, numbing its people. The December snows started with huge drifts, firewood was short and a second hard winter brought on a national disaster, which the 1315–18 accounts from Kibworth and many other English villages describe at the local level with compelling immediacy. As in modern famines in Africa the smallholders were the hardest hit. The surrender of tenements rose from an average of six a year to forty, as poor tenants gave up their strips, sold off gardens and then even their cottages. The final straw for farming people of course, then as now, was to sell off their animals and their gear. Such was the fate of many poor tenants up and down the country, dying as they had lived, in abject poverty. The Kibworth accounts, now in massive arrears, note the closure of a tenancy with laconic brevity: 'Death duty nothing to pay because he had nothing.' A farm diary from that year provides poignant details of the scenes that such people saw in their last days: 'extra hoeing – so many thistles'; 'peas fed to the pigs'; 'a great mortality of doves . . . snow drifts everywhere'; and – a last optimistic touch – 'roses late this year'.

In London the government had by now woken up to the scale of the tragedy, commandeering merchant ships to bring in grain from Gascony, Galicia and even Cornwall (which escaped the worst of the famine). In 1316 the Archbishop of Canterbury ordered the clergy to make solemn processions with the ringing of bells, the chanting of the litany and special Masses in which the people should atone for their sins and appease the wrath of God. For the rich there should be prayers, fasting and the giving of alms for charity to the poor. Pilgrimages were undertaken to the shrines of the saints of England to beg their intercession and prayers spoken in village churches throughout the land.

As always in such cases, there were high profits to be made out of the disaster. Merchants from Lincoln hurried down to Cambridge and Huntingdon, where there were rumours of supplies of surplus grain; dealers from York and Hull scoured the grain merchants' inns in Bishopsgate and Aldgate while some London merchants even travelled overseas looking for the one big consignment that could make their fortune. The government too intensified its own efforts to buy on the international market as grain prices went through the roof, hitting the ceiling unheard of in Leicestershire of 40s a quarter – a forty-fold hike. In 1316 the royal proclamation fixing prices had to be annulled as the Annals of London describe: 'the ordinance regarding livestock fowl and eggs should not stand because so few could be found on account of the derth and famine.' Even the Assize of Bread was redundant now: for if a quarter of wheat cost 40s, who now could afford a 'farthing loaf of best white'? In Harry the Hayward's almanac all that was left was gritty 'horsebread'.

In 1316 John Sibil turned fourteen and inherited the strips of his father Nick, who had died in the first winter of the famine (the college had administered his land for the first year while John was underage). Now in a soaking spring, according to the reeve's book, John sowed his strips with '7d worth of oats, 18d worth of wheat, 4 shillings worth of peas and 4s-6d of barley'. On Kibworth's heavy clays, allowing two bushels of seed an acre, it was going to be a thin yield. But with a widowed mother and younger siblings John was the breadwinner now.

This already dire situation was made worse by a devastating disease among the plough oxen. During the year a virulent cattle plague, which had started in Central Europe, ravaged herds from Devon to Scotland. The dreadful impact, both economic and psychological, comes out in an agonizing account from the time:

At that time there was a great famine and pestilence of humans, especially of the poor. But there was an unheard-of mortality among cattle which continued unabated for several years. And everywhere the poor animals stood still as if lamenting to the people looking on, howling as if in tears because of the terrible pain that gnawed at their inside . . . and then they would fall down and die.

Comparison with recent cattle plagues such as BSE and foot and mouth suggests a striking similarity between the Great Famine epidemic and modern outbreaks of rinderpest. Mortality rates among English herds probably averaged around 60 per cent and in some places they were wiped out. For a population already tormented by hunger, it was a horrendous blow. Between them the peasants of Kibworth had at least twenty plough teams, possibly as many as 200 oxen, and as many more cows and calves: in the autumn and winter of 1316 these must have been devastated.

In both 1316 and 1317 the famine and pestilence were exacerbated by outbreaks of enteric dysentery and typhoid which killed off tens of thousands of people. Writing in Leicester, Henry Knighton describes local conditions:

There was a horrific mortality of humans and a pestilence of animals throughout the kingdom of England; conditions were so bad that the surviving people did not have the wherewithal to cultivate or sow their lands, and every day they were burying as many as they could in improvised cemeteries . . . And so a great ruin seized the English people . . .

The numbed public response can still be felt in the protest poetry of the famine years. 'Sorowe spradde over all ure londe' wrote one balladeer, 'to binde all the mene [poor] men in mourning and in care . . . Come never wrecche into Englelonde that made men more agaste . . .' It would appear that 10 per cent of the English population died between 1315 and 1318 – between a half and three quarters of a million people.

The Great Famine ended in 1318 when, as a London chronicler remembered, 'good yer come agin and good chep of corne'. The poor inevitably had suffered most. The Great Famine was remembered even more keenly than the later plagues of the century, for it left a deeper psychological wound. The merchants had still profited, and supplies had been there which might have staved off calamity had the government been motivated to move them quickly. There had been one rule for the rich, as songs of the time observed: 'For miht is riht, and the lond is laweless.' The famine had been an act of nature but it was also a failure of government and an indictment of the rich. At fairs and festivals over the next years ballad makers would enlarge on this theme of 'the Evil times of King Edward II' and the potentially far-reaching consequences of social breakdown. A distant mirror, perhaps, of our own time.

Though battered through the 1310s and early 1320s, life in the village picked up in the 1330s: the government's poll taxes then give us an image of a community beginning to thrive again, a 'fair field full of folk' as Langland would put it. But this proved to be a cruel illusion: in fact, worse was to come. In 1347 Italian merchant ships brought plague-infected rats from Kaffa on the Black Sea to Constantinople, and on to the seaports of the Mediterranean. From its source between the Caspian and the Crimea a new pestilence ravaged the landmass of Eurasia. A Leicester man, Henry Knighton, who was a boy at the time, provides one of the most vivid descriptions of its arrival in Britain, with an electric sense of its unstoppable momentum: 'It started in Tartary,' he writes, 'and from there swiftly passed into the land of the Arabs; then it entered the land of Greeks, and finally came to the countries of the Christians. And in the year of our lord 1348 . . . it first came into England . . . a great terrible and unheard of affliction . . .'

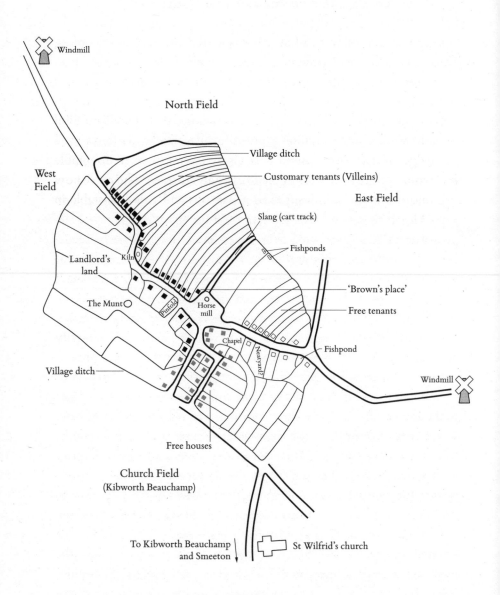

Windmill

North Field

West
Field

Village ditch

Customary tenants (Villeins)

East Field

Slang (cart track)

Fishponds

Landlord's
land

Kiln

'Brown's place'

The Munt

Pinfold

Horse
mill

Free tenants

Chapel

Neayard?

Fishpond

Village ditch

Windmill

Free houses

Church Field
(Kibworth Beauchamp)

To Kibworth Beauchamp
and Smeeton

St Wilfrid's church

Kibworth Harcourt in 1340, before the Black Death: at its greatest
population before the nineteenth century

## The Black Death: 1348–61

Spring 1348 was uneventful in the village, the court books recording the usual round of community business. There were new tenancies to be approved by the Merton steward, Simon Pakeman; fines were imposed by the manor court for encroaching on strips, or for dumping rubbish in the public street, or for making bad ale. Adam Sibil died; he was one of the senior men in the village and had often served as pledge and aletaster (useful perhaps as several of his redoubtable kinswomen were brewsters in the thirties and forties). The reeve now was another Polle: John's son Roger. He was chosen as constable in 1326, clearly tough enough (and canny enough too) to oversee law and order in the often dizzy world of peasant politics where neighbours' frictions over minor strip infringements and building rules, or simply perceived insults, could flare up at any time into feuds. Roger had been reeve for the last twenty years, solid and dependable, but in 1348 he was accused by some of his neighbours of maladministration and when this was referred to the fellows of Merton he stood down.

That summer the Kibworth villagers celebrated the marriage of William Carter and Emma Cok. Will was a villein, the grandson of Ralph, who held seven acres in the North Field and a narrow tenement and garden on Main Street; Emma was a young outsider from Great Glen. After the simple ritual and promises in church ('til dethe us departe' as Emma had to say) there were the usual festivities: sprigs of rosemary and a wheat garland round the bride's head; flowers strewn for their homecoming and a feast at Will's father's house with bride cakes and ale and a 'great noise of basins and drums'. Taking with them the traditional mother's gifts – a goose, a pot for the kitchen and perhaps even a chapbook if Emma could read – the newlyweds took a lease on the cottage next to William's mother, Alice. But in the fine weather that followed the marriage, dark rumours began to circulate from the south coast, perhaps first brought by the Merton bailiff from the college's estates in Surrey and Oxfordshire. Rumours of a new and terrible form of pestilence.

Contemporary witnesses agree that the plague first arrived with an infected Gascon sailor who landed in the little port of Melcombe Regis, in Weymouth Bay. The date was midsummer 1348, just before the feast of John the Baptist (24 June) according to the Grey Friars Chronicle. Ranulf Higden in Chester heard the same story, while Robert of Avebury gives 27 June, and at Malmesbury in Wiltshire they had 7 July. Hints of the plague's creeping progress across the country-side, these differing dates reflect the times when the first signs of infection in human beings were noticed, not when the plague first arrived. Allowing for a period of incubation of six or seven weeks, this suggests that the fatal boat came into Weymouth Bay around 8 May 1348. From then it moved with frightening speed. By the end of the following year the whole of England was in its grip, 500 days to cover 500 miles. That it spread so fast was due in part to the new-found mobility of English society which meant even Kibworth peasants travelled great distances to buy and sell. The commercialization of English society was well-advanced by 1348, even in the countryside, and hidden in tinkers' packs, merchants' bales and clothiers' wagons, the plague pathogen was able to race up the country at almost a mile a day.

Such an alarming pace must have seemed almost supernatural. Though the people did not know it at the time, the key to the infection was the bite of the fleas of the black rat. Fleas were something the peasants lived with every day and once bitten they no doubt thought no more about it after a good scratching, but after a while agonizing buboes began to appear in the groin and armpit. 'These tumours were the first sign,' wrote one eyewitness. 'Tumours that grew as large as an egg or a common apple, and from them this deadly affliction began to propagate itself through the body.' At that point, although some survived, death usually came within three weeks: 'These boils and abscesses on the thighs or in the armpits were the death bringers,' wrote an Irish friar. 'Some died frantic with pain in their head, and others coughing and spitting blood.'

By late 1348, the plague was wreaking havoc in the narrow tenements of London, by now the largest city in Europe, with some 80,000 people. Across the city and its suburbs 'with the aid of certain devout citizens' emergency measures were put in place to cope with the 'innumerable numbers of dead bodies'. The city's largest death pit, under Charterhouse Square, is thought to have held at least 10,000 bodies but was said to contain five times that number. The recent discovery of over 750 skeletons in a Black Death cemetery in East Smithfield, the first to be scientifically examined, has revealed a surprising absence of the elderly, with some 40 per cent being children, and a preponderance of young adults. (Strangely enough, this is the same profile of deaths in the 2009 swine flu epidemic.)

Once London had fallen into its grip, the contagion flowed out of the capital in all directions and soon became an inundation. By the end of 1348 it had spread all round the Cornish peninsula and up the Bristol Channel into the Welsh Marches and the Cotswolds (where the citizens of Gloucester fruitlessly barred their gates to keep it out). It made its way round the south coast and up into East Anglia travelling with merchant ships into the wool ports on the Stour, the Deben and the Orwell. In New Year 1349 undeterred by the cold weather it came by river to Sudbury and the surrounding manors, its path traceable in the court books and rentals of Earls Colne and little Cornard Parva (where six men and three women died – half the village). So remorseless was its advance that it seemed to some as if humanity was being stalked by invisible monsters – like the 'Babewynnes', the demonic creatures with bug-eyes, webbed claws and reptilian tails that populate the margins of their holy books, suggesting the vulnerability of their mental world. For to the fourteenth-century mind the world was indeed populated by phantasmal creatures, and the unseen was palpable and always threatening to burst over the threshold to terrorize the living, to snap them up, and pull them down into the abyss.

By Christmas 1348 the people of Kibworth knew that a monstrous jaw was closing on the open-field villages of Midlands England. Like all big settlements, Kibworth was surrounded by a ditch and hedge, a protection against wolves, defensible too against cattle raiders, or the outlaw gangs who plagued the Midlands, breaking houses at night. The constable and night watchman set bars on the road at the entrances to the village at night, on the king's road to Leicester and on the southern track to Smeeton and Gumley. They could attempt to keep the plague out, as some had tried to do elsewhere, but they had to let in food supplies and they had to let in their own people, the bread-winners who worked away – men like Will Chapman, the small-time travelling businessman who worked between Kibworth, Harborough and Medbourne market, or Adam Boton, who traded with William Falconer the horse dealer and broker at Lutterworth Fair. And then there was Brown the draper who bought bales of cloth over in Coventry. By now further alarming news must have arrived from the college bailiff, for that winter the plague ravaged Merton's manor of Cuxham in Oxfordshire with horrendous losses: perhaps half the tenants died. Cuxham was only three days' ride from Kibworth, and in mid-December Kibworth men were down in Oxford. In Harry the Hayward's omen book, the page for January has dark hooded figures spewing poisoned arrows; and this verse:

> The arrew smytes thorow the cloth
> that makus many man wel wroth . . .

The Black Death seems to have reached the village around the beginning of 1349. It was a cold wet New Year and the villeins had to spend extra time out of doors hoeing thistles in sleeting rain, feeding the dregs of their malt and a part of their peas to the starving pigs. It is just possible that Roger Polle's kinsman William was the first to die: his is the only death entered in the court book on St Lucy's Day in mid-December, incurring no death duty 'as he had nothing'. But the first death certainly caused by pestilence is recorded next door in Kibworth Beauchamp in March. Allowing for ten to fifteen weeks from the first infection, then time for the development of symptoms, and the course of the disease to death, this suggests that the first infective fleas arrived in Kibworth at Christmas 1348. Perhaps they were carried in clothes, or bales of cloth or saddle bags belonging to people coming back home for the festival. Or even with young Robert Church, who that December had made a journey to Oxford to plead in person to the fellows to be admitted to a holding of a few acres. Be that as it may, fourteen tenants' deaths are recorded in Kibworth Beauchamp in April. In Kibworth Harcourt though the first list of the dead is not entered until the meeting of the village court on St George's Day, 23 April, by which time the villages were in the grip of a nightmare. We have to imagine the dead rats in the streets and yards, sick villagers in agony with swellings and pustules; those suffering from pneumonic forms spewing blood; young children dying in their dozens; the desperate vicar, John Sibil, struggling to minister to his flock while knowing he was himself dying. While in a villein tenement on Main Street, the village midwife perhaps helped Robert Polle's newly widowed wife Alice give birth to a baby son.

The court meeting was chaired by the new reeve, John Church, perhaps in the open to avoid the 'infected air' which it was believed one might breathe fatally when in close proximity to the stinking and swollen plague bodies. With his curates Will Polle and John Palmer, John (who had just buried his father) now recorded the deaths of the previous few weeks. Between the New Year and April, forty-two deaths had been registered; two more in the August village court (with another four a year or so later). Among the dead were many familiar names: the newlywed Emma Cok and her mother-in-law Margaret, old Mr Heynes (village clerk for the last two decades), the Clerkes, the Alots, Alice Carter, Agnes Aron, John Church senior, Agnes Polle, Rob Polle (whose 'son is too young to inherit so his plot is taken into custody'), Nicholas Polle (whose lands were confiscated 'because he is a felon') and 'Godwine' – perhaps this is the reclusive John Godwine who had been tonsured without licence over thirty years back but had now in middle age returned to the village. It was a bright sunny late April in Leicestershire that year, but as someone observed at the time 'it seemed then as if the world would end.'

The deaths recorded in the rolls are only landholders and tenants, so to this number we must add an unspecified number of women, a generation of infants and young children, and also many of the landless men and women, the piecework labourers, pea-pickers and itinerants in their hovels up on the village edge by the windmill field, before we can reach a full estimate of the death toll. Among the dead too was the vicar, John Sibil, and his sister Constance. In time of plague vicars of course had the most dangerous job, tending the dying, administering the last sacrament, and trying to organize help and care for the most vulnerable survivors. (This is one of the few jobs that can be pinned down across the country as a whole – vicars suffered about 50 per cent mortality.)

As a microcosm of the great pestilence, the story of Kibworth Harcourt in particular puts this great event in the sharpest focus: with approximately 70 per cent, and possibly more, of its population dying, the death toll is unsurpassed in any court roll so far examined in Britain for the Black Death. Why these figures are so astonishingly high is hard to say. Was it because the village was on the main Leicester–London road? Was Kibworth already a place with inns where outsiders lodged as they did through the late medieval and early modern periods? How did Smeeton in the south of the parish avoid such heavy losses? Perhaps in the end it was simply bad luck.

That April the reeve and manor officials of the village court tried to keep routine and order, as people often do when faced with an irremediable catastrophe. The college steward, Simon Pakeman, and the reeve went through the list of dead tenants, listed vacant holdings and then invited survivors to take on the empty plots, offering them first to the relatives of the dead if there was no legal heir, and then putting it to the vote. Amazingly tenants were still found to fill all the vacant tenements, with some survivors taking advantage of the situation to acquire more land on favourable terms, their bargaining position sufficient to dictate to the Merton fellows and get them to waive the entry fines. When no immediate member of a family survived, the villagers elected the new tenants from among rival bidders and claimants: a novel procedure devised by the court in the face of conditions which had never arisen before. Many more men were eager to acquire land, so for the first time widows found themselves under pressure to remarry: half a dozen in the decade after 1348, some subject to fierce bargaining.

As demand for houses lessened in the village, plenty were left empty and a number converted into farm buildings and storage barns. Small properties attracted speculative buying: William Marnham for example took on two cottages in 1351 at a reduced rent from Merton, and then in 1354 three more; perhaps William was using them for the produce of his gardens or renting to incomers. It was the first indicator of what the long-term social effects of the catastrophe might be.

In Merton library today, under the warm red wooden polygonal roof, the rolls of Kibworth accounts take us through the balance sheet, 'the recknynge' as they would have said in the fourteenth century, in the spidery hands of Roger Polle and Heynes the village clerk, and John Church junior. The names of the dead cover two crumpled and stained membranes, in faded brown ink; crossed out and replaced by a sharper quill in darker ink. To the total of forty-four tenants who died in 1349, if we allow wives and children and landless labourers, then probably between 150 and 200 people died altogether. Add the other villages in the parish, Kibworth Beauchamp and Smeeton Westerby (for which full accounts don't survive), then upwards of perhaps 500 perished in this one small place – proportionally the highest loss known in any English village.

As for the disposal of the dead, the smell it was said 'could not be borne as a man walked by the open death pits'. The new vicar purchased a triangular field out on the Harborough road which the bishop licensed for a new cemetery, as was done all over the country. There, village tradition says, the dead of Kibworth were interred. If other death pits are anything to go by, the survivors were so scared of infection from the dead that they even left purses full of money untouched. The mound is still unploughed today.

What chance did one have to survive, and what if anything could the village doctor, Robert, have done about it, if he was still alive in 1349? Despite the best efforts of fourteenth-century surgeons, including Guy de Chauliac, who survived the plague and wrote a book about it, the fact is that our medieval ancestors had no idea how the infection was transmitted. They could distinguish between the bubonic and pneumonic varieties; they could observe the swelling of the buboes in the groin, thighs and armpits (these were the lymph nodes – the first line of defence against micro-organisms invading the body). But though they must have seen dying rats everywhere, and must have noticed that as the rats died the rat fleas aggressively turned on their human hosts, the clues were never put together. That had to wait until the Indian Plague Research Commission of Bombay in 1905. Then as millions were dying of bubonic plague in western India, the British medical team recruited a leading entomologist, an expert on insects, suspecting a connection between human infection and the presence of dead rats in and around the plague houses. Eventually they were able to prove that the agent of transmission, the vector, was the rat flea itself. The black rat lived around medieval people, just as it did in the packed shanties of Edwardian Bombay; houses, granaries, barns and mills are its favourite homes, just as grain is its favourite food. The IPRC showed that infection was from rats to humans, not (as the medievals believed) from humans to humans. The rat flea is a bloodsucker; the plague pathogen, which has much in common with a virus, is created by a blockage in the stomach of the flea, which makes it mad with hunger and causes it to regurgitate fresh blood and faeces into the bite wound. In 50–60 per cent of cases the plague bacterium eventually succeeds in overwhelming the lymphatic system and then bursts out into the bloodstream from the buboes. When that happens the victim has only a one-in-five chance of surviving.

Investigation of the Indian epidemic and its aftermath also established how the plague spread so fast from the city into the countryside. The people who carried the infective rat fleas in their clothing or in their bags or bales of cloth were often rural villagers who worked away but who fled from the plague in the city and came back home for safety. The same no doubt was also true in 1348 in Kibworth.

In Kibworth the story of one villein family can stand for all its people. The Polles had served in the village hierarchy as reeves, constables and ale-tasters since Henry III's day. Head of the family in 1349, as we have seen, was the one-time reeve Roger Polle, who was sacked by Merton for maladministration just before the arrival of the plague. In his late forties at the time, Roger lived a long life by the standards of the day: he died a peaceful death in 1369 having survived the Great Famine and the Black Death. His three sons, Robert, Nicholas and William, also survived the horrors of 1349 – a remarkable survival record for his household. Why, one wonders? Was it pure chance, or had Roger followed the later peasant wisdom about fumigating barns and houses and hunting down any rat as soon as it is seen near the house?

Roger's wider kin though were decimated by the plague. Two of his brothers, Robert and Nicholas, and his cousin Robert died in the first Black Death of 1349 along with his cousin Hugh Polle and his kinswoman Mabel. The next year at the tail end of the pestilence

Roger's third brother, William, also died. In the 1361 outbreak his cousin William and William's son Nicholas perished, while cousin Hugh's son Will went in the 1376 outbreak. Of these other branches of the family, only brother Robert's son, Nicholas, survived 1349 as a babe in arms. Young Nicholas lived till the end of century with his wife Felicia (born in the plague year; her name means 'the fortunate'), but if they had children, none is known to have survived. Roger's line then were the sole Polle survivors of the century.

The Polle family story is the tale of many families all over medieval England. They bred and multiplied in the boom time of the thirteenth century and entered the fourteenth century in great shape with four solid branches of the old family tree. But only sturdy Roger the reeve survived that generation. Of his three sons only Will and his wife Emma had children, and their descendants can be traced for eight generations in the village down to the seventeenth century, when the male line died out and the last Polle daughter married into the Clerke family. But not everyone is recorded in the Merton documents; some younger sons miss out because they left the village to marry and work elsewhere. In the Tudor period a Kibworth Polle became a leather worker in Harborough, where his kin thrived, another married the daughter of a yeoman farmer next door in Great Glen, and astonishingly some of their descendants still live in the area today, including one Polle who has returned to the ancestral home in Kibworth.

Back in modern Kibworth the bailiff's house where they lived for a time still stands on its ironstone plinth, with a frame of fourteenth-century timbers in its central hall. In the sitting room it has what the medieval carpenters called a 'dragon's tail' fanning out over the fireplace; and traces of soot in the hall roof which may be from the open fire in the days after the Black Death. There are surely few better examples of the tenacity of traditional English yeoman families, husbanding their patrimony in one small part of the countryside; loyal to what one Tudor testator in his will called 'the dear familiar place'. Between the 1260s and the seventeenth century, in all their property dealings, the Polles moved only a few yards along Main Street – and then back again.

# 11. Rebels and Heretics

After the huge disruption of the Black Death it would be easy to focus on the material life of the villagers, to look at the economy and labour relations in order to explain the dramatic transformations that now took place in English society. But there was a deeper reaction to famine and plague which became apparent in the next few decades: in the immediate aftermath of the Black Death, we can see the first signs of the spiritual, religious and psychological changes that would play their part in changing England from a Catholic to a Protestant state, and from a feudal communal order to a capitalist secular society – the first country in the world to be so.

These are the deeper undercurrents of English medieval history, the long-term changes that underlie the spectacular ephemera of events – the Hundred Years War, the brief but savage flare-up of violence in the Peasants' Revolt. Such events are often only symptoms of what is happening below the surface, and on the heels of the famines and plagues of the time now came profound social, economic and religious changes. As always, the villagers of Kibworth were involved in these transformations. Heretic preachers from the village wandered the roads of the Midlands preaching a revolutionary creed, and ultimately a dozen local men marched down to join a rebel army attempting to overthrow the king in London, where some of their number suffered a cruel death at the executioner's hands.

## A new vicar

The remarkable tale of Kibworth's involvement in the spread of heresy and dissent begins, at least as far as it is discernible in the records, almost twenty-five years before, at the end of February 1380 on the eve of the Peasants' Revolt, with the arrival of a new vicar in the village.

Riding up from Oxford to Kibworth that February, Thomas Hulman had much to reflect upon. The mood in the countryside was dangerous, and recent rumours warned of vagabond robbers on the roads and of armed gangs – lordless and landless men – preying on villages with frightening violence and random killings. The journey to Leicestershire was relatively short though, easily managed in two days, and the road was far less fraught with danger than the route to the college's northern estates. In the fourteenth century it took seven or eight days to the Merton manor at Ponteland, north of the Tyne, and the traveller was advised to ride in a large party and take weapons with him. The Merton accounts show that when their fellows headed into Northumberland they stocked up on crossbow bolts. But even though it was only seventy miles to Leicestershire it was not entirely safe and Hulman probably thought it best to ensure he had some spare bowstrings before he left Oxford, with a bow and a short dagger in the hands of his 'garcon'.

Thomas Hulman – MA and bachelor in theology to give him his full due – was a Merton man. Appointed vicar of Kibworth by his fellows, he was a West Midlander, and had already enjoyed a solid university career, matriculating fourteen years earlier in 1366, the year after another Merton man whom he knew, and who was later famously accused of heresy, John Aston. By now Hulman was probably in his mid-thirties and had been a fellow of Merton College for fourteen years, having been made a junior proctor of the university in 1370, the college bursar in 1373–4 and sub-warden in 1377. His career had gone well and he could look forward to a secure living as a bachelor of theology and a lawyer, perhaps even rising to enjoy royal favour.

Across the country the national mood was edgy, a sense that the pressure was growing, the political barometer rising. The old king, Edward III, the first English ruler to demonstrate real senility while in office, was dead and the young Richard II, a callow juvenile, had made a disastrous start. The government's unpopularity was reflected in a flood of popular ballads, songs and pamphlets, and there were reports of widespread discontent among the peasantry, especially in the richest parts of the country, the south-east, Essex and the wool villages of East Anglia. The fourteenth century was the first golden age of English political poetry, especially in the vernacular. 'In this wicked age England is perished . . .' wrote one balladeer, 'the world is turned upside down.' There were songs lambasting the friars and their lives of 'riote and ribaudry', and the attitudes of ordinary people to the medieval Church and the papacy were shaded by talk of privilege and corruption: 'covetousse bishops and proude prelates of the Churche', as one said, 'who only longed for possessions and temporal goods'. Such songs and conversations one might have heard in any of the coaching inns from Brackley to Daventry, complaints about the clergy and their expenses, their corruption and even (a peculiarly modern preoccupation) their sexual misconduct. 'If I had a house and a faire daughter or a wife,' it was joked, 'I would never let a smooth-talking friar in to shrive them' . . . 'er he a childe put hir with-inne – and perchaunce two at ones!'

Anti-clerical grumblings could be heard in any town in England in 1380. What was even more prevalent and striking was the seething discontent among the workforce, expressed in the exponential rise in labour disputes and peasant agitation. This kind of class conflict had been common for the last century or so. But now it was becoming organized. In 1377 the courts were inundated with cases in which peasants were taking their landlords to court. Those hostile to the peasants' movements grumbled that their actions were so widespread that they must have been centrally coordinated, specifically designed to clog up the system, making it impossible for the law courts to thwart individual actions and to contain the grievances. From that year cases contesting the rights of landlords became so widespread that talk now spread of far greater conflict, of massive social disruption and even of revolution. That year, the time of the first introduction of the hated poll tax, one Londoner who was no friend of the peasants was full of dark forebodings: 'Slothfulness has put the lords to sleep so they are not on their guard against the madness of the commons: they will allow that nettle to grow which is too violent in its nature.'

To experienced observers the crisis was coming fast:

He who observes the present time will fear that soon this impatient nettle will very suddenly sting us before it can be contained by justice or the law.

There are three things that will produce merciless destruction if they get out of control: one is a surging flood; another is a raging fire; but the third is the common multitude: for they will not be stopped by either reason or restraint.

Such were the views too at high table in Oxford, where the new colleges derived much of their income as landlords; in the ecclesiastical courts, for along with the king the Church was the greatest landlord in England; and in the law courts in London, where Hulman had travelled on business as Merton's junior bursar. So there was much to chew over on the road as he travelled towards Kibworth. The journey was usually made by the college agents three or four times a year, when making the annual audit, so he was setting out on a familiar road – 'going out of town', as they said, rather as today's students and dons might say 'up' to Oxford and 'down' to the country. The countryside he passed through was dotted with new spires, signs of the upsurge in popular religion after the Black Death. It was dotted too with gallows, for the lord of the manor in every place had the right to erect a gallows and try peasants, rebels, thieves and bandits. No one journeyed far in the fourteenth century without seeing a hanged man twisting in the wind, his eyes pecked by crows.

The journey involved one overnight stop, unless there was a reason to dawdle, and this stop was usually at Daventry, where the Merton accounts rolls note the customary expenses of a traveller on horseback: fodder for the horses, bed and candles, bread, beer, eggs, salted herring, codlings, nuts and salt; and if you were lucky, 'little fish' fresh from the local fishponds, served at the inns along the road.

The second day's ride took Hulman and his servant across Watling Street into the old Danelaw country at Gibbet Hill above the River Swift, then north-east through rolling countryside that since the Black Death had become the backdrop to many deserted villages – Bittesby, Stormsworth, Westrill, Knaptoft Misterton and Pulteney (the last a pleasant watering place for the fellows earlier in the century, on their long northern journeys). With an early start, they could be in Lutterworth (a few miles south-east of Kibworth) by mid-morning, its popular market on the River Swift much frequented by Leicestershire folk, and where the timber yards were stocked with wood from the Warwickshire Arden. Riding into Church Gate he saw a well-built town with good timber houses, the homes of prosperous local merchants. In the centre stood the fine church of St Mary, and on that chill February morning had Hulman walked inside and gazed up above the chancel arch he would have seen a great painted 'Doom', a vision of the Last Judgement, small white figures rising out of their tombs against a deep crimson background the colour of the stomach lining of hell, the ghostlike figures of the damned falling screaming into the abyss. And then even higher, separated by a dark black-blue wavy strip, the figure of Christ sitting on his rainbow throne surrounded by angels. The whole represented a stark warning of the ever-present threat of damnation, the promise of bliss and the fruit of sin. As Hulman would have said: 'Forgif us ure gyltas.'

The vicar here at St Mary's in 1380 was one of the most remarkable and controversial figures in England, indeed a man known across Europe: John Wycliffe. A former fellow of Merton, and no doubt already well-known to Hulman, Wycliffe was then living under government supervision. Prematurely aged now, thin and frail, John Wycliffe was an unlikely figure to have convulsed the English state and Church, arousing such hatred that the Pope had recently been moved to condemn him (and eventually after his death, in posthumous revenge, would command that his remains be dug up and burned, and his ashes cast into the River Swift).

Wycliffe – his family originated in the north Yorkshire village of Wycliffe on Tees – had enjoyed a glittering academic career: master of Balliol, fellow of Merton. He was still perhaps only in his fifties (though in the Middle Ages fifty of course was old), but his health was now deteriorating and he was soon to be partially paralysed by a stroke. As if he knew he didn't have long to live (for such strokes often announce themselves in minor attacks over the preceding months or even years) he was working ceaselessly, arguing against the main intellectual and theological currents of his time. A pool of pupils like John Aston in Leicester and the mysterious John Purvey, who lived with him in Lutterworth ('the fourth hieresiarch' as a hostile Leicester chronicler called him), were engaged alongside him in translating, copying and disseminating his works.

Among his pupils Wycliffe's 'unblemished walk in life' aroused great loyalty and affection. 'I indeed clove to no one closer than to him,' said one, William Thorpe: 'he was the wisest and most blessed of men whom I have ever met. From him I learned in truth what the Church of Christ is and how it should be ruled and led.' For Hulman then, that February, it was an opportunity perhaps to pay his respects to a much-loved old teacher.

Like most Oxbridge dons, Wycliffe liked a good meal and a good conversation, and there was much to discuss. Over a long and eventful career based on acute analysis of the biblical texts, Wycliffe had grown increasingly disillusioned with the Roman Catholic Church of his day and the vast edifice of scholastic theology that sustained the medieval ideologies of power, both spiritual and temporal. All these he felt had become both real and invisible chains on the minds of the people. Wycliffe believed simply that the scriptures were the only source of belief and doctrine, that the claims of the papacy in Rome were unhistorical ('there is no pope in the Bible,' he would say) and that the monastic orders, with their vast wealth and property, had become huge centres of privilege which were now irredeemably corrupt. He asserted that at the local level the widespread corruption of the priesthood invalidated the office, their actions and even the sacrament itself. In short, he said the Church must return to its roots, and the institution and its priests should be as poor as they were in the days of the apostles. In his person then, what had started out as an academic controversy, adjudicated in scholar's Latin, had become a national issue, whose implications for the ordinary people were very great indeed.

Wycliffe was not alone in his reflections, for there were parallel movements in Europe at this time, but in the Middle Ages these were dangerous paths to walk. Wycliffe himself was protected by wealthy and influential patrons like John of Gaunt, the Earl of Lancaster, but since 1374 a suspicious government had banished him to what amounted to a supervised internal exile in Lutterworth. There, convinced of his own rectitude, he had continued to preach against the

whole religious establishment, his words imbued with the quality of
his quietly spoken but scintillating lectures in Oxford and the sparkling sermons that had packed them into city churches in London,
where people of all classes had gathered to hear 'the wonderful things
that streamed forth from his mouth'. Such eloquence and intellectual
rigour had convinced a generation of educated scholars, learned
'clerks', to challenge the attitudes and behaviour of the Church.
The new ideas had percolated into the consciousness of the mercantile and artisanal classes – goldsmiths, drapers, parchment makers,
scriveners – who had every reason to resist seeing their wealth go
into the hands of a bloated Church while taking instruction on personal morality from a venal priesthood. In 1377 Wycliffe had been
condemned by the Pope himself for 'ideas erroneous and dangerous
to Church and state', and at home the orthodox decried his 'blasphemy, arrogance and heresy'. During this period Wycliffe's *Book on
the End of Time* contained some of his boldest flights of imagination,
sacred predictions for the time after the flawed old order had passed,
that even distantly seem to foreshadow a secular democracy as the
predestined fruition of Christ's mission on earth. What Wycliffe
envisaged was a new kind of commonwealth, and in very different
hands that idea was soon to be voiced too in violent revolution.

These were heavy debates that wore heavily on him now. Sitting
across the dining table in the old medieval rectory at Lutterworth
towards the end he was 'emaciated in body, and well-nigh devoid of
bodily strength', but still 'in temper quick, in mind clear, and in moral
character unblemished'. Unremittingly sharp towards his enemies,
like many a brilliant don he was cuttingly sure of his own views, but
never offensive: 'in demeanour and conduct he was very innocent,'
said one who knew him. Such qualities had inspired wide devotion.
'Many important people conferred with him', it was said. 'They loved
him dearly, wrote down his sayings, and followed his way of life.'

That February in Lutterworth, Wycliffe was still writing and
preaching. In fact he had never been on such a creative roll. His current project, tilting at the Pope's ban on vernacular translations of the
sacred books, was his English translation of the Bible, which would
be revised by his loyal pupil John Purvey. Thinking and writing

ceaselessly, he had produced an incredible amount of material (thirty volumes so far in the modern printed edition of his collected works). And although he himself could not easily travel, his ideas were spread (as he had envisaged) by a network of loyal friends and pupils, and once out there in the world, of course, his ideas were beyond his control.

Wycliffism was not just a dry scholastic argument. It was about the Christian way of life, and that is why his teachings appealed not only to intellectuals who followed the bold and challenging flights of his logic, but also to the artisanal and commercial classes in the cities, and the better-off free peasants in the Midlands who were moved by a vision of the Church purified and simplified, in which there was room for individual thought and expression – in effect, freedom of conscience. In his last years Wycliffe attacked the whole Church and the social hierarchy of the land, while growing more and more sure that the Pope and the Antichrist were virtually one and the same. 'The Church', he said, 'with Christ at its head offers one path to salvation. The Pope cannot say that he is its head, he cannot even say he is a member unless he follows the life of Jesus and the apostles.'

Although Wycliffe himself was not a social revolutionary, others at the time were in no doubt about the radical potential of his teaching. John Ball, the voice of the Peasants' Revolt (who made the famous sermon 'When Adam delved and Eve span who was then the gentleman?'), was said by the Leicester historian Henry Knighton to have been a disciple of Wycliffe. Directly or indirectly Ball took the social implications of Wycliffe's theories to their natural conclusion, a link that was understood in some quarters, where Wycliffe was virulently hated. The chronicler Thomas Walsingham unleashed a tirade of anger against the old man, calling him 'an instrument of the devil, an enemy of the Church, a sower of confusion in the common people, the very image of a hypocrite, the idol of heretics, author of schism, spreader of lies . . . a malicious spirit destined for the abode of darkness'.

So these were dangerous times for the kingdom of man and the kingdom of God. Men like Thomas Hulman shared a sense of impending crisis. Perhaps he felt uneasy as he said his goodbyes and set out from Lutterworth on the two-hour ride on a cross-country track through Peatling Parva and Bruntingthorpe, then through open fields across to Kibworth past the great post mill at Arnesby. From Smeeton Hill he got his first sight of the new spire of Kibworth, a great landmark for any traveller, soaring 160 feet above the peasants' houses, one of the finest smaller parish churches in England and long a source of pride to Kibworth people, the familiar landmark during their travels to the markets in the south of the shire, and a proud symbol of recovery by villagers who had poured their own resources into the rebuilding of their church – Christ's one true Catholic Church.

## Kibworth in 1380

The village where Thomas Hulman arrived at the end of February 1380 had seen many changes since the first great outbreak of the Black Death in 1349–50. The catastrophic fall in population had been arrested, despite further heavy losses from the plague in 1361, and again only the previous year in 1379. The village birth rate had shot up in the last few years, and the streets were full of children as he rode through Smeeton. The open fields were coming out of winter now, their furlongs still dusted with snow, the ploughmen preparing their gear as the first ploughing of spring corn was about to begin. The other side of Smeeton, Hulman passed through the village of dependent serfs and villeins owned by the Beauchamp family, their huge demesne yards on the right-hand side of the track, where the noise of a hundred plough oxen echoed in the barns; then down a little valley, across the stream and up to Kibworth church.

The village church stood, as it still stands, on open rising ground, on 'a considerable eminence' with a big graveyard and a clump of old yew trees; the medieval rectory was then on slightly higher land to the south. Surrounded today by housing estates, the church has lost some of its aspect now, the ridge between the villages straddled by the A6, though the land still shelves away to the south where the railway line now runs, its track formerly the bed of a little stream which was dammed to create the medieval fishponds that fed the peasants of

Beauchamp. The main structure of the church is much as it was in Hulman's day except that it is missing its late-fourteenth-century tower and steeple, which collapsed in the nineteenth century, today's imposing tower rebuilt in 1832. But the nave of the church survives with its wide aisles, flowing tracery and fourteenth-century octagonal font, giving a sense of the wealth of the parish at the height of the Middle Ages when Hulman was vicar and wandering Lollard priests from the village, such as the notorious Walter Gilbert, 'Walter of Kibworth', spread Wycliffe's seditious message through the villages of Leicestershire and the East Midlands.

The church is still entered by two fourteenth-century porches with their original iron-studded oak doors. According to village tradition, the south door is for Beauchamp and the north for Harcourt, and old Kibworth folk still tell of those who even in the recent past would not use the other door 'even for a wedding or a funeral'. At the east end the chancel is still essentially as Hulman knew it: the chancel from the early thirteenth century, green-tinged, local ironstone, the inside whitewashed as it has been since the Reformation, with a small, worn, thirteenth-century priest's doorway with simple dogtooth moulding through which Hulman would have left the church to make his way across the graveyard to his rectory. Today's church is thus essentially the same structure where Hulman and his predecessors spoke their sermons, donned their chasubles and prepared the Eucharist, wine and wafer for the Mass. A social as well as spiritual centre (in whose porches for example leases and contracts were made and charters drawn up by the village scribe), the church was the focus of life for the old village families we have met in the story since the 1280s, the setting for the rituals of their births, deaths and marriages, and the festivals of their agricultural calendar.

The interior of the church was richly ornamented, as befitted a village with a large and (by 1380) wealthy population. At festival time when the harvest had been gathered the nave was decorated with sheaves of corn, its columns were twisted with branches and flowers and the whole church wreathed with incense; for the peasants after weeks of backbreaking toil, going inside was to enter into a magical space. That colourful, glittering, almost garish world of medieval piety was swept away in the Tudor Reformation, but some of its structural features help us conjure up the world of the medieval village community. The nave, of course, like that in all English churches was originally open. The people, Nick Polle, Emma Gilbert, Adam Brown and the other characters in the village story, stood, knelt or prostrated themselves on the cold flagged floor. Surviving fragments hint at the elaboration and opulence of the decoration around them: the rich pigments of the murals, the painted panels of the saints, glowing in the lamp light during the evening Mass in winter. In the fourteenth century there was a two-stage rood loft above the chancel arch with stairs running up from the south aisle to a gallery for musicians and participants in the Easter pageants; above them hung a large painted wooden crucifix showing the suffering Christ with gruesome realism. This 'holy rood' above the chancel arch was perhaps made by a local carpenter, and the painting of heaven and hell on the wall above could also have been done locally, perhaps by the Kibworth man who turns up in the Merton documents as John le Peyntour.

Below the rood Hulman stood to speak his sermons, to sing and speak the Mass and administer the sacrament, helped by his chaplains and churchwardens. On big festivals when all the lights were lit he would raise his arms to chant the Gloria, one of the familiar comforting rituals sung in Latin but known to all the villagers, even to the unlettered. Behind him, dividing chancel and nave, was a delicate screen of polished oak; though repaired and restored by the Victorians this is still in part the original from the late fourteenth century, its traceried tops deep red with the wear, and the polish, of the centuries. In Hulman's day the open frames in the screen were filled with painted panels depicting the saints in bright colours with gilded haloes. These might have been paid for by local benefactors, well-off farmers like the Polles, Heyneses and Chapmans, who in the last few years had all gifted plots of land for the local chantry chapel. On the screen the congregation were reminded of the old stories that went back before the Conquest to the conversion of the English by St Augustine, to St Wilfrid, the father of the church, and local saints like St Wistan of Wistow. The cult of the Virgin Mary was strong in the village as everywhere in medieval England and here she had her own shrine as 'Our Lady of Kibworth', who was remembered by parishioners in their wills: perhaps she had a 'miraculous image' with its own local story. Pewter pilgrim badges have been picked up recently by metal detectorists in Kibworth, showing the faint image of Mary with her lilies, which perhaps had been brought back by villagers who had made the pilgrimage to the shrine at Walsingham where Mary was shown seated on the throne of wisdom, cradling the baby Jesus in her left arm, and holding a sceptre of lilies in her right hand. These 'toyes' were now condemned as idolatry by Wycliffe and his followers but the traditional Christian story was ingrained in the lives of most of the village community. Their cultural and spiritual references were the tales of English Christianity: Thomas of Canterbury, George and the Dragon, St Helena and the True Cross, stories whose calendrical commemoration marked their year, and whose exemplary heroes and heroines inhabited their lives.

## Traditions and controversies

Such things – images, statues, icons, paintings, the great wooden cross above the chancel arch, the painting of naked souls emerging blinking from the mouth of hell – were all viewed with hostility by Wycliffe's followers, who attacked the ludicrousness, indeed blasphemy, of worshipping a wooden statue or a relic: 'If the cross of Christ, the nails, spear, and crown of thorns are to be honoured,' they said, 'then why not honour Judas's lips, if only they could be found?' Indulgences, confessions, penances and chantries too were seen as latter-day corruption, as was the practice of money changing hands for prayers and forgiveness. These were merely 'false mawmentaryes' to extort money from simple people 'to sustain their idlness and luxury'.

After the Black Death such speculations were all part of the mood of the time. There was much meditation on the system of church patronage and on those rituals which people could use to approach God. Nearly thirty years before, some of the villagers had founded a prayer guild in Kibworth Harcourt and set up a trust to pay a chantry priest to say prayers for the dead. There was generally a strong devotional current in the hearts and minds of villagers as witnessed by the free chapels – run by chaplains, *capellani*, drawn from the village families – that were found in both Kibworths and in Smeeton. Local concerns were echoed in the broader literature, and at this time there was a surge of poetry about the crucifixion itself along with devout prayers, songs and jingles of heartrending directness, Jesus singing a lullaby to calm his grief-stricken mother, or telling the tale of his own crucifixion in vigorous dialect to his own loyal English people:

> My folk now answer me and say what is my guilt.
> What more might I more have done for thee
> That I ne have fulffilth?

In the late fourteenth century an outpouring of books of devotion, manuals for anchorites and anchoresses, religious handbooks and guides, popular songs and a spiritual popular poetry ran alongside the political agitation with deep antecedents in Old and Middle English devotional poetry. In all this the crucifixion was the core image:

> Jesus my sweet love my lemmon swete
> That diyedest on the Rode Tree
> With all my might I thee beseche
> For thy woundes two and three.

This devotional fervour with its intense psychological identification burst out in great popular pilgrimages and festivals, and was reflected in the main liturgy of the Church. The period between the Great Famine and the Reformation saw the heyday of traditional English Christianity as great festivals like Candelmas and Corpus Christi, along with pilgrimage and Pentecost processions, grew in popularity. This was the village world that Hulman entered, a world of popular piety, a rich imaginal world, but one also bounded by a plethora of concrete rules and regulations – tithes, fines and the payment of money from poor villagers to the wealthy mother church in Lincoln.

There are gift books still in Lincoln Cathedral's wooden library list-ing donations from all over the vast diocese from villages like Kibworth. Up to the Reformation the old families of the village like the Polles, the Carters and the Colemans can be seen leaving dona-tions in their wills of a few pence to Mary of Lincoln – the mother Church – and to their own church of St Wilfrid, 'in the name of the blessed Virgin Mary and the whole blessed company of heaven'.

But a new current discernible after the Black Death questioned all this, compounded by a growing literature of complaint reflecting ordin-ary people's increasing awareness of the law and their ability to use it. Vernacular poets of the period spoke of 'the evil times of King Edward II', the corruption of the friars and the ostentation of the rich. The world was changing. These were themes that Wycliffe sharpened, sensitized and formalized, and to which he gave intellectual fibre. But Wycliffe also championed the use of the vernacular in religion too, a split between the use of English and the use of French or Latin. A cen-tury before, clerics of Leicester Abbey had mocked the peasants of Stoughton near Kibworth as 'the most stupid people in the world', list-ing their uncouth names, mocking their women, using colloquial English to sneer at the vernacular speech of 'senseless rustics' in a Latin poem which ended on a resounding French tag, asserting that the status quo should go on for ever. But now English was on the rise and despite the great affection the mass of the English had for the traditions of the Church, its stories and the customs and the beauty of its liturgy, as with all working people, it still came down in the end to their hard-earned money, to tithes, dues, labour and power, and to the empowerment offered by the rapid spread of literacy. It was quite a time then for a Merton man to take up this living in the heart of open-field England, in a village where all these political, religious and psychological conflicts would come to the surface in the next forty years.

## The Peasants' Revolt

Hulman took up his duties as vicar in the rectory at Kibworth in spring 1380. He immediately found the villagers up in arms about the conduct of the government. The previous year an unpopular poll tax had been levied on the village; in 1380 another one was raised at a flat rate for rich and poor of 5d. Soon a third one was announced for 1381. In an atmosphere of vocal complaint, letters from peasant organizations were circulated calling for concerted action, and only a year after Hulman took up his new job the protests culminated in a full-scale rebellion – the Peasants' Revolt.

The wider background to the uprising is to be found in the social and economic conditions after the Black Death. The huge drop in the population left labour at a premium. Landowners like Merton and the Beauchamps at Kibworth faced the choice of increasing wages and competing for workers or letting plots and tenements go unused. Inevitably in the aftermath of the plague wages for labourers rose and inflation grew across the economy as goods became more expensive to produce. The landlords suddenly found themselves struggling in the labour market. Widespread anger and class-hatred among the elites comes out in the poet John Gower's very modern-sounding comments on labourers and their attitudes: 'they are sluggish, they are scarce, and they are grasping. For the very little they do they demand the highest pay.' The government had first attempted to prevent this in the first year of the outbreak with the 1349 Ordinance of Labourers, which effectively marks the start of English labour laws (and an ordinance, it is worth remembering, only repealed in 1863). Then in 1351, King Edward III summoned Parliament to pass the Statute of Labourers, which attempted to curb the peasants' demands for better terms of employment by pegging wages to pre-plague levels and restricting the mobility of labour. The statute also required all able-bodied men and women to work and introduced penalties for those who remained idle. The poll taxes of 1377–81 were thus imposed amidst a growing and nationwide sense of injustice in labour relations.

The revolt itself began in Essex at the village of Fobbing on 31 May 1381, when local gentry and free peasants refused to pay the tax. From then events moved with extraordinary speed, with different areas of revolt apparently in touch with each other. The Kentish rebels reached Blackheath outside London on 12 June. Two days later they met the young king and his councillors and demanded the sacking of unpopular councillors, the abolition of serfdom and, most enigmatically, 'that there should be no law within the realm save the Law of Winchester' – possibly meaning the Statute of Winchester in 1285, but more likely a golden-age reference by the peasant leaders to the days of Alfred the Great and his successors, who were viewed nostalgically by English people in the fourteenth century. For Chaucer's friend John Gower, however, the peasants' aspirations were the work of the anti-Christ: 'according to their foolish notions in the future there would be no lords but only kings and peasants.'

While the south-east was in uproar and the government tottering, up in Leicester Henry Knighton vividly conveys the near hysteria that gripped his town, probably as it did in most of England after the astonishing news of the rebels' entry into London. With the Essex rebels gathered at Mile End, the Kentish forces crossed London Bridge and stormed the Tower, beheading the archbishop and the king's chancellor. With the fate of the king himself in the balance, it must have seemed as if the whole order, 'justified and planked by God' according to the sermon makers, was about to collapse.

While things hung in the balance in London a messenger rode north through Kibworth towards Leicester, racing to tell the mayor that the Midland rebels were approaching and that their forces had reached Market Harborough. 'A detachment of the impious mob from London,' Knighton reports, 'would arrive in Leicester the next morning at the first hour of day. The mayor reportedly was most agitated and alarmed, and in a quandary as to what action to take in such a difficult situation. If he decided to resist them he might fail and be killed with his retinue, if he tried to receive them peacefully he might later be judged their accomplice.' That night inside the city walls, he called a meeting of 'neighbours, jurors, and other shrewd men', and eventually they decided to make efforts to defend the town. Knighton describes how the heavily armed force of 1,200 citizens massed outside the city, where for two days they waited fearfully to see what would happen, drilling as they awaited the rebels' approach, sending out mounted scouts down through Kibworth to the Welland to try to gather intelligence on the rebels' movements.

But the rebels never reached Leicester. Somewhere in the area between Harborough and Kibworth they stopped, and it was there perhaps that they got wind of the shattering news from London: the great meeting at Smithfield, the parley of 'the peasants' darling' Wat Tyler with the king, and his killing by the mayor of London. Losing their leader, and faced by a hastily raised levy of 7,000 troops, the peasant army backed off and eventually dispersed. The different local groups were then picked off by the vengeful government. The East Anglian rebels suffered a final bloody defeat at North Walsham in Norfolk on 23 June and soon the purges began, with a horrible fate handed out to the ringleaders. The priest John Ball (whom Knighton saw as Wycliffe's disciple) was executed in Coventry, hanged, drawn and quartered in the presence of the king.

The bitter fallout was chronicled in songs and new rhymes were found for 'the stool' – the executioner's block:

> Man be ware and be no fool;
> Thinke upon the ax, and of the stool!

★

The revolt had unleashed savage class antagonisms and exposed deep fissures between the rulers and the ruled. Despite the way it was depicted by royal chroniclers, the peasants' movement was organized and literate; it harnessed real grievances and probably involved a real programme.

Kibworth Beauchamp and Harcourt as well as Smeeton Westerby seem to have escaped the violence. Whether members of the rebel army in Market Harborough talked to the jurymen and other 'shrewd men' in Kibworth, we don't know, but perhaps for the people of these villages there was no advantage in joining the uprising. Their conditions were better, their circumstances not comparable to those of the peasantry in the villages of Essex or on the Winchester or St Albans estates, whose rage had led to the uprising. On the Merton estates up and down the country there was no great outcry to destroy the records of villeinage – the court rolls rentals and account books. For a century now the peasants in Kibworth Harcourt had been used to dealing with agents from the college, their bailiffs coming up to survey and negotiate, and as events unfolded they would take a different path to economic liberation and personal freedom.

As with all great events, the fallout of the Revolt set many changes in motion, some of them unforeseen, and most intriguing of these is the impact of Wycliffe's ideas among the old families of Kibworth: it is in the years after the revolt that we have our first really detailed evidence of matters of conscience and individual belief among the ordinary people of England, and, remarkably, some of it comes from Kibworth.

## 'I smelle a Lollere in the wynd'

Apparently untouched by the brief violent convulsion of the Peasants' Revolt, Kibworth's village court met that June to deal with the usual business, awarding new tenancies, imposing fines for field infringements and bad brewing, updating the list of runaways. But over the next thirty years other kinds of protest and acts of resistance made themselves felt in the village. Indeed, within months of the revolt a new name appears to describe those who spread heretical ideas, tarred by the brush of rebellion, and they will create a new current in English history which will overwhelm some of the people of Kibworth. They were called Lollards.

The name first appears in 1382 in Oxford. The first person to use it seems to have been an Anglo-Irish cleric called Henry Crumpe, who was duly suspended for committing a breach of the peace. 'Lollard' almost immediately had the force of a dirty word, but it stuck and in the minds of those in power came to cover all English heretics. In 1387 the Bishop of Worcester even used it for heretics in general, 'the disciples of anti-Christ and followers of Mohamet'. About the same time Henry Knighton used it specifically to describe the followers of Wycliffe. Whether the word was new then or had already spent some time unrecorded in the underground is not known. Its meaning has never been determined for certain, but in medieval Flemish or Dutch the word means 'to mumble', which suggests some of the connotations of the seventeenth-century radicals called Ranters. The Lollards would cause a crisis in the English Church and state that was never forgotten; fearing the whole edifice of their power would be shaken, the government would put huge energies into the detection of heresy, employing its agents and informants to 'I smelle a Lollere in the wynd' as Chaucer put it (the poet himself has been suspected of harbouring some sympathy towards the sect).

In the immediate aftermath of the Peasants' Revolt strange rumours spread in the Midlands and East Anglia of itinerant preachers, wearing red wool cloaks, carrying wooden staffs, some even going barefoot as they imagined the early apostles and missionaries of Christ had travelled. Their sermons in taverns and private houses preached Wycliffe's 'pestilential doctrines', which (so it was reported by the authorities) soon led to 'outbreaks and complaints of the commons', and what the medieval scholars called 'insurrectio et schismata in villis'. In London soldiers were brought out into the streets and in May 1382 the new Archbishop of Canterbury initiated a council to look into the increasingly worrying 'divisio et dissensio in Anglia'. In the immediate aftermath of the Peasants' Revolt the heresy was taken very seriously indeed. The teachings of Wycliffe were publicly condemned as seditious, and three leaders of 'the sect of Wycliffe' were detained, one of them a Merton scholar called John Aston who had preached up in Leicestershire. In Canterbury that summer in 'an inquiry against heretics' the new archbishop, William Courtney, 'head of all England, legate of the apostolic seat', set about investigating the spread among a minority of the English priesthood of these 'doctrines of eternal damnation, product of an insane mind . . . doctrines taught both in the schools *and outside* . . . pulling the wool over the people's eyes with sneering sophistry'. Several pupils of Wycliffe who had been active around Leicester, among them the canons Philip Repyngdon and Nicholas Hereford, and the Merton scholars John Aston and Laurence Bedeman were 'strongly suspected of heresy'. At Lambeth in June there was talk of 'conspiracy and confederacy', of a Lollard web all over England.

Unlicensed preachers were said to be spreading Wycliffe's doctrines all over England, and moves against them included a prohibition on teaching and discussing Wycliffite ideas within Oxford University, which had emerged as a centre of Lollard sympathies. A list of twenty-four condemned doctrines was compiled as the suspected or imagined ideological underpinnings of the revolt were examined. And among those summoned was, of all people, Thomas Hulman, the vicar of Kibworth.

## Inquisition at Canterbury

It was in this heated atmosphere that Hulman rode south from Kibworth to Canterbury to be questioned as an associate of Aston, and presumably as a witness to testify against him. Significantly the interrogators were aware that the two men knew each other and that Hulman himself had come into contact with heretical doctrines. On 27 June in the chapel at the archbishop's Kentish manor at Otford, Aston's hearing was held in front of ten theologians and six 'civil doctors', or, as we would say, lawyers. Crucial to the charges was Aston's denial of the presence of Christ's body during the Mass. (It was reported of Aston that he had pointed to a beautiful woman next to him and said that he was more able to see the beauty and presence of God in her face than in the host, the symbol of the Mass.) This was the topic on which in 1379 Wycliffe had written the work which had defined his split with the papacy. The manuscript of the hearing records Aston's disarming evasions on the question:

When I was required specially to say what I felt of this proposition, namely: 'material bread leaves [remains] in the sacrament after the consecration', I make this protestation that I never put nor taught nor preached that proposition, for I wot wil [I know well] that the matter and the speculation thereof passes in height my understanding.

Hulman was then questioned on Aston's views, and in the course of the discussion he appeared to approve of Aston's Wycliffite opinions, and was therefore placed under the necessity of clearing himself before the council. For the Kibworth vicar there was then a long and difficult session in the Chapter House in Canterbury Cathedral on 1 July. In front of nine masters of theology and two secular judges 'from nine in the morning till the second hour after dinner . . . the said master

Hulman was questioned . . .' In the dossier of heresies produced for the archbishop, Hulman's final recantation is preserved:

Guided by my Lord of Canterbury and of one opinion with the advice of his clergy, I now pronounce all these conclusions, together and singly, damnable and heretical and erroneous. And furthermore as my Lord of Canterbury and the other doctors of theology and experts in canonical and civil law with one council of clergy consider these heresies and errors to be damnable, so far as it is in me to do so, I condemn them, protesting myself that I hold and affirm the contrary to their conclusions, and in that faith promise to live and die.

In the face of the archbishop and committee of theologians, Hulman had backed down. It was not perhaps a point on which to risk one's life. Repyngdon and Hereford, on the other hand, regular canons of St Mary's, Leicester, refused to give way and sign the recantation. They were pronounced 'contumacious' and remanded to a fifth congregation at Canterbury, where Hulman himself was made to publicly condemn the twenty-four conclusions. With that he was allowed to go back to the village in time for Lammas and the August harvest.

## Back in Kibworth

How far had the villagers already imbibed these revolutionary ideas? And why did the Lollard heresy find fertile ground among the free peasantry of south Leicestershire? Hulman's role in all this will probably never be recovered, but can be guessed by the extraordinary number of villagers who supported the heresy in the next thirty years. He resumed his duties in the village but his card had been marked in the eyes of his archbishop and his bishop in Lincoln, John Buckingham, who would become an energetic hunter of Lollards. Hulman stayed on in Kibworth till he resigned in December 1385, when an anti-Wycliffite priest was put into the village by Merton, perhaps under pressure from above. But Hulman returned to the village in November 1387 and spent two more years there before apparently leaving – or perhaps dying – at Christmas 1389.

Wycliffe himself was dead by then, struck down by a stroke in the middle of hearing Mass in Lutterworth church on 28 December 1384: a turn of events his enemies not surprisingly read as a sign from God. He died on the last day of the year aged around sixty. The government no doubt breathed a sigh of relief in Westminster and Canterbury. To many it must have seemed that Wycliffe's death would lead to the end of the movement, but the remarkable thing was its transformation after his demise. From the late 1380s through the 1390s and during the first decades of the fifteenth century the spread of his ideas was now no longer chiefly through Merton men and scholars, but through ordinary people, and in this story the Kibworth villagers played a dramatic part. Members of farming families in Kibworth – the Browns, Gilberts, Polles, Carters, Dexters and Valentines – all appear in government inquiries as active disseminators or supporters of the heresy. It is on any reading of the evidence a remarkable haul from one village.

The Lollards' ideas were now increasingly anti-clerical and anti-Rome. In their sermons some said the Pope was an anti-Christ who had performed the remarkable feat of turning Christ himself into a heretic. And there were many who thought these theological disputations had a direct bearing on what we would call the political order, the 'community of the realm'. One John Corringham (another Merton man), preaching unlicensed in Huntingdonshire in 1384, along with the usual Lollard doctrines on the true body of Christ in the Mass, articulated pacifist ideas, arguing that even killing in self-defence was unlawful for Christians. He also disapproved of taxation to fund warfare outside the kingdom. These were radical ideas which have a powerful resonance even today.

That the religious crisis coincided with the aftermath of the Peasants' Revolt was no coincidence. Lollardy is often described as the direct outcome of learned controversy. No doubt this is true, but heresy was also part of the English people's revolt against the power structures which ruled their lives. It is easy to forget that this was a current in English life: eight medieval English kings after all were overthrown by revolt. For over a century there had been constant agitation at the grass roots. Peasants had contested their lords' demands before the law for 150 years, often with the support of the artisanal classes. Lollard rebels in East Anglia in the 1420s included millers, parchment makers, glovers, skinners, tailors, carpenters and of course a minority of priests. The appeal of the Lollards then was to literate people of some status in English society.

Whether older English popular religious traditions and beliefs also came into play is an interesting question. There is no question that Wycliffe shaped the debate but some of the Lollards' beliefs were ideas that could have been expressed if Wycliffe had never lived: they were part of an older popular vernacular current in English culture. The Bible, for example, was everything to Wycliffe and his follow-ers, so they thought it should be available to all in the English language. All the peasants in Kibworth knew some Latin: they could speak the Lord's Prayer and the Apostles' Creed in Latin. But in their daily speech they knew the wise saws and sayings of the Gospels in their own tongue. Rendering the Gospels into the vernacular after all was an old tradition in England. The first translations had been done in the Anglo-Saxon period and surviving manuscripts (from as late as the twelfth century) show that the text continued to be taught in English in church. Famous biblical proverbs known to the Kibworth peasants in English in the fourteenth century had a much more ancient pedigree: 'seek and ye shall find' – 'seceath and ye hit findath'; 'strait is the gate' – 'that geat is swythe wid'; 'you are the salt of the earth' – 'ye sind eorthan sealt'. The Old English version of the Lord's Prayer had already been part of the English language for centuries: 'Faeder ure thu the eart on heofonum, si thin nama gehalgod . . .' Behind the Wycliffe Bible, which was copied by hand in private houses near Kibworth, there lay an older current still of popular Christianity, emphatically English – and vernacular.

Among the issues that were contentious to the Lollards, however, use of the vernacular was not thought a make or break one. (Though Henry Knighton in Leicester, for example, strongly disapproved of translation: the 'language of Angli is not language of angels', he said, inverting Bede's famous story of Gregory the Great.) More important as we have seen was the corruption of the Church, its worldliness and wealth, its involvement in secular power. Some central theological doctrines also went against older custom. Transubstantiation was particularly contentious. The idea of the real presence of the blood and body of Christ in the Mass (still a central Catholic belief today) was only developed in the twelfth century by the papacy in Europe; prior to that it seems that the mystery of the Mass was capable of being understood metaphorically (and had been so by the Anglo-Saxons). So the Church orthodoxy was not a longstanding continuous doctrinal tradition and the fourteenth-century radicals' beliefs had not come out of the blue. Peasants after the sixteenth-century Reformation might look back fondly on the time 'when it was better when man ate his Maker at the Mass', but in the fourteenth century these were relatively new doctrines and in teaching them the Church encountered a wide variety of older custom and belief.

It all boiled down to the authority of the priest: who was a priest? Why should one have to be licensed by the Church in order to preach? Some Lollards asserted that 'any good man could be a priest – or any good woman.' A Lollard blacksmith in Lincolnshire memorably declared that he could make 'as good a sacrament between ii yrons as the prest doth upon his altar'. In a sense then the doctrinal crises of the time seem to have come out of a still little-known but deep current in popular spirituality: to some the heresy appealed to English vernacular roots.

## William Swinderby

In the years after the Peasants' Revolt these ideas spread across the East Midlands through local preachers who had been radicalized in the local community. In the early 1380s the people of Kibworth and neighbouring villages first became aware of a new kind of itinerant preacher. Wycliffe had aimed to do away with the existing hierarchy and replace it with the 'poor priests' who lived in poverty, were bound by no vows, had received no formal consecration and preached the Gospel to the people. After his death this happened. These itinerant preachers spread the teachings of Wycliffe. Two by two they went, wearing long dark-red robes and carrying a staff in the hand, the latter having symbolic reference to their pastoral calling, and passed from place to place preaching 'the sovereignty of God'.

They included formally educated scholars such as the Merton fellow John Aston. But the key people were local men like the self-taught blacksmith William Smith or, somewhat later, the itinerant Kibworth preachers William Brown and Walter Gilbert, who was known across Nottinghamshire and Derbyshire as 'Walter of Kibworth'. There were women supporters, too, including the anchoresses Anna and Maud (who was perhaps the holy woman Maud Polle who died around 1407, leaving land in Kibworth). Even the famous eccentric anchoress Margery Kempe on her travels through the area was interrogated by the town authorities in Leicester on suspicion of Lollardy.

The first key local figure seems to have been a charismatic preacher called William Swinderby. Known as William the Hermit, he had lived in a wood on the western edge of Leicester (where a cave is still known as 'Lollard's Cave'). Swinderby was a typical renouncer: he preached against the seductions of women, pride, adornments and loose living, and gained a reputation for holiness. He was visited by rich burghers, who provided him with food, and eventually, with the backing of the powerful John of Gaunt, Duke of Lancaster (who had a penchant for strange holy men), he moved into the town, setting himself up in a small cell adjoining Leicester Abbey.

From Leicester, Swinderby went out into the countryside on preaching tours, to Loughborough and Melton Mowbray to the north, and down the Market Harborough road south through Kibworth to Hallaton. Receptive audiences were easy to come by. In 1382 on Palm Sunday and on Good Friday he preached to large crowds at the chapel of St John the Baptist near the leper hospital outside the city wall. There conventicles were held and 'heretical ideas expounded': possibly the first reference to Lollard 'schools'. Swinderby attacked the whole edifice of the Church. In his reported words we can hear the kind of ideas that radicalized two generations of villagers in Kibworth over the next thirty years. To him image worship was idolatry; collective prayer was just 'blabbering with the lips'. It was worthless to pay money for the recitals of psalms or to pay for Masses. Only a person leading a good life has any value: 'such good living is prayer enough.' Alms for confession are accursed: 'No one should give alms to anyone they know to be wicked or corrupt; no cleric should have more than the bare necessities of food and clothes.' The Church should have no right to control (and charge for) marriage, as 'a union of two hearts' was all that was required. As for preaching, 'every good man or good woman' is a priest. As he grew in self-assurance, Swinderby promised that he would reform the people by his own teaching and asserted that he could preach at any church in Leicester without the licence of the Bishop of Lincoln.

These were dangerous ideas for they questioned not only the edifice of the Catholic Church, but the power structure of fourteenth-century England. This was precisely where heresy and dissent approached sedition: Swinderby attacked not only a corrupt and hypocritical clergy but announced that 'If lay lords are evil and do not mend their ways it is permissible for ordinary folk to correct them.' Coming in the aftermath of the Peasants' Revolt the idea of righteous peasants 'correcting' corrupt lay lords, as preached to villagers in Harborough, Hallaton and Kibworth, was to say the least concerning to the authorities. Swinderby refers several times to the 'law of the land' in the way the Peatling peasants had spoken of the welfare of the community of the realm: times had changed since the clerics of Leicester had sneered at the aspirations of the peasants of Stoughton and characterized them as 'pure villeins' who should know their place.

Soon we hear of Lollard schools in private houses. It seems hard to believe that there wasn't one, however informal and small-scale, in Kibworth. Here discussion groups were held, readings spoken, manuscripts pored over. The account of one gives a vivid sense of the grass-roots organization in this area of Leicestershire. This conventicle or school was founded by the self-taught Leicestershire blacksmith William Smith. Smith and his like were painted in black terms by their enemies. Just as Swinderby had been dismissed as volatile and shifty, Smith was portrayed as unstable and even mad, as well as 'deformed and ugly'. Henry Knighton, who remembered him, claims Smith took to his odd religious life as a result of being turned down by a young woman with whom he had fallen in love. Smith, it was said, renounced love and became a barefoot vegetarian, giving up both meat and alcohol (sure signs of mental instability to a fourteenth-century friar!). But Smith also taught himself to read and write and was later found to have been copying and gathering books in the vernacular. In a famous tale that would haunt Smith, on one occasion when he was cooking cabbages in his cell he broke up a wooden image of St Catherine and used it for his fire: 'a new martyrdom for St Catherine'.

Such people anticipate the strange fringe sects of the seventeenth-century English Revolution: Adamites, Seekers and Familists of Love. Of course, extreme religious renouncers often have a precarious sanity: finding their centre in rigid certainties. But peering through Knighton's sneering denunciation, we can see Smith as typical of a new kind of layman after the Black Death. Despite the hostile and sensational portrait devised by those who hated him, he was an interesting Englishman from the labouring classes of a kind we find in Kibworth too: critical, censorious, but eager through self-education and literacy to lead his own spiritual life – and to help others find theirs. Reading English texts, debating, rejecting outward shows of devotion, seeking what he saw as the true core of the Christian faith in a return to the simplicity of the primeval church, he was to many an attractive model to set against the rich and worldly clergy.

### The penance of Roger and Alice Dexter

Through the likes of Swinderby and Smith, by 1384 the heresy had spread through the huge diocese of Lincoln, into East Anglia, and to cities like Coventry and London. In the bishop's records in the medieval library in Lincoln Cathedral the voluminous hearings show that through the 1390s to the 1410s, the heresy swirled around the villages between Leicester and Northampton: Market Harborough, Kibworth and Smeeton all becoming centres of Lollardy. The Church reacted with growing concern. In 1401 there was a blanket condemnation of Lollard ideas; in 1408 a statute reaffirmed that to translate the Gospels into English was to commit heresy; in 1415 the Pope finally condemned the long dead Wycliffe as 'a stiff-necked heretic', banned his books and condemned all who followed him.

But it was all too late: the genie of heresy was out of the bottle. Swinderby by now had disappeared from the scene after multiple interrogations (he is last heard of in the Welsh Marches). But others continued. Thomas Hulman was back in Kibworth; and soon we meet ordinary people in the area who are strong supporters of Wycliffe's ideas. On 13 October 1389 the Bishop of Lincoln came up with a new series of suspects, among whom were close associates of William Smith: William Harry (John Harry was a reeve in Kibworth Harcourt at this time) and a married couple, Roger and Alice Dexter. The Dexters were then living in Leicester, but their name is found in Kibworth and that's where they went to live after the events which follow. With them were Smith and a chaplain, Richard Waystathe, who had been associates of Swinderby together with a number of people drawn from the middling sort: a scrivener, a parchmener, a goldsmith and a tailor (the parchmener was one of many Lollards associated with the book trade). They were accused of preaching against indulgences, confession, the worship of images and the payment of tithes, and were told to appear before the archbishop on All Saints' Day, 1 November 1389, at Leicester Abbey. But they hid, 'preferring to talk in darkness rather than in light'. After celebrating High Mass, Bishop Courteney excommunicated all who believed in such things, then, prompted by some orthodox citizens, named the eight individuals.

As the eight had not yet been apprehended by the mayor, the bishop now ordered their arrest. Ten days later Smith and two of his Lollard flock were detained and taken before him. The story was then told against Smith that he had burned the wooden statue of St Catherine as firewood. It was also reported that he had referred to two famous images of the Virgin Mary – the most popular pilgrimage destinations for the people of the villages round Leicester – as 'the witch of Lincoln and the witch of Walsingham'. Smith's fellow prisoners were the married couple, Roger and Alice Dexter – Roger had been reported by the faithful as having refused to venerate the crucified Christ, a common Lollard protest against what they saw as 'idolatry'.

Smith and the Dexters were under uncomfortable pressure now and agreed to abjure their errors. They were sentenced by the bishop to do appropriate penance: to attend in procession at the city church of St Mary Newark, William and Roger wearing shirt and breeches, Alice wrapped only in a sheet, all barefoot and bareheaded. In atonement William was to carry an image of St Catherine; Roger and Alice were to hold crucifixes in their right hands and lighted penitential tapers in the left. Three times in procession they were to 'stop and kiss the images in honour of the Crucified Christ, and in memory of his passion, and in honour of St Catherine', falling down on their knees on each occasion. Then they were to attend Mass in church. The following Saturday they were to repeat the whole ritual in the marketplace in Leicester and on Sunday for a third time in their own parish churches. Smith was also to recite an antiphon and collect to St Catherine, whom he had particularly 'insulted, defamed and desecrated'. Roger and Alice, who may have been illiterate, were simply to recite in Latin the Pater Noster and an Ave Maria. The weather was particularly cold, and for the services inside church the archbishop showed a touch of charity, allowing them not to strip to their thin undershifts, though they were still to go barefoot (a little hint of how chilly it could be going to church in the Middle Ages).

With the public confession of their error and stripped half naked in front of their many orthodox accusers among the citizenry, the humiliation of Smith and the Dexters was complete. But in addition Smith was accused of 'compiling and copying manuscripts in English', including 'books of the epistles and the gospels done into English and other works by the Church Fathers that he had spent eight years in compiling'. These he was now compelled to surrender so they could be burned. It was quite a collection for a blacksmith. Had such books survived, we would gain a fascinating insight into the learning of a self-educated blacksmith in the late fourteenth century – and for that matter the reading of the wandering preachers from Kibworth whom we will soon meet.

## *Survival: 1389–1414*

So it is in this period that we have our first really detailed account of matters of conscience and individual belief among the ordinary people of England. Something of Roger and Alice Dexter's later life can be restored from the Merton archive and from the bishop's records. After their 1389 penance the couple moved from Leicester to live in Kibworth: conceivably they had a family connection there (the name is found in the village). There is some indication that subsequently they had money troubles. The bailiff's accounts for 1394 drawn up by William Polle show an entry fine on a tenement due from Roger which was held over, suggesting perhaps that he couldn't pay. Then in 1409 the butcher John Pychard senior summonsed Roger for payment of a 40s debt. Most interesting, in 1403 Adam Brown of Kibworth Harcourt made a gift to Roger Dexter, of 'a housing plot with buildings, a curtilege lying in Kibworth Harcourt which he Adam holds from one John Wilcokson of Stretton Parva, and a plot 28 feet by 16 feet between that house and William Mann's house'. Adam Brown, as we shall see in the next chapter, came from an old Kibworth family; by 1403 he was a well-off draper living and working partly in Coventry. Some members of Brown's family had Lollard sympathies (one of them indeed became a wandering preacher), and it may be significant that a Coventry draper with Kibworth roots made a 'gift' of a house to Dexter. In his last appearance in the records, fourteen years later, Roger Dexter leases to Thomas and his wife, Joan Carter (the Carters were another Kibworth family with Lollard sympathies), the house and buildings he had got from Adam Brown. So in 1417 Dexter still held property in Kibworth; and it is touching to hear from one informer that Roger kept faith with Lollard beliefs 'until his dying day'.

The Dexters' story is direct evidence of the legacy of wandering preachers like Swinderby and Smith. Scholars such as the Merton man Aston and surely (though there is only circumstantial evidence from Kibworth) the vicar Hulman too had also played their part in the spread of Lollard ideas. By 1390 these ideas had spread through the villages between Leicester and Northampton. In 1392 the new Mayor of Northampton himself was a supporter and for some months the town was virtually a no-go area for orthodoxy. There among the seven reported ringleaders the anchoress Anne Palmer declared the Bishop of Lincoln himself 'an anti-Christ'.

How far all this was now being generated from the bottom has been a matter of debate among scholars. Close to Kibworth the Lollards found middle-class supporters among the gentry in Smeeton and Illston on the Hill. Nor did sympathizers at Merton lose contact. When the warden of Merton and some of the fellows stayed in the village to celebrate Easter in 1395, it would be strange if they did not preach in church, dine with the bailiffs, reeves and other 'swearing men' and their wives, and discuss not only the running of the manor but the meaning of Easter. In any case this meeting is an extraordinary example of exchanges between Oxford scholars and peasants. Did they talk at that time of what the Lollards called the 'True Law of Christ'? What would one give for a note of their private conversations.

## Oldcastle's revolt

Though the sect grew in influence in the thirty years after Wycliffe's death, spreading to the houses of the gentry in the East Midlands, to artisanal workshops in Coventry, to the wool towns of East Anglia and to book copiers in London, it was never a mass movement. But in 1413–14 it finally came to the national stage and swept up people in Kibworth. These events, culminating in the Oldcastle Rising of January 1414, were preceded by on-the-ground agitation in the area of Kibworth which, thanks to the government's apparatus of heresy detection, can be followed in some detail.

In spring 1413 a further round of inquisitions around Leicester picked up more unlicensed preachers, and more stories of banned 'books in English'. One man who was reported preaching between Thurcaston and Barrow on Soar down to Wigston and Kibworth was the *capellanus* William Brown, a native of Kibworth who perhaps had been chaplain of the little chantry chapel on Main Street. According to the government's inquisitors, William, who was presumably literate, had preached heretical sermons in the little church down by the River Sence at Wistow and in Kibworth Harcourt itself – possibly at the free chapel, perhaps at the parish church. His sermons do not survive but no doubt they were typical Lollard complaints: decrying idolatry, spurning pilgrimages to the 'witch of Walsingham and the cursed Thomas Becket', attacking the familiar corruptions of the priesthood. As Swinderby had preached, 'there will be no peace until the Church has been deprived of all its temporal goods . . . and know without doubt that God's vengeance will shortly come.'

Brown came from an old Kibworth family which goes back into the middle of the thirteenth century in the documents at Merton; one branch had risen in the 1380s and 1390s to be drapers and guild members in Coventry. Brown himself had been a pledge at the Kibworth manor court in 1412–13: a 'trustworthy swearing man' accustomed to serving on juries and speaking for the villagers. His preaching around Kibworth takes us to the villages south of Leicester at the end of winter 1412 and the early spring of 1413. Brown was perhaps the same unnamed Lollard preacher who arrived at Wigston, south of Leicester, on Sunday, 5 February 1413, after the Feast of the Purification of the Virgin. The tale unfolds in detail from the inquisitions of the Church made in the clampdown afterwards. The weather was bad – we may imagine swirling snowflakes and a freezing wind. After the church service Brown asked the vicar at Wigston whether he could preach to the people. But it was immediately apparent that the stranger was unlicensed. The village headman, the *caput parochiae* (the vicar, or the parochial chaplain), then protested but Brown spoke to the congregation inside the church: 'The village chaplain does not want me to preach here in the church; and therefore I am going out to the cross to preach there.' The parishioners though, in one of the most rich and populous villages in Leicestershire, wanted to hear him inside, claiming it was too cold to stand outside.

After his sermon the mysterious preacher had a surprise up his sleeve. He distributed ten marks to the poor – the equivalent of 1,600 pennies, nearly £7 of English money, and worth more than £3,000 today on the RPI, nearly £40,000 on average earnings. This was the kind of money that could only have come from a wealthy sympathizer among the gentry, someone like Thomas Latimer, the lord of Smeeton, whose house at Braybroke over the border in Northamptonshire was a refuge for Lollards and perhaps a place where 'English books' were copied. If so, it would be typical of the middling gentry's support for the movement. The tale too suggests what is also suggested by our evidence from interrogations in eastern England a few years later, that heresy was much more developed than has been thought: that there was some kind of organization in existence with schools, houses – and money.

### Walter of Kibworth

By various channels these revolutionary ideas thus percolated down to the villagers in Kibworth, Smeeton, Wigston and their neighbours. And this increasingly vociferous radicalism took Lollardy into deep water in the second decade of the fifteenth century. For a new and dangerous edge had crept into the rhetoric of the wandering preachers. Along with the anti-clerical attacks, there was now a growing opposition to the government itself. This would lead to a catastrophic confrontation with the Crown, and the death of Kibworth men on the scaffold in London.

In the spring of 1413 another itinerant preacher from Kibworth made his way from village to village on foot from Leicester to the Trent valley and into Derbyshire, where he was reported to the government as 'Walter of Kibworth'. His real name was Walter Gilbert, and he came from another old Kibworth villein family (his ancestor Emma had been a customary tenant of Merton back in 1280). In the summer of that year wearing the familiar rust-red cloak of heretical priests, Walter travelled through the villages of Derbyshire preaching Lollard ideas – and perhaps revolution. For now the heresy had moved into politics, and had become a source of increasingly acute anxiety to the government as threats were made to the king himself and to his office. They were right about the rebels' intent, though not about the real nature of the threat, nor its chances of success.

In July, Walter reached the village of Littleover (now a suburb of Derby), where he was given shelter by Henry Bothe or Booth, a lawyer and member of the local gentry, who would himself be accused of disseminating heresy. Gilbert was the kind of committed heretic who frequented the 'scoles of heresie yn privie chambres and privie plases of oures'. By now there was a new political dimension to his sermons. For in 1413 the idea was hatched of overthrowing the king to create a new Christian commonweath guided by Lollard ideals.

### Kibworth and the Oldcastle Rising

The old king, Henry IV, died in March 1413 while Gilbert was following his route between safe houses in Derbyshire. The king's son was crowned on 9 April at Westminster Abbey as Henry V. He was tall and ruddy-faced, 'with a look that flashed like a lion's', his long thin face scarred by an arrow wound sustained at the battle of Shrewsbury when he was sixteen. The coronation was accompanied by an unseasonable flurry of snow, which was interpreted by some as a bad omen. The first weeks were a nervous time for the new king: his father had been seen by many as a usurper so dissent within the royal house was a given; and the renewal of the war in France was in the air. Within weeks a rising was being planned against him by his old associate and friend Sir John Oldcastle, who had already been accused of heresy and become a focus of Lollard aspirations. Their quixotic hope was to depose Henry and make Oldcastle regent. Other rulers would be appointed at the will of the rebels, as a kind of commonwealth, 'a people without a head'. The plan was to coordinate the rebellion with men marching from various parts of England 'to the number of twenty thousand men'; to meet at St Giles' Fields in London on 10 January 1414.

In Kibworth, as we have seen, Lollard ideas had a long pedigree: vicar Hulman and the preachings of Swinderby, Aston and Smith had radicalized villagers like the Dexters and their friends; and Brown and Gilbert, the wandering preachers, had been active in the area too. The ringleader, Walter Gilbert, was able to elicit not only sympathy and money, but support. A dozen peasants from Kibworth, Smeeton and Saddington declared themselves for Oldcastle and resolved to travel to London to join the rebel army at St Giles' Fields. Messages must have been spread on some kind of underground system, possibly organized in cells like modern resistance movements, and in the village by now there clearly must have been something like the 'scoles of heresie' mentioned elsewhere. Behind the dozen men from Kibworth and its neighbours was the support of a substantial number of villagers, and not just family members, who provided money for food and accommodation. Among the local gentry some like Thomas Noveray, of Illston on the Hill next to Kibworth, sold their goods and made their wills before taking arms.

Among the rebels six Kibworth Harcourt men made the perilous journey south. Their names are preserved in the government's records, sometimes for obvious reasons using aliases. First is Simon Polle alias Carter, perhaps his mother's name – the two Kibworth families had long connections. Polle's family we have come to know in this story; he was a long-time tenant of the college. Henry Valentine came from another old family; tenants in the Merton rolls from the 1280s, they provided village scribes in the fourteenth century. John Blakwell's alias strangely was 'John Taylor of Lancashire', but the Taylors were another Kibworth family. John Barun 'alias Toogood, alias Scrivener' – a hint of his job perhaps – gave a Shangton address but from his name also belonged to the old Kibworth Harcourt family who had been free tenants from the thirteenth century. The sixth man, John Upton, described himself as a labourer of Smeeton.

The group thus included members of four old village families, all well-known in this story. Most prominent though was the chaplain Walter Gilbert, who was said to have induced the labourers to join them by bribing them with 20s, though perhaps this was not a bribe but expenses. Did the money come from well-wishers at the college? From rich family members like Adam Brown? Or from local landowners like Latimer or Noveray? The government's investigators were unable to discover.

With Walter was his brother Nicholas. The Gilberts were a longstanding village family, descendants of the customary tenant Emma in the 1280s. Their grandfather Nicholas is recorded in the Merton rolls making provisions for his mother Agnes, who remarried after the Black Death; her other son, Robert, appears in the poll tax of 1381 with his wife Emma as a 'merchant'. Their children William and Alice that year are taxed as servants; Walter and Nicholas may have been their younger sons.

The younger Nicholas had interesting connections with Merton College. He had been a tenant since the 1380s, and in 1394–5 his son John had carried letters from Kibworth to Oxford, at the behest of Warden Whelpingham, who visited Kibworth both years. By 1396 a minor official at Kibworth, Nicholas was a constant link between the village and the college. He was one of six upstanding men of the manor, an 'overseer of lands and tenements' entrusted with recording land transfers, encroachments and dilapidations of tenancies at the manorial court. Among the other rebels, Polle's and Valentine's families were old friends. There were those in the village of course who disagreed with them – Robert Gilbert was opposed to his brothers; the heresy seems to have split the Polles too. So maybe there were heated arguments behind closed doors in houses on Main Street. But no doubt too there were many sympathizers who gave support even though they were not prepared to take the momentous step of heading down to London to confront the king.

The journey to London could be made at a moderate pace on horseback in three days through Northamptonshire down to St Albans, reaching the northern edge of the city at Smithfield where the Peasants' Army under Wat Tyler had gathered thirty years before. (Tudor maps give a good idea of what they saw: though the city was slightly smaller in the middle of the sixteenth century than at its 1300 peak, when it had maybe 80,000 people.) As in a modern anti-war demonstration, parties moved on London from all directions: forty weavers and craftsmen on the road from Bristol, parties from Worcester, an Oxfordshire party led by a Woodstock glover with men from Handbrough, Baldon, Kidlington and Upper Heyford; a fuller, a tailor, a capper, carpenters, millers and masons singing songs. The urban sprawl of the city had spread outside the walls in the fifteenth century as far as the open fields beyond Clerkenwell, where wide drove roads brought in cattle from the 'champain' lands of Leicestershire and the Midlands to feed the insatiable appetite of the capital for meat and animal products.

The rendezvous for the Kibworth rebels was just beyond the northern edge of the built-up city, where over the rooftops at the end of the country lane that is now Turnmill Street rose the vast bulk of the Gothic cathedral of St Paul's with its giant spire, the tallest in Europe. In the fields of Clerkenwell was a huge inn called The Wrestlers on the Hoop, its yards and stables frequented by long-distance carriers and merchants; they could stable their horses and goods in the great cart yard opposite the stinking Fleet stream: it stood close to the Clerkenwell itself, whose stone wellhead still survives behind a modern shop front. There along Turnmill Street and Cow Cross were the inns used by drovers and merchants, including the Cock Inn, one of the longest-lived London inns on record: another Lollard safe house linked by a path across fields and allotments to St John's Gate. In this neighbourhood was a secret base for Lollard book copiers. From there the plan was that the peasant army would march round the suburb through open fields towards St Giles' Fields.

The government though had been warned by informers and was waiting for them with a heavily armed force. The young king was not yet the veteran of Agincourt but he had been bloodied ten years previously on the field at Shrewsbury. Brave and decisive, he knew how to manoeuvre troops, especially against disorganized and ill-armed peasants. Hopelessly quixotic, its aims confused, the revolt proved to be a damp squib. Where the Lollard leaders had called for 20,000 men, in the event nothing like that number gathered. They came in hundreds not thousands, the revolt was betrayed and the peasants who had risked all to come to London fled or were captured. The ringleaders, including the Kibworth brothers, were consigned to Newgate Prison to await King Henry's mercy.

In the event the young king was not keen to inflict brutal punishments on the rank and file, any more than he had been keen to kill his old friend Oldcastle. He wanted to make an example but not to take swingeing revenge. Pardons were issued for most of the prisoners. From Kibworth, John Barun was pardoned in May; Valentine and Polle had to wait in custody till the summer. Anxious to appear merciful, Henry and his councillors gave pardons on condition of acts of public penitence. But forty or so were hanged the following week, including some who recanted their heresy. A more terrible fate was reserved for heretics – they were hanged and burned alive. Among the dead were Walter and Nicholas Gilbert.

Oldcastle himself escaped from the safe house at the Cock in Turn-mill Street and fled west to the Welsh Marches, where he spent two years on the run while Henry made his name in the French campaign which climaxed at Agincourt. Eventually Oldcastle was hunted down and captured on the Welsh borders. He was tried and burned at St Giles' Fields in December 1417, at the same place where the Gilberts had died. The site today lies just at the end of Denmark Street near today's Dominion Theatre. At St Giles' church Oldcastle's name is still commemorated; he has also given his name to a pub on the old Fleet by Smithfield Market. In Tudor times he came to be viewed as a Protestant martyr and enjoyed a strange afterlife in Shakespeare's *Henry IV* as Sir John Falstaff, who was originally called Oldcastle in the play until a furore by Protestant hardliners brought an official reprimand, after which Shakespeare was nervous enough to issue an author's disclaimer. Even then Lollardy still carried a whiff of danger. For the Gilberts and friends there is no memorial.

But the Lollard heresy did not go quietly away. There were more risings, trials and executions in the 1420s and 1430s. The rising at Coventry in 1431 was the last major conflagration, but the beliefs survived across the Midlands and East Anglia and in the major cities. When Essex men marched on London in protest in the 1520s, they were persuaded to exchange their dog-eared handwritten Wycliffite texts for the new Tyndale testament. By then the Protestant Reformation was on the horizon.

### From Lollards to Nonconformists?

So yet again Kibworth found itself touched by the national story in a direct way. In the village, as in many places in southern England, the heresy split families, some of whom in the aftermath were barred from public office. In general though the impression one gets from the court documents is that such communities rubbed along together with a fair degree of tolerance, their lives always driven by the pressure of running the fields, of producing food.

But the Lollard protest had deep cultural and psychological roots. For orthodox Christian worshippers the images of the saints were justified as the books of the unlettered, their tales a source of deep affection and solace. But when literacy spread in a peasant society like Kibworth, as it did in the fourteenth century, the questioning of basic religious custom and practice was inevitable, especially when academic ideas like Wycliffe's percolated down through disciples, followers and even vicars. For the Lollards there was only one book: the Bible. 'There is no Pope in the Bible: Jesus consecrated no priest.' What mattered was the individual conscience and the individual reaching out to God through the Bible and his or her own prayers. For the Lollards this was worth all the masses, all the images and all the pilgrimages in creation.

The radical project of the Lollards failed miserably. But at a personal level the purely religious side survived, settling down to become part of the deeply ingrained down-to-earth religious sensibility of many English men and women. It continued at grass-roots level in villages like Kibworth for the most part unnoticed by government until later outbursts of persecution in the sixteenth century. In isolated close-knit communities there was always much mutual understanding, forbearance and tolerance, and a spirit of live and let live which helps account for the absence of persecution in the intervening years. And the same spirit kept persecution down to a minimum when it did raise its ugly head. That picture is inevitably conjectural: the historian cannot eavesdrop on the Polles, Peks and Browns through the fifteenth century behind their closed doors. But without such an assumption it is hard to understand how rapidly in parts of the country – especially in East Anglia and the East Midlands – the fundamental changes later imposed from above in the Protestant Reformation were accepted so swiftly.

In the tale of the Kibworth Lollards we have one of the earliest insights into the involvement of ordinary peasants in religious debate.

But it should not be a surprise that such ideas were imbibed at the very grass roots of English society to produce preachers like Brown and Gilbert and supporters like Roger and Alice Dexter. The community to which these people belonged with its alternative literacy was not the one that had come into being by permission of, or even by contained reaction to, those in power. It had grown first out of the necessity to cooperate in order to survive, expanding its ambitions as its horizons expanded, till the possibilities of different futures opened up. The ideas of the Lollards suggest the possibility of long-lasting continuities with the sixteenth-century religious radicals, with the seventeenth-century Quakers and Congregationalists and other dissenters who formed an academy in the village, and the Methodists and Nonconformists of modern times. Can it be a coincidence that the areas of strong Lollard support in Leicestershire, around Mountsorrel and Kibworth, would be great centres of Nonconformity after the English Revolution and in the eighteenth century? George Fox, the Quaker founder, was a weaver who came from Fenny Drayton, a village not far from Kibworth, and belonged to the same class as the Browns and the Gilberts. In Kibworth parish itself, Smeeton in particular in the late seventeenth century was an important Quaker centre against which armed force was used in the 1660s. At the same time Congregationalists were influential in Kibworth Harcourt, where a dissenting academy was founded in 1721. When the ebullient Edmund Knox, another Merton man, arrived as vicar in Kibworth in the 1880s he became well aware of the fascinating and complex religious history of the village, and with rueful humour relates the tale of one of his new flock who greeted him with a lecture on history and told him curtly that if he had his way he would 'blow the church up'.

In a nation which only recently declared itself the least religious society on earth, it is salutary to remember the conflicts that lie behind the secular democracy of today, which was largely won by the ordinary people of England – but, unlike us, they were God-driven.

# 12. From Villeins to Yeomen

England was the first society in the world to industrialize and historians from Marx and Engels to Weber, Tawney and others have long argued about the forces in society that brought this about. What were the conditions of work, class, family, marriage, labour relations, etc. that led the communally organized agricultural society of the fourteenth century to become the industrial society of the nineteenth?

We left Kibworth at the time of the Black Death with its feudal order, where the bulk of the population still worked the land and the peasants owed obedience, as well as labour and surplus, to a small elite. But how did the change then happen from a feudal order to a capitalist one, from an agrarian, close-knit society of self-sufficient peasants to an industrialized economy with a large, landless proletariat of wage-earners? And how did rural England become a diversified, regionally orientated society of commercial farmers, artisans and landless labourers who supported an industrial urban society?

Of course, social conditions in England in the Middle Ages differed from region to region – from the hill settlements of Devon to the mining towns of Northumberland – and in the English Midlands we have to take account of the remarkable proportion of smallholding freemen after 1086. But in the later Middle Ages a broad pattern of English history emerges from the south coast to the foothills of the Cheviots, in all villages that share the open-field system. The core idea behind the feudal order was that those with land and power claimed – and could enforce – the right to the labour and surplus of the bulk of the population. However, from the fourteenth century onwards there was growing pressure to abolish labour services and replace them with work for money. The final abolition of serfdom was a long battle; archaic renders survived for centuries on many estates, as did the resistance to change on the part of rapacious landlords. As late as 1549 the Norfolk rebels of Robert Kett urged in their petition 'that all bond men be made free, for God made all free with his precious blood shedding'. The capitalist system of course is also organized so that the rich and powerful may take part of the surplus of the workforce, and it could be said that this is still so for the mass of the population in the twenty-first century. But the broad story of England's history through the late medieval and early modern periods is of the freeing of the ordinary people from labour dues and the growth of personal and political freedom.

The Kibworth story is a microcosm of this great national movement. Indeed, the village records are so detailed that we can take individual family stories as examples of the whole tale. One particular case of self-advancement involves a Kibworth family who rose from being poor villeins in the thirteenth century to craftspeople and then mercers, aldermen and urban guild members in Leicester and Coventry in the fifteenth, with one branch of the family even making its fortune in London. Such revolutionary changes start to be traceable in the post-Black Death period, and they came about through education and literacy, through ideas about individual conscience, but also through mobility, the availability of money and changing patterns of work.

## After the plague

In the village the Black Death had devastated some of the long-standing families who hitherto had had a monopoly over the customary land in the open fields. Some like the Polles, as we have seen, never recovered, losing three of the four branches of their family by the end of the fourteenth century. Now smaller households with larger holdings made it difficult and unnecessary to maintain pre-1349 levels of arable cultivation, so the village began to see the evolution of new uses of land resources, and new ideas about work and labour relations.

In the village, conditions for survivors offered many opportunities if the gene pool of the family had held out. Here again the Merton documents from Kibworth Harcourt enable us to see close up how these changes happened. After the initial catastrophe of 1349–50 the new reeve, John Church junior, and his village officials had managed to fill all the tenancies despite the loss of two thirds of the tenants. But over the next two or three generations the plague continued to flare up with a frequency which must have caused the community deep and gnawing anxiety. As many as twenty-five tenants died in 1361, the faded brown of their names in the tithing list struck through, line after line in fresh black ink. Later notes in the Kibworth court books show that the threat remained for decades. In 1375 six more tenants' deaths are entered and there were more again in 1378–9. Between 1389 and 1393 nine tenants died of plague, a few more in 1395, and there was a last spasm in 1412. The three generations after 1349 then lived in constant fear of the return of the pestilence and there are many signs in the court rolls in Merton of growing hardship, with derelict properties and eventually a failure to take up tenancies which meant that rent revenues declined and rent arrears began to pile up for the college administrators.

Unlike the Polles, the Browns were one family who managed to ride out the storm. An old family in the village (their name is Anglo-Saxon) Robert Brown senior is the first member of the family to appear in the first Merton records in 1270. By the 1280s we find that there are three branches of the family, each with its own separate holding and house. Three of the male heads of the family are described as villeins. Robert had a house on 'the king's highway' (today's Main Street) with a garden and about fifteen acres in the open fields; his son William had a house and a virgate, thirty acres of strips in the field; and Henry also had a house and a virgate. But in the 1280s Robert's son William was also the holder of one of the coveted free tenancies, 'one messuage at a rent of one penny'. It was the beginning of the family's amazing tale of advancement.

In Kibworth over half of the landholding population had died out in twenty-five years between 1349 and 1374 but the village itself survived and within thirty years the 1377 and 1381 tax rolls give us portraits of villagers and the two generations of children that had been born since the plague, despite the aftershocks of the outbreaks of 1351, 1361 and 1375. Robert Brown junior of Kibworth survived the Black Death and held on to all his parcels of land. As survivors, households like his were ideally placed to ensure their genetic inheritance was passed down along with the family plots, and by 1377 poll tax returns show a surprising partial recovery of population and strong indicators that the drive towards diversification and economic change that we detected before the plague had not been halted. The documents indeed start to note more diverse job descriptions – drapers and merchants in the village, and ironmongers, slaters, skinners and drapers among Kibworth people working in Leicester. As a sign of the times, quite ordinary families now employ servants, twenty-five of whom are listed in Kibworth.

## Mobility, freedom and wealth

The Black Death also seems to mark a watershed in village life in terms of family mobility. As we have seen, English people even before the Conquest moved about. From the thirteenth century villagers moved, sometimes illegally, and sometimes surprisingly, in the case of the unmarried girl who left the Merton estate at Barkby and travelled all the way to St Andrews in Fife in the wake of Edward I's armies – not, it appears, for work but following the man in her life.

But after the Black Death the bonds that had lasted since the ancient world seem suddenly to begin to break down. With increased literacy, stronger political awareness and more personal commercial ambition, people travelled to find employment much more than they did before the plague. Members of old Kibworth families like the Godyers, the Coupers and the Wylmots moved to Leicester, following a number of village artisans and craftsmen – and women – from the village who appear in guild rolls and tallage lists in the city simply as 'of Kibworth'. Others, including the Heyneses and another branch of the Godyers, went to Coventry. Landlords' lists meant that in theory no unfree person could leave the village without permission and this rule had been strictly adhered to in earlier times, but by 1363 the attractions of the city proved too great and the college simply gave up trying to control the people who went away in search of new work and a new life: the injunction was abandoned in the face of day-to-day reality. Most people seem to have sought work within a five-mile radius of the village. The brothers Roger and John Man migrated to Shangton after the Black Death; they were perhaps the most mobile of any family that can be traced through the documents. They made ten moves in less than thirty years, probably looking for employment at the best rates, travelling around the villages in the area picking up seasonal work as labourers and servants and renting properties in other villages – a pattern of rural employment that would persist in England until our own time. In her late-twentieth-century memoir, the former landgirl Rose Holyoak describes working at fifteen different farms in a dozen Midland villages over a decade or two during and after the Second World War. The 1380s tell the same story, with John Man of Kibworth moving between the two Kibworths, Saddington and Stonton Wyville, and being taxed at Fleckney, for example, as a simple *operarius* – a worker. Through the early fifteenth century the Mans are simply what we would call agricultural labourers, but by the Tudor period the family had risen, with one of their descendants still in the neighbourhood and deemed to be worth £18 in goods, putting him in the middling ranks of freeholding farmers: an English yeoman.

So why, apart from money, were people like the Mans prepared to move away from the support of their family and neighbours, from the comfort of their village? No autobiography of a medieval peasant survives to tell us, but psychological concerns no doubt also played their part in persuading young men like Roger and John Man to give up the security of customary land in their own village and venture into the uncertainties of life as a newcomer – one of the sometimes mistrusted *adventitii* – in another community. Perhaps they preferred to make a living where they would be paid in hard cash, perhaps they wanted to find a wife; and maybe too they were attracted to the variety of the life and the sense of freedom not open to many at the lowest level of society in the Middle Ages. Their neighbours the Browns, though, rose not by travelling throughout the area but by systematically bettering their status through business deals, good marriages and then finally by permanent migration away from Kibworth, and theirs in some ways is a classic English story. In 1381 Adam Brown still had strips in the common field in Kibworth, though now employing servants and hired labour; but he made the move to the city and there he made it bigger than any of his neighbours.

## In the city is freedom

Urban life had boomed in England from the twelfth century and by 1400 many towns had more than 10,000 inhabitants. London had at least 50,000 or 60,000 (some have even argued twice as many). Leicester though was the first choice for Kibworth people with artisanal skills. Guild rolls and tallage lists in the fourteenth century show many Kibworthians, men and women, joining Leicester guilds as mercers, ironmongers, skinners, slaters, drapers and glovers; becoming residents of Leicester, but still defining themselves as 'of Kibworth'. The guild entries and tallage rolls are especially rich after the Black Death, as if the survivors were all the more active in seeking opportunity outside the village. 'John of Kibworth' is listed as a slater in the city in the mid-1350s; 'Richard of Kibworth' describes himself as being of both Kibworth and Leicester in the tallage rolls of 1359–60 and is noted again on the Leicester merchant guild roll of 1362. 'Robert of Kibworth' is listed as a corviser, while another Kibworthian, an ironmonger, is recorded as renting a shop in Leicester market in 1375. So although Leicester was only a comparatively small city, there were still job opportunities for people with skills, and it is also clear from the records that some of those who moved or worked there still retained links to branches of their kin who stayed in Kibworth. This was especially true of the Brown family, who found their fortune in the boom time of the late fourteenth century in the urban phenomenon of the day, Coventry.

Only twenty-three miles from Kibworth, Coventry was a day's ride on the old route south-west through Arnesby, whose tall post windmill on the long ridge was a landmark across miles of open-field countryside. The route to the city took the traveller through Lutterworth, crossing Watling Street into Warwickshire at Brinklow, from where the prospective fourteenth-century job-seeker could see the new spires of Coventry's great medieval churches.

The fifth-largest city in England, Coventry had doubled in size in just a few decades. Its rapid expansion was encouraged by an ambitious, self-confident town council that financed huge building projects, funded by a rapidly expanding wool and cloth trade. In its late-fourteenth-century heyday Coventry's get-up-and-go produced an ostentatious building programme that saw it far outstrip the old towns of the Midlands like Leicester. A burst of energy and optimism after the devastation of the plague saw the creation of what was effectively a new town with huge construction projects sponsored by the town council and the guilds. In a few years from 1355 they built two and a half miles of city walls, in fresh-cut red sandstone, twelve feet high and eight feet thick, with twelve gates and thirty-two towers. Inside the city a dramatic cluster of church spires rose towards the heavens: Holy Trinity, St John's, the huge Benedictine priory of Whitefriars founded in 1342, Greyfriars, whose steeple was completed in 1350, and the 300-foot spire of St Michael's (begun in 1371 though not completed in Adam's lifetime) that soared over jettied houses, courtyards, gardens and orchards inside the walls. Here was a city of money, status and opportunity; a city on the rise, inventing new civic rituals, with its mayors and aldermen, its craft and merchants' guilds, its mystery plays and midsummer processions.

In such a place, especially with kinsmen as fellow guild members, a freeman (or freewoman) could rise even from peasant status. The merchants' guild was founded in 1340, with St Mary's as their guild hall, a magnificent building set on a red sandstone plinth, its high roof embossed with angels, unicorns and swans, set literally in the shadow of St Michael's great spire. Three more guilds followed, to cater for the swelling ranks of merchants and craftsmen, and the city drew several Kibworth men to make their fortunes here after the Black Death. Again the Merton rolls allow us an insight into the beginnings of this great movement in English and British history which is still going on: the movement of the population away from the villages into the city, and from agriculture to commerce.

## The rise of the Browns

In 1363 Robert Godyer and John Heynes both arrived in Coventry from Kibworth after the second great outbreak of the plague had caused heavy losses in the village. Robert Godyer's son Roger arrived two years later and lived with (and was probably apprenticed to) Arthur the wiredrawer – making metal wire for jewellers by hand on a draw bench. But the people from Kibworth whose rise we can trace in the most detail are members of the Brown family.

To tell Adam Brown's story we need to go back to the 1380s and a house on Main Street in Kibworth Harcourt, which was long afterwards known in the Merton rolls as 'Browns Place'. Amazingly for a peasant's house, it has survived; the bailiff's house in the fifteenth and sixteenth centuries, then a yeoman farmer's house, it is still lived in today, known as the Manor House, though in fact it has never been the manorial residence. There has been a house on this site since Anglo-Saxon times, and from recent dendrochronological investigation it is now known that the oldest surviving part of the present house was built somewhere between 1320 and 1350. A new open hall made from huge oak timbers was added in 1385, perhaps by Adam Brown and his wife Joanna. The trees were felled to order and the builders used green wood (which is how the dendrologists can date the building so accurately – they were able to get a good core sample from one of the hall beams). No building account survives for the 1385 job, but later Merton accounts from the middle of the fifteeth century record the construction of a further extension to the house, perhaps the late-medieval range along the road (where there is a fine 'dragon beam' in the ceiling of the corner room, though no good tree ring sample was forthcoming). We have a good idea of what would have been involved in 1385: stone (for the house platform) carted from Medbourne, slate from Kirby, lime and plaster from Barrow on Soar; the big frame timbers from Temple Rothley woods, and lesser timbers for the joists and lathes from the timber market at Lutterworth. Tiles and nails would have come from Leicester, where a leading ironmonger was a Kibworth man.

The building of the 1385 hall looks like the rebuild of an old house to mirror the Browns' growing social status in the village. Only four years after the Peasants' Revolt had rolled like a black cloud on the horizon towards Market Harborough, the world had moved on and Adam Brown had much to be pleased with. He could look back on his family story over several generations, back to his ancestor Robert's days during the reign of Edward I in the 1270s. A young man at the time of the Peasants' Revolt, Adam had married Joanna and had young children. He was obviously a man of energy and initiative; he had diversified into other businesses in the two decades after the plague and in the 1381 tax returns, by then about thirty years old, he is already described as a draper. So he had a taxable income, he was comparatively well-off, and now he began to spread his wings. His trade first led him to the local market at Harborough, five miles to the south, where he mingled with the other mercers and the spicers and dealers who sold the dye he needed for his cloth. They in turn connected him to wider horizons and specifically to Coventry, where wool was imported and luxury fabrics exported. Coventry was home to many drapers, mercers and dyers whose Coventry blue cloth – 'true blue' – was sought after across Europe for its luminous purity and fixity of colour. And there Adam and Joanna's rise can be tracked, from free tenants holding a house for 1d rent in 1280, to burghers trading with the ports of the Hanseatic League.

Adam's rise happened, as such things often do in life, through contacts, friendship and marriage. We first pick up these connections in the 1390s. His life in Kibworth still involved him with his neighbours, the old families in the village, the Swans, the Peks, the Polles and the Parkers, in the day-to-day business of the open fields, the buying and selling of strips, the deliberations of the manor court; but advancement came through his wider circle of friends through his business dealings in Market Harborough. On 4 February 1398 Adam granted friends in Harborough, including Robert Michell of Harborough and the spice dealer Will Andrews, a tenement in Kibworth. This deed was witnessed by four of Adam's Kibworth friends, John Pek, Will Polle, Will Parker and Rob Swan. The Michells were an important family in both Harborough and Coventry who provided several

Coventry mayors in the fourteenth century. The Andrews family had eighty years' standing as dealers in Harborough – maybe they were old contacts (as we saw above, the family had dealings with Robert of Kibworth back in 1299–1317). But what this deed tells us is that by then Adam Brown had dealings in Coventry and his friends there were up-and-coming people, members of the town council, merchants, dyers, drapers and mercers; the kind of people who attended guild dinners and wore the ermine in the street processions at Corpus Christi.

By 1405 Adam is described as 'Adam Brown of Kibworth merchant' in the Merton documents, in one of which (a house purchase witnessed by the same Kibworth friends) we learn that his son William has married Agnes, the daughter of Richard Dodenhall of Coventry. Turning to the guild records of Coventry from the same time we now find that 'Adam and Joanna Brown of Kibworth' are both entered into the Guild of Holy Trinity in Coventry among the 'brethren' and 'sisteren' in the pre-eminent social group of the city. Membership of the guild was a real mark of Adam and his wife's status but more importantly it conferred the right to trade, and if they wished it even gave them docking rights – quayage – in the port of Bristol. Now they could make and sell cloth made from wool grown on sheep in Kibworth and dyed by Coventry dyers, and export it to Europe and perhaps the Baltic ports. The Coventry guild records also reveal the identity of Adam's daughter-in-law, for Adam's son William had married the daughter of Richard Dodenhall who had been Mayor of Coventry in 1383: a match unthinkable for the pre-Black Death Browns in Kibworth. The Browns of Kibworth were now linked to the civic life of Coventry with a web of connections through the city's guilds and the vast network of organized charities that played such an important role in pre-Reformation England.

The young William and his new wife Agnes Brown set up house in Erle Street, close to the cluster of churches in the centre of Coventry and a few yards from the merchant guild building of St Mary's, whose magnificent hall was finished in the 1390s. It was an area of wide lanes and jettied houses near to the cathedral, of which one tiny corner still survives at Bailey Lane – a little hint of the 'many fair streets builded with timber' described by later Tudor travellers. Erle Street survived into the Second World War along with a wonderful collection of medieval buildings in Old Palace Yard which was partly destroyed by the Blitz in 1940, partly (and more unforgivably?) by planners and developers in the 1950s. Here the Browns prospered and eventually moved house again. William appears in the Coventry tallage roll of 1424 as a draper living in Much-Parke Street paying tallage of 6s 8d for the king's war loan. William and Agnes soon had a son and named him Adam, after William's father.

William did not break his connection with Kibworth though: he still kept a house and land in the village, renting out strips, and employed servants or younger kinsmen. In 1434 he gifted some plots of land in Kibworth to William Wymondeswold of Coventry and his kinsman Thomas Brown of Kibworth. But by now William is described as 'William Brown of Coventry and Kibworth' – Coventry now taking precedence in the family picture of itself. It is a measure of his status now that the witnesses to the document, along with four Kibworth men, are John Michell, Mayor of Coventry that year, Robert Southern, bailiff, and William Donington, who was bailiff and recorder at Coventry for nearly fifteen years in the 1430s and 1440s. Donington was originally a Leicestershire man too, so perhaps a local network was still at work here: the medieval village by now had many connections beyond its immediate region.

Whether Adam kept in contact with other branches of the family back in Kibworth we have no means of knowing but of course it is more than likely that he did, and one story may illustrate this. As we have seen, one of Adam's kinsmen was the Lollard William Brown of Kibworth, who played a role as a wandering preacher before the rising of 1413. Recent research into the Coventry mercantile elites has shown that there were many Lollard sympathizers in the city from this time up to the 1431 Lollard Coventry revolt: among them the wealthy neighbour of the Browns in Erle Street, Ralph Garton, whose wife was executed in the aftermath. Garton had given financial help to impoverished Lollards from other towns who took refuge in the city. In this context a Merton document may be revealing

about Adam Brown's sympathies. In 1400 Adam made a gift of a
house in Kibworth to support Roger Dexter, a well-known Lollard
dissenter who, with his wife Alice, was forced to do public penance
in Leicester in 1389 (their story is told in Chapter 11). So Adam Brown,
a self-made man and pillar of the Coventry community, had connections with Kibworth Lollards – people with a 'lifelong commitment
to heresy'. Adam may have risen but he had not forgotten his roots or
his friends in Kibworth, and perhaps his Lollard kinsman William
Brown received financial support from his wealthy relative in the
Holy Trinity Guild at Coventry.

Such was the fruit of conversations hidden in the official sources:
the talk of men (as one Lollard said) 'sitting in taverns and talking at
table': the unspoken gaps that lie behind the dry formulas of medieval court books. Adam Brown's immediate family though never fell
foul of the law and the third generation after the Black Death saw
them firmly ensconced in the oligarchy of one of England's thriving
cities. With houses and land in Kibworth and a house in Coventry,
they belonged to both places, tenaciously holding on to strips in the
fields of their ancestral village, with friends and business partners in
both places. All of which shows how the horizons of a medieval village, which were never narrow in the first place, widened out in the
late fourteenth century. The land in William's grant eventually came
back to 'Adam Brown chaplain', who granted the land to the vicar of
Kibworth, whence it descended to Merton College in 1477. The
Browns finally disappear as Kibworth tenants in 1484, but in the sixteenth century their old family plot was still known as Brown's Place,
as if its former inhabitants still cast their influence over Main Street.

## London

The story of this particular Kibworth peasant family didn't end
though with an upwardly mobile marriage and a house in Coventry.
It didn't end with the Browns of Kibworth at a civic feast under the
star-studded roof of St Mary's hall, passing the loving cup with the

other guild members. In fact Adam's son William and his brother John also became councillors. Rich by then and a draper by trade, William was made bailiff and both were electors, members of the mayor's council who sat in chamber, two of the 'worthy men' for example who lent the Earl of Warwick a hundred marks towards his campaigns in France in the 1420s. William's second son (we are now in the third generation from our Kibworth draper Adam and nine generations from the free tenant William noted in the documents in 1280) was called Thomas and is described as both a weaver and a draper. He was rich enough to contribute cloth towards the needs of the army fighting in Normandy when war resumed in the summer of 1449 (Rouen fell that October and the English were driven out of Normandy for good the following year). In 1451 Thomas is described as a 'linen draper', one of the worthies of the city called on to consider the state of the town's fortifications on the eve of the Wars of the Roses. Then the next generation of Browns sees Nicholas as warden of the city in 1478 and a member of the town council; he was an elector in 1483–4, around the time when the family finally disappear from the Merton records for Kibworth as tenants, leaving only a branch of their kin as wage labourers holding a rented cottage.

In the following year of 1485, however, there is one more clue to the family fortunes. That year the Coventry recorder's office became vacant and was offered to John Brown, who was perhaps Nicholas's son or brother, in the event that one Thomas Kebell did not accept it. (Kebell was a Londoner who also had land in the Kibworth area and was probably part of the Browns' old circle of friends.) The letter making the offer survives in the Coventry Leet Book, one of the most magnificent civic documents from any English town in the Middle Ages. The mayor was Robert Only and his letter is dated January 1486:

Ryght worshipful sir I recommende me unto you in my most herty wyse desiring your welfare, praying you that ye wyll gyff credence to the bryngher of this letter . . . writtyn at Coventre Your true lover Rob Only Mair of the Citie of Coventre

To the right worshipfull John Brown be this deliverd

John's reply is also preserved in the city's Leet Book. It begins with the lovely formalities of fifteenth-century letter writing:

> Right worshypfull and my verray good maister, I recomende me to you, thankyng you in full hertly wyse for your letter, and that it hath pleased you so to remember me as ye have don; and of me never in eny wyse deservyd . . .

Regretfully, however, John Brown turns down the request: 'I think myself full unable thereto,' writes John, saying that he has been so long in London that he now knew nobody intimately in Coventry save Robert Only himself and Mr Symonds, who had been mayor in 1477, so he could not help:

> but I trust it shal-be my fortune hereafter som-thyng to do that shal-be to your pleasure:
> writtyn at London the Monday next after the fest of the Circumcision of our Lorde
> Yours
>     J Broun

This is not the first letter written by a Kibworth person in the medieval period, but it contains a fascinating story. By 1485, the year of the battle of Bosworth, John Brown is a Londoner and will indeed rise to become an alderman and knight, having made the same journey as so many ordinary English people over the coming centuries, a journey from the village, to the city and then to the capital. As an English yeoman family's tale of advancement it could hardly be bettered.

But this is still not quite the end of a story that has taken us from thirteenth-century farming in Leicestershire to the City of London. Adam Brown's family was last seen in Coventry in 1497; they disappear from the records of the city in the 1490s in the reign of Henry VII. By then Coventry was in grave economic decline, its troubles the subject of street songs and popular ballads. Just the time perhaps for the family to move on and seek new pastures. The timing suggests that the Browns had not lost their knack of knowing how to look after themselves and when to make their move. Just as they had left Kibworth in the stagnation of the early fifteenth century when opportunities in the village were at their thinnest, making an advantageous marriage into a leading Coventry family, in London at the end of the century there was also a grand marriage. Then William Brown, mercer, merchant of the Staple of Calais, a rising star in the cloth trade and son of John Brown, knight and alderman of the City of London, married a wealthy heiress, Katherine, daughter of Edmund Shaa, knight, and his wife Juliana. Was this our John, author of the letter to the mayor, the Coventry draper whose ancestors had come from Leicestershire and whose distant cousins still paid seasonal labourers to work on their strips 'under Blacklands' in the East Field of Kibworth Harcourt? We cannot be absolutely certain – the name after all is a common one – but the circumstances and the timing fit perfectly, and there could hardly be a more perfect story of the rise of an ordinary English family in the late Middle Ages.

# 13. The End of the Old Order

At the turn of the fifteenth century the Kibworth reeve, William Polle, like his neighbours the Browns, the Sibils and the Botons, could look back on five or six generations of family success, back to the days of Henry III and the *horrida bella* of the thirteenth-century civil war that had changed the village for ever. The villagers had divided feelings about the government and the commons, though they were loyal to the king himself as the personification of England, fount of the law which they knew was there to serve them too. In the collective popular memory of English history, the time of Henry's son, Edward I, when Merton became their landlords, had been a time when 'peace returned, and weapons were put aside; when dark clouds blew away, and sunshine came.' For William Polle (perhaps through the stories told by his grandfather Henry), the family memory easily went back to those years of Edward's reign before 1300 when 'the English were joyful', in the palmy days before the Great Famine, the 'evil days of Edward II' and the horrors of the Black Death.

Much had changed since his grandfather had been buried in the churchyard of St Wilfrid on the eve of the Famine. Still with his wife Emma, William by now had been reeve for fourteen years, just as his father Roger had been reeve for twenty years till his death in 1348, also having served at times as constable and ale-taster. The family took pride in having been long-standing officers in the village, just as in his turn William's son Robert would be. But the years of famine and plague had taken their toll across his wider kin. Plague had become an almost permanent presence in the village in the last half-century. Two thirds of the village had died in 1349, but more deaths had followed in a steady wearing away of the manpower and morale of the community over the next five decades, to culminate in a final savage spasm in 1412. A man who carried in his mind (as reeves must) a detailed picture of the village population and the interweaving of its kin groups over recent history, William was all too well aware that in his time, over the four branches of his own family, the names of seven male members had been struck through in the tenants' lists, in addition to many kinswomen and children, all victims of the pestilence.

At the turn of the century in 1400 there were complaints across the nation about the failures of Henry IV's government, and its exactions. Henry, it was murmured, was an inauspicious usurper who had overthrown Richard II unjustly: 'aboute this tyme the peple of this land began to grucche [grouch] agens kyng Harri, and beer him hevy, because he took thair good and paide not therefore; and desired to haue ageen king Richarde.' Stories even circulated among travelling brokers on the road that Richard was not dead, 'wherof moche peple was glad . . .' The local abuse of power renewed talk of Magna Carta, 'that no one should be arrested or imprisoned without response, or due process of the law . . . which the charter has confirmed in each parliament'.

The national mood then was grim: above all because of a general economic decline, which is vividly revealed in the manorial rolls for Kibworth. The great changes in employment patterns now becoming evident across the country had been under way before the Black Death, the heavy rent arrears in Kibworth for example already mounting up in the 1320s after the Great Famine. But everything was accelerated by the plague, and among the survivors it was the same whether one migrated or stayed put in the village. As William Polle and his kin saw it, the plague had hit the family hard, with the loss of so many of its menfolk. The oldest branch was headed by his cousin Nicholas and his wife Felicia; now the fifth generation after Robert (a freeman who is named in the Hundred Rolls in 1279), they had no children who survived to adulthood. Cousin William died of plague with no male heirs; as did another cousin Nicholas. The plague also killed three brothers in the third branch – Roger, Will and Robert – leaving only their sister Alice. So only our William came through, living a long life through the Black Death to 1406. William and his son Robert held the key village office of reeve for an astonishing fifty-six years between them. Clearly the Polles were generally respected and trusted, despite the inevitable village feuds with the likes of the cantankerous butcher John Pychard junior, who seems to have been able to pick quarrels with his neighbours almost at random.

As he entered the first quarterly court rentals arrears of the new century, William was well aware of the physical decline of the village. Adam Brown (now happily in business in Coventry for part of each year) may have raised his neighbours' eyebrows with his fine new house by the Slang in Main Street in 1385, and other free tenants of old families kept good homes, but many of the customary villagers, let alone the serfs, of whom there was still a handful in the village, lived in increasingly depressed conditions. The loss of so many villagers in 1349 and during later outbreaks of the plague had left a surplus of rentable housing, barns, sheds and farmhouses. Of these many are now described in the court rolls as 'empty', 'in need of repair', 'derelict' and even 'ruinous'. Over the next two generations many better-off survivors accumulated more property and land at low rents, then rented them out to other villagers, or farmed them with seasonal labour or with their own servants. But needless to say they no longer wished to be held to every term of the customary manorial conditions of rent, especially the landlord's onerous repair clauses.

The last years of the fourteenth century, then, had been a time of economic hardship, rising prices and social unrest, when the real long-term effects of the Black Death made themselves felt. And in 1401 a dangerous level of confrontation was reached in Kibworth Harcourt. Rent arrears when William took over as reeve had been nearly £15, the highest since the plague year of 1361. As this situation persisted, the college now threatened twelve tenants with steep fines if they did not repair their houses. Most of these tenants had two or more houses by this date (accumulated as the result of tenancies left vacant by plague) and this was not seen by the villagers as a fair or reasonable demand so they refused. At the same time thirteen other tenants surrendered their holdings as a joint protest. It is clear that Polle sympathized, for the rent arrears were not collected.

Through this time, from the Peasants' Revolt to the middle of the fifteenth century, a continuous thread in the court books (which is

found in many other places over the country) is a feeling of dissatis-
faction with the system in general. For poets and balladeers of the
time, now using English to speak on behalf of the ordinary people, it
was a common theme: 'The world is like a false lemman [lover] ffayre
semblant and much gyle . . . God made lords governors to govern
people in unity . . . Each king is sworn to governance, to govern god's
people in justice.' The treasury of a kingdom was not only the outward show of kings and their chivalry, rich merchants and learned
clergy, but 'corn stuffed in store' and 'a rich commons', wrote a poet
in 1401. A king without commons was no king:

> A kyng withoute rent
> might lightly trussen ['pack up'] his treasure.
> For commons maintaith lords honour, holy church and religion,
> For commons is the fairest flower
> That ever god set on earthly crown.

One important by-product of this time of stagnation and plague
outbreaks was that the birth rate dropped and population stayed low
in the country as a whole: indeed there were still only 2.5–3 million
when Elizabeth I came to the throne in 1558, half what there had
been in 1300. This story is mirrored in Kibworth. In the village,
people were marrying later and having smaller families. Some indeed
were not marrying at all, a surprising fact in any traditional rural society where heirs are always needed to work the farm. To take William's
family, his cousin Nicholas had died in middle age in 1396 with no
heir, his uncle Nicholas had died celibate in the 1380s (highly unusual
for a medieval peasant) and his three cousins produced just one daughter between them; a dramatic drop in the fertility of the family. So by
the fifteenth century the family lands became concentrated into the
hands of one branch, the reeve William's descendants.

It is at this time that we begin to see the change from a traditional
extended peasant kin group with several branches in one village to a
much smaller nuclear family practising prudential marriage, the men
and women marrying late (in their mid- to late twenties) and having
smaller families. This is the English pattern of prudential marriage,

husbanding the patrimony, what will become known as possessive individualism, which historians now see as one of the crucial social changes in the rise of capitalism (though it was a pattern fatally broken for the Polles by the inheritance strategies of William's great-grandson John, the wealthy village bailiff in Henry VIII's day, who unwisely split the family land between his four sons).

Though the fifteenth century saw a long period of stagnation, there were dramatic changes in labour relations across England. The consequence was a change from the feudal order to capitalism, from an agrarian, communally organized, close-knit society of self-sufficient peasants to a diversified, regionally orientated society of commercial farmers, artisans and landless wage-earning labourers, supporting a growing urban and commercially minded society. What happened in Kibworth is revealed in extraordinary detail in the Merton archive. As we saw, during the summer of blood of the Peasants' Revolt the Merton rolls betray no hint of political unrest in Kibworth, unless it be Nicholas Gilbert (the reeve in 1381) silently and tactfully remitting the tenants' arrears that summer. In fact the villagers were already embarked on their own plans for reform of lord and tenant relations. In this they were ultimately successful; it took time but not blood.

The confrontation between the peasants and the college in 1401, with the organized action over repair clauses, had been the first step. The surrender of their holdings by thirteen tenants as a joint protest had only been a token as in practice they continued to hold their lands and the college continued to collect their rents. But all this was a dress rehearsal for full-scale action by the community of the village. In the next few years the Merton archives reveal more cases of the villagers rejecting the custom of the manor. For example, since the very beginning of Merton's tenure of Kibworth Harcourt the village court had been required to record and investigate *fugitivi*, runaways from the village who left the lord's lands without permission of the college. But as we have seen, this kind of migration increased after the plague, with many villagers travelling away to seek work, even settling down as paid workers in cities like Leicester or Coventry. In 1407 the tenants refused to present to Merton the names of men who had left the

village without the lord's permission; and after 1409 the listing of
absconders and absentees was finally abandoned altogether by the
new reeve, Robert Polle, son of the old reeve, William. From this
time the college documents show the fellows were still in legal arguments about the legal status of some of their tenants: one bundle
records a lengthy investigation into the villein status of the Polles,
tracing their ancestry back (some as freemen, some as villeins) to the
college's acquisition of the village in 1270.

The old bonds of villeinage then were becoming unworkable
simply because of changing times and conditions, but chiefly because
the peasants refused to make them work. To make matters worse, in
1413–14, as we have seen, the Lollard heresy which had been a bub-
bling undercurrent in village life for the last thirty years flared into
life: another disturbing development for the fellows of Merton, who
themselves had already been implicated in Wycliffism. Among the
peasants from the Kibworth area who declared their allegiance to the
Lollard leader Oldcastle were men from old families with wide kin
networks and real presence in the administration of the village:
Browns, Polles and Valentines. The ringleader, Walter Gilbert's
brother Nicholas, had been a long-respected college representative in the village. Both men were among those hanged and burnt
a week later in St Giles' Fields. To the fellows of Merton, long a
source of suspicion to government and Church for their Lollard
sympathies, the village was proving to be a little too free-thinking
for comfort.

Things continued to go from bad to worse. In 1422, while Henry V
was away fighting on two fronts in France, many tenants at home
were finding themselves ruined or impoverished. At this point their
feudal lord, the Earl of Warwick, demanded a feudal aid of £16 from
Kibworth Harcourt, a war tax on all the tenants. For the reeve, Robert Polle, it was the last straw. By the end of the year sixteen tenements
were in his hands: one third of the manor was without tenants. In the
manorial court Robert struggled to let small parcels of land at low
rates to help balance the books, but over the next decade the college
lost £95 in rents – a large sum for the time, getting on for £50,000
today. Needless to say the tenants felt deeply aggrieved and now as a

group they finally put their foot down over the question of customary dues. On top of national taxes and war aids, the double bind of labour services and rent increases, with extra landlord's costs, was no longer supportable, or – as they perceived – enforceable. In discussion with the reeve and the college steward they let it be known that they wanted traditional labour services regularized across the board to straight money transactions. Eventually the college gave way.

First, in 1427 the college agreed that henceforth all eighteen customary virgates (villein tenancies) were no longer to be held *in bondagio*; from now on they were to be held *ad voluntatem*, 'at the will of the lord', in other words on the basis of a negotiated contract paid in cash. Customary status then would no longer be the determining factor in labour law. At the same time the college also consented to reduce the rent by 3s 4d per virgate per annum (a rental which would remain fixed till the eighteenth century!). A great deal of reorganization was required as a result of these changes, and negotiations and adjustments occupied the village court in the court rolls for over ten years until 1439. Arguably, this was as big a change as the enclosure of the open fields in 1779, perhaps greater, for in effect it signalled the end of the feudal order in Kibworth.

Over the next few years through the manorial court under their elected reeves the peasants negotiated the new conditions of employment with the Merton fellows and their agent, who came up on regular visits to meet with tenants. Finally in October 1439 a special Court of Recognition was held at Kibworth, chaired by the bailiff and the reeve, to finalize and record the mutual consent of both parties – the college and the tenants – to the new tenurial arrangements. This kind of thing was happening all across England in the late fourteenth and fifteenth centuries, though it is rare to be able to see the minute details as we can here.

The document is now on paper instead of vellum, itself a sign of the times. At the top it reads 'The Sunday after the Feast of St Dionysus a Court of Recognition between the customary tenants of Kibworth and the house of scholars of Walter of Merton at Oxford'. Then comes a list of all eighteen customary tenants by each of which

in the margin the scribe has written 'ad voluntatem'. They are familiar names: Robert's cousin Simon Polle, John Chapman, Robert
Brown (cousin of the Coventry drapers), Tom Saunders, John
Pychard the butcher and other members of old village families, the
Heyneses, Peks and Swans. More than 170 years on from Merton's
assumption of the lordship, the village community was still a coherent group run by the same families.

In English medieval law, status – as legally defined with recorded
precedent – was everything. It determined freedom, work, education and movement. Hence some earlier writers had railed against
'those foolish men that would allow serfs an education'. Back in the
bad old days close to Kibworth at Stoughton a legal case had concluded 'once a villein always a villein' as a triumphant shriek from a
sneering landlord. A Merton investigation into the villein status of
the Polle family in the fifteenth century produced a complete account
of the family history in an attempt to prove their ancient villein status (though Robert in the Hundred Rolls of 1279 was clearly free, as
was the head of another branch of the kin, Nicholas, a free tenant in
1280: the great-great-grandfather of our Robert, who was reeve
between 1406 and 1443). Others, though, had been 'customary tenants' or villeins. The 1439 Court of Recognition meant the abolition
of villein status and the de facto adoption of primogeniture, with the
acceptance of leasehold, indentures and transfers; in other words,
personal and economic freedom for most of the villagers. Also abolished was the legal category of 'bondman' and of certain land being
described as 'bondland'. In the past to hold bondland, *in bondagio*,
could make you a bondman. Gone too were the labour services
attached to bondland. There were now just fixed rents, which could
not be raised by arbitrary will of the lord.

The Kibworth 1439 agreement also had a long-term effect on farming practices and the organization of the open fields. It confirmed the
amalgamation of customary half-virgate tenancies (the small peasant
holdings for one family) into single and multiple virgate holdings.
This meant that tenants could hold unequal amounts of land in the
three open fields and could keep double the number of beasts on the
meadow, or more. So the administration of the farming cycle had to

become more flexible and the need for by-laws began to assert itself. (Oblique references to by-laws became common in the rolls; the first by-law was enrolled in 1430, the first ones still written in Latin, later in English.) This process continued so that by the seventeenth century the open fields in Kibworth were already much diminished after well-off yeoman farming families like the Heyneses and Rays had consolidated sizeable individual holdings in the open fields, amalgamating field strips over time. It may be for this reason that there was little push for enclosure in this part of Leicestershire during the Agricultural Revolution in the eighteenth century, and the enclosure of the open fields, when it came to Kibworth Harcourt in 1779, was arranged with little disturbance. The process had been going on for a long time and the last flickering was due in part to satisfy the desire of the college to tidy things and come up to date.

## Social change: 1400–1600

The 1439 agreement had far-reaching effects. It even brought changes in the look of the village, with extensive rebuilding over the next few decades, increasingly using brick, as families improved their own homes. The modern village is well on the way as it first appears in visual representation in a 1609 Merton map, with brick houses and chimneys. The late-fifteenth-century farmer's house known as Priory Farm is typical of the new style of English domestic architecture: no longer a medieval open hall but a long house with a second floor and private bedrooms. Out in the fields too the industrially farmed landscape of the High Middle Ages was changing: the great brown swathes of open fields, without hedgerows or trees, was giving way to mixed farming with a shift away from arable to pasture. With greater flexibility open to them now, some tenants concentrated on stock and others on arable. Large areas of arable land went down to permanent pasture in the three open fields. Commercial farming had arrived.

Almost immediately a greater differentiation between economic groups is revealed in the college archive: a number of thirty- and sixty-acre holdings emerge, soon to become a hundred acres or more, held by husbandmen, yeomen and eventually by gentlemen. This is the real beginning of the class of free English yeomen farmers who will be such an important agent for economic growth and cultural and religious change in the Tudor period, especially in the East Midlands and East Anglia. A social class below the rich shire gentry of the fifteenth century, these people (like the Polles, Clerks, Browns and Peks in Kibworth) are the well-to-do middling farmers whom we have traced through this story in detail from the thirteenth century (many of them clearly descended from the free peasantry in Domesday Book). In court cases of the Tudor period some of these people could accurately recall a dozen or more generations by name back to the early-fourteenth-century poll taxes. Altogether a greater diversity of class and status began to emerge in the village: gentlemen, lawyers, clergymen, yeomen and husbandmen, and artisans who lived in cottages but were not necessarily poor. Genuinely poor were the day labourers looking for work at the hiring fair on the Bank at Beauchamp and the widows and others living in cottages in the mud houses on the insalubrious edge of 'the Marsh' at the eastern end of Kibworth.

In the Merton archive the 1448 building accounts for a house still standing in Main Street may perhaps be seen to epitomize these changes in wealth and class. The identification of this house in the Middle Ages is not certain, but it is likely that this is the site called Brown's Place in the Merton records where, as we have seen, a surviving range is dated to the decade or two from the 1320s and a hall from 1385, very likely built by Adam Brown, the successful draper who made his fortune in Coventry. In 1448 a new big range with a hall and farm buildings was constructed running along Main Street on a large ironstone platform on the slope where the droveway goes out to the open fields by the horse mill and pond. After many rebuildings no firm dendrochronological dating could be gathered from this part of the house, but a fifteenth-century 'dragon beam' still holds up a jettied upper storey at the corner by the Slang. The house was occupied by the families of reeves and bailiffs through the fifteenth and sixteenth centuries, including the Peks, Clerks and Polles. The 1448 accounts are entitled 'Expenses at hand of John Caunden ordered the administrators of Merton College' and list in full the construction costs for a hall with chambers and outbuildings, itemizing wages to twenty villagers for cartage and labour, including carpentry, plastering and painting. Over fifty entries give a great impression of the intensive labour on one fine village house:

To John Parke for the carriage of lime
For the carriage of timber from Temple Park [Rothley]
Idem Slate from Kirby
Idem Stone from Medbourne
To John Simkin for the carriage of lime from Barrow on Soar
To Thomas Wynllof carriage of timber from Temple Park
To John atte Hulle for readying the ground for the hall
To John Cawnden carriage of timber and lathe from Lutterworth
And ten cartloads of stone bought at Medbourne
To Will Peek 'for painting of the woolhouse'
'The plasterers for their labour'
To John Reynolds for 800 big timber nails
700 'pricking' nails
4000 lathenayle [lathe nails]

Extra payments were made to masons and carpenters for labour on the hall, the chamber and the stable, and on other barns and outbuildings. There are also records of payments for bread when the carters were carrying the stone to Kibworth (the equivalent today would be sandwiches) and for pork and veal, and ale.

So just before the outbreak of the Wars of the Roses the reeve, now generally known as the bailiff, had a very substantial house, where perhaps the fellows of Merton and their agents would stay when they made their regular visits to the village. By now the bailiff had become a man of real substance and influence in the village.

In the early Tudor period, from the 1490s to the 1530s, we can get our first really good impression of the furnishings of such 'middle class' houses through villagers' wills and their attached inventories. Wills or deathbed testaments began to be used widely among this yeoman class in the late fifteenth century – over 20,000 survive from Leicestershire alone from the 1490s to the 1590s but this is a pattern common across England as a whole. Discussed in detail in the next chapter, they offer a close picture of these upwardly mobile farming households with their furniture, clothes and material possessions and luxuries, using hired servants (as many as six in the Polle household), sending younger sons away to study law or enter commerce and giving their daughters generous dowries.

The will of Amy Polle is typical with its detailed inventory of house contents listed room by room. Amy (or Amice) was the wife of John Polle, the bailiff from 1520 till 1536, and she lists the 'gret coffer that stands in my parlour' and her set of best bedlinen – coverlets, pillows and bolsters – together with 'one feather bed with hangings thereto'. There are many kitchen pots and pans, and a fine collection of gowns and kirtles, fitting for a bailiff's wife. We learn that she employed no fewer than six servants, probably including a gardener for the vegetable plots behind the yard. Typical of the Kibworth villagers, she also made numerous charitable bequests, including a gift of corn to 'every poor family in Kibworth'. For a family descended from peasant holders of a virgate in the thirteenth century, the Polles had risen in village society. Some of Amy's neighbours like the Colmans and Iliffes are recorded from Tudor times till today, and still live in the village. Other very long-lasting families like Amy's are long gone from the village now, though they have surviving collateral branches in the region.

### Education: 1300–1500

So many of these stories about reeves, bailiffs and clerks – not to mention Lollard preachers – suggest a level of literacy in the village that might appear surprising given the way we tend to view the lives of medieval peasants. But there has been a persistent underestimation of peasant literacy in the English medieval village. It is very likely that there were literate people in Kibworth even in the eleventh century – a priest or a parish clerk, perhaps, for such a sizeable community; and, indeed, it is not impossible that there were literate laity there in Anglo-Saxon times, when town reeves were expected to know the lawbook. The first literate villager appears in the records in the 1160s – 'William the clerk of Kibworth', the village scribe.

By the 1200s everyone in Kibworth, as in most of England, was in contact with reading and writing. You went to church, where the priest used a book and the church had wall paintings carrying poems, songs and religious texts. You knew the Lord's Prayer and the Creed in Latin. As a freeman or freewoman, and even perhaps as a villein, you may have 'signed' a lease of land in the church porch, affixing your own seal. If you went to Leicester to join the merchants' guild as a draper or ironmonger or wool brogger, you will have kept accounts, which may have required of you some basic literacy and numeracy. And by the end of the thirteenth century there were chantry chaplains in Kibworth drawn from peasant families who must have had a basic reading ability.

There was a long succession of villagers with the title of *capellanus* or *dominus* ('sir'), such as John Godwin in 1280, William Polle around 1300, and John Polle and John Sibil later in the century. Such men appear in the court rolls through to the Reformation; they came from old village families and clearly had some kind of basic education. But how did they become literate? Who taught them? A village school is recorded from the sixteenth century, with a permanent building in the 1620s. But when did it start?

## The secrets of the school box

'On the Sunday next after the feast of St Helen, in the 27th year of King Edward III' – that is, on 18 August 1353 – a meeting was held at Kibworth Harcourt, perhaps after Sunday church, maybe in the north porch of St Wilfrid's, or in the bailiff's house on the Slang, whose northern wing still survives from before this date. The witnesses included William Polle, 'chaplain', and Roger 'the clerk' along with Roger Polle, Will Heynes and others. In an agreement, Robert Chapman of Kibworth Harcourt and John Dere of Saddington placed a small amount of land in a trust to be administered by trustees: 'a house in Kibworth next to Nicholas Polle's old house in Church lane; a rood of land lying above Middlefurlong next to the strip held by Nicholas' son Henry and abutting the boundary of Kibworth; a rood of meadow in Bradmere'.

Along with two other deeds from the 1350s, this agreement is the beginning of the story of Kibworth Grammar School. It turned up in what became known as the 'school box', the first document in a parchment and paper trail that extends over 600 years and which is now being catalogued for the first time. The original purpose of the gifts, in which the Polles and Chapmans appear to have been instrumental, was not to found a school. It was to set up land and property to provide an annual income supervised by a trustee apparently, although never specified in the deeds, for a little village guild, with a preacher or chaplain who would chant special masses for the souls of the members' ancestors, a typical arrangement of the fourteenth century, especially in the traumatized time after the Black Death.

By the seventeenth century these lands were known as the 'School lands', and they provided an income for a grammar school which survived until the twentieth century. The lands were rescued from expropriation during the Civil War, and during the enclosures of 1779 were consolidated with the agreement of local landowners, with three fields still earmarked for the support of the school. Though the school finally closed in 1960, amalgamated by the local education authority, the lands are still known as school lands and their income still supports school trips, such as to the First World War battlefields, for today's Kibworth High School.

A 'grammar school' at Kibworth Beauchamp is first mentioned in 1559, but the village tradition was that it was founded by Richard Neville, Earl of Warwick – 'Warwick the Kingmaker' – during the Wars of the Roses. The early history of the school is very shadowy, but at a hearing over the endowments in 1651 it was believed that the school's endowment of land had been preserved at the time of Henry VIII's dissolution of the chantries during the Reformation through the intervention of John Dudley, Duke of Northumberland, who was then lord of the manor of Kibworth Beauchamp. The documents in the school box show a board of feoffees, all local farmers, going back to the fourteenth century; in later times, from at least 1559 to 1877, land and houses at Kibworth Beauchamp were held by feoffees in trust 'for the maintenance of a free school'. These feoffees acted as sole governors, received the rents of their tenants, and appointed the schoolmaster, who until 1907 was always a clerk in holy orders.

It is hard to prove there was a school, or even a teacher, before Tudor times, but there were clearly many educational possibilities in the village much earlier. One lay in Kibworth's relationship with Merton College. Merton was the first formal college at Oxford: the founder's idea was to create an academic community of university scholars who had a first degree and who wished to study for the MA or degree in civil law or theology. At the same time the statutes of 1270 also provided for the education of another group, of 'boy scholars' studying grammar with a status lower than undergraduates and with a master paid to teach them. From 1270 an additional group of twelve poor 'secondary scholars' (*scolares pauperes secundarii*) appears, paid for by money donated by wealthy benefactors. Even before 1277 there are further references in Merton rolls to the 'poor scholars of Kibworth'. These were evidently boys learning grammar rather than undergraduates. And in the early accounts of Merton from the 1280s and 1290s there are one or two further references to 'poor scholars of Kibworth'. Presumably some of these boys who learned Latin grammar became clerks and chaplains in the village – which helps us to understand the high degree of literacy among village officials, reeves and *capellani* drawn from families like the Polles and Sibils.

Clearly there was some kind of reciprocity between the college and Kibworth from the start. But was there some kind of medieval village school, with a teacher? It is certainly possible – teaching might have been held for example in an aisle of the church or in a private house. This might account for educated villagers like William Brown and Walter Gilbert being able to preach with the help of English texts, rather like William Smith, the self-taught Leicester smith, with his compilations of 'English books'. Though Roger and Alice Dexter were most likely illiterate, Adam Brown the Coventry draper may well have been literate, as his grandson certainly was. The same might go for some village women: like the three Kibworth women, Margaret and Mary Harcourt and Maud Polle, from a small nunnery down the Welland near Stamford, who in their wills, which also found their way into the school box, donated lands in Kibworth for the purposes of prayer (Margaret died in 1407). In this context a fascinating and perhaps unique survival in the archives of Merton suggests that, exactly as tradition has it, there was already a teacher of grammar in the village as far back as the early fifteenth century.

## Pychard the Butcher

In the summer of 1447, John Pychard, the Kibworth Harcourt butcher, was feeling 'vexyd and trobuld gretely' and furious with his neighbour Robert Polle in particular. Pychard was maybe in his forties, a butcher (and grazier?) like his father before him. He had a cottage and half a virgate on Main Street with his wife Agnes and his teenage son, John junior. He was clearly a quarrelsome figure. His tendencies earned him frequent entries in the court rolls – he had more than once drawn blood in brawls.

Off he went in August to one of the village scribes, and got things off his chest by composing a long letter addressed to the Warden of Merton. What follows is part of the text lightly modernized with a little added punctuation. It is perhaps, remarkably, the earliest English letter by an English peasant to survive:

Most worshipful and reverent lord I commend me unto your worthy lordship desiring to hear of your prosperity and bodily health, the which almighty God preserve and sustain unto his pleasans and your wealth and welfare. And if it be pleasing to your worthy lordship that I that am your own poor servant and man unto my power in what service that lieth in me abide upon your lord ye will with all my heart.

The issue bothering him sounds like a typical village conflict, a dispute which John says 'cost me more than forty shillings'. His complaint was that the Kibworth bailiff had fiddled the court roll in his own favour – and once something was set down in writing in the medieval system, one imagines it was very difficult to gainsay it without a lot of time, expense and personal appearances at the manor court – even, as had already happened to John, a nine-mile ride to Leicester to petition a higher court. 'And now foully and wrongfully am I put away from it by record of Robert Polle and all my neighbours.'

At the end of the letter comes the surprise that takes this letter out of the typical mundane world of the medieval manorial court:

And furthermore sir we have a young man with us, the which is a goodly scholar for a grammarian [grameryen] after the form of the country, and a likely man of person to do you service. And truly sir he is the son of one of your tenants that is to say the son of Agnes Palmer.

Will Palmer was twenty. His father John died in 1448, and was perhaps sick when Pychard wrote this letter to the fellows of Merton. Pychard's letter continues, 'not stopping on his points':

And truly sir the man deserved to have cunning [knowledge] over all thing notwithstanding he might have masters in the king's house and in diverse places but he wolde evermore have cunning. And truly sir we pray you all your tenants everyone that ye would cherish him for truly sir he shall be at you in haste and forsooth you will like his conditions have you assayed him a while both for governance and person. No more at this time but almighty god have you in his keeping. Written at Kibworth in the feast of St Hugh the Martyr.

He your own man and poor servant John Pychard.

Pychard's letter takes us right into social relations in Main Street in the 1440s, into village politics and relations between families. What was his relation with Agnes Palmer? Why had he taken young Will under his wing? And how had Will already in his teens acquired the skills to be accounted a 'grameryen'? Evidently Palmer was not one of the poor scholars of Kibworth at Merton, otherwise the fellows would already have known him, but he had obviously already taken the first steps up what medieval schoolmen called the 'tower of learning'.

Pychard's interest in him (for all his cantankerous character) recalls later injunctions by Tudor educationalists that 'no man goeth about a more godlie purpose, that he is mindfull of the good bringing up, both of hys owne, and other mens children.'

The letter is a clear indication that there was indeed a teacher of grammar in the village by this time. Most likely he was one of the chantry priests paid for by the villagers' gifts of fields that remained in the school's possession from the sixteenth century until modern times. Our village story is the same as so many across England in the Middle Ages. To administer the fields and strips Nicholas Polle used writing. Lollards like Gilbert and Brown read vernacular books. The estate manager made notes itemizing nails, boards, plaster and slate on strips of parchment or paper sent in a bundle to Merton. And the butcher (on behalf of 'all your tenants') recommends a neighbour's young son for higher education. For the ordinary folk of England education was a passport to wealth, to changing status and freedom, and to new mental horizons.

## The horizon of the fifteenth century

Complex changes in history are thus revealed in the fortunes of ordinary families. This slow crystallization was already under way before the Black Death but accelerated after the plague, with changes in employment, in the culture of the people, in personal self-awareness and in religious autonomy (as is evidenced in the Lollard heresy). Education and literacy too played a part in a process which emerges from the lower reaches of society, instigated by the villagers themselves. By the late fifteenth century the manorial labour discipline and all its implications were gone, and Kibworth had taken its first steps on the way to becoming a modern village.

The changes in the mentalities of the English people in this period were psychological and material. Both played a part in the transformation of society which would lead England to become the first capitalist society in history. Historians now agree on the broad picture, but till recently they have been in the dark over how agrarian society changed at grass-roots level between the late fourteenth century and the eighteenth, laying the basis for the swift and radical social and political changes that transformed England from around 1700. Only in recent years as the court rolls of villages across the English Midlands have been examined has it become clear how these things happened. It is clear now that the change was not only in laws and structures of government imposed from above: by 1500 new mentalities are apparent that would shape England's future path. And these were created not only by the rulers, the jurists and the authors of medieval management texts, but by the peasants themselves.

# 14. The Reformation in Kibworth

In the summer of 1535, with candles burning before the image of Our Lady of Kibworth, the light from the stained glass glinting on the painted rood above him, the vicar William Peyrson had to make an extraordinary series of church announcements to his parishioners. During the previous months Henry VIII's Parliament had enacted a short piece of legislation which would have a significance to the English people out of all proportion to its length: an Act of Supremacy asserting that 'the king our sovereign Lord his heirs and successors kings of this realm, shall be taken accepted and reputed the only supreme head on earth of the Church of England.' With that the Pope, whose predecessor Gregory the Great had sent the famous mission to convert the English almost a thousand years before, was no longer the head of the Christian Church in England.

This was the crowning moment in a religious revolution which had gathered momentum over the previous five years. King Henry's Reformation had begun earlier in the 1530s over his divorce from Katherine of Aragon and his love for Anne Boleyn, but had now become an issue for all in his realm. How it was to be interpreted on the ground at parish level in Kibworth was now Peyrson's responsibility. That summer of 1535 the government abolished 'the abuses of the Bishop of Rome. His authority and jurisdiction.' The English clergy were ordered to teach the doctrine of Royal Supremacy to their parishioners and:

to cause all manner prayers orisons, rubrics, canons in mass books, and all other books used in the churches, wherin the said Bishop of Rome is named or his presumptuous and proud pomp and authority preferred, utterly to be abolished eradicated and erased out, and his name and memory to be nevermore (except to his contumely and reproach) remembered.

In the chancel behind the medieval oak screen, Peyrson now had to watch his curate apply a metal scraper to the ink in his old vellum mass book, scraping out the Pope's name and titles. From now on there would be no mention of the holy father in Sunday prayers.

Up to that point Kibworth had been still a traditional society: a community where the rich local brand of late-medieval Christianity was still robustly thriving after many centuries. Inside the church there were the old familiar images, the glowing stained glass and brightly painted rood screen, the incense and the lamps; and there too were practised the old familiar rituals, the saint's day processions and relic cults, the church alms and masses for the dead, the suspended moment in time when the Host was raised and the Body became present in the Mass. From Kibworth there were visits to Walsingham and to the 'mother church' in Lincoln (which no Kibworthian omitted to mention in his or her will); and to the network of local shrines: the holy well at Hallaton and the shrine of St Wistan with its little painted statue of the royal prince and martyr, whose golden hair, it was said, waved each year at the end of May in the long grass of the water meadows below Kibworth.

It is likely that so far, as elsewhere in England, the parishioners of Kibworth took these new developments in their stride. They had their lives to get on with; in an agricultural community life was bounded by work. Matters of supremacy were something for kings and ministers to worry about, not the man who cuts the hay or the woman who brews the ale. But the same year a heavy new tithe was imposed on all parishes and as the dissolution of the great monasteries began, through the summer of 1536, reformation of religious practices at local level gathered momentum. One new law abolished all holy days which fell in the law term and the harvest period, with a handful of exceptions; it was claimed they were damaging the country's economy, stopping vital work and impoverishing workers. Services could be held, but people must work as usual. As might be imagined, there was widespread anger over this attack on traditional religion, with some daring to call King Henry and his henchmen a 'false secte of heretiques'. In the north the response was a mass armed rising which came close to toppling Henry's government, and news of these sensational events, along with disturbing omens and prophecies of further threats to the Commonwealth, no doubt reached Kibworth.

In September 1538 Peyrson again addressed his parishioners from the pulpit to inform them of a new and still more hardline series of injunctions. There was to be a new Great Bible (or 'King's Bible') kept on a chain in each parish church; to be read out aloud in church services; the first authorized Bible in English. The vicar was now required to make a register of births, marriages and deaths for the parish in a vellum manuscript to be carefully kept in church, effectively gathering information on the conformity of the people. He was also to conduct regular examination of the laity in the principles of faith, to see that they were not slipping back into 'childish superstition'. But most disconcerting to Peyrson and his flock was the ferocity of the government's new language against traditional English piety. For in their pronouncements now was a sneering contempt for the old customs and practices of the faith which had sustained ordinary English men and women for so long: pilgrimage, devotion to images and worship of saints, the old rituals of confession and absolution, the masses for the dead. To a traditionalist like Peyrson this must have been a devastating blow. He was now instructed to exhort the people of the village 'not to repose their trust in any other works devised by mens phantasies, as in pilgrimages, offering of money or candles or tapers to images and relics . . . or in kissing or licking them, or such like superstitions'. To avoid the 'detestable sin of idolatry' he should remove from his church all such 'feigned images', even the beloved Virgin of Kibworth herself. Though Peyrson could perhaps not see it yet, with that the process was set in train which would lead inexorably to the rubbing away of the traditional spirit world of the English.

Will Peyrson was a conventional clerk, son of a staunchly Catholic mother, a man who lived and died in the Old Faith. Devoted to the cult of Mary, as he put it, 'to Our Blessed Ladye, Most Purest Virgyne, and to all the companye of heaven', he was punctilious in observing the solemn rituals of the past, and among his possessions was a little stone crucifix plated with silver which he used for prayer in his own chamber. Not surprisingly he could not conceal his anger about these new developments. That September in Kibworth church an argument over the government's reforms took place in front of the parishioners and led to Peyrson making an outburst against King Henry. This was reported to the authorities by some of them, led by a man identified in the offical report only as 'R. O'. The core of R. O.'s information was that 'Peyrson the priest in Kybworth church most devilishly spake these words: "If the King had died seven years agone it had been no hurt."' Wishing the king dead of course could be construed in many ways and was not wise given Henry's malevolent obsession with crushing any kind of dissent. Peyrson was hauled off to Leicester and thrown in prison by Henry's local enforcers, one of whom, Sir John Beaumont, wrote to Henry's chief minister, Thomas Cromwell, concerning the case: 'The wretch is in prison. His accusers are sworn before the sheriff.'

The tale would be repeated up and down the land over the next few years. Peyrson was an old-fashioned country vicar: his traditional regime of memorial masses, miracle plays, pilgrimages and church alms was not to the liking of the new order in the shires whose inquisitions will soon enough dismiss men like him as 'unsound in religion . . . massemongers who useth incantation . . . and who dice and play games'. One Midland vicar was even said to be 'a drunkard and dumbe, and it is thought a sorcerer'. Peyrson's chief accuser, Sir John Beaumont, on the other hand, was typical of the unscrupulous 'new rich' partisans of Cromwell: he acquired the lands and buildings of Grace Dieu Priory for himself after claiming two nuns had been guilty of fornication and had given birth to children. He was eventually dismissed for corruption and misappropriation, though too late to save Peyrson's career.

But who were the Kibworth informants who had been so angry with their vicar that they had informed on him, and did they genuinely hold more Protestant views? 'R. O.' perhaps was Robert Oswin, who lived at the end of Hog Lane by the village ditch (his plot is occupied by a modern house today, but the arable just north of it is still called Oswins Leys). Unless there was a personal animus against Peyrson, the tale suggests that Henry's reformation of the old religion already had some supporters among old families of the village, and perhaps even (though this is harder to quantify) that some of the dissenting ideas spread by the Lollards might have been still current in the village. As in the early fifteenth century there may well have been splits in the village, and even in families, over religion. But these were increasingly uneasy times and when talk went astray there was no telling where 'Scandalous, Seditious and Treasonable Speech' might end.

## The reign of Edward VI: 'commocion tyme'

The writing was on the wall. Nevertheless Henry's Six Articles of 1539 reaffirmed the centrality of the traditional mass and even threatened its critics with burning. So the English religious establishment for now continued as a compromise with a part-Protestant, part-Catholic prayer book. As far as we can tell from wills of the time, most of the people in Kibworth as in England generally were still satisfied with the old religion and were devoted and generous to their local church and clergy. The turning point came with Henry's death in 1547. The new king, Edward, a pious and cold-hearted swot, was ardently Protestant, and with the evangelical party triumphant in Court, rumours spread across the country like wildfire through 'markets fairs and ale-houses' of 'innovations and changes in religion'. Within months the commissioners moved into the regions with a draconian set of enquiries. A root-and-branch reform was to take place of the people's 'blindness and ignorance', which was founded on 'devising and phantasising vain opinions of purgatory and masses'.

Over the next five years Edward and his advisers imposed sweeping changes on the fabric, furnishings, customs and liturgy of the parish church. Images, stone altars and rood lofts were taken down and destroyed. Whitewash and biblical texts replaced the gorgeous medieval wall paintings. And with this physical desecration came the destruction of the valued local institutions – chantries, free chapels and guilds – which had provided teaching, dispensed charity and performed anniversary masses. In Kibworth the little free chapels of St Leonard in Smeeton, St Lawrence in Beauchamp and St Cuthbert in Harcourt were closed down and demolished, their rubble sold off for building stone.

So Edward's reformation became a wholesale wrecking of the old church at parish level, and an attack on the traditional beliefs and rituals long followed by the English people, even striking at that most natural and intimate of human needs: the remembrance of the dead. And though Catholicism was briefly and bitterly restored under Mary in 1553, the Protestant religion was finally settled under Elizabeth after 1558 when the last phase of iconoclasm began – a third change of regime and religious policy in twelve years. No specific information survives on this from Kibworth, but it is very likely that it was in Edward's day that the interior of St Wilfrid's parish church, with its fourteenth-century rood lofts, screens, saints' panels, wall paintings and altars, was effaced, leaving what is seen today. No doubt there were those who were glad to see these 'marks of idolatry' destroyed, but to others it was a time when 'all godly ceremonies were taken out of the church . . . all goodness and godliness despised and in manner banished . . . when devout religion and honest behaviour of men was accounted and taken for superstition and hypocrisy.' The argument between those two points of view would take centuries to resolve – and is not over yet.

## Living through the Reformation

How did the Reformation work itself out in the village? How did our villagers cope? We can track the ups and downs of the vicars: Peyrson's hatred of Henry VIII leading to his imprisonment and dismissal; the subsequent refusal of later Tudor vicars to accept enforced change from either the Protestant or the Catholic side; the enmity between High Church and Puritan rivals in the Civil War. But what of the people themselves? As we have seen, there may have been a long undercurrent of anti-clericalism and dissent in the village, going back to the turbulent years of the early fifteenth century when such questions even split families, such as the Polles, Browns and Gilberts, stalwarts of the community. The Oswins and others may have approved of Henry's reforms in the 1530s.

What happened during these great changes between the late 1530s and the 1560s cannot be tracked in detail in Kibworth as the church-wardens' accounts have not survived. The parish registers cannot help us either as they start only in 1574 and are missing at least eight or nine years: they may have begun at the start of Elizabeth's reign. The enormous quantity of administrative material in the bishop's registers in Lincoln has yet to be trawled. But what we can do in Kibworth is suggest some of the changes, both material and psychological, in a new source for the village story, the wills of the villagers. Twenty thousand of these survive for the shire from 1490 to 1600 in the County Record Office, and many more after. Often accompanied by inventories of possessions, these provide a vivid insight into the people's lives. At earlier stages in the village story some kind of intimacy has been possible, for example in letters like that of John Pychard, but in the wills we can find hints of the villagers' beliefs and concerns, their attitudes to work, houses and possessions, and even to luxuries; but especially to friends, family and neighbours.

The villagers' wills begin within living memory of the Wars of the Roses, early in Henry VIII's time, and many of the community then still belonged to the old families we have followed from the thirteenth century, such as the Carters, Browns, Sanders and Iliffes in Harcourt, and the Reynalds, Hyndes, Colmans, Gambles and Wards in Beauchamp. Drawn up in 1516, early in the reign of Henry VIII, is the will of a woman from another old family that we have found was well established in 1279: the Polles, who at this time lived in the bailiff's house, now known as the Manor House, on Main Street. As we have seen, until the 1530s England was a Catholic country, and the will follows traditional formulas ('Sir' before Katherine's son's name is the traditional honorific for the village curate; a trental is thirty requiem masses to be recited by the vicar):

In the name of God Amen the eighth day of the month of April 1516 I Katherine Poll of Kibworth Harcourt sound of mind and memory make my Testament in this manner. Firstly I leave my soul to almighty God and the Blessed Mary, and my body to be buried in the churchyard of St Wilfrid's in the parish of Kibworth. Item I leave to the Mother Church of Lincoln 4d. Item I leave for the repair of the parish church of Kibworth aforesaid 20s.

19. Culture: theatrical tradition was strong in the village, from mummers' plays to visiting professional theatre companies. This poster from 1790 advertises a topical anti-slavery play, *Inkle and Yarico*, whose sponsor lived at the Manor House in Kibworth Beauchamp.

20. Plough Monday processions and dances were an old East Midlands tradition still performed in Kibworth in the 1930s.

The coming of the railways saw the transformation of Kibworth from a rural community to almost a small town.

21./22. *Top and middle*: navvies photographed by the Leicester photographer Sidney Newton.

23. *Bottom*: opened in 1857, Kibworth station was closed over a century later.

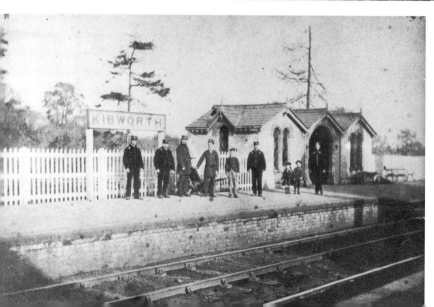

Shopping: by the 1860s Kibworth had drapers, grocers, sweet shops and a newsagent's.

24. Dalton's shoe shop. Albert Dalton in the doorway of his Reliable Boot Stores. The shop is now the village fish-and-chip shop.

25. George Lynn (*far left in the picture above*) standing outside his shop, the main general store from late-Victorian times till after the Second World War.

26. Eli and Floss Bale outside their draper's shop, around 1900.

ROSE & CROWN HOTEL
KIBWORTH, LEICESTERSHIRE.

27./28./29. Drink: there were once twenty-three inns and drinking houses in Kibworth. The four survivors include the now rebuilt Old Swan; the Rose and Crown, a big coaching inn which is now Raitha's Indian Restaurant; and the Coach and Horses, where Thomas Cook famously waited for his ride.

30. Like most English villages of any size Victorian Kibworth had a rich cultural life, music being especially important. The brass band was a fixture in village life from the 1860s.

31. Sport too was a great feature of Victorian working-class culture: cricket in Kibworth goes back 200 years, with the cricket club founded in the 1840s but only recently becoming national village champions; the village ground (seen here in the 1950s, but today with a spanking new pavilion) is a venue for women's internationals.

32. Politics and dissent: 1897 jubilee flags in front of the Old House, home to Kibworth's famous dissenting academy in the eighteenth century, and where the poet, feminist, anti-slavery campaigner and pioneer children's writer Anna Laetitia Barbauld grew up.

33. Radical politics: the 1905 Leicester unemployed march on London was the forerunner of the Jarrow march. Three heroic figures in the workers' struggle: Amos Sherriff, the Rev. F. L. Donaldson and George White.

34./35. War: forty village men died in the First World War. George Maynard Ward, aged eighteen in 1917 (*left*), and Percy Bromley, killed in France with his brother Cecil in 1918 (*right*); both families have been in the village for over 400 years.

36. Kibworth: 'Our grumbling friendly warm-hearted village', as Leslie Clarke put it in the wartime village newspaper, photographed by the Luftwaffe in November 1940.

37./38. The Home Front: Rose Holyoak, ploughing as some of her medieval women ancestors did. In the Second World War, Kibworth had a Home Guard unit, a POW camp and a Landgirls' hostel and sheltered evacuees from London.

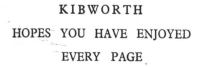

KIBWORTH
HOPES YOU HAVE ENJOYED
EVERY PAGE

"To love the little platoon we belong to in society is the germ of all public affection."—BURKE.

THE KIBWORTH NEWS
and FORCES' JOURNAL

No. 1 NEW SERIES 1944

*KIBWORTH*
*sends affectionate New Year Greetings to our Lads and Lassies on sea, land and in the air, to the sick and suffering and those who tend them, and to all Prisoners of War.*

*1940—1944*

Sent Free to all
serving in H.M.F.

All others
6d. each.

39. The *Forces' Journal*, which was sent to all serving villagers, a 'memory chain link' with 'that certain village back home in dear old England'.

Item I leave for the repair of the Chapel of St Leonard of Smeeton 3s 4d. Item I leave to Margaret my daughter 53s 4d. Item I leave to Sir William Polle my son to celebrate one trental for prayers for the health of my soul and all the faithful departed 10s. Item I leave to each of the priests who celebrate my exequies 6d. Whatever truly remains of my goods I leave my executors Sir William Polle and Thomas Clerke of Kibworth Beauchamp to despose of as they think fit for the good of my soul and to be supervisor of my testament Sir Walter Lucas Rector of the church of Kibworth.

The text is brief and to the point, as might befit an ordinary farmer's wife, but it suggests the rich detail of local religious life: Katherine's devotion to the Virgin Mary and to the mother church of Lincoln; the trental of thirty requiem masses to help her soul through purgatory; the evidence that her son 'Sir' William was a curate or chaplain in the village, and hence (though from a peasant family) literate and 'book learned'. The gift for 'each of the priests' who were to perform her funeral procession and service suggests that Katherine had requested a full old-fashioned country funeral with the tolling of the 'Great Bell'. Katherine's bequest of money for the repair of the little chapel in Smeeton tells us of her devotion to one of the little free chapels which had sprung up in the later Middle Ages across the parish where village families paid for regular prayers to be recited for the souls of their ancestors. Such was the village world on the eve of the Reformation.

The next will comes from Katherine's cousin, John Polle. John was the bailiff in Kibworth Harcourt from 1520 to 1536, so he and his wife Amice lived through the beginnings of the crisis with Henry VIII. Long a pillar of village society, he was counted as the richest farmer in the village in the 1524 Lay Subsidy, where he was assessed at £33 in goods, as against some of his middling neighbours who were rated at a mere £3 or £4, and ten more who were taxed on wages of only 20s per annum, including members of some old families like the Colmans. John could count back seven or eight generations to his forebear Nicholas in 1280. Again his last testament is a traditional Catholic one, with prayers to the Virgin Mary (the most popular cult in the village) and 'all the company of Heaven', and like Katherine he asks for a trental of thirty requiem masses to be recited for his soul in St Wilfrid's church. Taken down in wonderfully idiomatic English, the text is presumably what John spoke when he made his will in August 1536, 'by the visitation of almighty god' confessing himself to the vicar of Kibworth, 'my ghostly father', who is none other than William Peyrson, whom we met above. The original will would have been taken down by the village scribe and is a fine example of the looseness of English spelling at this time (some breaks in the manuscript have been filled, spellings have been modernized, abbreviations expanded and light punctuation added):

In Dei Nomine Amen I John Polle of Kibworth . . . by the visitation of almighty God: make my will after this manner following, having my perfect mind, and bequeath my soul unto all mighty God Beseeching him to have mercy and our Blessed Lady to pray for me and all the company of heaven. And my body to be buried In the churchyard of the forsaid Kibworth and secondly my wife and my son William Polle I make my executors and John Brian to be my supervisor. Thirdly as concerning the dividing of my goods: In primis I bequeath unto Our Lady of Lincoln 6d. Item unto my parish church I bequeath 20d.

Item onto my ghostly father's house a trental. Item It is my mind and will that my wife shall have her [due portion] With all thereto pertaining onto her haven Be hove And lyke manner my son William Poll to have his onto is behave. Item I give and bequeath onto my son Thomas Polle one messuage and two yardlands which I purchased of John Russell of Rothwell after the decease of me and my wife whichever us it pleases god to live the longer. Item unto the said Thomas I bequeath half a score of ewes and lambs. Item I bequeath onto every one of his children a ewe and a lamb. Item I give and bequeath onto my son Richard Polle two messuages with all appurtenances which I purchased of Richard Ray after the decease of me and my wife. Item I bequeath onto the said Richard Polle four heifers And five marks of money. Item bequeath unto my brother Thomas Poll a gown and a noble of money And to both of his children a ewe and a lamb. Item it is my mind and will that my sister shall have a cow and a howse herd after decease of her husband. Item I bequeath onto every one of my god children 4d

The will of a long-serving bailiff and an influential man in the village, this suggests the straightforward country Catholicism of a well-to-do farmer in the 1530s. His family had given service in the village through the Great Famine, the Black Death and many other major events in village history. His ample personal possessions are not mentioned as they went straight to his wife Amice, who was still living in the house.

From the same period but from the opposite end of the social scale, there is the will of Thomas Colman, John's neighbour. Thomas was a smallholding husbandman whose descendant 'Widow Coleman' was a well-known village smallholder in the 1630s, and whose later descendants still live in the village of Kibworth Beauchamp today. Tom is typical of the small farmers and husbandmen in the Tudor village. In the 1524 hearth tax he is taxed in Kibworth Beauchamp but in his will he mentions kinsmen who live in Harcourt too. He is valued at the lowest band of 20s annual income, along with thirteen other smallholders – the lineal and sometimes biological descendants of the freemen and customary tenants of the thirteenth-century surveys. Tom's will comes on the heels of Will Peyrson's imprisonment and the installation of a new vicar, Robert Mason, but it is still thoroughly Catholic in its devotion to the Virgin Mary and the 'holy company of heaven', a traditional formulation by a Catholic village priest. Tom's was a pious, old-fashioned English village Christianity, exemplified in his provisions for the untimely death of his son. His reference to 'some *poor* priest' is noteworthy: his slight reticence about giving money to a well-off priest perhaps a hint of old opinions in the village about the unmerited wealth of the clergy? But a bushel of wheat and 4d to every poor person in the parish is generous, as is the gift to his parish church. Robert Mason, the curate named by Tom, was later the vicar who became notorious for a sex scandal in the village in 1541. Finally, Tom's will also offers a fascinating glimpse into the personal possessions of a small farmer. From them we may imagine his house (perhaps fifty or sixty feet long), with an open hall in the middle and a chamber with a bedroom floor at one end and a kitchen at the other. He would have had an outhouse, a workshop and a yard with hay barns, cattle stalls, a stable, a well and a privy. Tom's descendant Wayne, by the way, is the care-taker of the Old Grammar School hall today:

In Dei Nomine Amen I Thomas Colman of Kibworth husbandman of good mind & perfect Memory makes this my testament & last will in manner & form following. First I bequeath my soul to God almighty, Our Lady Saint Mary & to all the holy company of heaven & my body to be buried within the churchyard of Kibworth. Item I give to the mother church of Lincoln 4d. Item I give to my parish church of Kibworth 6 shillings and 8d. Item I give to my sister Katherine Colman one stick of wheat, one stick of malt, my rose red coat & my violet coat. Item I will the said Katherine Colman to have three roods of barley land: three roods of peas land to be part ploughed & sown at my costs & charges for one year & I give to her also one rood of wheat readily sown & one young calf. Item I give to any poor man within the town of our Kibworth 4d. Item I give to whomever (poor) person one bushel of malt. Item if my son John Colman shall shortly depart then I give to some poor priest to sing for my soul & all Christian souls for a quarter of a year's space 20 shillings. Item I give to my sister Alice Baly of Wigston one strike of wheat, one strike of malt & I give to her husband two jerkins & one pair of hose. Item I give to Sanders' wife, Cooper's wife, Alice Wood Peters' wife, Alice Bukes 4d apiece. Item I give to William Coleman cowherd my second rose coloured coat, my best doublet & 4d of money. Item I give to Robert Frisley one Kersey doublet & 4d of money. Item I give to each one of my godchildren that be alive one ewe lamb. Item I give to James Eastwood my . . . 12d. Item I give to 'Sir' Robert Mason my curate & godfather 13d. The residue of my goods my debts paid & my Will performed I give to Alice Colman my wife & John Colman my son whom I make my executors to distribute them to the pleasure of God and to the health of my soul & all Christian souls, this to witness Sir Robert Massey parish priest of Kibworth Richard Moor of the same, John Park of the same William Colman of the same with others more & I will the said John Park to be the supervisor of this my last will

Anno Domino 1538

Appended to Thomas's will is an inventory of his goods. From this can be seen the basic possessions of a small-holding farmer on the eve of the Reformation in Henry VIII's day. A summary note of house-hold goods lumped them together as 'stuff in the house'. Then his 'horses and carts: ploughs: and the gear for the plough teams & all things belonging to them'. The most valuable part of the estate as assessed by his neighbours was 'the dairy herd young and old' (worth 40s); his sheep flock (worth 40s) and 'the crop within the house', the stored grain, also worth 40s. All of which made him worth £11 6s 8d, about a third of John Polle's estate.

Although Tom possessed some good clothes (his two 'rose-red jackets' sound more than farming gear – could they have been his Sunday best?), his and Alice's household was clearly not one where luxury, fancy clothes and furniture were the norm. Tom's was an ordinary Kibworth working family of the Tudor period: pious, anx-ious about prayers for his soul in the hereafter; concerned that the new vicar and curate do well by his eternal soul, and that his kinsmen and neighbours protect his estate. But he was also motivated by char-ity. Like many of the wills from Kibworth at this time his charitable provisions for the poor people are noteworthy for a man who was not well-off, and other personal stories may lie behind his bequests. The cowherd William Colman, for example, may be a handicapped relative mentioned in another neighbour's will as 'poor Will Col-man'. A persistent strand in the wills is the community's sense of duty to its sick or impoverished members.

## 'Slander and scandal'

Tom Colman died in 1538, at the moment when the dissolution of the monasteries was under way and when the Kibworth vicar, Wil-liam Peyrson, had been arrested for expressing opposition to the king's religious reforms. It was at this time too that 'Sir' Robert Mason, the curate named in Tom Colman's will as his godfather, also found himself in deep trouble with the church authorities. Mason is the first schoolmaster of Kibworth about whom we have some details, but he fell foul of the Bishop of Lincoln on quite another matter. On 14 March 1540 the bishop instigated a church commission at Kibworth to 'reconcile' the church after an alleged scandal. The story is almost incredible. Witnesses said that Mason had 'defiled' St Wilfrid's church by having sex with a married woman inside the church; not mere cuddling or kissing but ('as it has been asserted') full sexual congress with 'emission of semen' with Isobel Green, the wife of John Green of Kibworth. (The Greens were tenants living in Kibworth Beauchamp: the previous year John had been marked down as a billman in the military muster of the village.) Whether the story was entirely true of course is another matter. The case of Vicar Peyrson less than two years before shows that enemies of traditional religion in the shire – men like John Beaumont – were willing to concoct slanderous stories whenever it suited. Sexual innuendo had been particularly effective in blackening the Catholic church: Beaumont himself had fabricated the tale of two nuns giving birth. It is possible then that Mason was a victim of false accusation. But not entirely false perhaps: it seems unlikely that within such a closed community Isobel Green would have been publicly exposed without some truth to the liaison being acknowledged by the village.

The church was duly cleansed with the appropriate prayers and rituals, and Mason subsequently witnessed land purchases in the village: a charter of that year in the school chest bears his name ('this charter was written by Sir Robert the priest'). But it seems that 'Sir' Robert didn't long survive the scandal since there is no later record of him. If he had indeed made love to a parishioner's wife, then his standing with the village had gone. He was succeeded by a clergyman who did have some standing, Richard Pates. But in these increasingly heated times, within a year or so of taking office, in 1541 or 1542, Pates also forfeited his benefice at Kibworth and was attainted for high treason because he failed to 'accommodate himself to the varying beliefs of those in authority'; that is, to Henry VIII's religious reforms. In Pates's case we know a little more about the reasons for his demise, which were more directly 'political' – he had committed the offence of corresponding with Cardinal Pole, a committed Catholic who was then in exile. Pates was a clerical diplomat and Kibworth was only one of his benefices, so he was probably not in regular residence in the old rectory on Church Hill. Fortunately for him, he was abroad when his guilt was proclaimed. He did not return to England until Mary's reign, when he was confirmed as Bishop of Worcester.

So Kibworth vicarage again became a pawn in the bigger game of national politics. From spring 1542 to summer 1553 the vicar was in government terms a safe pair of hands: a Protestant, William Watkyn, who saw Kibworth through the troubled times of Edward VI. But after Mary came to the throne and instituted a return to Catholicism, Watkyn was imprisoned in his turn and deprived of the benefice because of his refusal to comply with Mary's directives on religious worship. Between 1553 and 1554 Watkyn languished in jail and Kibworth parish was again vacant, administered by its curate and churchwardens. A letter from the Privy Council to the Sheriff and Justices of the Peace in the county of Leicester in 1554 gave permission 'to set at large William Watkyn, personne of Kybwoorth, out of the gaole of Leicester, yf he be not indicted or attaynted'.

This tale reveals something about local as well as national politics. Some parishes (famously Morebath in Devon) had the same vicar over the whole period from the 1530s to the 1570s, trimming with the wind to steer their parishioners through these great psychological changes. Here one after another they go. But though there may have been religious differences in the village, in some areas the people seem to have been united against the interference of self-seeking grandees like Beaumont. One such was the school. The smaller and poorer religious houses in the Kibworth region were mostly dissolved in 1536; a few continued until 1538–9 along with a few hospitals and almshouses. But the abolition of chantries (by the Acts of 1545 and 1547) had a direct effect on the village school, for the chantry lands provided an income for the chantry priest, who doubled as a schoolmaster. The 1547 Act in fact had stipulated that lands used for the upkeep of a chantry priest could be used in future for the upkeep of a schoolmaster, but in the property grab by government cronies they usually passed to private individuals, and even when village schools survived they often lost their endowed lands. The 1547 Act completely suppressed more than 2,000 chantries and guild chapels. But the school at Kibworth managed not only to survive but to keep most of its endowments. The lord of the manor of Kibworth Beauchamp,

John Dudley (Earl of Warwick and later Duke of Northumberland), had an interest in education, and a number of schools owed their survival to him. A hint at Kibworth's debt to him is found in a witness statement in a seventeenth-century lawsuit. Robert Ray, in giving evidence about the origins of the school, stated:

He has heard Thomas Parker, one of the ancient feoffees of the School, say that the Earl of Northumberland, then lord of the manor of Kibworth Beauchamp, made claim to certain lands in Kibworth and being informed they were employed to so good a use as the maintenance of a school said God forbid I should have them.

## 'So that there remain no memory'

On Monday, 17 November 1558, Elizabeth Tudor succeeded to the English throne. The following Sunday after Mass the people of Kibworth poured out of Harcourt and Beauchamp doors to light a bonfire in the lane at the church gate and to hand out a dole of ale, cheese and bread to the poor of the parish. Like every parish in the land Kibworth had celebrated the coming of a new ruler of England with the traditional rituals. That Sunday, the first in Advent, the leading villagers had stood in St Wilfrid's church and proclaimed the new queen and prayed for a happy and prosperous reign for her. They would have recited 'Our Father' and Hail Marys, and their vicar would have chanted the Latin litanies and collects suitable for a Catholic ruler. The mood of the congregation was perhaps nervous after so many reversals of national religious policy in such a short time. Some neighbours and friends were Protestants, some leaned towards Puritanism, many were old Catholics, but the village community had lived with its religious differences for a long time, in the main rubbing along fine.

Elizabeth herself was a sincere Protestant but not a zealous reformer: she had no wish to force people to take communion (she did not want, she said, 'to open a window on men's souls'). But she and her advisers were determined to bring her father's stalled Protestant revolution back on track. In July 1559, Elizabeth's government brought in injunctions for the final suppression of 'superstition' and 'to plant true religion'. Parish priests (still mainly of Queen Mary's Church) were instructed to accept new rituals, a new prayer book and the authorized Protestant Bible; altars and images which had so far escaped destruction were to be removed along with surviving wall paintings, stained glass, ritual clothing and chasubles. In many parts of the country churchwardens were required to prepare a document containing an inventory of all the 'church goods' together with 'all the names of all the houselling people in the parish and the names of all them that were buried there since midsummer and was twelve-month Christened and wedded' ('houselling' – a word Shakespeare puts into the mouth of Old Hamlet's ghost – meant people who take Catholic communion). For a while some of the pre-Reformation customs which had been outlawed or suspect under Edward were briefly allowed to reassert themselves: the old Rogationtide processions along the parish boundaries, the quaffing of 'parish ales', the old ritual of 'churching' women who had just given birth – they were isolated for a month after birth, then purified in church, after which a family feast was held. For a while these were seen again in Main Street, but the net was tightening on the old religion.

In Kibworth church, as we have seen, it is not certain whether the Catholic imagery had already gone in Edward's time. But if not we must now imagine the final changes: the whitewashing of the walls, the selling off of the vestments, chasubles and maniples, some of them probably beautifully embroidered gifts by women of old village families 'in white damask, and blue velvet' – what the Puritans liked to call 'the relics of the Amorites'. What was done in the middle of the sixteenth century can be seen from what remains, especially the stone supports for the rood loft which was dismantled by workmen. The great lifesize painted wooden Christ was perhaps burned on a bonfire outside the church along with the painted image of Our Lady of Kibworth with her blue gown and halo of gold: in the aisle of the nave today a stone washing basin or piscina marks the place where her shrine stood.

The royal injunction had required 'the removal of all signs of idolatry and superstition, from places of worship *so that there remain no memory* of the same in walls, glasses, windows, or elsewhere within their churches and houses'. For the vicar and his curates and church-wardens, and the village jurymen, it was, one imagines, now a matter of accepting things calmly and getting on with it. The members of one parish in Devon threatened with excommunication because they had failed to remove their rood loft and its crucifix, met and sadly agreed to do it: 'Foreasmuch as we be excommunicate for not pluck-ing down the rood-loft let us agree together and have it down, *that we may be like Christian men again of holy time.*' The likes of Tom and Agnes Colman and their neighbours no doubt would have agreed.

### *Thomas Ray*

Only a few months after these developments Thomas Ray died: he was a well-to-do farmer, and his is the first Kibworth will from the days of the new order of Elizabeth. Ray was typical of 'modern' farmers and lesser gentry: an incomer to the village who was very different from the homespun farming class of the Colmans. He even had a 'feather bed'. The will was made in October, less than a year after Elizabeth's accession and following the Act of Uniformity. It is stripped of the old Catholic references to the 'company of heaven' and the Virgin, still less 'Our Lady of Kibworth', though the mother church is still remembered with a small donation. There is no longer any reference to 'trentals' of prayers for the soul, nor to intercession from 'my ghostly father'. But another dimension emerges in Thomas's will, and that is of private wealth. The will describes a private house with different rooms – parlours, halls and chambers – whereas the Colmans, for example, probably lived in the simple hall house of any ordinary farmer. Thomas's provisions to the poor (as with many Kibworth wills of this period) are generous. Michael Coxon, who was not at that time a freeholder in the village, is probably Thomas's foreman or farm manager; though he could be his wife's brother. Particularly touching is the provision made in case his wife Margaret should remarry and go 'away from the farm'. As their only son, Nicholas, was still a juvenile, it may be that Margaret was quite a bit younger than Thomas:

In Nomine Dei the year of our lord God 1559 the 18th of October, I Thomas Rey of Kibworth Harcourt In the County of Leicester, gentleman, sick in body but thanks be to God in perfect mind & memory, make & ordain that my last will & testament in manner following. First I bequeath my soul to almighty God & and my body to be buried within the church of the said Kibworth. Item I bequeath to the mother church of Lincoln 4d. Item to the poor of the parish ten shillings. Item I bequeath to Michael Coxon two kine [pigs] and eleven hoggerylles [piglets] one featherbed & all things belonging unto it with part of my apparel at the discretion of my wife, my debts and funeral expenses discharged The residue of my goods unbequeathed I give to Margaret my wife and Nicholas my son whom I make my full executors of all my goods moveable & unmoveable to be distributed betwixt them too by equal portions; also I will that Nicholas my said heir the lease of my farm when he cometh to lawful age with all his goods & if it fortune my wife to marry away from the farm then I will that Michael Coxon have the occupation of that said farm till my son cometh to lawful age & if it fortune that God call my son to his mercy before he come to lawful age Then I Will that his goods be divided equally betwixt my wife & Michael Coxon aforesaid. Also I do make Nicholas Cloudsley superviser that this my last will and testament be performed And for his pains I give him an old ahsell [a donkey?] for a token

The will is witnessed by Rob Carter, Tom Bryan, Michael Coxon and 'Sir' Robert Barton the curate, and attached to it is an inventory drawn up by Thomas's neighbours, Will Clark, Robert Carter, Tom Bryan and Tom Brees, who after his death went round the house with the village notary. The inventory contains fascinating detail of a well-off Kibworth farmhouse in the middle of the Reformation period: a house with new kinds of domestic arrangements, with an upper floor and private parlours and bedrooms. Very likely it is what is today called the Manor House in Main Street, which was then the bailiff's house. From the inventory Thomas evidently had a brewhouse for brewing ale for the family and its servants and for the agricultural workers; the dyeing of cloths was also done on site. First though are Thomas's animals and farming gear:

| | |
|---|---|
| One stud horse & seven geldings | [£10] |
| Two mares and two foals | [£4 6s 8d] |
| 14 pigs 6 heifers & 2 bulls | [£22] |
| 7 heifers of two years old and four yearling calves | [£4 10s] |
| One boar & 12 fatted hogs | [40s] |
| Three sows & eight shoytes | [46s 8d] |
| Twenty small hogs | [£15] |
| Geese and pullen | [20s] |
| One bee hive | [3s 4d] |
| One iron bound cart & one bare cart & two ploughs with cart gear and plough gear | [£3] |
| Plough timber and axle trees | [33s 4d] |
| Six harrows | [12s] |
| Timber boards and firewood | [£8] |
| Wheat & rye | [£6 13s 4d] |
| Barley & malt | [£18] |
| Peas | [£13 6s 8d] |
| Hay | [£10] |
| Cattle pens and & pigsties | [40s] |

**Stuff in the hall**

| | |
|---|---|
| One frame table with a carpet two chairs and seven buffet stools | [20s] |
| One cupboard with a carpet and nine cushions with the hangings | [30s] |

**Stuff in the buttery**

| | |
|---|---|
| One set of platters and dishes, ten candle sticks, four porringers [eating bowls] | [£3 10s] |
| One thassyn dish two salts & a basin and ewer, one brass mortar & a pestle | [10s] |
| Three pewter basins & a ladle with other implements thereto belonging | [20s] |

**Stuff in the new parlour**

One standing bed with the appurtenances, one
cupboard with a carpet one pallet bed, two
coffers with the hangings [£10]

**In the old parlour**

One standing bed with the appurtenances, four
chests, one presse with the hangings [£6 13s 4d]

**Fine linen cloths**

One table cloth of diaper & one towel [40s]
Twelve table cloths three dozen of napkins [£5 16s]
One dozen & a half towels [40s]
One dozen of cupboard cloths [40s]
26 pairs of sheets [£40]

**The meyne [poor] linen**

28 pairs of sheets of the coarser sort [£10]

**The chamber over the parlour**

Ten carpet cloths for tables [£10]
Five pair of fustian blankets [£6 13s 4d]
Seven pair of woollen blankets [£4]
Two divan beds & four feather beds [£16]
Three 'flocke' beds six bolsters sixteen pillows [£9]
Eight counterpayntes, two of them scarlet [£20]
Two quilts the one of them covered with scarlet farsenytt [40s]
One standing bed with tester curtains of farsenytt [40s]
Five little stools & two chairs & eight cushions [20s]
A great chest & what is in it [£20]
One presse & two cupboards one coffer & a
trendle bed [13s 4d]
the hangings there [£6 13s 4d]

**The chamber over the buttery**

Two bedsteads one cupboard and one coffer with
painted hangings [13s 4d]

**The chamber over the hall**

| | |
|---|---|
| One bedstead one whol harnes & hangings | [40s] |
| Two stones of wool with other certain stuff | [£3] |

**In the store house**

| | |
|---|---|
| Iron and iron ware with spades & pitchforks & shovels with other implements of husbandry | [40s] |
| Stuff in the milk house & larder house as salty trosses [for salting meat] cooking dishes & things | [20s] |
| Stuff in the brewing house | [6s 8d] |

**Stuff in the kitchen**

| | |
|---|---|
| Two brass pots & one brass pan | [40s] |
| Three cauldrons, a pan, a cooking dish, three gridirons | [13s 4d] |
| Two pairs of cupboards & five spits and two dripping pans | [13s 4d] |
| One hand Iron a fire fork, two pairs of tongs two pairs of bellows and two fire shovels & a clev[is] | [14s] |
| Stuff in the maid's parlour | [6s 10d] |
| Stuff in the mens' chamber | [6s 8d] |
| One steeping vat & a hare [rough] cloth for the cleaning & a fold of flax | [£1 6s 8d] |
| His apparel | [£20] |

From Ray's will we can see that in Kibworth the changes in the middle of the sixteenth century are not only psychological but material: no sooner is Purgatory fading away than a possessive individualism is making itself felt. A great rebuilding of domestic housing was well under way now, and for the middle class, people like the Rays, that was accompanied by a sharp rise in the standard of living. Old habits were changing: privacy was more and more sought after; possessions were becoming a mark of status. For those old enough to remember the days of Henry VIII, as was recalled in Ray's time, 'three things are marvellously altered in England within their sound remembrance.' These were the ubiquity of chimneys and fireplaces for private rooms (so striking on the first pictorial depiction of Kibworth from 1609); the accumulation of private possessions in houses; and the variety that middle-class people now expected on the table. In the old world into which Tom Colman's parents were born, the family lived in a communal hall, where they slept on straw pallets with 'a good round log under the head' (pillows were 'for women in childbed'). In Ray's house, albeit a fine place for the bailiff on which Merton had lavished considerable expense over 200 years, there were a hall, a buttery, new and old parlours with chambers above both, a kitchen and a domestic storehouse, in addition to all the barns and animal sheds. Indeed, Ray even has a 'maids parlour' as well as a 'mens chamber' so he kept maids as well as male servants. Employing servants had been customary in the village from the fourteenth century (and of twenty-five servants named in the 1381 Poll Tax nine were women), but Ray's will seems to mark a new period in the village story. In other houses on Main Street and neighbouring lanes, inventories attached to wills show the same picture: tapestries and painted cloths on the walls, pewter on the table, fine linen and brass, and wooden furniture: a custom 'now descended yet lower', said a writer from the 1570s, 'even into inferior artificers and many farmers who have learned also to garnish their cupboards with plate, their joined beds with tapestry and silk hangings, and their tables with fine napery'. The world of Tudor interiors had arrived in Kibworth, at least at the better end of Main Street.

## 'A woman is a worthy wight'

Our last example from the Kibworth wills is the testament of Elizabeth Clarke of Kibworth Beauchamp, which comes from 1580 and is an indicator of the status of a woman in the late-Tudor village. By now the Reformation had passed through several phases and in some regions the Counter-Reformation was making a fightback with Jesuit missions. But in most parts of the country the establishment had triumphed by 1580, and there is no trace of these conflicts in Kibworth. What comes out of Elizabeth's will is still the typical Tudor concern with charity for the poor as well as her relationship with other women, including her sisters, and her friendships within the village. The detailed inventory of her household goods gives a fascinating insight into a woman's possessions in Elizabeth's reign, with bolsters, bedlinen, coverlets and tablecloths. Sadly no books are mentioned (if she possessed books they may not have been valued by assessors Rob Brian and Richard Sharpe, who were middling farmers used to assessing farming estates). It is possible though – even likely – that Elizabeth was literate. In the East Midlands and East Anglia in her life-time it was not uncommon for women of this class to possess chapbooks and primers, and to read their Matins in English; and there was even a market for devotional books like Whitford's *A Werke for Householders* or Nicholas's *Order of Household Instruction*. Further back in time Lollard books must have been available in Kibworth, and the importance of Lollard literacy among women may just have left some kind of tradition among the women of the village.

Elizabeth's gift to the poor represents half a year's wages for a small husbandman (about £2,500 today on the average earnings index). Elizabeth's husband was dead at the time of the making of her will (as, it appears, was one of her daughters), and though there is more detail about house furnishings and tableware than about the harness for her ox team, it can be assumed that like all women of her class she knew her way round a farm and knew what was in her barn (spellings have been lightly modernized – by 1580 we are very close to modern spelling – but the language is hers):

In the name of God Amen. I Elizabeth Clarke of Kibworth Beauchamp on the first of June in the year of the lord 1580 and the 22nd of the Queen's reign being of sound and perfect memory, praised be God, make this my last will and Testament in manner and form following; first I bequeath my soul into the tuition of Christ Jesus my creator and redeemer and my body to be buried in the churchyard of Kibworth. Furthermore I give to the church of Lincoln 2d, I give to the poorman's box 12d, I bequeath also to Agnes my daughter 46s and 8d and 20 shillings that was her sisters part either in money or money worth, to be paid unto her at the day of her marriage. I give to her two pair of flaxen sheets, four pairs of hempon and harden sheets, a flaxen board [table] cloth, a harden board cloth; one bolster and two pillows, a pair of blankets, four napkins, one towel, a green hillinge, two platters, a pewter dish and a saucer, a brass pot or a noble in money, a brass pan, or 10s in money. A candlestick or 16d in money . . .

After a similar bequest to her second daughter, Elizabeth, she then turns to her neighbours:

I give to Alice Chapman's children Anne Wood and William Wood 6s and 8d equally to be divided between them and to be paid them at the age of 16 years. I give also to Alice Chapman's children Margaret and Thomas 3s 4d between them and to be paid them at the age of sixteen years. I give also to John Clarke 26s 8d to be paid within one year after my decease and 20s among his children to be paid within four year after my departure. I give to Thomas Clarke one half acre of barley and to the children one ewe and a lamb or 5s in money. I give to my two godchildren 6d apiece. I give to Margery Gourde my Sister 12d. I give to Luse [Lucy] Greene my sister 12d and one sheet or 2s. I give also to Alice Poole half a strike of malt, half a strike of mylne corne. I give also to Thomas Martin, Thomas Papennere, John Wright and Richard Heywood every one of them one tolfoot of mylne corne. All the rest of my goods unbequeathed, my funeral expenses being discharged, I give to Laurence my son whom I do make my full executor of this my last Will and Testament. I will that Richard Sharpe and Robert Brian be supervisors to see this my will performed, and they to have for their paines 6d apiece. These being witness Nicholas Decon, Hugh Sothel, John Clarke, with others.

## The passing of the old order

Elizabeth's funeral was held in the churchyard of St Wilfrid's towards midsummer in 1580. We don't know how she died, but as most medical cures offered by the village doctor would have been ineffective in relieving pain, it is likely that if she went through a long illness she experienced months or even years of suffering – a time to contemplate her impending death. Like all religious women of her class the art of 'dying well' was an important life lesson to be learned. You could even read self-help manuals on how to 'learn to die' like Thomas Becon's *Sick Man's Salve* of 1561. With the old certainties no more, an enlarged personal Christian strength and resolve had to be cultivated. Pious women especially were held up as 'comfortable testimony of godly resolution'.

Her children and close family would have attended her through her last days. But one of the more profound effects of the Protestant Reformation was in the long term to sever the relationship between the dead and the living. Though many traditional beliefs and customs took a long time to fade away, the new Protestant orthodoxy enshrined in the Kibworth vicar's funeral service was that dead Protestants were now beyond the reach of prayer. Most of the traditional Catholic intercessionary rituals after burial were swept away. Familiar customs that were second nature to the villagers in Henry VIII's day – trentals, masses, dirges and prayers for the dead – were resolutely set aside. In Elizabeth's own mind perhaps there still lingered the old familiar prayer which vicar Peyrson had recited for the older generation of the village (it survives in his own words) committing 'my soule into the handes of Almyghtye God my Creator and Redemer, to Our Blessed Ladye, Most Purest Virgyne, and to all the Holy Companye of Heaven'. But the church ceremony for Elizabeth and her family would have been very different from the pre-Reformation rituals performed by 'the ghostly fathers' like Peyrson for Katherine Polle or for Tom and Agnes Colman.

In the old days, as Elizabeth's older neighbours would have remembered well from their own parents' funerals, the procession entered the church with the coffin while 'Sir' William sang psalms before the great wooden crucifixion above the chancel arch, and wished the soul Godspeed on its journey while sprinkling the body with holy water and censing it with incense:

Almighty and everlasting God we humbly entreat thy mercy, that thou wouldst commend the soul of thy servant, for whose body we perform the due office of burial, to be laid in the bosom of thy patriarch Abraham; that

when the day of recognition shall arrive, she may be raised up, at thy bid-
ing, among the saints of thy elect.

There over her coffin he and his curates and the village chaplains
would have sung the 'masse and dyrige by note accordyng to the use
and custome of the sayd churche and every prest and clerke of the
sayd churche . . .' And at the end, while candles shimmered around
the gilded image of 'Our Lady of Kibworth', as had always been
done, 'the great bell shalbe ronge for the space of 6 oures accordyng
to the custome of a knell.'

Elizabeth's funeral though was an altogether starker affair, in a
whitewashed church with a Protestant minister in sober black. A version of the committal survived to 1549 – without holy water or
incense – but reference to the soul was finally removed under Edward
VI in 1552 and was never officially reinstated in the Church of England.
The soul went straight to its reward, needing no intercession, com-
mendation or committal. All that was committed was the body to the
earth. One bishop's set of rules for funerals in the 1570s inadvertently
reveals the continuing pull of the old country rituals at this time:

no superstition should be committed in them wherein the papists infinitely
offend; as in masses, dirges, trentals, singing, ringing, holy water, years',
days', and month-minds, crosses, pardon letters to be buried with them,
mourners, de profundis sung by every lad that could say it, money for the
dead, watching of the corpse, bell and banner, and many more that I could
reckon.

The Protestant Reformation thus radically revised not only the
rituals but the process of salvation itself: as one might say, its concep-
tual geography. Where do souls go now? The question was of great
personal moment in an age tormented by religion: no less an intellect
than Hamlet will later frame it, deftly catching the public anxiety.
The prayer book of 1552 and its Elizabethan successor which vicar
Beridge used at Elizabeth Clarke's funeral assert that the soul of the
elect will immediately live in the Lord, 'delivered from the burden of
the flesh . . . in joy and felicity'. Instead of petitioning God for

favours, he simply rejoiced that 'it hath pleased thee to deliver this Elizabeth our sister, out of the miseries of this sinful life.'

So the trental of masses paid for by her fellow villagers for almost a thousand years to help the soul through Purgatory was a thing now of mere 'childish superstition'. Inevitably such things were so ingrained a part of religious practice that it took several decades of preaching, discipline and punishment to draw them to a close. Though 'not permitted by the laws of this realm', funeral feasts still persisted in Kibworth as elsewhere; provisions for obits and prayers for souls are still found in local wills in the thirty years before Elizabeth's death and even after. Anniversaries and communions for the dead may have survived, and of course belief in ghosts took much longer to be done away with. We don't know whether Elizabeth's children cast the prohibited flowers on her coffin; though many vicars up and down the land, including perhaps Beridge, made concessions to their parishioners' feelings as they helped them adjust to 'the revolution of the time'.

With Elizabeth's funeral we leave our sketch of the impact of Henry's Reformation on Kibworth: fifty years in the life of a community about which we can tell little from the official sources. But these last testaments of the villagers give us in their own words a few precious clues to the changes they were living through. In a sense, though, it is the old imperatives of the community which are most vividly revealed in these documents: the continuities of farming life in Kibworth; the importance of land, family and inheritance; the strong links with neighbours and their children; even the care of the poor. But also detectable now, as the old communally organized world is gradually transformed, is the growth of new ideas about property, wealth and individualism which would shape a different future for the people of Kibworth – and, of course, the people of England.

# 15. A Century of Revolution

The heavy snows of the first years of the seventeenth century provide us with images as vivid as those from the eighth century or the early fourteenth. In London the Thames froze over, and the bitter winters have left their trace in poetry of the time in images of 'wind fanned snow'. On frozen and rutted roads travel proved especially difficult. The main road north to the Trent was notorious as 'one of the worst kept roads in the kingdom', impassable in winter, and when wet 'loaded with mud to the footocks', so that wagons must be 'dragged on their bellies'. Travellers in the East Midlands remarked that it was so hard to get them properly repaired that an entirely new road system 'as Romans did of old' might be the answer: 'so heavy the loads, and so numerous the carriages that a great number of horses are killed each year by the excess of labour.' Daniel Defoe noted on his travels a little later that the road beyond Northampton through Harborough to Leicester, which ran through Kibworth, was 'perfectly frightful to travellers . . . where there is no provision for repair, and in some seasons dangerous'. The winter of 1606–7 was the worst: the poet John Marston, who travelled this road through Leicester to write a masque for an aristocratic house party near the city, describes noble ladies on their struggling carriages, their hair shining with 'glittering icicles all crystalline, . . . periwigged with snow, russet mantles fringed with ice, stiff on the back'.

Kibworth suffered heavy losses from plague in 1605–6, then shivered through the long winter. Almost every house now had chimneys burning coal in bad weather. Taxed in the seventeenth century on the number of hearths, it was still normal for villagers to have two or three; many had four, and some like the Rays had as many as eight. At this time the village population was on the rise. The revival of population in England after the calamities of the

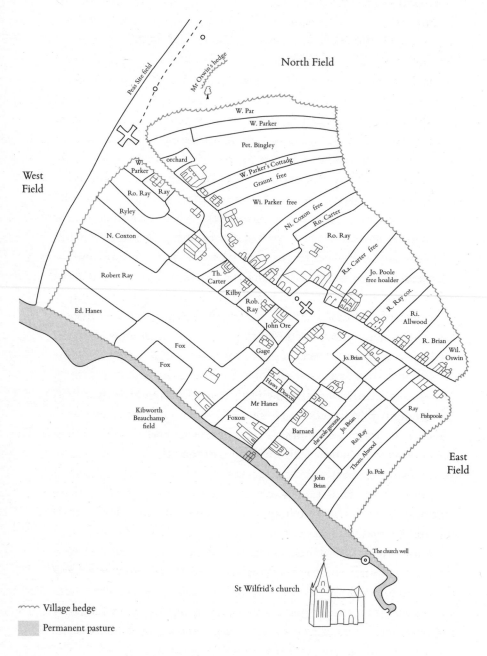

North Field

Peat Site field

Mt. Oswin's hedge

W. Par

W. Parker

Pet. Bingley

orchard

W. Parker's Cottadg

Graunt free

West
Field

W.
Parker

Wi. Parker free

Ro. Ray

Ray

Ni. Coxon free

Ro. Carter

Ryley

Ro. Ray

N. Coxton

Ra. Carter free

Jo. Poole
free hoalder

Robert Ray

Th.
Carter

R. Ray cot.

Kilby

Ri.
Allwood

Ed. Hanes

Rob.
Ray

R. Brian

John Ore

Wil.
Oswin

Fox

Gage

Jo. Brian

Fox

Haws Deacon

Ray

Fishpoole

Kibworth
Beauchamp
field

Mr Hanes

Foxon

the scole ground

Jo. Brian

Barnard

Ro. Ray

East
Field

Thom. Alwood

John
Brian

Jo. Pole

The church well

St Wilfrid's church

~~~~ Village hedge

Permanent pasture

Kibworth Harcourt in 1609, from a Merton Estate map:
it was still surrounded by the open fields

fourteenth century continued apace during the first half of the seventeenth – from an estimated 4.1 to 5.3 million between 1601 and 1656. In Kibworth Harcourt there was a slow but steady increase, but development had not gone beyond the bounds of the village reached in the fourteenth century. In a beautiful map from this time of the open fields of Harcourt, held at Merton, the houses still lie behind the old hedge as they had for centuries, the tenements and gardens running back from Main Street. The Rays are in the former bailiff's house; the Coxons are in Priory Farm; John Polle (the last of the male line of Polles) is on Hogg Lane, and Rob Brian (son of Elizabeth Clarke's trusted friend) and Oswin are at the end of Hogg Lane by the village hedge.

For the parish as a whole the population had risen in Elizabeth's reign from eighty-two taxable households in 1563, perhaps 500 people, to 444 registered communicants at church at the end of the reign. These were people over fourteen, which suggests an increase in population to about 600. By the middle of the seventeenth century there were nearly 200 households evenly divided between the two Kibworths and Smeeton, perhaps 800 people. These increases took place despite severe mortality from disease over the century. Typhus, influenza and plague continued to leave their mark, and the danger of bad harvests and famine was ever present. There were three great periods of mortality between the later years of Elizabeth's reign and the 1690s. In the plague in the 1590s sixty-two men, women and children died; and there were even more heavy losses in 1605–6 with seventy-nine deaths. That summer alone thirty-three men and thirty-four women were buried in the churchyard, though the villagers were successful in protecting their children, only two of whom were lost. A last major outbreak in Kibworth between winter 1657 and summer 1659 caused fifty-seven deaths, among them sixteen children. But the community managed to cope with all this and avoided starvation in the years of the extraordinarily bad harvests of 1612 and 1639. Only in the 1698 famine year did the village see high mortality.

## *Rural revolt*

The conditions of rural life in England were still as precarious as they had been in the fourteenth century. A string of bad harvests after bad winters and heavy rains brought the rural poor in the Midlands to their knees in the first decade of the century. There had already been sporadic violence in Midland towns against recent enclosures as avaricious landlords ploughed up the hedges and the common field strips for sheep farming. The old communal society of the Midland 'champain' lands was beginning to dissolve. In the first week of June 1607, major rural riots flared up across Warwickshire and Northamptonshire, with several thousand peasants and agricultural workers demonstrating against the enclosers. In Leicestershire rural revolt flared to the south of Kibworth at Cotesbatch, where crowds of workers tore out fences and hedges. These rural rebels called themselves 'Diggers', and as they marched the Diggers of Warwickshire sang songs brimming with workers' patriotism:

> From Hampton-field in haste
> we rest as poor delvers and day labourers
> for the good of the Commonwealth till death . . .

The Diggers had produced a written manifesto to put their case to the local authorities – the JPs and freeholders – portraying themselves in an almost Shakespearean image as one limb of the English body politic, still loyal to their king:

Loving friends and subjects under one renowned prince, for whom we pray long to continue in his royal estate . . . his most true hearted Commonalty . . . We as members of the whole, do feel the smart of these encroaching tyrants, which would grind our flesh upon the whetstone of poverty . . .

At Hill Norton 3,000 rebels gathered to protest against 'the incroaching tyrants who grind the faces of the poor'. In response local JPs and gentry assembled armed bands and erected a scaffold in the centre of

Leicester. On 8 June over the shire border at the village of Newton in Northamptonshire a crowd of almost 3,000 peasants was attacked by a private army raised by the local authorities. The rebels were easily dispersed, leaving fifty or so dead. The leaders were hauled off to Northampton, where they were summarily condemned to death, and hanged, drawn and quartered on a scaffold in the centre of town.

Across the Midlands many were shocked by the brutality of the retribution. On 21 June in Northampton a sermon was preached by Robert Wilkinson, who used the Diggers' metaphor of the body politic to preach against all violence, including that of the rulers 'who reformed wickedness with a greater wickedness'. The smell of burning was in the air, with prophecies of greater conflagrations ahead. Kibworth itself had so far escaped big enclosure battles; the amount of land still farmed as common fields and pastures almost 200 years later shows that it remained till the end an open-field village. But around it many other such villages had already gone, and across England the voice of the workforce, suppressed in Elizabeth's day, was now clamouring to be heard, more vocal, more self aware and increasingly literate. The changing nature of the proletariat then, coupled with the changing nature of what they called 'the middling sort' – people who wanted more say in local affairs than a franchise based only on gentlemen of the shire – were developments that set the scene for the Civil War. And in the background of the revolutions of the seventeenth century was education.

## A literate society

The sixteenth century had been an era of turbulence and change in England – in politics, religion, economy and society. The Reformation had broken down many medieval institutions that had served the community. But the Tudor period had also seen huge advances in education. During the reign of Elizabeth, 160 grammar schools had been founded, making England the most literate society the world had yet seen. After Henry VIII and his son Edward had dissolved the

monasteries, and abolished guilds and chantries, the traditional institutions of charity and social welfare had found themselves pillaged
by a rising gentry and middle class profiting from a spectacular property boom. In Kibworth there had long been a grammar teacher,
possibly even some kind of 'school', which village tradition said had
been founded in the time of Warwick the Kingmaker, during the
Wars of the Roses. In the early days the 'grammar school' in Kibworth (like most village schools) consisted of nothing more than a
chantry priest teaching children in the corner of the church nave, or
in a private house in winter, but this arrangement had been financed
by the rents from 'school lands' originally gifted by local farmers for
a chantry. During the Reformation, as we have seen, these had been
saved by the intervention of the Lord of the Manor of Kibworth
Beauchamp, John Dudley, who, according to the Kibworth gentleman Robert Ray, shrank from grabbing lands 'employed to so good
a use as the maintenance of a school'.

Kibworth school's surviving feoffment charter from 1595 provides
the names of eighteen men then appointed to act as trustees. It is
a telling testimony to the range of social classes working together
on the school's management: two knights, four gentlemen, nine
yeomen and three husbandmen – a real mix of the Elizabethan
'community of the village' and all, presumably, interested in the provision of education for their sons and happy for them to share a
classroom. The knights and gentlemen were largely from outside the
village (and the involvement of eminent men from across the county
testifies to the importance of the school in its wider region). Of the
four gentlemen, only Robert Ray (grandson of Thomas, whose will
we saw above (pp. 290–95)), was himself a Kibworth resident. Seven
of the yeomen trustees were local: Thomas Fox and Richard Polle of
Harcourt, John Iliffe of Beauchamp, and Zachary Chapman, Arthur
Cloudesley, Richard Bryan and James Wright of Smeeton Westerby –
all of them respected and respectable 'swearing men' who farmed
their own land. The labourers were William Frisby and William
Smeeton of Beauchamp and William Goode of Smeeton Westerby. It
may seem surprising to find sixteenth-century farm labourers serving on the board of a grammar school, but a mark of the 'community

of the village' in that time was the respect afforded to ordinary freemen in local society. They may not have all been literate themselves – half a century later a few of the school trustees still signed their names with a single initial – but they appreciated the value of literacy, and aspired to it for their children.

In 1601, two years before Elizabeth died, measures were taken by the government to address problems and abuses in the administration of private charities which had arisen during half a century of upheaval. The Poor Relief Act of that year put the administration of poor relief in the hands of municipal authorities (one by-product of the Reformation had been the collapse of the great edifice of medieval charity provided by the religious houses and guilds). The Statute of Charitable Uses, meanwhile, called for an investigation into the state of existing charitable endowments, seeking to ensure that bequests continued to be utilized for their intended purpose, and putting ultimate supervision in the hands of the state. The legislation's preamble spoke of the widespread abuse known to have occurred as monastic and chantry lands were bought up by well-placed individuals. It sought to redress 'the Abuses, Breaches of Trustes, Negligences, Mysimploymentes, not imployinge concealing defrauding misconvertinge or misgovernmente of land and money heretofore given to godly and charitable uses'.

Among the many such charitable uses specified in the act were the maintenance of 'Schooles of Learninge, Free Schooles and Schollers in Universities'. As a village with an established grammar school maintained by charitable bequest, Kibworth was on the itinerary of the commission of enquiry finally appointed for Leicestershire in 1614. The following year four commissioners visited Kibworth, and spent time looking into the origins and current maintenance of the school, hearing evidence from those locally with information – including, no doubt, the then schoolmaster, the Reverend Richard Kestyn, who retained the position for more than twenty years between 1611 and 1634. They established that 'certain messuages, farms, closes, cottages and lands' had been bequeathed for the maintenance of the school and its schoolmaster at a point 'before the memory of any of the villagers then living'. The land documents in the 'school box' in fact, as we have seen, go back to 1353, probably originally rents provided for a local prayer guild or chantry chapel whose priest may have doubled up as a teacher of grammar for village children like Widow Palmer's son in the 1440s (see p. 271).

Much is known about the running of the school in the middle of the seventeenth century, because in 1647 a book of rules or 'constitution' was drafted for the school, on the model of one that had been drawn up in 1630 for Market Bosworth Grammar School. The Kibworth governors carefully studied the Bosworth regulations before adapting them for use in Kibworth. The school, which had about thirty pupils, was free, and consideration was to be given to the status of many of the families concerned. The governors did not prescribe text-books, but stated that the schoolmaster should teach 'none but authentical authors and *because the School standeth much upon poor men's children*, whose parents are not able to buy many books, that they read unto them few books and them throughout, if conveniently they may'. Children accepted into the school had already to know their 'letters', in other words their grammar, and to 'be somewhat well entered into the spelling of words'. (This primary education would be provided by small infants' schools run by villagers – often women – in private houses over the next three centuries.)

The grammar school feoffees themselves undertook to examine the children to assess their progress: along with the rectors of Kibworth and Church Langton, they were 'on the Thursday before Whit to examine the children, hear them dispute and observe their proficiency'. Those who failed to progress might be discouraged from continuing: 'the schoolmaster shall certify the parents of such children as they shall find unapt for learning or indoceble, to the end that said parents may prevent their loss of time and expenses.' Nor did the regulations exempt the schoolmaster himself from examination. He had in the first place to be well-educated, with an MA or BA, and free from infectious diseases; he was expected to devote himself full-time to the school and to set a virtuous example to his pupils. Vices from which he was to abstain are methodically set out: 'gaming and night-walking' among the excluded behaviour. And he was prohibited from excessive violence with his charges; he must not 'strike any scholars about the head or face with his hands or fist or with a rod, book, or any such like thing'. (Vigorous corporal punishment had been the norm in English schools since the Anglo-Saxon period.) If anger got the better of him, he was to pay a fine into the Common Box. Older boys were given the responsibility to police the conduct of their younger schoolmates; these monitors would 'observe the scholars in the upper school and present them that swear or use any unseemly talk'.

Standards must have been high. The school box suggests that literacy was widespread among the yeoman farmers of the parish in the seventeenth century, and under the schoolmaster James Wright, who was appointed in 1639, we learn of boys from Kibworth school gaining places to continue their studies at the universities of Oxford and Cambridge. As an insight into how one English village tried to take care over the future of its children, the Kibworth school box is the pre-modern story of English education in microcosm.

## The coming of civil war

The 1630s were an unhappy decade on both the local and the national scene. Poor harvests – with associated malnutrition and disease – came bunched together, accentuating a sense of gloom and foreboding aggravated by an increasingly overweening government. Charles I's 'personal rule' after his dissolution of Parliament in 1629 was widely viewed as an 'eleven-year tyranny', and it rankled in Kibworth, as elsewhere in England. Fighting unpopular wars with France and Spain, and with enormous expenditure on the court, the government looked to increase revenue by the revival of archaic taxes such as Ship Money which was extended for the first time to inland territories in 1635. This was a particular grievance in a distinctly un-maritime county. Leicestershire was expected to fund a 450-ton ship, a tax that partly fell on the taxpayers of Kibworth who only recently, in 1628, had had a Lay Subsidy levied on them – the village incomes and goods had been noted, starting with the richest man in Harcourt, Robert

Ray, then going down to the likes of ordinary freeholders such as the Colmans, Iliffes and Carters. Anger at the tax was heightened by the assiduity of Henry Skipworth, the staunchly loyal Sheriff of Leicester, who aspired 'to be the first Sherriffe that should paye in his whole somme'. His efforts were effective but stirred furious resentment. Skipworth lamented the 'soe manye complainers & opposers' and accused Puritans in southern Leicestershire of stirring civil disobedience. At Noseley, a few miles east of Kibworth, the fiery Puritan Sir Arthur Hesilrige sent Skipworth's men scuttling from the area as they tried to extract payment by confiscating property. Hesilrige's election in 1640 as a senior knight of the shire was a sign that local support for the monarchy was ebbing away.

## Religion

Mistrust of the king in the country also stemmed from his religious policies, his High Church leanings and his Catholic marriage. A very important aspect of the seventeenth-century revolutions was religious dissent, and the national conflicts over the next decades were mirrored in Kibworth. The village became a major centre of dissidence; it is not yet possible to say whether such opinions had remained as an undercurrent in village culture through the Tudor period, but in the seventeenth century religious independence suddenly emerged in a flood of debate. The immediate roots of these movements in England lay in the growth of Separatist and Independent groups in the 1590s, Protestant denominations which demanded a return to what they saw as a plainer, purer form of Christianity. In this the literate free peasantry of the East Midlands proved to be a particular hotbed of ideas: the Pilgrim Fathers came from the region and George Fox, the founder of the Quakers, was a weaver from Fenny Drayton, to the south of Kibworth. Whether such groups had already made headway in the village before the Civil War has not yet been discovered; though the strength of Independents, Dissenters and Quakers in Kibworth in the early 1660s suggests they had a longer history in the village. Their insistence on independence from the national church, on 'purer' forms of worship and even, later, on anti-slavery and women's suffrage represents a strand in village culture which would survive robustly into the twentieth century. These ideas came to a head nationally and locally in the Civil War period.

Layered on top of these grass-roots movements was the national situation. King Charles's Church of England was itself in turmoil, and though the majority of Kibworth people were loyal to the national church, the measures taken by Archbishop Laud to enforce High Church ceremonies smacked to some of a covert return to Catholicism. They provoked further tension in a county already deeply divided in spiritual matters. In this south-east corner of Leicestershire there were strong Puritan communities, but also a conservative, Laudian element. The evidence for religious tendencies in Kibworth during the decades prior to the Civil War is fragmentary, but what there is suggests a village that was deeply divided, and this came out in thirty years of conflict over the post of vicar.

Early problems arose with the appointment in 1634 of the Reverend James Weston, who had been curate at Tur Langton, as schoolmaster of Kibworth Grammar School. His religious inclinations seem to have been Puritan. Archbishop Laud closely supervised matters of practice at a local level and an ecclesiastical visitation in 1634 resulted in Weston being presented for 'defect in canonical habit' – probably a refusal to wear the surplice. The following year he was appointed as curate in Kibworth, but in 1639 he had his licence to teach revoked by Laud for the propagation of unsuitable doctrine.

Some of the feoffees who managed the school, however, are known to have been staunchly Church of England in their outlook – and would adhere closely to the king's party in the troubled years ahead. The Beridge family – whose son John went up to Jesus College, Cambridge, in 1642 – were both lords of the manor of Beauchamp and occupants of the church living for several generations from the 1570s. During and after the Civil War they were loyal to the Stuart regime. On the death of the vicar William Beridge in January 1640, the gift of the living was passed to the king, who appointed an outsider, William Hunt, as rector. Hunt would not forget – and neither would his parishioners – that he was a king's man. Thus began a sequence of events which saw the rivalries and controversies of the Civil War played out at a local level in the parsonage house and the streets of Kibworth.

Like many Kibworth rectors of the period, Hunt seems to have enjoyed several benefices and been often absent – employing a curate, Joseph Foster, to run the church week to week. Foster, no doubt, was a man after Hunt's own ecclesiastical taste, and if later charges are to be believed, the two of them 'observed ceremonies' in Kibworth church, suggesting an obedience to the crypto-Catholic rituals that had riled the Puritan element. The 'ceremonies' of which Hunt was accused in Kibworth would have centred on the performance of sacraments: the hearing of confession, for instance, and the respectful kneeling to receive holy communion. The communion table in St Wilfrid's would have been shunted from the middle of the church (where, for Puritans, it symbolized the democracy of worship) to the east end, where, railed off like a Catholic altar, it emphasized the God-given intermediary role of the priest. Hunt himself would have worn the traditional white surplice – retained under the Elizabethan compromise, and staunchly defended by Laud, but furiously denounced by Puritans for its evocation of Roman tradition. To the Calvinist or Independent, the Nonconformist or Dissenter, such practice in the parish church reeked of popery, and was intolerable.

## Civil war

As tension mounted nationally between the king and his Parliament (which Charles was finally forced to recall in 1640), local issues and rivalries became overlaid with the broader passions of a divided nation. The long-running feud between the dominant Hastings family of Leicestershire and the rival Greys re-clothed itself in the colours of the impending Civil War – but such tussles were often about local power as much as the political future of the nation. One thing was for sure: Leicestershire was a divided place in which royalist and parliamentarian gentry families intermingled – a county which had 'many Bickerings one with another'.

For the inhabitants of Kibworth during the three years after 1640 the dominant hope, as for ordinary men and women throughout England, was that the storm clouds massing in the political realm might pass over and leave them undisturbed. For the people of Leicestershire in particular there was a strong feeling of being, in the words of a petition sent to the king in 1642, 'in the middest of your Kingdome of England, and in the middest of our great feares and apparent dangers'. Few felt an allegiance for either cause decisive enough to induce them to leave the county to fight in the armies. The common people, it was often remarked during these years of turmoil, loved 'their pudding at home better than a musket and pike abroad, and if they could have peace, care not what side had the better'.

In Kibworth itself, the sense of living in a polarized county was keenly felt. Only four miles to the north-east, at Noseley Hall, lived Sir Arthur Hesilrige, the tempestuous radical MP whose attempted arrest by Charles I (along with four other members of the Lower House) had heightened the sense of an impending conflict. Meanwhile, a short downhill walk along a track to the west brought the villager to Wistow, the seat of Sir Richard Halford, one of Charles's most loyal and influential supporters in the county (and a feoffee of Kibworth Grammar School).

In the early months of 1642 the stakes dramatically increased. The sense of crisis was brought home to the provinces of England as king and Parliament scrambled to secure the allegiance of the country's feudal levies – the 'trained bands' of borough and shire – which still constituted its only standing army. Historically such bodies were at the command of the king. But mounting distrust of Charles's intentions led to Parliament issuing, without royal assent, a Militia 'Ordinance' – an unprecedented move which further polarized opinion and enraged the king, for whom this trampling upon his customary rights seemed 'the fittest subject for a King's quarrel'.

In the Kibworth area Sir Arthur Hesilrige of Noseley was at the centre of these developments. On 4 June he was despatched by Parliament back to Leicestershire to assist with the mustering of the county militias. Under Henry Grey, the Earl of Stamford, appointed by Parliament as Lord Lieutenant of the county in place of his great rival, the royalist Henry Hastings, Hesilrige oversaw plans for one muster in the borough of Leicester and one, on successive days, in five of the hundreds of the shire: 'in such convenient places as might be most for their ease, and least chargeable'. The muster for the Gartree Hundred was appointed to take place at Kibworth – more accessible from Leicester than Market Harborough (a key consideration given that Grey, Hesilrige and other parliamentarians were riding frantically back and forth from the county town to coordinate activities and counter the similar efforts of royalists).

King Charles, meanwhile, tried desperately to regain the upper hand. Having issued a proclamation from York forbidding the raising of troops without his express command, he sent Henry Hastings back to Leicestershire on 12 June with a 'Commission of Array', authorizing him, with Sir Richard Halford, Sir Henry Skipwith, Sir John Bale and other loyalists, to raise the local trained bands in the king's name. In her memoirs Lucy Hutchinson would recall that time vividly in a period metaphor:

Before the flame of the war broke out in the top of the chimneys, the smoke ascended in every county; the king had sent forth commissions of array, and the parliament had given out commissions for their militia, and sent off their members into all counties to put them into execution. Between these, in many places, there were fierce contests and disputes, almost to blood, even at the first; for in the process every county had the civil war, more or less, within itself.

At Kibworth, a second muster was held by the king on 15 June. 'A very good appearance' was noted, 'with above an hundred volunteers' – 'except', an interesting caveat, 'some of the Clergy'. The Reverend William Hunt may have exerted some influence in Kibworth in the king's cause, perhaps denouncing the actions of Parliament from the pulpit, but he was wise enough to keep his head down while the muster was taking place. There is no indication that he was specifically singled out by Parliament in 1642, when across the shire those who made attempts to frustrate the parliamentary musters were reported by villagers and drew retribution from London.

The parson of neighbouring Ibstock, for instance, was among those 'forthwith sent for as delinquents for opposing and giving obstruction to the execution of the Ordinance of the Militia in the county of Leicester'. For now, Hunt would watch which way the wind would blow.

The war began when Charles raised his standard at Nottingham on 22 August 1642 (decorated with the motto 'Give Caesar his due'). The two sides first came into conflict at Edgehill in October, and the next three years saw armies moving and recruiting through the Midlands, though the Kibworth area was spared the worst depredations. Like most regions, though, it was subject to the punitive costs of garrisoning major towns – a double taxation, as both sides sought to extract maintenance and supplies from the same population. The general sense of fear and upheaval which pervaded this most anarchic of English decades is conveyed in Kibworth's parish register, which has several blank pages introduced by the following note:

Anno Domini 1641. Know all men, that the reason why little or nothing is registered from this year, 1641, until the year 1649, was the civil wars between King Charles and his parliament, which put all into a confusion till then; and neither minister nor people could quietly stay at home for one party or the other.

The first phase of the war came to a climax in the late spring of 1645. With the outcome of the conflict still in the balance, Leicester found itself suddenly surrounded by royalist forces and presented by Charles's nephew, Prince Rupert, with an abrupt summons to surrender. The townsmen sought desperately to buy time while they threw up earthworks to patch the decrepit medieval walls, but they were soon subject to an intense bombardment by the royalist artillery established on a ruined Roman aqueduct to the south. A breach was quickly opened and rampaging royalist troops poured through, unrestrained by their leaders in retribution for the town's failure to surrender. Many hundreds died that day inside the town.

Meanwhile out in the countryside to the south a parliamentarian cavalry regiment under the mercenary John Dalbier was quartered at

Kibworth. Dalbier's soldiers, it was said, were 'the most unruliest of all the Parliamentarian soldiers quartered in Leicestershire' and their stay must have been an unpleasant experience for the villagers. (In the archaeological dig of 2009, Civil War stone cannonballs were found on Main Street by the old marketplace.) The troops would at the very least have taken water from the village wells, and demanded fodder and grain from their barns; but perhaps a lot more besides. Domestic robbery no doubt was commonplace. A hint of what things were like over that late spring of 1645 for the Colmans, Chapmans and Carters living in the middle of the village around the market cross at the junction of Hog Lane and Main Street is given by a remonstrance received by the parliamentary Committee of Both Kingdoms concerning the behaviour of Dalbier's unit: 'for the last two years they have been damnified by free quarter, taking of horses, and other charges not imposed by Parliament . . . Many of the troopers of Dalbier's regiment are returned into the county to the intolerable burden of the inhabitants.'

There had been, the committee noted, 'of late within three days 200 robberies committed in the county by soldiers, which has much disheartened the country in the Parliament's service'. While billeted in Kibworth, Dalbier's troops also learned of the vicar William Hunt's royalist sympathies. At Whitsun (25 May that year), 'they threatened Mr Hunt they would not leave him worth a groat.' With Hunt's reputation as a royalist and High Church to boot, and given the destructive record of parliamentarian forces elsewhere, especially if they were Puritans or religious radicals, it would be surprising if the interior of St Wilfrid's survived this episode unscathed: what little had survived the Reformation iconoclasts no doubt went now.

But the decisive battle was now at hand. Having captured Leicester on 31 May the royalist army moved south through Kibworth towards Market Harborough, fanning across the countryside to scavenge supplies from the beleaguered villages. In the path of the army on the main Harborough road, Kibworth (as its vicar later noted) was now afflicted by raids and plundering from the other side, as the royalist troops replenished their stores and quartered themselves on the population. Prince Rupert's cavalry had been based throughout the siege of Leicester at Great Glen, two miles from Kibworth. On 6 June 1645 the Earl of Manchester reported to the House of Lords, 'that the King marcheth Southward, his Forlorn Hope at Harborough, the main Body following; their Foot Quarters about Kybworth, Noselye, Scevington, and Tilton'. On 4 June, King Charles stayed at Wistow Hall, seat of his ally Sir Richard Halford, and it was around this date that the main royalist foot moved through Kibworth. The king's cavalry was reckoned at 3,600, his remaining infantry at around 4,000. If this was not, as Clarendon observed, 'a body sufficient to fight a battle for a crown', it was no doubt enough to strike fear into the long-suffering villagers, and to drive them indoors praying for deliverance from this 'unwanted war'.

The main parliamentary army under Fairfax and Cromwell now moved north to intercept the king. On 14 June the decisive battle was fought to the south of Kibworth at Naseby and Charles was comprehensively defeated. This 'very great victory' was hailed by the Committee of Both Kingdoms as a mighty providence from God: 'the King's army in which he was in person is wholly broken and destroyed.' As the royalist forces retreated in chaos north towards Leicester – Charles himself pausing at Wistow to change horses and saddles (the conspicuous crimson and gold one he left behind still remains in Wistow Hall) – they were pursued by Cromwell's cavalry. 'Our horse,' the committee reported, 'had the pursuit of them from four miles on this side Harborough to nine miles beyond, even to the sight of Leicester, whither the King fled. Our army quartered last night at Harborough, and this day are marching both horse and foot towards Leicester.' It was said that the first eleven of the fourteen miles through Kibworth to Leicester were littered with hundreds of Cavalier dead, scythed down from behind as they fled, pursued by a body of 'the enemyes horse and loose scowters to Great Glyn'. It had been, as one survivor noted, 'a dismall Satterday'.

Among the overheated and bedraggled royalists fleeing desperately north on the road towards Leicester was the rector of Kibworth, William Hunt. Hauled later before the parliamentary committee for sequestration, on suspicion of having been in the royalist army, Hunt pleaded simple ill-fortune. He had, he said, unwittingly set out on

horseback from Kibworth for Leicester at about two or three o'clock
on the day of the battle and found himself caught up with the defeated
royalists: 'the king's forces were then so scattered that they rode up
and down the country about Kibworth, so that a man could ride no
way, but he must needs ride in their company.' It was, to say the very
least, unfortunate timing.

Hunt's hearing, however, opened up a major religious split in Kibworth. The charge sheet brought against Hunt was later catalogued
by the royalist John Walker, in his compilation of the 'Sufferings of
the clergy of the Church of England who were sequester'd, harass'd,
&c in the times of the Great Rebellion'. Having had his property
sequestered initially on 17 August 1644 (though he evidently remained
in Kibworth after that date), Hunt was fined the substantial sum of
£150 in November 1645 for being in Leicester when it was a royal
garrison. 'While at Leicester', it was alleged, he 'got protections from
Prince Rupert for some parishioners, but left others to be plundered',
implying a loyalist community in Kibworth whose interests he had
sought to protect. Hunt was accused of having ridden in arms with
Cavaliers and of having been 'one of those who fled after Naseby',
suggesting – and it would not be surprising – that fearful royalist
sympathizers in Kibworth followed in the tail of the fleeing Cavaliers. But he was also, as we have seen, charged with observing
'ceremonies'; also of refusing to read parliamentary notices and of
avoiding taking the Covenant – an oath in support of Parliament. He
had, moreover, even 'employed a scandalous curate' in Joseph Foster,
who had, the constable of Kibworth reported, been several times
seen drunk. In the aftermath of a war, the story is a measure of how
central religion was seen to be in the conflicts of the time.

The evidence was enough to condemn Hunt. In 1647 the parliamentary Committee for Plundered Ministers – set up to replace
ministers loyal to Charles – ordered that Hunt be removed and nominated in his place a Cambridge Puritan vicar for Kibworth, John
Yaxley. But Hunt would not go without a struggle. Finally, after an
appeal, on 16 July 1647, the Committee for Sequestrations ordered that
his eviction proceed. Interestingly they did so, 'on parishioners' petition', suggesting that if there was a royalist contingent in Kibworth,

there was also a body in the village hostile to Hunt and his 'ceremonies'. Hunt remained obstinate and barricaded himself into the 'fortified parsonage house', the medieval rectory to the south of St Wilfrid's. The parliamentarians responded robustly. A party of soldiers was despatched and they 'broke down part of the house "not without bloodshed" and gave Yaxley possession'.

Hunt continued his fight at law but failed to wrest the living back from Yaxley, though the dispute rumbled on bitterly for several years. In 1654, Yaxley complained that Hunt was still trying to sue him even though, he indignantly protested, he had now been the village vicar 'quietly' for seven years. On 27 June that year the Committee for Compounding ordered that the county commissioners should 'use all lawful means to quiet Yaxley in his possession of the rectory'. Finally, on 9 February 1655 an agreement was reached by which Yaxley kept the living on condition that he returned all of Hunt's possessions and paid him £120 for the first year and subsequently £80 a year for life. The generosity of these terms – and the passion with which Hunt fought for them – shows how lucrative the Kibworth living was. And if this dispute dragged on longer than most, it is a pointer to the degree of religious turmoil at grass-roots level during these years that roughly two in five of Leicestershire's parish incumbents in 1642 had been obliged to resign by Puritan committees.

If Hunt, his curate Foster and their 'ceremonies' had been a divisive presence in Kibworth, the same was also true of the new man, John Yaxley. A zealous – indeed militant – Puritan, Yaxley was (even his admirers conceded) not an easy man to live with. Even apologists for Nonconformist preachers after the Restoration hint at his uncompromising approach: 'He was a sincere, plain-hearted, humble, pious man; a faithful friend, and very communicative. While he was in the church he was very zealous in promoting reformation, both in his own parish and in the whole country.' Such men though could be 'exceptionable characters and turbulent spirits', one admitted, 'and Justice obliges us to acknowledge that Mr Yaxley appears to have been of this description.' Riding with the army as a captain in 1648 with his own troop, Yaxley was 'a great disturber of the peace, by day and night, searching for cavaliers and making great havoc and spoil of people's goods'. Back home in his Kibworth pulpit he 'constantly preached and prayed against the Stuarts'. In Kibworth, needless to say, with its rich and often diverse religious life, such an inflexible approach to his parishioners could only stir up trouble.

Yaxley's Puritan fundamentalism was felt in Kibworth from the start. The fourteenth-century font was cast out from the church as a 'relic of superstition' and wound up doing service as a horse trough in the yard of Robert Brown, a local man of presumably similar views who had served as an officer under Yaxley. (Later buried in a field, it was recovered in the 1860s and today is once again used for the village baptisms.) A similar attitude was taken towards other details of ornament or ritual which offended Yaxley's sensitive nose for papistry. But such was the drift of the time. Elsewhere even the tomb of Walter of Merton was rudely assaulted, as a Latin inscription commemorating its subsequent repair makes clear:

In the year 1662, during the custody of the nobleman Thomas Clayton, the warden and scholars of Merton College in Oxford University, by virtue of their devotion and gratitude towards its founder, restored this tomb, which had been damaged and almost destroyed by the madness of the fanatics (which mad rabble, for a period lasting beyond the recent civil war, directed its rage against this tomb in just the same way as it was accustomed to do on a monstrous scale against the churches themselves, and against the relics of heroes and saints piously established therein).

Up and down the land in these bitter decades it was not only lives but history which was lost: in Kibworth too, where the once numerous memorials in St Wilfrid's were mistreated.

Yaxley meanwhile eagerly assisted the wider work of the Puritan regime, which with a virtual 'thought police' sought to stamp out licentious behaviour or blasphemous opinions (the latter category of course including any perceived disaffection towards the government). In August 1654, Cromwell passed an ordinance, in his newly assumed capacity as Lord Protector, 'for ejecting Scandalous, Ignorant and Insufficient Ministers and Schoolmasters'. A panel of commissioners was nominated for each county: on that for Leicestershire sat Sir Arthur

Hesilrige as well as Cromwell's fourth son, Henry. This was assisted by a subsidiary panel of eighteen ministers deemed impeccable in their Puritan rigour, one of whom was the Kibworth vicar John Yaxley.

Together they worked for the 'setlement of a godly and painful Ministery', sniffing out any such wrong thinking as contravened the 1650 Act against 'Atheistical Blasphemous and excrable opinions, derogatory to the Honour of God, and destructive to humane Society' – as well as licentious behaviour: not only adultery, fornication, drunkenness and fighting but also frequent playing at cards or dice, 'Whitson-Ales, Wakes, Morris-Dances, May-poles, Stage-plays . . . or such like Licentious practices, by which men are encouraged in a loose and prophane Conversation'. Republican England, then, was not a place for jollity. Liberty did not on any account mean *licence*. And Kibworth, with Yaxley at the helm, was in the front line of the campaign for a brave and godly new world.

By the late 1650s, Cromwell was dead and his son Richard installed as Lord Protector, as was noted approvingly in the Kibworth parish register. But many in England, even those once enthusiastic, were wearying of the Republic. As support for the regime dwindled, Yaxley led a delegation of thirty-eight Leicestershire ministers to deliver a petition to Parliament. His was the first name affixed and he delivered the preamble, testifying to the desire of all 'the true Godly of the Land, to strengthen your Hands in the Work of the Lord', and rueing the late lapse of erstwhile allies: the ministers 'could not but with shame, and bleeding of heart, bewail that Cloud of darkness, which had lately overspread divers of their old professed friends, who at first deeply engaged with them'. The House thanked Yaxley and his fellows for a petition in which they discerned 'a Gospel-Spirit of Meekness, Sincerity, and Holiness'. But many of them sensed clearly enough that, for the English Republic, the game was up.

## Restoration

From the moment that Charles II landed at Dover on 25 May 1660 and processed to London, there were those in Kibworth who sensed that the game was also finally up for their vexatious minister. Unfortunately for Yaxley, the return of the king gave his local enemies all the security they needed to avenge the violent eviction of William Hunt thirteen years earlier and much else suffered by villagers in the interim. One need scarcely doubt that, if there were Puritans in the village who shared Yaxley's mindset, there were many others profoundly unhappy with the turn their community's religious life had taken. (In 1658 even the schoolmaster of Kibworth Grammar School had resigned after only two years in the job, fed up with the minister's busybodying.)

But Yaxley did not go quietly from Kibworth. As Charles arrived in London, Yaxley delivered an apocalyptic commentary from the village pulpit: 'Hell is broke loose, the devil and his instruments are coming to persecute the godly.' From the time of the Restoration, it was alleged, Yaxley preached that 'the King was a Papist, and went to mass twice a day, and that Popery and Profaneness increased apace'. Finally, at dawn on 17 August 1660, William Beridge, whose family had been popular vicars from the 1570s, and his village friends took the law into their own hands.

For what happened next we have conflicting accounts delivered in petitions to Parliament: that of Yaxley's sworn witness on the one hand (a man given simply as J.D. who was staying at the Rectory while Yaxley was away); and, on the other, the reply of the local Justice, Sir John Pretyman, who lived near to Kibworth and who was summoned to the scene after the initial drama had taken place. According to J.D., Beridge came to the parsonage at sunrise with two other men, Richard Clark and John Brian, both middling Kibworth farmers. They drew the latch and entered, Beridge armed with a drawn sword and a cocked pistol, Clark with a cocked pistol and a fork. Having turfed the maids out of bed they entered the room where J.D. had been sleeping and threatened to run him through with a sword if he did not rise and leave quietly. They then entered the chamber of Mrs Yaxley, breaking down her bolted door, hauled her from the room in her petticoat and thrust her down the stairs and out of the house.

J.D. testified that Mrs Yaxley then went to her sister's house in the village to borrow a coat before returning and shouting through the parlour window to be allowed to collect some clothes. Yaxley later seems to have claimed that his wife had been frantic at being unable to collect her granddaughter, who was asleep in a cradle in the house – and that she had shouted through the window: 'You villains, will you kill my child?' Both agree, however, that she was then shot at through the window and badly wounded in the face by the gunpowder and broken glass, which left her sightless and – as J.D. delicately put it – 'more like a monster than a woman'. It was a harsh punishment for her husband's unpopularity.

Yaxley moved to Smithfield in London, where he continued preaching until he died in 1687. It is interesting to compare his case with that of William Sheffield, another Puritan preacher installed by Parliament. In contrast to Yaxley, Sheffield became so respected by his new parishioners that a successful petition to the court was organized after the Restoration – signed by over a thousand people – requesting that he be allowed to continue in his role. But in 1662 the Act of Uniformity imposed the ritual and liturgy of a new Book of Common Prayer – a measure which led to the resignation of some 2,000 clergymen, including Sheffield, who could not comply with its terms. On his resignation William Sheffield retired to Kibworth Harcourt, where he owned land and where he lived the rest of his life. For eleven years he 'constantly went in the morning, with his family, to the parish church, and preached in his own home in the afternoon', becoming a lynchpin of the burgeoning Nonconformist community in Kibworth. In 1672, Sheffield licensed his house behind the Old Crown on Main Street as a place for Presbyterian worship with himself as preacher. The Civil War had seen the uniformity of the Church of England that Henry VIII and Elizabeth had sought fragment into scores of sects. Ecclesiastical discipline had almost entirely broken down, and thanks to war and division a generation had grown up quite unused to regular attendance in the established church. 'Nonconformity', as a local phenomenon and as a national movement, was born.

## Nonconformists

The explosion of radical and dissenting groups after the Civil War is one of the great features of English seventeenth-century history. What contemporary directories of heresy had listed with loathing was now in the open: Quakers, Ranters, Independents, Millenaries, Sabbatarians, Seventh-Day Men, Brownists, Children of the New Birth, Sweet Singers of Israel and so on. Their legacy in Kibworth can be seen in chapels dotted around the village, many now redundant, and in the beautiful slate tombstones in the grounds of the old Congregational Chapel on the A6.

It was after Charles II's Restoration in 1660 that Kibworth suddenly emerged as a great centre of dissent. We know from the surveys ordered by Gilbert Sheldon, Archbishop of Canterbury from 1663, that Kibworth Harcourt in particular was already a centre of Protestant dissent. The episcopal returns of 1669 report a startlingly big community, a 'conventicle' of about 200 Presbyterians and Independents of the 'middle sort of people' meeting there together – an astonishingly large number, unsurpassed even by larger centres of dissent like Market Harborough. It was reported that these dissenters met in the houses of ordinary husbandmen, Isaac Davenport, Will Johnson and Will Jordan, and the returns list four preachers in particular who preached to this community: Matthew Clark, John Shuttlewood, an 'ejected minister called Southam' and 'a husbandman called Farmer', along with William Sheffield. In a trend that quickly came to define Nonconformist practice, however, most ministers were itinerant, and of these only Sheffield actually lived in Kibworth. Clark was particularly tireless, 'preaching up and down in Leicestershire and the neighbouring Parts'. In 1669 he seems to have been preaching at no fewer than fourteen Leicestershire parishes.

The atmosphere was particularly hostile for Nonconformists during the first decade of Charles's reign. In 1664 the Conventicle Act forbade religious assemblies of more than five people not under the aegis of the Established Church, driving some pastors and their congregations to hold services in the open air. Three times Clark was imprisoned in Leicester jail 'for the Crime of Preaching'. He was evicted from his 'very lonesome house in Leicester Forest' by the terms of the 1665 Five Mile Act, which forbade clergymen from living within that radius of a parish from which they had been banned. He was later fined and excommunicated, and had his possessions seized. A community as large as that in Kibworth Harcourt must have been subject to routine observation, harassment and inquisition. Not for nothing has this period been referred to as the 'heroic age of Dissent'.

Something of a let-up occurred in 1672 when Charles issued a Royal Declaration of Indulgence, which suspended (though it did not repeal) the penal laws and permitted the construction of registered chapels run by pastors who were officially vetted and licensed. William Sheffield was granted such a licence that year, and his house in Kibworth was recognized as a meeting place.

There were certain groups, however, to which no such forbearance was shown. One, surprisingly, was the Quakers. This sect had been founded during the 1640s by a weaver's son, George Fox, who came from Fenny Drayton near Kibworth. They called themselves 'Saints' (to mark their intended revival of the early Church), 'Friends of the Truth' or simply 'Friends'. But after a judge mocked this group as 'Quakers' who 'tremble at the word of the Lord', this label was proudly adopted. In contrast to their later reputation, the early Quaker communities were seen as dangerous and subversive, particularly by the Restoration regime alarmed by their rejection of monarchy and the established social hierarchy; but even Puritan preachers who now led Nonconformist groups were furious at the disruption the Quakers caused (and at their rejection and ridicule of all priests and ministers). During the 1650s William Sheffield himself had twice written to the Protectorate to report 'a great concourse of those people called Quakers'. They acted 'under pretence of peaceableness,' he wrote, '. . . yet some of them were accidentally seene to have pistols at theire sides under theire cloakes and in their pocketts'; he himself had been threatened with the 'lowse-house' (slang for a cage). By toleration for such, he argued, 'godly people [are] discontented, that the government should be soe much asleep as to suffer such in their insolency, which is falsely called a liberty, for as they manage it, it is not only disturbing but distructive to the civill and Christian libertyes of others.'

Measures were taken against the Quakers during the Interregnum, and more systematic suppression was carried out by the government of Charles II, which in 1662 introduced a Quaker Act, requiring people to swear an oath of allegiance to the king – all such oaths contravened Quaker principles. Such persecution led many Quakers to emigrate to America, among them William Penn, who founded the Commonwealth of Pennsylvania with unprecedented religious freedoms. But a remarkable document in the Leicestershire County Archive preserves the suppression of one Quaker community unrecorded in the official Quaker histories and which based itself in Kibworth parish at Smeeton.

As ever, it is in the official attempts at suppression that traces of these groups survive. In this case the County Lieutenancy Book preserves an order sent out to a Lieutenant Bales, at the head of a militia troop overseen by Captain George Fawnt, on 3 December 1668. It notes information passed to leading men of the county to the effect that 'there are great numbers of persons commonly called Quakers that assemble and meete together *under the pretence of joyninge in a religious worship* at Smeeton in the parrish of Kibworth and divers other places [. . .] in the Hundred of Gartree.' (As we have seen in the case of William Sheffield, informants were plentiful against a group whose conduct offended even the Nonconformist conscience.) Regardless, action was enjoined: muscle was to be provided, with as many troops as seemed necessary, to Mr Oliver, one of the Chief Constables of the hundred, 'to bring all the said persons or the chief of them before his Majesty's Justices of the Peace'. Unfortunately the local quarter sessions of the period are missing, so full details of the dissenters, the charges against them and their punishments are lost.

## The Kibworth Academy

Kibworth, however, continued to grow as a centre of Nonconformity. In the wake of the 'Glorious Revolution' by which William of

Orange deposed Charles's Catholic brother, James II, the 1689 Toleration Act relieved dissenting communities of some of the punitive
restraints imposed upon them (though exclusions from political office
and the universities would long remain). During the course of the
eighteenth century small communities of Independents, Presbyterians, Baptists and Methodists would establish themselves in Kibworth
Beauchamp and Smeeton Westerby. Kibworth Harcourt, however,
remained the hub of Nonconformity in the parish. Soon after the
regime change, in 1690, a private chaplain called John Jennings, Welsh
by birth, who had himself been evicted from a living in 1662 and subsequently gathered an independent congregation at nearby West
Langton, relocated to Kibworth. When he died in 1701 he was succeeded by his son, another John Jennings, who established a small but
highly influential dissenting academy. When Jennings moved to
Hinckley in 1722, the house – in the yard of the Crown Inn – was
bought by the congregation, and his pupil Philip Doddridge, then
only twenty years old, took the helm. During this period a list of
Dissenters in Kibworth, Glen and Langton gives an astonishing 321
'Hearers' and forty-one 'Voters' in Doddridge's congregation.

Three years later Doddridge was asked, by one Reverend Saunders, to provide an account of Jennings's teaching at Kibworth, which
he did in full, from memory and with reference to a letter he found
in which Jennings himself had set down his methods. The syllabus he
details seems astonishingly diverse and open-minded, not least in
comparison with the resolutely unmodernized education provided
by the old universities in the early eighteenth century. (The impera-
tive to run academies in the first place was provided, of course, by the
exclusion of Dissenters from Oxford and Cambridge – subscription
to the Act of Uniformity and the Thirty-Nine Articles being a condition of university admission.)

'Our course of education at Kibworth,' Doddridge recalled, 'was
the employment of four years, and every half year we entered upon
a new set of studies.' He then detailed a curriculum, stage by stage,
which was remarkably utilitarian and broad-minded in its embracing
of the latest modern disciplines as well as theology (which itself was
taught in a manner which encouraged freedom of opinion). Science

was strongly represented, with lectures on mechanics, algebra, geometry, anatomy, physics and astronomy; modern history reading included not only works on Britain and Europe but the latest studies of Africa, Asia and the Americas; French was studied as well as Latin and Hebrew; logic was taught using a system Jennings had largely derived from John Locke. At all turns, Doddridge observed, Jennings 'made the best writers his commentators'. When in later years, after the academy had relocated to Northampton, students were admitted for a general education as well as in preparation for the ministry, its popularity and success mounted. Jennings also strongly believed in women's education, and it is no coincidence that his sister's daughter, the poet, feminist and anti-slavery writer Anna Laetitia Barbauld, was born and raised in Kibworth. Also a pioneering writer of children's books, Anna enraged Wordsworth and Coleridge by her anti-war stance, and, though she left the village when she was fifteen, she is one of the most interesting and symptomatic products of Jennings's Nonconformist curriculum.

Doddridge himself thrived on Jennings's example and relished his time in Kibworth for the leisure it gave him to study and reflect, in addition to his work teaching and ministering to his congregation (which included the composition of numerous hymns, some of which, like 'Oh Happy Day', remain popular among Nonconformist communities even now). When in 1720 a friend consoled him for the assumed tedium of being 'buried alive' at Kibworth, Doddridge memorably contradicted his correspondent:

Here I stick close to those delightful studies which a favoring Providence has made the business of my life. I can willingly give up the charms of London, the luxury, the company, the popularity of it, for the secret pleasures of rational employment and self-approbation; retired from applause and reproach, from envy and contempt, and the destructive baits of avarice and ambition. So that, instead of lamenting it as my misfortune, you should congratulate me upon it as my happiness, that I am confined in an obscure village, seeing it gives me so many valuable advantages to the most important purposes of devotion and philosophy, and, I hope I may add, usefulness, too.

## Grievous crimes and carnal concupiscence

There was much of profound interest, then, and of a modern cast, in the religious and intellectual life of Kibworth during the early eighteenth century. One less appealing aspect though was the enforcement of morality. It had long been a tenet of the Church that behaviour contravening the Christian moral codes endangered the salvation not just of the individual sinner but even of the wider community. In the absence of criminal sanctions for such moral lapses as pre-marital sex or adultery, punishment took the form of ritual humiliation by the church congregation. Cases were referred to the Leicester archdeaconry – and in Leicester Cathedral to this day there remain the furnishings of the consistory court in which such 'crimes' were addressed.

In the county archives numerous cases survive from Kibworth, as from across the archdeaconry, which attest to the importance of such moral policing in early eighteenth-century English society. The majority of such 'crimes' were cases of defamation or pre-marital 'fornication' – with the guilty couple almost invariably subsequently marrying, either by choice or through family and community pressure. Less frequent but not unusual were instances of the more serious lapse of adultery. In 1702, for instance, Esther Sturges of Kibworth was charged with committing adultery with another villager, William Swinglar. Her penalty was to appear on successive Sundays in January and February 1703 in the parish church of Kibworth, and in the neighbouring churches of Burton Overy and Great Glen. There, at the beginning of morning prayer, she was to 'stand upon a stool before the desk in the face of the congregation then assembled', dressed (in the winter cold) in nothing but a white sheet, and holding in her hand a white wand – the sheet a symbol of a return to baptismal purity, the wand an acceptance of the rod of discipline. In this humiliating position she was to recite her humble confession:

Whereas I Easther Sturgis not having the fear of God before mine eyes but being led by the instigation of the devil and mine own carnall concupiscence have committed the grievous crime of adultery with the above-named Wm

Swinglar to the great dishonour of Almighty God, the breach of his most
sacred laws, the scandal and evill example of others and the danger of mine
own soule without unfeigned repentance for the same I do humbly acknowledge and am heartily sorry for this my heinous offence. I ask God and the
congregation pardon and forgiveness for the same in Jesus Christ and beseech
him to give me his Grace not only to enable me to avoid all such like sin and
wickedness but also to live soberly righteously and godly all the days of my
life and to that end I desire all that are here present to joyne with me in saying the Lord's prayer. Our Father which art in Heaven . . .

On the back of the charge sheet, which was passed to the village rector
or curate, a note was made confirming that the confession had been
made in the prescribed manner, before the sheet was returned to the
archdeacon for filing. In the case of John and Sarah Monck, and John
and Mary Reddington, whose penance was carried out on the same
day in April 1719, a note was made by Will Vincent, the rector of Kibworth, that the confessions could not be recited sooner 'upon the
account of the women's lying in': both couples by then had married.

   Such ceremonies seem to us now the stuff of repressive fundamen-
talist fantasies, but they were performed routinely in England during
the eighteenth century, as similar rituals had been for hundreds of
years previously (Esther's penance, for example, unmistakably echoes
that of Roger and Alice Dexter in 1389 (see p. 226)). After a more
live-and-let-live attitude in the late medieval and early Tudor period,
where pre-marital sex was widely accepted among 'engaged' couples,
these rituals became more common after the Reformation as congregations sought to return to the 'purer' practices of the early Church.
By enforcing them, it was believed that the Church could thus secure
a forgiveness of sins for the penitent by the community. During the
course of the eighteenth century, however, such moralizing zeal waned
under the influence of new ideas and a more relaxed religious climate.
Cases of penance continued in Kibworth church until late in the century, but they became less frequent, and had disappeared altogether by
the early nineteenth. The religious fears and tumultuous passions
which had driven the events of the Tudor and Stuart periods had
begun, finally, to subside.

# 16. Agricultural and Industrial Revolution

Between the early eighteenth century and the middle of the nineteenth the society of Kibworth, as of England as a whole, once again went through dramatic change. This change had its roots far back in time, in the agrarian crises and labour disputes after the Black Death when a society of communally organized peasants gradually became a commercially minded society of yeoman farmers under a county gentry, their economy increasingly tied to urban and industrial centres beyond their immediate horizons. A sign of the times was the coming of the turnpike road between London and the west of Scotland, built in 1726. Now the A6, this road followed the old road through Market Harborough and Leicester which had been created in the twelfth century. At first it was paved with gravel and small stones, later with granite sets, with little toll houses, some of which survive today. When a fast and regular public coach service to London began in 1766 there was a revival of coaching inns in the village, and the London road (Main Street in Kibworth Harcourt) soon had eight coaching hostelries with accommodation, yards and stables. With that the modern age was on the horizon.

At this point Kibworth was still a cluster of agricultural communities but its society had already been transformed from the late-medieval village. Harcourt in particular was a typical 'closed' village, with a small circle of gentlemen and yeoman farmers, a growing number of tradesmen and craftsmen, a few husbandmen or small farmers, and a group of landless labourers for whom housing was provided by their employers. The old and retired tended to live under the same roof as the younger generation, but there was still the need for a gradual increase in housing for the poorer members of the community (who will loom much larger in the village story during the eighteenth century and whose names we come to know now through the records of the Poor Law commissions and the charitable clauses in the huge number of surviving wills). For these people new houses were built on the few remaining patches of waste land and along the verges of the road; one group, which became known jokingly in local speech as 'the City', comprised small houses of mud and thatch on the edge of the village. Here, for example, lived the Perkins family in the late eighteenth century. These people were not migrants, newcomers or seasonal labour. They were the indigenous poor who from now will be a constant in the story, typical of the new British proletariat.

But the visitor to Kibworth would still have seen the same shape of the village recognizable since the thirteenth century. The hamlet at Smeeton, with its well-built brick farmhouses, was smaller than it had been in the fourteenth century. Beauchamp, with its Tudor manor farm and its new grammar school building, still straggled along the high street with its workers' cottages down by the fish-ponds below Church Hill. In Harcourt the Polles were gone now, but the Parkers and Brians, Oswins, Carters, Rays and Haymes continued. The Colmans too still thrived. Providing literate village 'registrars' during the Commonwealth, they no longer held significant land but Will Coleman will be an important figure in the many wrestlings of the parish with the Poor Laws in the early nineteenth century – and indeed the family still live in the village today. The aspect of all three villages was much more of red brick now, with chimneys everywhere (for fireplaces burning coal), but Main Street was still lined with big medieval and Tudor farmhouses along the northern side, facing a row of neat little cottages down to the village pump. Here stood the grand late-seventeenth-century Old House where the poet Anna Laetitia Barbauld grew up and where the dissenting academy in the eighteenth century offered a curriculum that would have been the envy of the universities.

The most significant changes in the village in the eighteenth century came in its agricultural life, for these profoundly altered the social order. Ever since the village had been founded in the Dark Ages the life of its people had centred on the cultivation of the fields. But from the Tudor period onwards there was a movement across the country on the part of well-off landowners to enclose the common fields and move from arable to pasture. In Kibworth the old communally organized open fields still survived, as they did in most places in the English Midlands, but there were wealthy graziers among the local farmers 'whose lands and tenements were so dispersed in the fields that in their present situation they were incapable of any considerable improvement', as a Kibworth man was later to remark. On all fronts though this was an age of improvement. And wherever they could, such men were already trying to buy up parcels in the common fields, meadows and pastures with a view to gathering their scattered holdings together, usually through private agreements with other landowners, and enclosing them with hedges. From the seventeenth century, and particularly during the eighteenth, Parliament became involved in the process, enabling a majority of proprietors who were keen on the development to override the objections of a minority. In such economic rationalization lay the path to the future. Though some small yeoman farmers were still to be found in the area before the Second World War living in the old style, from now on the writing was largely on the wall for the old ways. The process came to a head with the enclosure of the common fields of the whole of the parish in 1779.

## The enclosure of the common fields

On the evening of Wednesday, 21 April 1779, William Peters, the innkeeper of the Crown Inn on the main road in Kibworth Harcourt (now an Indian restaurant), had a big crowd in for a midweek night and did a roaring trade catering for a noisy meeting of local land-holders. The assembled group were there to discuss the issue which had dominated talk in the parish for months: the enclosure of the open fields in the lordships of Kibworth Beauchamp, Kibworth Harcourt and Smeeton Westerby. Needless to say, no more than at any other time were these developments conditioned only by local concerns: just as in the Middle Ages, the reorganization of the countryside came at a time when society as a whole was undergoing rapid change. The population of England rose from five and a half million in 1688 to more than eight million in 1801. Huge urban centres were now growing up, especially London, of which an increasingly educated farming community was well aware through travel, business and the beginning of regional and local newspapers. Change was in the air.

Among local landholders, including ordinary small yeoman farmers like Will Perkins on Main Street, who still held land in virgates and yardlands, the issue of enclosure had already rumbled on contentiously for some years. The process of obtaining a Parliamentary Enclosure Act required the prior support of at least three quarters of the local proprietors, as well as agreement about who would act as commissioners to oversee the process and the compensation to be paid for tithe and manorial rights. In most places this was a drawn-out process, descending to light bickering at the very least. By 1779 it was achieved in Kibworth, and the necessary Act of Parliament was passed that year. If there was ongoing tension at the Crown that evening it may have stemmed from the owners of the eight out of the 148 'yardlands' in Beauchamp who had declared their opposition to the process. Typically it was in Beauchamp, the proletarian half of the parish, that resistance was most felt.

The purpose of the meeting was for the appointed commissioners to debate the many practicalities arising from the Act's execution, such as the definition of public roads and paths across the village land. Some of these had been customary ways for centuries: the Slang, from the horse mill out into the North Field; Mill Lane, westwards out of Beauchamp from which one could reach the west fields of both Smeeton and Beauchamp; the old ox tracks out into Ridge Field and Nether Field in Smeeton and on to the even more ancient furlong of the Gric. The new Act meant that the old pattern of the countryside was to be swept away.

The landscape they were measuring and valuing was owned by many landowners, the most important of which was Merton College, which leased lands in the open fields of Harcourt to farmers both big and small, some of which had been passed by father to son over many generations. As we have seen, the open-field landscape of Kibworth was the product of centuries of development and change since the fields were first laid out, probably in the tenth century, and then expanded up to 1300. Rights to use the land were shared

between the landowners – Merton in Harcourt and various manorial lords in Smeeton and Beauchamp. The commoners had the
right to graze their livestock when crops were not being grown.
Some of these rights had eroded over the previous couple of centuries, and some areas of the parish had already been enclosed by
well-off landowners working together. But still in the 1770s most of
the land consisted of the remains of the three big fields, the common
haymeadows and a series of closes, paddocks, orchards and gardens
dotted around the village which had come down over time for
common use; and also the common waste, the pasture and rough
lands on the very edge of the parish. In 1779 this patchwork system,
with its scores of field names going back to their medieval and
Viking ancestors, was still part of the common mental world picture
of the villagers. But with the sanction of the state, by parliamentary
Act, these common lands were now to be fenced off and divided,
with deeds and titles awarded to private owners, ending the centuries-
old traditional common rights.

Throughout the summer that year the Enclosure Commissioners
worked in the open fields of the ancient parish of Kibworth, walking
with local jurymen, 'dividing, allotting, and inclosing the Open and
Common Pastures' and measuring and staking out all public roads
and tracks which traversed the open land. On 28 August a formal
notice was printed in the local press, and pasted prominently around
the village, detailing the various 'Carriage and Drift Roads and Bridle Roads' to be retained. Thus, for instance, 'the present Turnpike
Road [now the A6] leading from Market Harborough to Leicester, in
the same track it now goes over the Fields, is marked and staked out
of the breadth of sixty feet.' (Other carriage roads in the parish were
forty feet wide; bridle roads twenty.) The commissioners' clerk, William Wartnaby, announced a subsequent meeting at the Crown,
scheduled for 9 September, which would give villagers a chance to
voice objections to the proposed routes.

Kibworth's enclosure took place during the most important period
of enclosure in Leicestershire: during the 1760s and 1770s two thirds
of all the enclosure acts for the county were passed, at an average of
five or six per year. In the parish of Kibworth some 3,900 acres of

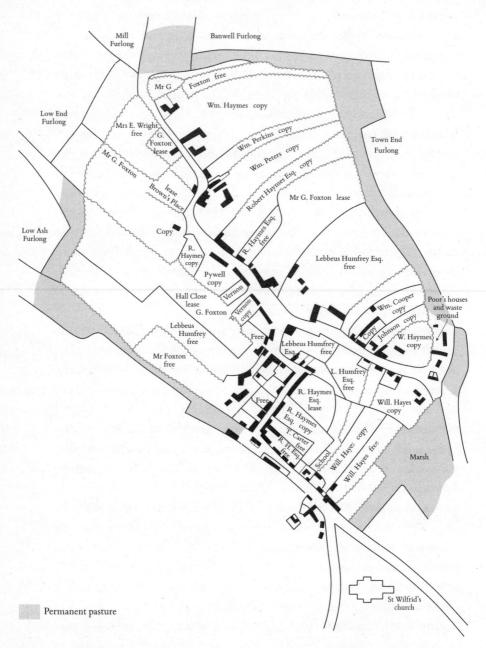

Mill Furlong

Banwell Furlong

Low End Furlong

Mr G. Foxton

Foxton free

Wm. Haymes copy

Mrs E. Wright free

G. Foxton lease

Town End Furlong

Mr G. Foxton

Wm. Perkins copy

Wm. Peters copy

Robert Haymes Esq. copy

Mr G. Foxton lease

lease

Brown's Place

Low Ash Furlong

Copy

R. Haymes Esq. free

Lebbeus Humfrey Esq. free

R. Haymes copy

Pywell copy

Vernon

Hall Close lease G. Foxton

T. Vernon copy

Wm. Cooper copy

Poor's houses and waste ground

Copy

Johnson copy

Lebbeus Humfrey free

Free

Lebbeus Humfrey Esq.

Lebbeus Humfrey free

W. Haymes copy

Mr Foxton free

L. Humfrey Esq. free

Free

R. Haymes Esq. lease

Will. Hayes copy

R. Haymes Esq. copy

T. Carter Esq. free

R. H. Esq. free

School

Will. Hayes copy

Will. Hayes free

Marsh

St Wilfrid's church

Permanent pasture

Kibworth Harcourt in 1781 after enclosure, from a map in Merton College, Oxford: the three great open fields and the old customary holdings have now gone open farmland, unsegregated by hedge or fence, were awarded to twenty-seven proprietors in Beauchamp, twenty-three in Harcourt and thirty-five in Smeeton Westerby, according to the number of 'yardlands' they had previously claimed in the parish. The subsequent erection of fences and cultivation of hedges to demarcate individual plots would change the appearance of the surrounding country for ever, shaping today's patchwork field system which we now think of as archetypal English countryside.

The most powerful local owners, Lebbeus Humphrey (a relative newcomer) and Robert Haymes (from a village family which rose in Tudor times), did best out of this process. The popular mythology of enclosure quickly became that of a 'Great National Robbery': a land grab by the powerful at the expense of the impoverished tenantry, whose access to any remaining common land was much reduced if it was not removed entirely. Dr John Aikin, a descendant of the Reverend John Jennings and born and raised in Kibworth himself, expressed the view of many radicals when he wrote: '[the poor man] has resigned to the landlord all his share of the ground, which his own hands cultivated, not reserving to himself as much as will bury him . . .' A child in the 1860s, F. P. Woodford remembered the bitter opinion of many working men in the village:

the surrounding landowners said that it would be very advantageous if the fields, meadow and pastures were enclosed (for *ever*). Amazing candour! Agreeable and acceptable to all concerned no doubt, totally ignoring the poor man, whose rightful heritage they were, and whose need was more pressing than theirs (rank robbery, and discreditable to all concerned).

Historians have been more divided. Large-scale enclosure was both symptom and catalyst of broader economic change. As population growth increased the demand for food, and improvements in transport facilitated the movement of produce, so the incentive grew for landowners to pay the costs of enclosure in return for gains in productivity. In Leicestershire, at least, there do not seem to have been widespread outbreaks of violence as a result of parliamentary enclosures during the eighteenth century (the only instance concerning the South Field of Leicester in 1753) – though the much earlier Mid-lands Revolt of 1607 which affected the region to the south of Kibworth was sparked by the enclosure of common land. That said, there is certainly some evidence that the dramatic changes prompted by enclosure in Kibworth were the cause, directly or indirectly, of increased suffering among the growing numbers of rural poor.

## The creation of a landless proletariat

In 1797, less than a decade after the parish of Kibworth was enclosed, Sir Frederick Eden published his remarkable and pioneering three-volume survey *The State of the Poor*, the predecessor of great works on the English working class from Engels to E. P. Thompson. Prompted by the hardship he observed among the labouring classes in 1794 and 1795, when harvests failed and prices rose steeply during the war with France, Eden set out to survey conditions among the poor all over England. Doing some of the fieldwork himself, he gathered information from the clergy, as well as designing a questionnaire which he sent out with 'a remarkably faithful and intelligent person', John Housman. Housman gave brief accounts of his tours in the *Monthly Magazine* and observed the rapid decline of arable now in the Leicestershire area where 'the farmers graze most part of their grounds.' A major change in English economy and society was under way before his eyes.

In Eden's book Kibworth features strongly. The detailed picture Eden provided for the village in the 1790s noted that some nine tenths of the land had become pasture, while no common or waste land (such as described in 1086 in Domesday) now survived in the parish. Before the fields were enclosed, people in Kibworth told Eden, they were 'solely applied' to the production of corn; the poor then 'had plenty of employment, in weeding, reaping, threshing, &c and could also collect a great deal of corn by gleaning'. 'There is,' Eden concluded, 'some truth in these observations: one third or perhaps one fourth of the number of hands which were required twenty years ago, would now be sufficient, according to the present system of agriculture, to perform all the farming work in the parish.'

He may have exaggerated the extent to which the open fields in Kibworth had been exclusively arable – a portion at least of the open fields had been set aside for 'ley' (that is, grass for grazing) and the 1779 enclosure survey of the fields shows many already as 'Old Inclosure'. But there is no doubt that pasture significantly increased as a result of enclosure and that this drastically reduced the available farm work for landless labourers. The 1801 crop returns gave the relatively low figure of 348 acres of surviving arable land for Kibworth Beauchamp, of which the largest constituents were beans, wheat and barley in that order. It cannot have been coincidental that annual expenditure on poor relief in Kibworth Beauchamp soared during this period: from £72 in the year ending Easter 1776, to £147 in 1785 to £423 in 1803 (getting on for £350,000 today in terms of the average earnings index).

Eden discussed in detail the economic situation of one Kibworth labourer in particular. In August 1795 he was forty years old, and had a wife and five children from fourteen down to eighteen months to support; at fourteen the eldest girl earned two shillings a week spinning, but neither the labourer's wife nor his other children earned; his second daughter, who was twelve years old, suffered from fits. He worked part of the year as a canal navvy, and at other times picked up casual labour. Lacking the regular seasonal agricultural work on which his ancestors had relied and which he might have expected to perform for much of the year, the family were often dependent on the extensive system of charity organized by the parish – one of the features of Kibworth life as far back as records go. 'The parish pays this man's house-rent, finds him coals, occasionally gives him articles of wearing-apparel, and, for the last two weeks past, has given him an allowance of 2s. a week.' The labourer gave a detailed account of his family's basic diet:

[He] says that they use little or no milk or potatoes; that they seldom get any butter; neither do they use any oatmeal; that they occasionally buy a little cheese, and sometimes have meat on a Sunday; that his wife and daughters consume a small quantity of tea; but that bread is the chief support of the family and that they have far from a sufficiency of that article at present; that they should use much more, if they could procure it; and that his children are almost naked, and half-starved. He adds, that he has lately worked many days with only bread diet, and that many weeks have elapsed since he has tasted any beer.

With its journalistic approach to factual detail Eden's approach, which is typified by this 1795 interview with a poor Kibworth labourer, is the pioneer of the flood of great nineteenth- and twentieth-century literature on the condition of the English working class, from Marx and Engels to Priestley and Orwell. In his book the signs are unmistakably on the wall. Over the next century the population of England will quadruple; our nameless worker and his family, it might fairly be said, represent a new turn in English history.

## Canals and industry

Fortunately for him, and many others like him in Kibworth, at this particular moment, when the enclosure of the village fields severely reduced the available agricultural work, an entirely new source of labour – albeit temporary – had appeared in the region. 'Many labourers,' Eden noted, 'can, at present, get work at a canal cutting in the neighbourhood; otherwise, the [county poor] rates must have been much higher than they even now are.' The labourer reported that he was working at the canal for about half the year, earning 2 shillings a day, when the weather allowed. Money was money, with a family to feed, but digging canal trenches by hand, with hand picks and shovels, and with overseers intolerant of slacking, was work which must have been painful and draining almost beyond endurance on a meagre diet of bread and gruel.

For the region, though, this was a momentous development. Economic growth in Leicestershire had always been constrained by the fact that this part of the Midlands was unserved by navigable waterways. By now coal was an important part of the local economy, for industry and for domestic heating, since there were few sources of wood close by. In fact the Merton court rolls show that coal was already used in Kibworth in the late thirteenth century, when the peasants' dues included carting the lord's coal across the county. But the poor quality of roads and tracks made Kibworth dependent on local supplies of coal, which were more costly and inferior in quality to that produced in neighbouring Derbyshire. The roads were so bad in places that even local coal was brought to Leicester on the back of horses and mules. Goods from London, astonishingly, were still conveyed to Leicester by sea, in coasting brigs which travelled down the Thames, north around the Suffolk and Norfolk coasts to the Lincolnshire mouth of the Trent, and then in 'Trent boats' as far as Loughborough, before they were finally carried overland by wagon.

Though strong vested interests opposed the building of canals – not least the Leicestershire coal merchants – sufficient weight in favour was eventually secured to overcome resistance. The success of river 'navigation' schemes in the north of the county was followed in the early 1790s by the canal mania which gripped England as a whole. An ambitious plan was drawn up to create a water link – later dubbed the 'Grand Junction' – from London to the Oxford Canal and ultimately to join the Trent and Mersey Canal to Liverpool. This led to a 'Union Canal' project which would link the Midland towns of Nottingham, Derby and Leicester to this wider network. In spite of tortuous negotiations, and a dip in canal fever as the French wars continued, the project went ahead on a route which ran north-west from Market Harborough, round the southern edge of Smeeton Westerby, towards Leicester. Less than a mile to the west of Smeeton a major tunnel, 880 yards long, was dug through rising ground at Saddington, whose huge spoil tips are still visible along the edge of Smeeton fields. As the English canal revolution was launched, villagers in Kibworth had a box seat.

For the locals, though, this had pros and cons. On the one hand, employment in the village, which had dried up with the enclosing of the fields, could find an outlet on major local engineering projects. On the other, works on this scale required more labour than they alone could provide. Much of this labour was provided by gangs of imported 'navigators' or 'navvies' who lodged in temporary encampments on the edge of the village or in local accommodation if it could be found cheaply. The unruliness of many of these newcomers, who were often Irish, made them highly unpopular with the communities on which they descended. The height of canal mania in the 1790s was also a time of war in Europe, and since the Irish had a history of alliance with the French, xenophobic passions made it a particularly combustible time in the village. One incident recorded in the *Leicester Journal* for April 1795 became long remembered as the 'Kibworth Riot'.

On Monday, 30 March 1795, the Mayor of Leicester was brought word that a large number of men who were working on the Union Canal had assaulted a detachment of Leicester 'Fencibles' (these were temporary home guard units called up during the war). Having liberated two deserters being held by the soldiers, the navvies were now rioting in Kibworth. The mayor promptly summoned one Captain Heyrick and ordered him to organize a military response. Between three and four that afternoon, as the *Leicester Journal* reported, Heyrick blew a horn in summons and the Leicester troop of Volunteer Cavalry duly formed up, armed and equipped, in the town's marketplace. Having been informed of the situation and given their orders, the troop rode off for Kibworth with bayonets fixed, while an infantry detachment followed shortly afterwards armed with muskets. When they reached the turnpike at Oadby, word reached them that a group of the rioters, along with the two liberated deserters, had moved on to Newton Harcourt, a small hamlet to the north-west of Kibworth which was also on the line of the canal earthworks. Arriving there the troops traced a group of the rioters to the Recruiting Sergeant public house, where they appeared defiantly at the door armed with long pikes and 'seemed determined to resist'. The local JP, Justice Burnaby, who had been summoned to the scene, read out the Riot Act – the measure of 1713 which allowed local authorities to order any group of twelve or more to disperse or face punitive action. For the process to be lawful the text had to be read accurately, audibly and in full:

Our Sovereign Lord the King chargeth and commandeth all persons, being assembled, immediately to disperse themselves, and peaceably to depart to their habitations, or to their lawful business, upon the pains contained in the act made in the first year of King George, for preventing tumults and riotous assembles. God Save the King!

Once the Act had been read, a group of cavalrymen were ordered to dismount and to search the public house for the two deserters, who were not found, though four of 'the most desperate' of the rioters were seized and sent to Leicester under armed guard. The remaining cavalry then scoured the neighbouring country, following the line of the canal south-east to Fleckney, Smeeton and Kibworth, where they met up with the infantry detachment at around seven o'clock in the evening. The following day the cavalry again rode along the canal route, accompanied by a sergeant and another of the Fencibles who had been injured during the fighting in Kibworth the day before (and so knew their men). Nine more of the rioters were identified and apprehended: 'amongst them was *Red Jack* and *Northamptonshire Tom*, two fellows notorious for being a terror to every country they have resided in.' All taken were examined on the Thursday before Justice Burnaby, when nine were freed and four – Jack and Tom presumably among them – committed.

The Union Canal became operational from Leicester to Kibworth in 1797, when the nearby Debdale Wharf officially opened for business, though not until 1814 was the full Union project completed, with the opening of the huge staircase of ten canal locks at Foxton, south-east of Kibworth – one of the most dramatic engineering projects of the canal age. In general those canals built earlier than 1790 were more successful than the many conceived afterwards in what has been described as 'a spirit of excited optimism'. In Leicestershire the subsidiary side canals in the north of the county were almost all failures. However, the main north–south line, linking London, Birmingham and Leicester with the Trent – a key element in the massive network which now linked the capital with the booming industrial cities of the north-west – was ultimately important enough to pay dividends and had a lasting impact on the local economy. The 'fuel famine' which had for so long held back the development of this part of the Midlands was resolved by regular, and cheaper, supplies of coal; and even the back kitchens of Kibworth houses were now stacked with lumps of 'Derbyshire Bright'. The population of Leicester itself began to rise rapidly, from just under 17,000 in 1801 to 30,000 in 1821, and it continued to grow at the rate of 10,000 per decade until 1850. In town and country, industrial England was on the move.

## The Industrial Revolution comes to Kibworth

The effect of the canals on Kibworth itself was dramatic too. As we have seen, the village had been one of the most populous in the area since the eleventh century; it had had perhaps 600 people in 1381 and by 1670 the village population had returned to its highest medieval level. In the early eighteenth century there were 150 families in the parish – perhaps 750 people – but from then on like many places in England it experienced a steep rise. The 1801 census, which is not a complete record, gives a population of 1,232 people, and this almost doubled in the next century. And yet again the story of national historical change is mirrored at this point in the life of the village as the old agrarian world is transformed and industrial society begins to enter the village with small-scale industry, brick works, textile factories and especially framework knitting.

Framework knitting had begun with the invention of the knitting frame in the Midlands in the 1590s. Strongly concentrated in Leicestershire, Nottinghamshire and Derbyshire, it became a massive industry during the Napoleonic Wars, employing nearly 100,000 workers, not counting children. Their product was not only plain and fancy hose, but also gloves, braces, mitts, blouses, pantaloons, cravats and miscellaneous articles. Leicester itself was a centre of fine work – 'spider net' blouses, fancy hose and best gloves. In Kibworth basic hosiery was produced both in private houses and later in small factories, whose remains are still dotted around the closes and back lots of the village. These were confined to the 'open' villages of Beauchamp and Smeeton. Across the road the closed village of Harcourt resisted such inroads: farms, cottages and coaching inns still characterized that part of Kibworth.

The reason why Beauchamp and Smeeton in the south of the parish became so heavily a part of the hosiery industry, but not Harcourt, lies in their different histories. As it had been since 1270, Merton College was still the owner of the fields and many of the houses in Harcourt, and it was still an agricultural place, a 'closed' village, as indeed it was until very recently. Smeeton's seven manors had broken up in the early modern period into private holdings open to speculation; and Beauchamp was a proletarian place where an underemployed workforce was ripe for industrial exploitation. Perhaps it is not too fanciful to think this pattern an old one. In Beauchamp in the fourteenth century there had been twenty-four villein families, three cottagers and eighteen families of serfs – a population of well over 200 unfree or semi-free peasants. The pattern continued. In the late-fourteenth-century poll taxes there was still only one free couple, Thomas and Amice Swan, but already there were thirty-one married couples who were former villeins now holding the land as tenants 'at will', along with seven servants, a 'labourer', a 'craftsman', eight cottagers and a widow, Juliana Ward (whose descendants still lived in the village in the seventeenth century, when there were forty-five families in the 1664 Hearth Tax). So Beauchamp's history from early times suggests a dependent landless proletariat: not freeholders, but tenants and workers. Here in the early nineteenth century widespread unemployment after enclosure and new production opportunities led to the growth of an industry which would change Kibworth for ever, turning it into what was almost a small town, with cottage industries and workshops, and eventually, in the mid-Victorian age, working men's clubs, pubs and small factories.

The adoption of framework knitting spread fast in the first decades of the nineteenth century, pushed by the demands of the war abroad and the fashions of the rising middle class at home. By 1850 it was the major source of employment in Kibworth. The reasons are not hard to see: after the enclosure of the common fields, once the stopgap of labouring on the canals had dried up, the lack of work in the village fields became severe. If direct employment on the land in Kibworth declined as a result of increased pasturage, however, the rearing of sheep in ever-growing numbers in Leicestershire did indirectly create new jobs. 'With regard to the collective interest of the nation, and not the particular benefit of the parish,' Eden wisely noted, 'I much doubt whether the wool now produced from the Leicestershire inclosures does not employ more hands (though not perhaps in Leicestershire) than its arable fields did formerly.' In fact, as Eden would have seen had he returned to Kibworth a couple of decades later, some at least of the additional jobs did remain in the parish.

The fleeces of Leicestershire sheep had long been prized, as John Leland had remarked back in the 1540s. While on his famous tour of Great Britain in the 1720s, Daniel Defoe observed that the sheep bred in Leicestershire were 'without comparison, the largest, and bear the greatest fleeces of wool on their backs of any sheep in England'. Since Queen Elizabeth's day shifting fashions had seen an increasing demand for long stockings or 'hose' – silk for those who could afford it, wool or later cotton for those who couldn't. Initially they were knitted by hand, but the invention of the stocking frame – generally credited to William Lee of Calverton in Nottinghamshire – created a large-scale industry which came to be concentrated in the East Midlands from the late seventeenth century. (Initially, in what would be a recurring pattern, this technological innovation was angrily resisted by hand-knitters, who feared for their livelihood; when the first frame was brought to Leicester in the 1680s it is said to have been operated in secret in a cellar for fear of retribution.) While its Midland neighbours focused on silk (Derbyshire) and cotton (Nottinghamshire), Leicestershire in particular specialized in products made from worsted (fine-combed woollen) cloth. Daniel Defoe visited Leicester in 1705–6 and wrote two decades later in the account of his tour:

A Considerable Manufacture carry'd on here, and in several of the Market Towns round for Weaving of Stockings by Frames: and one would scarce think it possible so small an Article of Trade could employ such Multitudes of People as it does; for the whole County seems to be employ'd in it: as also Nottingham and Derby.

In Kibworth it was the poor families of the parish, once the field labourers, who took up this cottage industry which could be carried out at home, with the frame being rented. Knitting occupied the whole family: the father operated the frame with its heavy treadles, the mother seamed together the stockings, and the children assisted by winding the threads – though they might themselves be put to work the frame from the age of ten or eleven. Some at the time romanticized this employment in which all the family worked together, but the reality was anything but romantic: as one framework-knitter retorted, for all members of a family to be engaged in order to scrape a meagre living was a sign of poverty and wretchedness rather than well-being.

At the time of his survey a few years after the enclosure, Eden did note 'a little stocking weaving' in Kibworth Beauchamp, but this was clearly the sort of old-fashioned hand-knitting or weaving which women customarily practised to supplement a family's income, while the spinning of worsted thread which he also recorded as a 'principal employment of the women' involved the preparation of the raw material rather than the finished clothing. A few decades later, however, much had changed. In his survey of Leicestershire of 1831, the curate John Curtis reported that many of Kibworth Beauchamp's 1,372 inhabitants were employed at framework knitting. By the gazetteer of 1850 'the majority' of Kibworth Beauchamp's people were engaged in the industry, and the character of the village had been changed for ever. Even today the visitor to the village (and to Smeeton) will see the distinctive weavers' cottages with enlarged upper-storey windows which admitted enough light to work the frame.

After a relatively good period for wages in the late eighteenth century, much harsher conditions after the Napoleonic Wars led to deep social unrest, and the struggle of the framework-knitters played a key role in what has been called the 'Making of the English Working Class'. In this Leicestershire was an important part of the story – it is no coincidence that Ned Ludlum (Ludd), who gave his name to the Luddites, came from just outside Leicester. After the Napoleonic Wars conditions for workers in the industry were often poor and sometimes perilous. A huge increase in the number of frames for hire, demand that fluctuated with fashion, a faltering economy and an uncertain international situation all conspired to put the individual worker and his family in the hands of the capitalists. Grievances especially turned on the ways in which unscrupulous hosiers sought to economize on labour and cheapen production, particularly by the hated practice of 'trucking', in which payment was not made in money but in supplies, or tokens redeemable only in shops of the owners (which were often not a fair equivalent). The frames were substantial – the height of an upright piano, if a little narrower; they were generally hired and the frame rents had to be paid consistently, regardless of the work available. Hosiers or their middlemen, for whom such rents constituted a substantial portion of their income, were suspected of deliberately hiring out more frames than were needed for the available work. Between 1812 and 1844 the number of frames in use in the East Midlands doubled to almost 50,000.

A serious deterioration in the industry took place from the late 1830s and this struck the village very hard. In 1840, at the worst point of the depression, a third of the frames in Leicestershire were said to be unused, and in Kibworth Beauchamp the dire situation saw many single men queuing up once more at the old weekly hiring fair on the Bank, and a flood of applications to the local Poor Law board, many from bemused older workers who had never experienced such cutthroat work practices. Three years later a petition was presented to Parliament signed by over 25,000 framework-knitters in the three Midland counties, which led to the appointment of a Royal Commission to look into the industry in 1844. The subsequent detailed report by R. M. Muggeridge largely confirmed the petitioners' belief in worsening conditions and gives fascinating detail on the conditions of workers in Kibworth.

Among the witnesses whose interviews were transcribed in the report were five framework-knitters from Kibworth and Smeeton. John Mawby of Beauchamp reported that he worked for seventeen or eighteen hours a day to make two dozen pairs of hose a week, for which he was paid 4s 3d a dozen – but he had to pay frame rent and seaming costs as well as for the candles he needed to work by night, and the soap or oil with which to grease the worsted. His eldest, crippled, child did a little seaming, and his nine-year-old daughter he had already put to operate a second frame, though she struggled to cover the cost of renting it. Thomas Iliffe was another (he came from an old Beauchamp family prominent in the village in the seventeenth century, and even earlier in Saddington). Iliffe declared that he had recently been seriously ill for a year and able to work only at a fraction of his normal rate, but he had been allowed no reduction in his frame rent: 'the master stated that the frame had stood still while he wanted the work, and that being the case, he should not take any rent off.' Job Johnson of Smeeton similarly bemoaned the rental burden: 'I think it is a very extravagant price we have to pay for frame-rents.' He worked fourteen hours a day to keep his wife and five children, whom he could not afford to send to school, a misfortune similarly lamented by John Lover, also of Smeeton:

There is no race of people under the sun so depressed as we are, who work the hours we do, for the money we get. It would be my delight to bring my family up to a school; I cannot bear the thought of bringing a family up in ignorance so as not to read a little.

The report had critical words about the use of trucking. This had evidently continued to be a serious problem, even after the Truck Act of 1831 had outlawed the practice. It affected a fifth of town workers, the report estimated, but as many as four fifths of those in the country. In the parish of Kibworth the problem seemed to have eased only in recent months in the wake of prosecutions of offending hosiers. Job Johnson claimed to have been paid 'nearly all in goods' until the Christmas past; goods which, as John Lover made clear, they were 'obliged to receive at a price, I believe, extortionate to what the other shops were selling them'. Lover would, he thought, 'have been completely starved this winter, if that system had not ceased before Christmas'. Many of them reported relying for food on potatoes grown on allotments they had been granted by the parish, a system which 'had always proved a very good thing'. (The allotments incidentally are still there, and very actively tended, below the former workhouse and the frameworkers' tenement at Smeeton Terrace.)

Real wages had declined significantly since the war years. Middlemen

increasingly interposed themselves between the local knitters and the
hosiers in Leicester: they saved the knitters from travelling to and fro,
but spread the work too thinly and it was felt took rather more than
a fair cut. One manufacturer who lived in Smeeton, William Ward,
freely agreed that these 'undertakers' or 'bagmen' were having a
highly pernicious impact; the hosiers, he said, used such middlemen
to beat down prices when demand was a little flat:

They know those are the men to do it; they do not like to do it with the
single hands themselves, and so they do it through them . . . [The under-
takers] know that things have been so middling lately that the poor people
are obliged to work at any price, or else they would have nothing to do . . .
When the hosiers could not have the barefacedness to offer it themselves,
they get those men to do it for them.

That this sort of man-powered work continued at all in a village like
Kibworth might seem surprising given that in other parts of the
country the production of textiles had become mechanized and
factory-based. The knitting and seaming of stockings had been,
however, relatively resistant to steam power, with the result that the
Leicestershire hosiery industry in the early nineteenth century did
not share in the dynamic growth (albeit combined with deplorable
working conditions) experienced in Lancashire. Moreover technological innovation, when it came, continued to be treated with the
utmost suspicion and hostility by frameworkers, who saw in it only
a further reduction in their chances of employment. Back in 1773 a
stocking frame reputedly capable of producing a dozen pairs of hose
at once, when put on exhibition at the Leicester Exchange, was
destroyed by a crowd of workmen who obliged the hosiers to promise not to introduce such a machine. An invention for mechanized
spinning of worsted yarn had led to serious riots instigated by the
hand-spinners in 1787. (The fact that many large-scale manufacturers in the region came from the dissenting community led to a
widespread rallying cry: 'No Presbyterians, no machines.') The
Luddite machine-breakers of the 1810s were busy in Leicestershire,

smashing many hundreds of stocking frames inspired by the now legendary Ned Ludd.

The shocking conclusion of the 1845 commission report was that as many as three quarters of all Midland framework-knitters were either out of work or 'seriously under-employed and dependent on parish relief'. For those out of work and impoverished, their plight seemed worsened by the changing nature of this relief since the Poor Law Amendment Act of 1834. The 'Gilbert's Act' of 1782, named after the MP Thomas Gilbert, had liberalized the parish-based workhouse system so that 'poorhouses' were established purely for the old, sick and infirm, while able-bodied paupers were to be provided with outdoor relief and employment near their own homes (at the discretion of the parish poor guardians). In a precursor to the council housing system, parishes like Kibworth owned a number of cottages which could be let at low rates to the poor. There was also, in Smeeton, a purpose-built poorhouse: a large, three-storey building which still stands. Under the terms of the 1834 Act, however, control of poor relief was taken away from individual parishes and centred on regional 'Poor Law unions' which answered directly to the Poor Law Commission in London. For Kibworth, this meant the transference of control over poor relief to the Market Harborough Union.

A fascinating insight into the local running of the Poor Law over the period of transition from the old to the new system – at a time of particular economic hardship – is provided by the papers of the Market Harborough Union in the National Archives in Kew: part of a still largely untapped archive of more than 16,700 volumes of papers, reports, submissions and letters which together constitute a source of social history as rich as the national censuses. In a series of handwritten letters to the Poor Law Commission in London, for example, a group of elderly Kibworth paupers complained bitterly that the local parish guardians were failing in their obligation to find work for the unemployed.

'We the undersigned,' they wrote on 11 January 1835, 'beg leave to inform you that we are poor men belonging to the parishes of Kibworth Beauchamp and Kibworth Harcourt in the county of Leicester and being out of employ we have applied to the guardian repeatedly for work but he invariably refuses to employ us.' Gilbert's Act, they insisted, had made clear that no guardian could refuse to employ destitute men unable to find work. Even more loathed, however, than the haphazard nature of the old system was the new workhouse regime under which the able-bodied unemployed could be forced to do residential labour in the Harborough workhouse in return for the most basic subsistence:

We beg further to state that in no place are the poor so much oppressed as at Kibworth. They have actually sent poor people to the workhouse and they have worn their linen 11 weeks with only once washing during the time until they have literally swarmed with vermin . . .

The letter was signed by Richard Tolton of Kibworth Harcourt (upwards of seventy years of age), William Tolton of Kibworth Beauchamp (nearly seventy years of age), and Samuel Guest and William Jackson, both of Kibworth Beauchamp and both nearly sixty years of age. Though all were near or past today's retirement age, they were nonetheless insisting on their right to work – and their desire to do so.

The Poor Law Commission in London responded with an argument which sounds familiar today:

the amount of relief, you must be aware, ought not to be such as to render the situation of the pauper equal to that of a person living by independent industry: a practice of making allowance for idleness equal or nearly equal to the wages of industry [. . .] must tend to make pauperism preferable to independence.

This was beside the point, the four Kibworthians alleged. The failure of the local authorities was a consequence of persecution against them because they were religious dissenters. As was typical of Nonconformists, their letters were rich in biblical allusions: those that held back relief from poor disciples would be sentenced to eternal damnation; 'blessed is he that considereth the poor; the Lord will deliver him in time of trouble' (Psalm 41); while the Israelites had been forced by the Egyptians to make bricks without straw, the Poor Law overseers expected the manufacture of bricks without clay. Residence in the workhouse, moreover, was particularly abhorrent for conscientious men and women of religion:

You may rely on it that men will not submit to be incarcerated in a Workhouse merely for want of employ. If that were the case the marriage ceremony must be altered for instead of man and woman being joined together until death separates them it must be until parted by the work-house master . . . No dissenter can submit to be transported into such dens of iniquity, we have lately collected information respecting one of those dens of iniquity and we consider it worse if possible than West Indian Slavery.

What is perhaps most remarkable about these letters is the level not only of literacy and general education, but also of specific knowledge about the precise terms and clauses of government legislation. It is abundantly clear that the ethic of education and learning among the Nonconformist community in Kibworth had remained strong since the days of Jennings' and Doddridge's Academy: a thread of literacy in the village story which goes back to the likes of the fifteenth-century butcher John Pychard and the village clerks and reeves from the time of the Black Death.

One Jeremiah Jackson, meanwhile, wrote from Leicester, whence he had moved from Kibworth in a vain search for work, to complain likewise of the hard line taken by the local Kibworth guardians:

I am by trade a framework knitter and have a wife and one child, one I have lately buried and my wife is far advanced in pregnancy – and being utterly destitute of work I applied to the relieving officer of the Harborough Union as I belong to the Parish of Kibworth Beauchamp . . . I understand all parishes except Kibworth relieve the poor at this distressing time when out of work . . .

The commission in London confirmed that his case had been dismissed on the grounds that he was now a non-resident pauper, but did state that 'should the depression in the markets continue, the Board would have no objection to rehear his case'.

Also among the Harborough Union papers are the documents pertaining to the selling off of those local cottages owned by the parish for the use of the poor. In Kibworth Beauchamp alone there were sufficient cottages, some of them divided, to house fifteen impoverished families, among them owners of some long-surviving Kibworth surnames: a freehold cottage in Smeeton Lane, for instance, 'now used as three dwellings and in the respective occupations of Joseph Fletcher, William Carter and William Green'; another freehold cottage in Smeeton Lane 'in the occupation of William Holyoak'; and a freehold cottage in Wire Lane 'now used as two dwellings in the respective occupations of Robert Lea and Sarah Coleman'; or a freehold cottage in Wire Lane 'now used as two dwellings and in the respective occupation of Joseph Holyoak and Samuel Butcher'. All were to be sold off, and the tenants evicted, with the proceeds used to pay off parish debts and contribute to the new union workhouse. A similar list of property to be sold in Smeeton Westerby included Smeeton Terrace, the 'large building formerly used as a workhouse' but now divided and let along with a group of cottages or tenements adjacent to it to, among others, Matthew Woolman, Robert Freer, Robert Iliffe and Job Johnson, the framework-knitter interviewed for the commission report.

The process of evicting these sometimes long-standing tenants was painful. In 1837 John Jackson, the son-in-law of William Holyoak (who had evidently died some years back), wrote plaintively to the commission:

In the year 1803 I married the daughter of the late William Holyoak and she being housekeeper to her father I went and resided with them, and have continued to reside in the said house ever since . . . I have had no relief from the parish several years and the late Mr Holyoak absolutely gave me the house. Under all these circumstances I am at a loss to conceive what claim the parish can have on this house . . . As I have always considered that every Englishman's House were his castle, I feel therefore determined to defend mine to the last extremity . . .

The parish, however, had ordered the properties to be sold and Jackson's understandable distress was unavailing. (One of those wealthy landowners who took the opportunity to purchase the cottages was Robert Haymes, whose grandfather had done so well out of the enclosures.) Among those who supervised the new Poor Law system, the attitude was ingrained – as it would be in England for centuries – that poverty was an indication of moral weakness, since work, in a natural equilibrium, would always be available for those who sincerely sought it. In this some of the debates of the time seem strikingly contemporary. In 1836 Thomas Symes, the Vice-President of the new Harborough Union, reassured the commission in London regarding the complaining paupers of Kibworth:

The true cause of their pauperism being want of character and inclination to work, their worst principles being fed by the ready aid administered to them by the old law; I have ever contended, and I doubt not it will now be found so, that within the limits of this Union, we have no more labourers than work.

Together the guardians of the union testified in 1837 to the 'great benefit which the new system has introduced into this union – not only as to the reduction of the rates but as to the moral improvement of the labouring classes . . .'

Not surprisingly the labouring classes of Kibworth did not in the main see themselves in need of moral improvement – and they were perfectly willing to turn to any form of work to earn a fair living. This comes out vividly in a remarkable letter sent late in life by Jonathan Jesson of Kibworth to Lord Feilding, after he had heard the latter speak at a meeting at Fenny Compton in Warwickshire. Jesson was a well-known Kibworth character who was fondly remembered even on the eve of the First World War for his dancing on Plough Monday (an ancient East Midlands festival still observed in Kibworth in the 1930s). He had requested that his letter be returned, but Feilding's wife considered it sufficiently interesting to transcribe it and retained her copy. At sixty-five, Jesson wrote, he scarcely need bother himself in detail about the political matters

Feilding had addressed in his speech: 'but I cannot help but take an interest in it'. The letter gives us a mid-Victorian working man's autobiography.

Born in 1825 in Fleckney, barely a mile and a half west of Kibworth, Jesson was raised in poverty with ten siblings by his widowed mother: 'during that time we was glad of three meals of wasted potatoes a day & nothing but a bit of salt to them.' Between the ages of nine and thirteen he drove a plough before declaring that he would buy his own bread, or starve. He worked cleaning turnips; then took a job in service, which allowed him to provide a little help to his mother and crippled sister. He worked on a railway line at Stamford, walking twenty-six miles home with beef for his family at Christmas. In 1850 he married Ann, the daughter of Samuel Butcher (who had lived in one of the parish poorhouses on Wire Lane in Kibworth Beauchamp), and at this point moved to live in Kibworth. In the 1851 census he was living with his wife and child in Pudding Bag Lane, just off the Bank where the roundabout is today. Family health was not good and his wife was bed-bound for six months with rheumatic fever, though, Jesson says, 'no one gave to us.' 'I have told many a poor man to persevere in his labours & be punctual to his payments, if that won't carry him thro' life nothing will.' He worked at one of the framework knitting 'factories' in the village – perhaps the long two-storey workshop close to his house which still stands behind number 24 on the Bank; such places were little more than a collection of frames under one roof. Later he went into the 'fish & rabbit trade', pushing a truck-load from Kibworth to market in Leicester. Though his wife remained sickly, he spurned suggestions that he fall back on charity: 'some people will try to console a man by telling him to trust to providence, but I dare not my spirit won't allow me, it always says go & look for work.' In the end through perseverance he did well enough to become involved in the building boom in Kibworth as the 'new town' took shape in the late nineteenth century. As a working man's tale, literate, self-reflexive and realistic, adaptable and tenacious, it is no doubt typical of many of the age. Where his ancestors had worked the land as peasants, *nativi* or villeins, he was now part of what had come to be known as the working class.

## The village in the 1860s

From the enclosures of the 1770s the villagers had lived through a time of European war, agricultural and industrial revolution, and social change. The patterns of work and life in the village – as in the country as a whole – had changed for ever. But for all the upheavals, the village community had shown a remarkable tenacity – the social glue that bound people together had not been dissolved: the role of the church and the many dissenting chapels, the importance of culture, sport and music, the role of the parish in education, charity and social welfare, in provisions for the poor, and even for their health (which in some respects appear today as a precursor of the NHS).

The transformations of the mid-century are recorded for Kibworth in the 1851 census and in the district gazetteers, which, rather like a Victorian Domesday, testify now both to the growing commercial and industrial life of the village and to its place in the new Victorian order of Poor Law unions and local government and law and order. According to White's gazetteer, Kibworth was now a parish of almost 2,000 people with over 3,000 acres 'mostly given over to pasturage' rather than arable – far less acreage than in 1300: 'Many of its inhabitants are framework-knitters employed chiefly in weaving worsted stockings for the Leicester manufacturers. The Leicester and London Railway, which was opened in 1856, passes through the parish and has a station at Kibworth Beauchamp. The Union canal traverses the western side of the parish, and passes under a hill about one and a half miles S.W. of the village by a tunnel more than half a mile in length.' In such a portrait, no less than that of 1086, great historical change is encapsulated. It is a sketch of a populous agricultural community transformed by the industrial age, its traditional communally organized rural workforce now representative of the new working class of the industrial age. In the previous seventy years many of its people had suffered loss of status, work and freedom, and had often experienced degradation, but their Victorian descendants would create a culture and political consciousness of real vitality – and with it, as we shall see in the next chapter, a vigorous and democratic popular culture.

# 17. The Victorians

Though far away from the imperial conflicts in India, China or Africa in the Victorian age, the people of Kibworth nonetheless were not untouched by the great events of the day. Like any English village the drama of the national story impinged on people back home. Thomas Gamble had been on the blood-soaked decks of the *Temeraire* at Trafalgar. Will Post and Robert Shaw had been with Wellington in the Peninsular War, fighting 'Boney and the Mounseerrs'. Even more exotic, William Fletcher and David Roddis had rejected a life of framework knitting or digging canals to sign up with the East India Company in the wilds of 'Hindustan', marching the sweltering plains of north India from 'Muttra' and Cawnpore in the Maratha wars and spending the year of Waterloo in Ghazipur, where the British established their biggest opium factory. Mrs Knapp went out to the Crimean War with her husband and came home with tales of the savage winters when she contracted the chronic rheumatism which left her bent double as she walked to the shops. John Chaplin, later the founder of the Kibworth golf club, won the village's only VC, at the siege of Taku fort in China during the second Opium War in August 1860, planting his regimental colours on the smashed bastion by the Hai River over spreadeagled heaps of Chinese dead.

Living in mid-Victorian England, even in the countryside, it was impossible to escape the presence of the empire, whether across the counter in the village shop, in the milliner's store, or at the newsagent. Veterans like Roddis and Shaw regaled wide-eyed village children with their stories of 'wonderful doings in a mystic past', smoking their long clay pipes on the railway bridge on Station Road on summer evenings while the kids threw their cloth caps into the air as the engine smoke whooshed into their faces above the parapet. For the likes of Will Fletcher, who had signed up when he was fifteen, and returned nineteen years later after more than half a lifetime in

India, there must have been an unsettling sense that the 'dear familiar place' was no longer the village they had left. But this was no mere effect of age and distance. All history is change, but it was the pace of change that observers remarked: Kibworth was indeed changing fast. This after all was a village which still had many mud houses such as had been lived in by its medieval occupants; its people still performed the traditional St George and the Dragon mummers' plays and danced in their Plough Monday processions; yet this was also the new world of railway timetables, telegraphs and daily newspapers.

## The coming of the railways

During the Victorian period the population of Kibworth rose steadily, from a total for the ancient parish of 1,232 in 1801 to 1,975 in 1871. The population of Smeeton Westerby reached a peak figure of 567 in 1841, which it has not attained since. But the most rapid rise was in Kibworth Beauchamp, which was most marked in the years 1851–81, when it passed the thousand mark. The village's position on the main route from Leicester to Market Harborough and onwards to London ensured that, for a rural community, Kibworth remained literally on the fast track. And just as the transport revolution of the canal age had reached Kibworth parish, so did the much greater and more lasting revolution, ushered in by the coming of the railways carved directly through the village on the line from the East Midlands to London.

The plan produced in 1836 proposed driving the track through between Harcourt and Beauchamp, down the little stream bed in the low ground where Beauchamp's medieval fishponds had been, south of the church and the rectory. By the time that the railway surveyors first appeared in Kibworth in 1845, it was fifteen years since the opening of the Liverpool and Manchester Railway – the first line running a fully timetabled service of steam locomotives – had inaugurated the railway age. By this time railways had been built from Italy to Russia and from Canada to Cuba, but Victoria's England was at the forefront; and whereas elsewhere government often played the leading role, the British Parliament looked on only as arbiter (and not always an assiduous one), allowing private enterprise to develop a national system that was almost entirely haphazard and opportunistic in its growth. From the mid-1830s, and particularly at the end of the 1840s, handsome dividends being paid by the pioneering railways drove a railway fever as infectious as the canal mania which had preceded it, and a good deal longer lasting.

In May 1844 three previously competing companies, the Midland Counties Railway, the North Midland Railway and the Birmingham and Derby Junction Railway, merged by Act of Parliament to form the Midland Railway Company, led by the unlikely pairing of the Leicester Quaker and reformer (and later MP) John Ellis and the dynamic but less scrupulous 'Railway King', George Hudson. It was the surveyors of this amalgamated company who descended on Kibworth in 1845 to assess the route of a proposed line from Leicester to Hitchin, which would pass through Wigston and over the 'Kibworth summit' to Great Bowden Junction. As had been the case with the canals, by no means all locals were in favour of this dramatic new development in the village – particularly those owners and tenants whose land was directly affected. And the canal proprietors, whose predecessors had been outraged fifty years previously at hidebound opposition to their schemes, were outraged in their turn at this new and threatening technology. Coach proprietors, turnpike trustees and the keepers of Harcourt's dozen coaching inns were also alarmed: their livelihoods depended on the twenty-four coaches a day that stopped in Kibworth and which they foresaw, correctly, would dwindle with the impact of the railway. Far from endeavouring to appease these protesters, some of the surveyors behaved with arrogant disdain, refusing to give their names and blithely levelling crops and hedges in the presence of disgruntled landlords. Fearing significant unrest, a police unit was placed on standby. (This was another new development in a fast-changing country: the Leicestershire Constabulary had been created only six years previously, in 1839 – one of Britain's first professional county forces.)

The bill for a Leicester & Hitchin Railway – joining the Great Northern Railway at Hitchin to run into London's King's Cross –

was passed in 1853 and the first barrow was filled with Kibworth earth on 1 June 1854. Each Sunday during the following weeks crowds of villagers wandered down to the line to inspect the progress made during the week, leaving infuriated church and chapel preachers bereft of their accustomed audience. Eventually the Methodist preacher, drawing no doubt on the tradition of outdoor services in the Nonconformist community, resorted to preaching in the 'gully hole' near the line in an effort to stem the outgoing tide of his congregation. So once again, as they had during the construction of the canal during the 1790s, teams of 'navvies' descended on Kibworth, providing custom for the tradesmen as well as disruption and unease for the inhabitants generally. It was reckoned that a navvy might move up to twenty tonnes of earth in an average day; and, paid once a month, not surprisingly he would spend his earnings straight off in the local inns, unwinding afterwards by rioting and fighting in the streets. Camped in tin huts erected alongside the line, a dozen or more to a hut, the navvies stood out by virtue of their customary dress: moleskin trousers, canvas shirts, velveteen coats, coloured waistcoats, hobnail boots and felt hats. Many shared their huts with 'wives' married according to their own unconventional ceremony, in which the couple jumped over a broom and straight into bed as the party continued around them.

On the evening of 2 July 1856, the first engine came through Kibworth on a trial run, and 200 people from the village massed above the line to see it. The following April, Kibworth station – built in typical mid-nineteenth-century ecclesiastical gothic – was formally inspected, along with others on the line, by a local dignitary, Colonel Yolland. And on 7 May 1857 the line was officially opened, with some 5,000 tickets being sold for inaugural trips on special trains. A normal timetabled service commenced the following day. And just as the local innkeepers had feared, the last of the stagecoaches from Harborough to Leicester had rattled through Kibworth on the previous Saturday.

Initially no through trains were run to London; villagers wanting to travel to the capital alighted at Hitchin and bought a ticket for the Great Northern train which took them on. But as passenger numbers boomed, along with the strength of the Midland company, in 1862 it was decided to build a new line into London which passed through the Chilterns at Luton before skirting Hampstead Heath to arrive at a new terminus between King's Cross and Euston: a soaring Gothic hymn to the railway age completed in 1868 – St Pancras station.

Back in Kibworth the impact made by the railway's arrival in the village was far-reaching. Special sidings with cattle pens were built outside the station where local graziers' herds could be loaded straight on to cattle wagons to be taken down to feed the ever-growing demand for meat in the capital; so finally ended the centuries-old custom of the Midland cattle-droves down to Smithfield. In decades to come noisy crates containing tens of thousands of chickens from the hatchery on Harborough Road would also be despatched by rail from Kibworth station. Coal, timber and other goods were brought into the village much more readily, deposited in large sheds by the sidings and handled by local merchants, among them Tom Iliffe, who, as Francis Woodford recalled, was the local coal carter in the 1860s. Small factories and businesses, furthermore, could now base themselves in the village and rely on the railway to deliver their raw materials and their finished products.

The railways also of course affected the ability of the villagers to travel. The inhabitants of Kibworth could now move with unprecedented ease to the local towns: Leicester, in less than thirty minutes; Harborough, only eighteen minutes; and even down to London, five hours. The surviving weekly shopping receipts for the Grewcock family shop, preserved at Market Harborough Museum, testify to the normality of routine visits to the local towns.

And of course the railways saw the birth of that characteristically modern creature – the commuter. The middle-class element in the population of well-situated villages like Kibworth now grew as urban people sought the tranquillity of rural living, which, as they read in their periodicals, was now within easy reach of sedentary jobs elsewhere. In August 1875 the *Market Harborough Advertiser* noted that the population of Kibworth 'unlike that of many villages in the county, has, during the last decade, considerably increased' (though this was more true of Beauchamp than it was of Harcourt). Earlier the paper had commented on the much increased value of property in Kibworth, which had now become 'a desirable neighbourhood for villa residences'. For the local builders John Loveday and John Mason these were boom years and the former in particular rose to a position of considerable prominence in the village. But it was Mason who built a row of six fine houses with walled gardens for the affluent middle class above the railway in the 1870s; they are known to this day as 'The Villas', and were commended by the *Advertiser* as 'not only eminently commodious and convenient, but an ornament to the village'. With them, modern middle-class housing arrived in the village, just as it had in previous eras with Brown's Place in 1385, and Priory Farm in the early Tudor period, or the brick and stucco Old House in the days of William and Mary.

Last, but not least, the trains running through the village provided a fine source of diversion for young and old alike. Woodford remembered the railway bridge as a place where 'old men congregated to smoke and talk', while boys massed to watch the trains – 'a never ceasing wonder then' – or to 'occasionally throw a cap over in order to see it blown up again by the snorting monster, sometimes to lose it altogether by its being blown on to the moving train'.

Momentous as it was, the railway was not the only element in the communications revolution which transformed the Victorian village. The postal service was another, which from the earliest days of rail shaped its needs to the rail network. A variety of limited regional and national postal services had existed in Britain since the Civil War. But it was the radical reforms overseen by Rowland Hill, who in 1840 introduced the affordable penny post, prepaid using a system of adhesive stamps, which inaugurated the first modern postal service. Opposite Kibworth church the nineteenth-century Rectory Cottage served as the village's first post office until about 1900. At about the same time the electrical telegraph system came into use – much popularized by the successful arrest in 1845 of a murderer thanks to a message telegraphed to London that he had boarded a train dressed 'in the garb of a kwaker' (the machine did not accept Qs). This too further mitigated the sense referred to by Philip Doddridge a century before of being 'confined in an obscure village'. On 7 December 1869 the *Market Harborough Advertiser* reported:

It is now some years since a 'Royal Mail' was seen in the streets of Kibworth but on Monday week there was one came to the Post Office here with workmen to prepare for the connecting of the telegraph with this office. No doubt Kibworth will be a place of considerable business. Letters are now received here twice a day, and it would be a further improvement to have two dispatches a day, as there is every convenience by railway.

At the same time modern technological progress was being brought to bear on the daily experience of life in Kibworth itself. One key change was the introduction of gaslight in homes and on the streets. Public street lighting had been demonstrated in London during the Napoleonic Wars, and the Lighting & Watching Act of 1833 gave councils the right to install street lighting if they so wished (as well as to establish a paid local police force). But it was in the early 1860s that the question became a live one in Kibworth. The fact that agreement would be required to fund the amenity by the local rates ensured that in Kibworth – which was as disputatious a village as any, and perhaps more than most – the matter was cause for fierce controversy.

In January 1862 the turnout for a vestry meeting to discuss the issue was so large the rowdy gathering had to adjourn to the schoolroom. In Beauchamp at least the leaders of the progressive camp – John Loveday, the builder, and Thomas Macaulay, the village doctor – secured the necessary support, and the streets were lit for the first time in the winter of 1863. A lamplighter was employed whose task it was to light each lamp at dusk before returning around 10 p.m. to turn them off. An attempt in 1864 to convince enough people that the village should adopt the Lighting & Watching Act so that street lighting could be provided through the municipal rates failed, however, and the lights were paid for by private subscription. Evidently enough residents objected to what would have been an increase in rates for an 'improvement' which it was felt would benefit some more than others.

In Kibworth Harcourt, meanwhile, darkness continued to prevail, it proving impossible to raise the funds by subscription. The contrast in ethos between the neighbouring halves of Kibworth seems as marked as ever in these years, when the new railway line through the centre left the rival villages quite literally on opposite sides of the tracks. A local paper reported that:

the inhabitants of Kibworth Beauchamp often laugh and chaff those of Kibworth Harcourt, or more properly speaking those of 'dark' Kibworth, as it is now very familiarly called, because they cannot, or will not, raise the £15, which is all that is required to light the few street lamps in that part of the village.

The fact that the local gas company, having installed lights in Harcourt, then proclaimed its intention of removing them since the necessary money to run them could not be raised was recorded with withering scorn in the *Market Harborough Advertiser*: 'That this proceeding should be necessary in the present age of progression and general acceleration is certainly no small stigma on the inhabitants of this aristocratic and so-called enlightened village.' When the lights briefly returned in 1873 the paper suggested that the village would appreciate an end to a 'total eclipse' by lighting 'which people in their right mind would never have submitted to have done without'. In Harcourt the dispute dragged on, or erupted sporadically, until after the First World War.

As the pace of change increased, similar amiable or less than amiable rivalry between the two villages recurred on all manner of issues, serious or trivial. In 1885 when the new vicar, the ebullient Bangalore-born Merton man Edmund Knox, took on the parish of Kibworth, the rivalry between the two Kibworths was one of the most striking, and challenging, aspects of his new living. Beauchamp, he noted, the home of 'stockeners' and predominantly 'radical', was in stark contrast to Harcourt, 'the home of the sporting squirearchy and retired businessmen of Leicester'. Between the two 'was kept up a half-playful antagonism', with even the most minor disagreement eliciting 'fiery eloquence' poured forth with 'passion such I had never heard in Oxford'. On one occasion, he recorded:

The vestry debated warmly the plan of a sewer which was to run down a road that divided the two villages. It was even suggested, with a fine disregard of costs, that two parallel sewers should be constructed, that the sewage of one village should not be 'contaminated' by the waste of the other.

## Woodford's 'Personal Reminiscences'

As always in history, the raw sources of the 'official' history of the time – censuses and gazetteers, local government, education and Poor Law papers – can take us only so far. What the historian really hopes for is some sense of the inner life of a community. For Kibworth an account like this survives in a vivid portrait of the mid-Victorian village which was written by F. P. Woodford at the beginning of the First World War and published in 1916. Woodford's book is a description of the village in the 1860s, remembered house by house, with portraits of many of the 'characters'. The village he describes is an agricultural place remembered in a young person's imagination in an affectionate and it might be thought idealized fashion but for a realistic undercurrent of class tension, especially his dislike of the pretensions of the rich and powerful, 'enlightened and obliging authorities ever ready to bow the knee to wealth'. Woodford for example preserves a stark village tradition of the 1779 enclosures as having been 'sheer robbery'. He is frank too about drink and violence: the club feasts at the Old Swan at Whitsun for example were an excuse to get 'beastly drunk and quarrelsome', with the biggest fights adjourning to a nearby field, where things could get quite out of hand. Though a churchgoer, Woodford was not hostile towards Nonconformists, many of whom he liked. And like many a reform-minded Victorian Protestant he had a real admiration for radical politicians like the builder John Loveday. But most of all he was sympathetic to human foibles. His main design was simply to record house by house who lived where, and what they did, and in doing so he gives an intimate portrait of a village on the cusp of modernity: a village with railways, telegraph and newspapers but which only did away with its stocks and whipping post in 1865 and which still had Plough Monday dancing and mummers' plays.

Kibworth in the 1860s was a still agrarian society which had moved into the world of Victorian retail shopping: there was Branson's grocery store, Mrs Weston's sweet shop ('where she sold sweets of her own making, whose flavour and sweetness readily induced any youngster to part with any cash they possessed') and Wardle's newspaper shop, the only one which sold papers in Kibworth. Miss Weston ran a high-class milliner's shop, 'a large millinery and dress making establishment who employed a number of young lady apprentices who generally lived with her, and from whose establishment two or three romantic elopements were made'.

There were a surprising number of schools, including the old grammar school, the parish school, chapel schools and three schools for infants, run by the Goodales, by Mrs Kesson and Miss Cotton, and the best-known headmistress, Mrs Allen. For a time there had even been a girls' boarding school, whose failure had led to the suicide of the head, Miss Brake. There were a village constable, a stationmaster, and a popular nurse and midwife, 'Nurse Warrington'; there were two surgeons, two chemists, a plumber and glazier, a fishmonger, a saddler and an expert woolwinder; in Beauchamp, where there were many framework-knitters, the framesmith did a lively trade mending frames. 'Dizzy Green' was the proverbially honest rag and bone man who died in the workhouse. The village had shoemakers, seamstresses, a vet, a tailor, three coal hawkers, and the carpenter and cabinet maker John Wilson, who did the beautiful restoration of the fourteenth-century oak screen still to be seen in St Wilfrid's church.

Most of those shops and businesses reflected the new times and have their equivalents today. But mixed with these there were still many workers, artisans and craftspeople whose jobs are mirrored in the village documents as far back as the thirteenth century. Mrs Mattock, for example, was the laundress and, just as Alice 'the washerwoman' did in the 1280s, in good weather put the wet clothes on a drying ground behind her house. Doctors too were no new thing in the village: there was one in the village in the thirteenth century; and one of the two chemists or druggists, Mr Potter, was, says Woodford, 'a good model of the now extinct apothecary' (an early Merton charter is witnessed by a 'Henry Hwen apotacarius'). Among other traditional workers the miller was still important: the Smeeton miller, Ebenezer Weston, lost his mill in the Great Storm of 1860, leaving only Charles Smith at the post mill on the Langton road which ground its last grain in 1925, and still stands. There were also still smiths, masons, coopers and wheel-wrights, a brewer and a sheepwasher, David Atkinson, who was much in demand in neighbouring villages. And in a village where there were still several old-fashioned yeoman farmers, there were still full-time agricultural workers, including a trio of mowers who used not the new-fangled mowing machine, but scythes, 'swinging along in rhyth-mic time . . . with the musical swish of their scythes'.

Woodford identified with the churchgoers, virtually all of whose placings in the pews he could remember fifty years on; but Noncon-formity then was also very strong; as represented by the Bromley family, for example – Eileen today is a preacher at the Methodist chapel – who were 'one of the oldest families, here for more than 400 years'. A cluster of the Bromleys' poor cottager neighbours are described as 'sturdy Nonconformists, worthy descendants of Cromwell's best men – straightforward, honest and afraid of no man'. Their beliefs Woodford contrasted with the spread of 'Socialism and irreligion', which he saw as an inevitable result of injustice and oppression, and of the progressive growth of disparity in wealth since enclosure. 'The time will come,' he wrote, 'when the possession of great wealth will be looked upon not only as a disgrace but as a great crime.' The death of one framework-knitter evidently made a par-ticular impression on the young Woodford: Joseph Bailey, who hawked his homemade socks and stockings round neighbouring vil-lages, froze to death when caught out in the countryside one night during the terrible winter of 1860–61, the worst for fifty years.

Striking in the narrative is the mix of old and new. In the very heyday of empire of course many village people had seen other worlds. Many of the men had fought in imperial wars across the globe, the curate Phillips had worked as a missionary in India. But back home the old still remained for now. The mummers' play was still done as it was in ages past with certain families like the Bromleys traditionally playing particular roles. (Harry Bromley was the dragon in Woodford's childhood.) Plough Monday and harvest festival were celebrated in the 'old English way'. There were many annual village events, of which the most famous locally was the flower show. Kibworth still had an open-air village feast in the 1860s; there were 'club feasts' at Whitsun in Beauchamp at the Old Swan and at the Admiral Nelson in Harcourt. Traditional customs were also observed among the farmers such as George Gray, who was 'the last one whom I remember used to celebrate harvest home in the old English way, decorating the last load of corn with green boughs duly sprinkled with water and poppies, finishing up with a supper to all his hands'. Gray, said Woodford, 'was one of the few farmers by the 1860s who regarded the Mosaic law by not reaping the corners of his fields, which he left to be gleaned by the poor'.

The Victorian village also had many organized sports and leisure activities. Cricket had been important from the 1840s, as it still is. There were Whitsun games and wrestling tournaments on a platform at the Bank (a 'brutal exhibition of holding and kicking', says Woodford). There were several accomplished painters and, as might be expected given the strength of church and 'chapel', music was also a very big feature of village life: several villagers were excellent instrumentalists, among them Fred Iliffe the organist, who went on to Oxford to study music. The village had many good singers and a twelve-piece brass band, which still continues today. There had also been a long tradition of theatre in the village. In the late eighteenth century visiting companies played Shakespeare and Sheridan and topical shows like the anti-slavery play *Inkle and Yariko*, apparently in one of the inn yards which had a gallery and pit. But in Victorian times there seems also to have been a vigorous amateur theatrical tradition at village level; in addition to the mummers' plays, and the 'travelling players' who did shows in a large old brick barn off Main Street, Woodford mentions penny concerts organized by the village.

In its resolute ordinariness as a portrait of the world before radio, television and mass newsprint, Woodford's account makes fascinating reading. Our view of Victorian England tends to be dominated by the picture of the city created by journalists and writers like Dickens. A large rural village like Kibworth had its share of class conflict, wild drunken brawls and 'fierce fights between the rowdy boys of Kibworth and Smeeton'. But it had its sports and plays and festivals; and it also had a huge amount of voluntary public service from the likes of Edward Cayser, an 'old fashioned draper', a cricket umpire, shareholder and supporter of the new village hall, and chairman and contributor to the village Penny Readings, 'a popular and useful man, and one of those people who did so much to make village life pleasant and attractive.'

Alexis de Tocqueville had observed thirty years before of the English that they were a nation of clubs and societies, where a huge amount of social action at a local level was voluntary. One gets the same impression from Woodford, from the elementary schools to the flower shows and musical tuition. But perhaps there is something more: he also shows 'strange and diversified scenes' of which a Victorian novelist might make a vivid picture. May we call it English eccentricity? Or is what he describes really typical of many modernizing societies at the point when they are still in touch with their peasant roots? The quality of life we catch in Woodford, despite the enormous social differences of the period, has a great deal of diversity, tolerance and eccentricity, and a notable amount of personal expression: nonconformity not just in chapel but in personal mores: the blind fiddler Billy Parsons, 'dressed in old fashioned cord knee breeches buttoned at the knees', with his worsted stockings, heavy nailed shoes and scarlet waistcoat topped by an 'old fashioned beaver hat', sang his strange songs about the poor; the mummers performed their medieval mystery play; the storytellers were Mary Miles and Mrs Linnet the seamstress, who was 'possessed of a wonderful imagination and an unfailing supply of witch or fairy tales'; Sam Burditt, the jolly and kindly shoemaker, was an instrumentalist in church, but, so the child Woodford had heard, was an atheist and hence really 'a very wicked person'; Ebenezer Weston, the miller, grew vines and made wine and in front of his house had a carved ship's figurehead showing a woman; Robert Shaw, the Peninsular veteran, invariably got roaring drunk on pension day, and told fantastical tales of his days as 'eddy camp' (aide-de-camp) to the Iron Duke no less, 'and could himself have been a Dook!' One of the most affecting village characters was the eccentric and peculiar deaf mute Burgess, who each year published his homemade almanac and was 'locally regarded as a fair guide for the weather'; he transfixed children in the street by gesturing to the sky and conveyed his meaning with 'peculiar sounds and shakes of the head'. A cleaner and mender of clocks and watches, Burgess was also a green-fingered gardener who always produced the first peas and potatoes in the village.

Best of all in this gallery of characters worthy of Dickens is perhaps the blacksmith John Collins, a Heath Robinson inventor who made all his house furniture himself out of iron. Collins wore a black velvet coat with buttons made of silver fourpenny pieces; his working vest was buttoned with copper farthings; and he had soled his boots in iron so the eerie clack of his boots on the cobbles always heralded his approach. Collins was a self-taught genius eccentric, 'a very clever allround man' who made his own tools, shod horses, could tackle any mechanical job, from locks and keys to complicated machinery, and was a great admirer of Spurgeon's sermons – the populist preacher of the day whose weekly penny sermons were bestsellers; these 'he would underline with quotations of his own written in hieroglyphics decipherable only by himself'.

Perhaps there was nothing out of the ordinary in such people, within the wide range of mid-Victorian society. But such characters reinforced Woodford's childhood sense of the society of the village as a kind of wonderland still in touch with a 'mystical past', where fairy tales mixed with deeds of derring-do at Corunna and Cawnpore, and where archaic rural customs were tenaciously maintained that, as he observes, mostly died out in the last half of the nineteenth century. His glimpses down the Kibworth lanes of his childhood reveal strange scenes: John Carter, the coalman, who kept two 'Egyptian frogs the size of small cats like those which came up out of the Nile at the command of Moses'; and Carter's lodger, William Noble, 'a famous local negro comedian and one of the principal and favourite entertainers in the village', who sang American minstrel slave songs. 'Jonty' Jesson, the former frameworkknitter, is perhaps typical: 'a unique character' whose autobiographical letter we encountered earlier. Jesson was especially prominent as 'a character and a dancer' in the Plough Monday processions with his friend the scythe mower, Tom 'Mate' Tolton. Tolton, 'dressed as a countrywoman and fairly primed with drink, would dance grotesque country dances with his partner Jonty Jesson till fairly tired out'.

Vital, boozy and anarchic as well as conformist and 'chapel'; with its reading rooms and political agitation – this all realistically suggests a robust working people's culture which was perhaps typically the product of a village with such distinct halves, 'country' in Harcourt and 'radical stockeners' in Beauchamp. Sex is the only thing about which Woodford is reticent. As a snapshot of Victorian village England, the record of one insignificant place, Woodford's account is a window on to something so close to us, only 150 years distant, yet which seems a lost world; except that with its cricket and clubs, allotments and eccentricities, its popular entertainments and the generally tolerant humour of its hustings, it is still perhaps recognizably Kibworth – and, indeed, still recognizably England.

## Education, education

More serious though, and more deeply divisive, were the matters of political and social reform. One such was the Education Act of 1870. Up till the nineteenth century, the village, like most places in England, had made its own provisions for the education of its children, just as it had organized its own charity, albeit hand in hand with the Church. Ever since the 1620s there had been a permanent school building in Kibworth, with a fine new grammar school built in 1722. Traditionally the school had been administered by trustees drawn from the village, a mix of ordinary farmers and wealthier local gentry. But in the later Victorian age there was a massive shift towards state control over these areas of life, and the 1870 Act laid the basis for universal elementary education between the ages of five and twelve. By the terms of the Act, local ratepayers could petition the Board of Education to investigate educational provision in their area, comparing the number of available school places with the number of children of school age; in the event of a significant shortfall, a school board would be set up to create and run additional non-denominational schools.

The dominant role of the Church of England in providing school-
ing, and its influence on the education given, provided strong
motivation for dissenting opposition. For a village like Kibworth,
with its large Nonconformist congregations – which had a strong and
longstanding culture of education – the issue was an explosive one.
The reforming contingent in the village was led by the socialist builder
John Loveday. Loveday was described by an admirer as 'one of the
earliest and most energetic supporters of the Franchise, Free Education Act, the Nine Hours Movement, and kindred measures; a man of
ready wit, unfailing good temper and full of energy.' Supported by
many village 'sturdy radicals', Loveday made several attempts to win a
vote for a school board in Kibworth, but these were repeatedly frus-
trated by what was openly called the Church party, including the
long-serving rector, Montagu Osborn. In 1872 the staunchly conservative *Market Harborough Advertiser* reported a parish meeting held at
the village hall to discuss the matter, brought to a head for the second
year running by the 'turbulent spirits' in the village. Defeated in his
motion at the meeting, Loveday requested a poll of all the ratepayers.
The paper was withering. This local 'Solomon', it commented:

aims to be the political saviour of the working men of the parish, and on
their behalf he undertakes most absurd things. This is striving to gain popularity with a vengeance, and in a way which none but a rustic 'Buzfuz'
[a verbose barrister in *The Pickwick Papers*] would ever dare to adopt. It is
a great pity that there is not a proviso in the Act, so that individuals,
factiously putting a whole parish to expense, when they have no chance
of gaining their end, and simply to be thought clever and active – should
be mulcted in the whole expense themselves!

The poll was held on Whit Monday (20 May) and the village was
energetically rallied by the opposing factions. As the magnificently
partial *Advertiser* observed:

Loveday and his motley crew tried all kinds of efforts, persuasive and otherwise, to bring voters to the poll . . . considerable excitement prevailed in
the parish; vehicles of all kinds were brought into requisition to fetch up

voters, and visitors from Harborough, Wigston, and other places testified to the general interest felt in the proceedings.

The final result was 71 votes in favour of Loveday's motion, 131 against – 'a sound drubbing'. Opposite the hall, said the *Market Harborough Advertiser*, the school bell 'tolled out the termination of the School Board farce'.

Across the country similarly acrimonious debates were held in the wake of the 1870 Act. In the subsequent decade well over 3,000 schools were either founded or taken over by newly established school boards. In some places, as in Kibworth, the creation of boards was delayed by local votes; elsewhere boards were set up, but church-men and their supporters secured seats on them in order to obstruct the creation of secular board schools and to divert funds towards the church schools. In 1880 primary education was made compulsory to the age of ten – but the school boards were abolished by a Conser-vative government's Education Act of 1902 (roundly opposed by Nonconformist campaigners), in favour of some 300 Local Education Authorities.

The Education Act of 1870 was the product of wider movements in British society at both national and local level. In some degree, the Act of 1870 was a response to a fundamental political reform of three years earlier: the 1867 Reform Act, which sought to quell growing unrest by a significant further extension of the franchise. The inclu-sion of most of the urban working class, as well as a county franchise dependent on a £12 property qualification, caused concerns among the governing class about the competence of the new electorate to exercise its democratic right. In the light of the 1867 Act, the Liberal politician Robert Lowe famously remarked that it became necessary 'to educate our masters' – a view which successfully challenged the long-dominant assumption that education for the lower orders was both unnecessary and potentially destabilizing (since an educated working class might chafe at their inferior station). In Kibworth the villagers' literate medieval ancestors – village clerks and chaplains like the Polles and Sibils, book-reading Lollards like Walter Gilbert and William Brown – would no doubt have agreed with the idea that it was the 'masters' who needed educating.

By the time of the 1870 Act literacy was already quite widespread in the village, helped in part by three small private infants' schools run by village women which offered basic instruction in reading and writing. The ethos of self-improvement, which was so strong in Victorian culture, particularly in the Nonconformist community, had produced already in Kibworth a reading room for the benefit of the 'working classes'. Based initially at the National School, after its founding in 1853, it moved to the village hall (that characteristically Victorian institution) when the latter was built as a joint stock venture in 1866. After the reading room's members took over its management, its library was increased by over 200 volumes and it took twenty daily and weekly papers: testimony, itself, to the profusion of print journalism in Victorian England. It was open daily from 9 a.m. to 9 p.m. and (in concession to less intellectual, if still cerebral, relaxation) possessed 'well-occupied' dominoes, draughts and chess sets.

For a village as engaged, and divided, as Kibworth, the 1867 Reform Act only increased the political temperature. As the population continued to expand, efforts were made by the rival contingents to ensure that as many of their persuasion as possible were enfranchised. On 25 March 1873, Joseph Arch, the controversial president of the influential National Agricultural Labourers Union, spoke at a meeting at Kibworth Village Hall, where he discussed for the benefit of local workers their best means of acquiring property and so gaining the franchise.

In July that year an organization was founded which called itself the Kibworth and Smeeton Working Men's Association and Land Society, electing the indefatigable John Loveday as its chairman. Its aim was to buy up unused land on the edge of the village which could be used for building small houses (which Loveday, a successful builder himself, could oversee). Its early successes were flamboyantly proclaimed, to make sure that local opponents took note. After a drawing of lots for properties on the first estate, which was held at the new

Working Men's Institute in January 1874, the society's sixty-odd members processed to the ground, led by the Kibworth Brass Band playing 'You Dare Not Turn Us Out'. There Loveday and other leaders held aloft a yellow banner proclaiming 'Unity in Strength'. Needless to say, the rival Conservative grouping was quick to follow suit, buying land and building properties of their own for sale only to those who could be relied upon to use their vote 'responsibly': that is, for the Conservative Party.

So Kibworth 'New Town' was created on the western edge of the village over a few years in the 1870s and 1880s in an atmosphere of intense political partisanship. The houses (which still stand) were plain red brick terraces for working people. The names of the newly laid-out streets tell their own reforming story: Rosebery Avenue, Gladstone Street, Palmerston Close, Peel Close, Disraeli Close. Jonathan 'Jonty' Jesson, the engaging framework-knitter whom we met earlier, managed at this time to earn and borrow enough to acquire a plot of land on Fleckney Road on which he built four houses. These he prominently named 'Beaconsfield Cottages', in tribute to the Conservative Prime Minister Benjamin Disraeli, Lord Beaconsfield – another political gesture in partisan Kibworth. But for decades afterwards, in spite of the efforts of Jesson and others, the New Town was known locally simply as 'Radical' Kibworth, a name still remembered among older members of the community.

Among certain of the middle and upper class of the village – especially in Harcourt – there was nervousness at the workers' response to the rising tide of radical ideas in the early 1870s. The difficult conditions which produced what Marx referred to as the 'Great Awakening' of agricultural workers in 1872 were capitalized on by the national union agitator Joseph Arch. A benevolent supper at the Rose and Crown on Main Street (reported by the *Market Harborough Advertiser*) was organized for the labourers by the local landowner (and Methodist preacher) Mr Haymes, who dispensed fatherly words of advice with the beef and pork pie. He 'cautioned the men not to join the Unions and be led away by agitators, who only wished to set class against class'. In the countryside this was a particularly difficult time, when farming and other industries were depressed, as is suggested by the heightened level of antipathy to itinerant Irish farmworkers who appeared looking for work at harvest-time. Among long-favoured forms of protest were outbreaks of 'incendiarism' and the posting of anonymous threatening letters, such as one that was found attached to a bush in Kibworth in July 1870 and was reported in the *Mercury*: 'If you don't raise wages this week, you won't have a chance next. If there is any Irish left here after this week they will have to have a fresh gaffer. This is the last week of low wages.'

But if political rivalry and division could at times be bitter, and class tensions resurfaced at times of economic hardship, it seems that personal relations in the village were not invariably soured by Kibworth's passionate political engagement. In spite of the derision heaped upon him by hostile elements of the local press, John Loveday was remembered long after as a well-meaning and good-natured man who would 'talk and argue with his heated opponents with greatest good humour'. He was, Francis Woodford recalled, 'in seventh heaven when expounding his views to the large audiences which used to gather to hear him, either in the Village Hall or from a platform erected at his own expense on the Cross Bank', where he was well attended by admirers – Tom Iliffe, John Grant 'and other sturdy Radicals'.

## Leisure pursuits

Political rivals met, moreover, at the increasing range of social events and entertainments which characterized Victorian life, as statute limitations on working hours began to create for the mass of the population the reality (and indeed the very concept) of leisure. The 'weekend' came into being for the first time as a secular concept, still incorporating the religious sabbath but also involving free time to be spent in pursuit of worldly pleasures. It was this era which bequeathed, to England and to the wider world, the lasting legacy of organized competitive sport which has come to play such a significant role in modern culture. Association football and rugby football were both popular in Kibworth – two sports whose rules were codified in the

Victorian age from the numerous local forms which existed in the days before the railways.

But it was for cricket that Kibworth acquired significant local renown during the nineteenth century, though the fortunes (and indeed existence) of the club ebbed and flowed. As early as 1847 the Leicester press carried references to a Kibworth Cricket Club, consisting, the *Leicester Journal* noted in May 1848, 'of many of the farmers, as well as the tradesmen and the working classes'. It seems indeed that the social division between 'gentlemen' and 'players' for which the Victorian game is renowned was felt in Kibworth only by the 'gentlemen' absenting themselves from the action – sticking, though in a different season, to the fraternity of the hunting field, for which Leicestershire in general and Kibworth Harcourt in particular were well known. At an annual dinner in 1880, the cricket club secretary, Frank Loveday (John's son), regretted that 'many of the upper-class people of Kibworth would not support the club.' But it is doubtful whether they were much missed. A match organized, for instance, between 'the Framework Knitters' and 'the Builders' in 1877 (won comfortably by the former, belying their reputation for poor physical conditioning!) testifies to the interest of working men in the sport, which also attracted many of the middle class of the village.

Cricket was not always the gentlemanly pursuit we might imagine. In 1873 the *Leicester Chronicle* reported 'disgraceful proceedings' at a match between Kibworth and Gumley, which had degenerated into a pitched battle: 'the fight went on for some time until at length a perfect riot took place, and bats, which for some time had been flourished in the air, began to alight on the nasal organs of the combatants.' But in this case, as in so many similar, an excess of refreshment was held responsible: 'the greater portion of the rioters were apparently maddened by drink; and their conduct will probably induce the members to forswear the future admission of intoxicating drinks on the ground.'

For many in Kibworth such a tale would have seemed no laughing matter. The popularity of the many inns in the village, particularly no doubt on days of 'leisure', was the cause of much agonizing for a strong local temperance movement, which founded a Band of Hope club and held tea meetings in the village hall as often as other groups enjoyed less abstemious dinners in the Old Swan. The village stocks may have been gone for decades, but public exposure as a drinker could still be quietly embarrassing. Thomas Knapp, a framework-knitter who was accustomed on pay day to making a lengthy visit to the Old Swan, suffered the indignity of having his teetotal wife Harriet coming to sit accusingly next to him in the pub while he drank, until he felt sufficiently shamed to come home.

The temperance movement in Britain grew fast, inspired by Joseph Livesey's movement in Preston in the 1830s, and religious Nonconformists were at the forefront, with many Baptist and Congregational ministers advocating abstinence. (Just as beer and the Established Church were associated with the Tory party, so temperance and Nonconformity were associated with the Liberals.) One enthusiastic Baptist and temperance campaigner who was active in Leicester and Market Harborough, and preached regularly at Kibworth's Baptist chapel on Debdale Lane, was – legend has it – waiting for a stagecoach in Kibworth in 1841 when he had what would prove a world-changing idea: an excursion by train for over 500 temperance campaigners from Leicester to a rally at Loughborough. The man was Thomas Cook, and the tourist business for which this campaign outing was the seed would have a vast impact on the changing tastes and expectations of the British public. Package tours to the British seaside (a remarkable innovation from inland Leicestershire), and even to the Continent, attracted soaring numbers – though the temperance roots of the English package holiday ceased, at quite an early stage, to exert a defining influence on the future shape of mass tourism.

More local entertainment of a reliably edifying nature was laid on by the committee who ran the village reading room, in the form of a regular series of concerts, or 'penny readings', held at the village hall and often chaired by the vicar. A variety of performances were given by villagers: classical recitals, readings from Dickens, Mark Twain and others, popular songs, including 'English and Irish songs, Scotch and Welsh ballads, comic and "buffo pieces" . . . the whole forming a brilliant and amusing entertainment'. Their efforts were written up in unfailingly flattering reviews in the local press which cast a fascinating light on Victorian village entertainment:

A string band gave some pieces, and Mr Macauley gave a reading 'How to Cure a Cold' on which he, as a professional gentleman, could speak with authority. Mr E. Miles gave the song 'The Goose Club' which was rather amusing and was encored, being similarly complimented when he sang 'The Old Bachelor'. Mr Taylor gave two recitations and Mr Caysar a reading. Mrs Osborne, Mrs Heygate and Mrs Allen gave a trio. Miss Turner sang 'The Bird of the Wilderness' with great taste and received a deserved encore. Mrs Taylor sang with great precision 'Silver Threads among the Gold'. Mrs Taylor, Mrs Allen and Messrs Aitkinson and Bryant sang 'The Belfry Tower' and 'The Skylark's Song'. Miss Redsall and Miss Martin gave the 'Qui vive' duet. The whole entertainment was quite a success and no doubt will prove so to the society.

At times the reading room committee laid on an improving lecture, though this wasn't always as big a draw as had been hoped. In November 1872 the Reverend Hipwood gave 'a lecture, or missionary address, illustrated with diagrams on the Indians of North America' – but the hall was half empty: 'At the close, Mr Kirby proposed a vote of thanks to the lecturer and regretted that so few attended to hear it, while for anything light and frivolous there was generally a large attendance.' Strangely enough though, a talk on 'Arab Life and Manners' drew a packed house, perhaps because of its theme as 'an illustration of eastern life and Bible customs'. The speaker was one Seyyid Mustafa ben-Yusuf, an Arab convert studying medicine at Cambridge who spoke in full Arab costume having roped in 'some dozen natives (not Arabs) dressed in Arab and Turkish costumes'. Seyyid Mustafa brought with him a collection of interesting Near Eastern objects, including a hookah, a Damascus spear, an Arab musket, a Muslim prayer carpet and even a copper coffee pot. Whether the hookah was actually put to use is not stated, but the people of Kibworth were perhaps fortunate that their committee took a less frosty attitude than was taken by the nearby vicar in Market Harborough, who made plain at a similar event there that 'the object of these meetings be to afford instruction and amusement, and that they be called "Penny Readings" and not "Popular Entertainments"' – and that singing or reading 'in costume *must be excluded*'.

More to the general taste was one popular local performer, William Noble, who was long remembered as a 'famous local negro comedian'. No photograph of Noble has yet turned up but he was almost certainly a white man 'blacked up' in the style of the minstrel groups whose popularity had spread from the US in the 1840s, and which remained successful in Britain well into the twentieth century. (Many thousands of black men did arrive in Britain in the late eighteenth century, in return for fighting in the defeated colonial armies in America, but they congregated overwhelmingly in London or the port cities.) At a concert given at the village feast in November 1873, the *Market Harborough Advertiser* reported, 'the well known popularity of Mr Noble again secured him a full house . . . Mr Noble, who is always at home here, sang several fresh songs, causing much laughter.' Kibworth also welcomed visits by the 'Kentucky Minstrels' of Leicester. One local man, James Hawker, recorded later in life how he had joined a minstrel troupe in Oadby, on the main route between Leicester and Kibworth, playing bones (castanets) along with a banjo player and two violinists – charging threepence admission for performances in a local pub.

Such was popular entertainment in an English village before the age of television, and a strange and wonderful mix it is too, from anthropological lectures to comic turns, from Mark Twain and Dickens to Haydn and temperance songs. Contrary to what one might now assume, minstrel entertainments, now so insensitive and demeaning, were at the very respectable end of the spectrum, and were loved for their pathos, their humour (they are an important source of modern stand-up comic routines) but also for their sometimes egalitarian themes. The world of 'music hall', however, in which bawdy songs and risqué jokes were performed in an atmosphere thick with tobacco smoke and enlivened by purposeful drinking, took off during the second half of the nineteenth century, and served to sharpen the disapproval with which some viewed stage entertainment. If such evenings took place in Kibworth, then they were certainly not in the village hall, under the chairmanship of the vicar – and nor were they politely recorded in the local press! But no doubt the village inns, like the huge and now decaying Rose and Crown on the London road, played host to performances of a less decorous nature. The coming of the railways, indeed, and the resultant collapse in the stagecoach net-work, left former coaching inns with unused outbuildings, which it paid to rent out for social events. The vicar and the local temperance society would not have approved, but even in a village dominated by 'chapel' there were no doubt many working men who enjoyed a rougher and less moralizing kind of amusement.

## 'Brave, voteless women'

While entertainments in the village hall appear to have been fault-lessly respectable, the venue also played host to political meetings of which many in Kibworth must have disapproved – like the visit of Joseph Arch, the controversial founder of the National Agricultural Labourers Union and an energetic franchise reformer. Early in the new century, however, a new kind of political gathering was held in the hall which raised many eyebrows, even though the message was squarely within the village's proud radical and dissenting traditions. On 5 March 1910 a meeting was organized there by Mrs Mary Taylor, who for over ten years had lived at Westerby House – a large, red-brick Georgian residence on the old boundary between Smeeton and Westerby. Mary – or Nellie as she was known – was a suffragette, and that day in Kibworth the largely female audience listened to passion-ate addresses by the suffragettes Alice Pemberton-Peake and Dorothy Pethick. On 19 March a second meeting was held in Kibworth, and on 22 April open-air meetings were organized across Leicestershire. During the early months of that year large groups of women trav-elled from Leicester to villages around the county, by a means of transport as radical in its design as it was in its social impact – the bicycle – bringing with them the message of the Women's Social and Political Union.

On 4 March, the day before the first Kibworth meeting, the paper

*Votes for Women* paid tribute to the preparatory work of Mrs Taylor, in language which aptly expressed the movement's quasi-religious zeal:

The Mission is occupying all the workers' thoughts as the next piece of work which they have to accomplish. More canvassers are urgently needed to bring to women householders a personal invitation to the Mission to learn the moral and social meaning underlying the movement. Will volunteers call at the office? This week new ground has been broken at Kibworth, where great interest has been aroused by a local member, Mrs Taylor, who has worked hard in canvassing and speaking.

Nellie, who came from an old Nonconformist family herself, must have found sympathetic ears within the non-Anglican congregations which had long been attracted to social radicalism and even to the rights of women. In 1911 the WSPU promoted a boycott of that year's census. All-night entertainments ensured that women were not at home, and Nellie Taylor and her daughter Dorothea are duly missing from the Smeeton return. The census document was filled out by her supportive husband Tom, who entered himself and his two sons before writing defiantly across the bottom: 'Women absent protesting No Vote No Census.'

The campaign for women's suffrage had in fact been gathering momentum over the last forty years. In 1869 the philosopher and MP John Stuart Mill published an essay, 'The Subjection of Women', calling gender discrimination 'one of the chief hindrances to human improvement'. But his fellow Parliamentarians — all of them men — were resolutely deaf to such arguments. The Third Reform Act of 1884 extended the borough qualification of the 1867 act to the countryside, but still left some 40 per cent of men and — the more fundamental omission — *all* women without the vote, though the Married Women's Property Acts of 1870 and 1882 had done away with the argument that since married women did not own property in their own right, they could not qualify for a property-owning franchise. In 1897 seventeen groups merged to form the National Union of Women's Suffrage Societies. It was members of this organization, led by Emmeline Pankhurst, who left six years later to form the Women's Social and Political Union, believing that waning interest in the issue required the adoption of more sensational tactics. When hopes of a compromise agreement under the Liberal government came to nothing by 1911, the temperature further increased.

At 10.29 p.m. on 4 March 1912 Nellie Taylor sent a message by telegraph from Victoria Post Office in London to her husband, who was in Nottingham with their three children. It read simply: 'Quite safe but business satisfactorily completed. Nelly.' No doubt Tom knew, at least in broad terms, what this 'business' was. The following day he received a letter from Westminster Police Court:

Dearest Tom and my dearest children. I was arrested last night with Miss Crocker and Miss Roberts for breaking the windows of Knightsbridge Post Office. I understand we are to receive fairly heavy sentences this time, so that I think you must be prepared for me to get a month's sentence . . . Goodbye my darlings, your loving mother.

A report survives, filed by Ernest Bowden, the detective who followed her on the night as Nellie, with two fellow suffragettes, Nellie Crocker and Gladys Roberts, left a restaurant on the Strand used for WSPU meetings and walked towards Charing Cross. The women knew they were being followed. They took the tube on an indirect route, emerging eventually at Sloane Square, where they ducked into the Royal Court Theatre and entered the auditorium. Shortly after the performance had begun, at 8.38 p.m., they rose quickly and left, walking across Sloane Square towards the King's Road. They had not shaken off the assiduous Detective Sergeant Bowden though, who reported seeing the women run suddenly across the road towards the post office and smash its large windows with hammers concealed in their clothing.

Arrested and taken to Gerald Row Police Station, the three women appeared next day at Westminster Court (Nellie having given the false name Mary Wyan), where they were denied bail and taken to Holloway Prison. The three-month sentence they later received was stiffer than Nellie had expected. They were far from alone: over

200 women were arrested in early March during a window-smashing campaign in London, many of them sentenced to terms in Holloway. Emmeline Pankhurst heralded this 'time-honoured method of showing displeasure in a political situation . . . The argument of the broken pane of glass,' she urged, 'is the most valuable argument in modern politics.'

Nellie's letters from prison were later deposited by her daughter at the Women's Library in London and reveal a loving wife and mother driven to extreme measures by her faith in the suffragette cause. (It was perhaps more than just a wry joke when she entered her religion on prison documents as 'Votes for Women'.) On Westerby House notepaper she bid her children farewell for the duration of her sentence: 'Goodbye my darlings, it is not for long. Keep the flag flying.' After they had visited her in prison she confessed to struggling at first:

I was so glad to see you . . . I felt rather bad the first day – but I think it was caused by the effort to bring oneself up to the point of breaking a window at all. I believe it was the strain of this that left its after effects. I feel better now.

She was shocked though by prison conditions – 'the most extraordinary system' – and became an advocate of reform: 'You feel more like a little child . . . the place looks more like one would imagine a lunatic asylum might look like.' The suffragette cause and prison reform became associated in her mind: 'the whole [prison] system will be swept off the face of the earth when we get the vote.'

Photographs exist of Nellie and other suffragettes taken as they walked in the prison yard at Holloway by a police surveillance camera concealed in a van. As it happened, this was the first such camera that Scotland Yard owned. Prisoners had been routinely photographed since 1871, but as suffragettes increasingly refused to pose (in one shot, a jailer's arm is seen round the neck of the Manchester suffragette Evelyn Manesta – clumsily doctored to look like her scarf – while she grimaces to distort her face), a request was put in for a Wigmore Model 2 reflex camera and an 11-inch Ross Telecentric zoom lens. The Home Secretary personally authorized the purchase, 'to be used for the purpose of photographing suffragette prisoners'. Police then compiled photographic lists of known militants, with the aim of combating their acts of vandalism. So Nellie Taylor of Smeeton was the proud subject of one of the first surveillance photographs in British history.

Protest continued within the prison. Cell windows were smashed, and many – Nellie included – went on hunger strike when visiting and correspondence privileges were withdrawn. Her subsequent letters are etched in tiny handwriting on small squares of paper smuggled out by sympathetic fellow prisoners who passed them to visitors of their own. 'I must not write it long,' she penned in miniature, 'as there are so many to pass through.' She drew succour from her faith in the cause, from the contact with fellow campaigners, and by clinging to small pleasures: 'The moon shines into my cell. It looks glorious. They can take the small things away from me but they cannot take away the big things which we all share in common.' Her proud husband Tom, meanwhile, hammered out at his typewriter a stream of letters to newspapers and leading politicians. The latter, he concluded, were 'afraid of the pluck, determination and resource of these brave voteless women'. No protester by temperament, he steeled himself to heckle Lloyd George at a public meeting and was hustled out of the room by a 'horde of hooligans', his glasses knocked off and rudely trampled on. He tried to explain his conduct to his devout Nonconformist mother:

I am afraid that you and the others find it difficult to understand and impossible to approve my action . . . You can well believe that to a modest self-conscious man all this publicity is hateful as I know it is to refined suffragettes. But there comes a time when, as with Christ, it is necessary to do the hateful thing in order to maintain a principle and express an idea which makes for progress.

During 1913 across Britain the bitterness of the struggle escalated, as the 'Cat and Mouse Act' allowed hunger-striking prisoners to be released to recover, then be rearrested. Emily Davison, notoriously, ran under the King's horse on Derby Day – and was captured on film doing it. The suffragettes' increasingly violent and vociferous campaign, however, was brought to a sudden end by a much more serious crisis, the outbreak of the First World War. The Great War (as it would become known) would mark the true dividing line – psychological, cultural and political – between the age of Victoria and the twentieth century.

As if already aware of this, it was during the first year of the war that F. P. Woodford, who had grown up in a cottage close to the church in Kibworth, set down his remarkable account, based on his own memories, of the Victorian village in the 1860s. At this point in the winter of 1915, the very idea of civilization itself, so confidently appropriated by the Victorians, had become profoundly problematic: a source even, as one great contemporary put it, of deep anxiety, even of 'mourning and melancholy'. Woodford had set out to write a simple History of Kibworth but to this he appended his 'Reminiscences of my Childhood 1860 to 1868', which is a far more significant document. His detailed look at one place, his native village, became a comment on what England was, or at least what it was believed to be, and in particular what made the English village community tick. By then Woodford had moved away with some regrets, and change was his theme: the transformations of time and society. 'The old seasonable customs,' he wrote, 'rapidly began to lapse and disappear' after the 1860s. He acknowledged social and political change (and was grateful for much of it), he mentioned the political battles and sometimes bitter class antagonisms, as well as the unquestionably hard life of many of his poorer childhood neighbours, the framework-knitters and coal-hawkers; as we have seen, he was scathing about the greed of those rich people who were not motivated by feelings for the community as a whole. But Woodford still portrays the village, warts and all, in the mid-Victorian era as almost a golden time. He is sensitive to what one might call the givenness of the past, the continuity of life lived in that place, what he calls the 'unseen presence' of the people of the past: this idea no doubt lay behind his compulsive recording of every person in the village. 'If it were possible to obtain a glimpse of

Heaven on earth, surely it was to be found there.' It is hard perhaps to recognize that image in the Kibworth depicted in the raw archives of the Victorian era: the Poor Law volumes, the censuses, the newspaper reports from the village he portrays so touchingly and affectionately. But he was a good observer, and the core for him evidently was in the community itself, and the glue that bound it together, and he was surely right in that.

# Epilogue:
# The Twentieth Century

For the first time in the history of Kibworth a military funeral has taken
place in the village. On Thursday afternoon upwards of 2,000 people
assembled in the streets and at the cemetery for the interment of Private
Bertie Pell, aged 20, of the 2nd Leicesters, eldest son of Mr and Mrs B. H.
Pell, of Fleckney Road, Kibworth. He passed away in hospital in England
last Saturday from injuries sustained in May while in the firing line. He
had been previously wounded, in March, and recovering, went again to
the front. The cortege was headed by a squad of 12 1st and 2nd Leicesters
(all of whom had been wounded at the front), under the commands of
Sergeant-Major Read and Sergeant Sands, together with Bugler-Drummer
Sharpe. The coffin, covered with the Union Jack, was borne by four of the
deceased's chums . . . The deceased was a chorister in the Parish Church, a
Boy Scout, and a prominent footballer. He is the first Kibworth Grammar
School boy to lay down his life for his country.

*Market Harborough Advertiser*, 6 July 1915

In the village the hosiery factory and shops, and the grammar school,
had been closed for the afternoon. The boys from the school lined the
route to say farewell to their former schoolmate. They sang 'Fight
the Good Fight' and afterwards the soldiers fired off three volleys of
shots by the graveside. A bugler sounded the Last Post in the summer
sunshine while a light breeze stirred the old yew trees in the churchyard. Pell was the first of forty men of the village to die in the mud
and horror of the Western Front. With Private Pell's death we have
reached the modern era: what would become known as the Great
War marks a dividing line in the history of the village. The story of
the last century in Kibworth would merit a book on its own: an
enormous amount of material is being gathered from local archives

by the Kibworth History Society, and recorded from old people in the village, funds of knowledge about the social life of the place during the transformations of the last fifty years as the village expanded to become as it is today, almost a small town. Here as an epilogue we can only highlight a few of the stories of the village since those now almost unimaginably far-off moments, the Jubilee of 1897, Victoria's death in 1901 and the beginning of the First World War.

During Victoria's reign the village had doubled in size, with a particularly big expansion towards the end: the growth of Kibworth Beauchamp in the late nineteenth and early twentieth centuries is particularly noticeable today in Station Road and at the western end of Fleckney Road, where almost a new small town sprang up after the establishment of Johnson & Barnes's hosiery factory there in 1901, close to the Working Men's Club and Institute. The Johnson & Barnes factory produced fully fashioned cashmere hose and exported in particular to Canada and Scandinavia until its closure in the sixties. During its heyday before the Second World War it provided employment in Kibworth but also in outlying villages: in the early thirties two busloads of workers came each day from Great Glen and Fleckney. The factory also provided a lot of outdoor home-based work for women in the form of 'lining' or 'seaming', that is, stitching the toes of the stockings and attaching the foot to the leg. The women took their work home in bundles by bike. With its hosiery factory, gas- and brickworks, railway station and sidings, and sizeable shops like Lynn's general store, Kibworth now was well and truly part of the urbanized economy of the twentieth century, and the factory-based workforce in the 'town' now outnumbered those who still worked as agricultural labourers on the land.

Troops from the village fought and died in the big battles in Flanders, as part of the Leicester Regiment and also the Sherwood Foresters. Eileen Bromley's father was among them and he vividly conjured the terror of the night before the 'Big Push' on the Somme in 1916: 'I will never forget that night as long as I live . . . we retired under heavy fire, shells and bullets. What sights I saw, I shall never forget them: there were dead and wounded everywhere.' There were those though who stuck to the village's old Nonconformist tradition. The draper Eli Bale was a conscientious objector:

All through my life I have tried to be a follower of Christ and a Christian and I have a conscientious objection to all military service. I consider human life to be sacred, and under no circumstances would I take the same. These views I have held all my life. I have been a Nonconformist local preacher, a teacher in the Sunday School, and will ever serve my principle . . . I don't believe Jesus Christ would take part in any military affairs and therefore I cannot.

This story was typical of the village, where (though Bale was in a very small minority) all opinions seem to have been represented.

Life on the Home Front meanwhile went on. In December 1916, while the boys endured the miseries of winter in the trenches, the proprietor of the village general store, George Lynn, published for the thirty-fourth year running his free almanac. This gives us a little window into the material life of the village, which for all its industry was still at heart a farming community. In its pages there is advertising for wire netting, dolly tubs, buckets, roofing felt, rat traps, poultry feed, and pig and chicken powders. The monthly calendar is illustrated with photos of horses pulling seeding carts, the village vet at work and the horse-drawn milk cart stacked with huge churns setting out on Lynn's rounds. With his recently installed telephone, Lynn could now take orders and offer deliveries to villages all over the area, from Gumley to the Langtons.

The preface to his almanac offered news on the government's rationing of sugar (recommending corn syrup or honey as substitutes), along with adverts for Collis Browne's cough medicine (that year Kibworth had seen a prolonged and very trying winter with a great snowstorm in February). Pages of 'useful facts' include a calendar for 1917 with key dates, and tips for gardeners and vets. There are pages of postal charges, useful foreign phrases, tax tables and pension charts. National pensions were new: the maximum pension was 5s per week for anyone earning less than £21 (5s today is about £12 on the retail price index; £70 on average earnings). In the calendar for 1917 the dates of the hunting season are marked (Kibworth was a hunt area), as well as the anniversaries of the recent battles of Verdun, Jutland and the Somme, together with older imperial landmarks such as the Black Hole of Calcutta and the battles of Quebec and Sebastopol. From Lynn's adverts one might also infer that for the gentry and landed aristocracy life in the countryside was not too bad: he stocked Irish butter and Danish bacon along with French champagne, Jamaican rum and Spanish red wine.

The First World War marked the village as it did everywhere in England. Even now Armistice Day is commemorated in St Wilfrid's by a packed church with standing room only. The mental geography of the ordinary people of England had been changed. Previous imperial wars in the Crimea, South Africa and elsewhere had been far away. The First World War was closer to home: the thunder of guns on the killing grounds could be heard in Kent. And everyone knew someone who had died.

Patriotism continued to be drummed into the young at school. In Kibworth, as one villager remembered, Empire Day on 24 May 'was celebrated at school by an assembly of all classes for the singing of patriotic hymns, followed by half a day holiday'. The 1935 jubilee of George V and Mary was another great patriotic event, with the village hung out with bunting and a huge bonfire. In school, chapel and church the villagers imbibed the myths of empire and with them, at least for a time, a sense of the superiority of English culture over outsiders; in whom, nonetheless, there was a great deal of interest, and from whom and about whom much was learned. 'Every nation', it has been observed, 'is a semi-permeable container, washed over by many different forces and influences from beyond its shores', and this was especially true of imperial Britain.

Beyond the forty lost lives, the war had a much wider and longer-term impact on the village: few village families were untouched by these wider changes. The old agricultural world of Kibworth, which had been gradually eroding since the 1789 enclosures, was now almost entirely gone. Land was concentrated in a handful of large farms in Beauchamp and Smeeton, with the fields and farms in Harcourt still rented from Merton College. Most smallholding farmers were gone and the old families of smallholders and husbandmen who survived in the village, like the Bromleys, Clarkes, Iliffes and Colmans, were mostly no longer in agriculture. Nonetheless the physical aspect of the village was still rural. As one Kibworthian who lived through the thirties, G. A. Ringrose, observed:

Had anyone contemplated taking up residence in Kibworth between the wars, their reaction would have been that the village had not suffered excessively as a result of the Industrial Revolution. Compared with other villages within the county Kibworth was still relatively unspoilt; a large village certainly, and as it had in the past possessed two markets, it often became the subject of argument regarding its qualification for town status. The agrarian influence was never as obvious as in Smeeton Westerby, nevertheless a rural atmosphere prevailed. Everyone seemed to know everyone else, the neighbourhood was a more tightly knit community than it is today, due perhaps to the fact that no one at that time thought in terms of a classless society; a strict line of demarcation existed within the social strata and it is doubtful if anyone considered crossing it.

(The division between the Kibworth of the 'stockeners' and the 'hunting and fishing' side was still pronounced and would ebb away only in the last decades of the century.)

Though the war had brought changes for the better, including the extension of the franchise, the late twenties and thirties were a time of economic depression, remembered by more than one Kibworthian as a period which though happy for children was hard for many adults: 'it was a common sight to see and hear an unemployed man standing in the middle of the street playing a musical instrument.' Some were young, some were old, but they all had one thing in common – hardship – since National Assistance was a thing of the future. During this time the Jarrow marchers came through Kibworth on their way to London and gathered on the Munt, with tea provided by the locals, to listen to a speech from Ellen Wilkinson MP. But in the thirties the village also saw significant changes in its material life: in the fields the old ways went fast between the world wars, with rapid mechanization. The surviving post windmill in Harcourt ground its last bag of flour in 1925; handploughing died out in the thirties with the arrival of the tractor. The first public telephones arrived with the famous red 'Jubilee' box in 1936; radio had come to most houses by the end of the decade.

Another important change was the arrival of a piped water supply. The wells and springs along the Kibworth ridge had sustained life for generations, but a debate over the quality and reliability of the water had begun with the Public Health Act of 1875, in the wake of cholera epidemics in London. The act required all new housing to include running water and internal drainage. But it took a long time for Kibworth to catch up. In bad dry seasons (as in the drought of 1884) many houses in Kibworth had gone without water for weeks on end. Now, as the population of the village grew, the problem became critical. In the First World War Kibworth still relied on public pumps, and many houses were without a proper supply. As with so many places in rural England, the time had come for Kibworth to leave this aspect of its medieval past behind.

As with electric lighting, however, mains water was not eagerly taken up by the villagers. Those who had a good pumped supply were not keen to pay for those who didn't, and the debate was only resolved in the 1930s, by which time the water of four out of five of the village wells had been condemned as unfit for drinking by modern standards. (In Britain as a whole at this time, more than half of all houses, about 7 million dwellings, lacked a hot-water supply, 6 million had no inside WC, and almost 5 million had no bath.) By May 1938 most of the village was connected, though village and private pumps continued in use for many years after the Second World War. At least one house relied on water from its own well until the drought of 1976 forced the owner to accept a mains supply, and even today wells in the three villages are still in use. As was the case for most of Britain, the arrival of water on tap, hot and cold, with baths (let alone showers), is a comparatively recent phenomenon.

## The Second World War

After the Munich crisis of 1938 a village meeting was held in the Oddfellows hall, when villagers were fitted for gas masks. The Kibworth Air Raid Precautions handout was circulated on 27 March 1939, several months before the British declaration of war, but by then, as older villagers remember, war already seemed inevitable (Germany had invaded Czechoslovakia on 15 March). The document was drawn up by the much-loved headmaster of the old grammar school, J. E. Elliot. On two typed and cyclostyled sheets the five wardens' posts are enumerated, together with the first-aid point (the village hall) and the 'Air Raid report centre' (the grammar school). Over one hundred Kibworth people were mobilized, with first-aid teams, a rescue and demolition squad, ambulance drivers ('Canon Eacott, Mrs Potts . . .') and sixteen auxiliary firemen, including some old village names (John Iliffe was the deputy chief auxiliary fire officer, and two of his brothers also served).

From then on 'fear of conflict was ever present', wrote G. A. Ringrose, 'and no one was surprised when war broke out in September 1939.' Kibworth was immediately involved. That same weekend the first frightened child evacuees arrived by train from London, carrying their small belongings and a cardboard box for their gas mask, about to spend the next years of their lives far away from the back-to-backs of the East End in the rolling fields of Kibworth and Smeeton. In time the village would even have a small camp for Italian prisoners of war, who saw out the war working on local farms, and at least one of whom subsequently married a local girl.

Black-out rules were brought in immediately – and so effectively that 'it was easy to get lost in one's own village.' The village appears in Luftwaffe photographs. Close to the US airbase at Bruntingthorpe, and on the German bombers' flight path into the Black Country, it even saw a little action. The most famous event is still remembered by old people in the village. On a Sunday afternoon in October 1940, a low-flying German Dornier bomber strafed the High Street in Kibworth Beauchamp. Bombs also fell on the village on the night of the Coventry Blitz in November 1940, perhaps from a plane which had failed to reach its target and dropped its load on to the darkened countryside. That night an orange glow spread across the sky from the fires of Coventry, which could be seen clearly from the bedroom windows in Beauchamp. Then came the raids on Germany, when, as G. A. Ringrose remembered, 'through 1942 in the evenings it was a familiar and almost unforgettable sight to see the skies over

Kibworth literally full of bombers.' Rose Holyoak, who worked as a landgirl driving tractors in a number of villages, remembers that her Uncle Vic, the chief mechanic at the Johnson & Barnes hosiery factory, supplied his own kitchen table to provide a base for the air raid siren which was mounted on the factory roof. (It remained there until the factory was demolished in July 1993!)

The village had its Home Guard unit ('Dad's Army') based at St Wilfrid's church; it was led by 'Captain' Blake, who painted his prized red Singer sports car in camouflage colours so effective that on more than one occasion he lost it and had to send out search parties – much to the amusement of his 'platoon'. Through the war the village entertainments were kept up, with the dramatic and choral societies doing shows in the village hall, where patriotic and 'morale-boosting' government films were also shown. These were received by the villagers with sceptical humour. '"Morale",' says Ringrose, 'became a standard word, followed by "utility"!' In the village there was deep scepticism about some of the government's 'propaganda' campaigns, especially as they came in class accents. J. B. Priestley's plain north country accent went down better than exhortations in plummy Eton tones. 'Everyone felt sure that we would win the war,' remembered one Kibworthian, 'we didn't need to be told to be cheerful: we were cheerful.' As Ringrose recalled it: 'wartime society in the village was disciplined and people were allowed to enjoy themselves without being victims of someone's psychopathic condition!' Being told to do their duty, in short, was felt to be not only unnecessary but impertinent. From the village newspaper it can be seen that from the start of the war Kibworth people, like the British population as a whole, saw a higher purpose than Churchill's narrow rhetoric about empire: namely a community of interest with the people of Europe to counteract Germany's 'New Europe'. Even in 'little' Kibworth they saw that.

That was the Home Front. But, of course, many young men and women of the village fought in all three services throughout the war in North Africa, Italy and Normandy, in battles on land, at sea and in the air. Their experiences and feelings are brought into sharp focus in a home-produced village newspaper which was sent out to the 'lads and lasses' of Kibworth serving on all fronts during the war: at its peak in 1944–5 over 350 men and women. *The Kibworth News and Forces' Journal* was sent free to all villagers in the forces with a motto from Burke: 'To Love the little platoon we belong to in society is the germ of all public affection'. The paper was edited by a former First World War soldier, Leslie Clarke. It includes stories, letters, poems, competitions and illustrations, with pages of news from the village, including a record of all baptisms, marriages and deaths. 'Our desire,' wrote Clarke, 'is that every issue of the *Kibworth News* may be a "memory chain link" reminding you of your home and village.' The Christmas 1944 issue carries greetings from over thirty village organizations, clubs and societies, from the Working Men's Club to the Women's Institute. 'Kibworth sends affectionate New Year Greetings to our Lads and Lassies on sea, land and in the air, to the sick and suffering and those who tend them, and to all prisoners of war.' Each issue also contained a roll of honour of those who had lost their lives from Dunkirk to D-Day.

The letters from the troops speak with great affection of 'that certain village back home in the Midlands of dear old England', and the cover of the bumper victory issue of December 1945 has 'Christmas Greetings, Happy family reunions, Good luck and success in Civvy Street'; there is a photo of May Holyoak chosen as 'Lady Kibworth' at the village carnival; and a rich letter column reminisces about the 'Dear Old Village' from India, Italy and Africa, with a poem from a grateful Kibworthian in Iraq, 'Bagdad Blues':

> I want to feel the rain again, and mow a tennis lawn
> I want to mess about in boats, and watch the bitter dawn . . .
> I want to scurry home again as quickly as I can
> To settle back in Kibworth, and be an ordinary man.

## Post-war new world

Until the Second World War, it has often been said, the visible agencies of the state were just the policeman and postman, with the taxman unseen in the background. But the draconian wartime powers on the

Home Front and the Labour victory in 1945 led to a dramatic increase in state control after 1945, and these changes across post-war England as a whole saw a world transformed: the rise of housing estates, the influx of new waves of immigrants, the end of the old industries like mining, shipbuilding and steel; the arrival of mass media and new forms of popular culture. A new England emerged: its population doubled during the century as all over the country former villages were swallowed by city suburbs. In Kibworth it was in the late forties and fifties that the signs of development which would turn the place into a small town were initially noticed. The first post-war housing scheme consisted of 150 council houses built opposite the church. Kibworth was still separated from Leicester, ten miles away, by open countryside, but as one villager remarked of that time: 'We were becoming urbanized.'

Further far-reaching changes came in the sixties. More housing estates were built, but there was also a big change for the town's workforce: with the closure of the hosiery factory in 1961, Kibworth's long association with the knitting industry ended. 'When the factory finally closed,' wrote Ringrose, 'it was as if a part of the character of Kibworth had vanished . . . scenes which had been commonplace for years disappeared: the workers on factory corner at Fleckney Road and Dover Street; children in the thirties returning after their mid-day break, the second shift coming on at 3 p.m. till midnight.' Not long afterwards the railway station was closed, in the aftermath of Dr Beeching's cuts. There was also a major reorganization of education, which led to the closure of the old grammar school. The Education Act of 1944 had laid down that 'no fees were to be charged in respect of admission to any School maintained by a local education authority', and though the grammar school gave some free places, it had only survived on feepayers. Between 1944 and 1954 the head, Mr Elliott, made a bold effort to revitalize the school, increasing the roll from 300 to over 500 pupils, and bringing Kibworth back to what its medieval or Tudor founders intended – a Free Grammar School. But after much agonizing, it was eventually decided that the school was too small to continue.

Your committee reached its conclusion with the utmost reluctance. It could contemplate the discontinuance of a school of Kibworth's long tradition only with the most profound regret . . . but the inexorable fact is that if the Wigston Grammar-Technical School is built it is impossible to find sufficient children suited for the grammar school type of secondary education to keep Kibworth Grammar School in existence.

In 1964 the old premises of Kibworth Grammar School were closed and Kibworth High School was founded on a new site, and has now become a large and thriving school as the population of Kibworth has continued to expand since the sixties. As for the school box, the records going back to Kibworth's Tudor schoolmaster and the medieval farmers whose gifts became the 'school lands', these testimonies to the story of education in the village over the centuries now rest in the County Record Office in Wigston.

## *The village today*

Kibworth today is a thriving place of between 5,000 and 6,000 people. Typical of many large villages in modern England, many of its people work in shops and offices outside the village, some in Leicester, some even commuting through Market Harborough to London, which can now be reached by train in an hour. It still has several large farms, and one or two smaller ones. Merton College, though it sold its houses off in the 1970s, still rents out the fields which formed the large part of Walter of Merton's original endowment of 1270. It still has a relationship with the village: the warden comes up every three years for a visit, and the college choir performs in St Wilfrid's church. As it has been through history, the village's main urban link is with Leicester, which these days is fast expanding southwards. Leicester is possibly the most multicultural city in modern Britain, and has managed the most recent waves of newcomers to England more successfully perhaps than anywhere else. (In 2009 the city announced that it would declare all ethnic groups minorities, even the 'white'

English.) Kibworth itself is still a predominantly white place, but as members of the successful and vibrant Asian and Caribbean communities in Leicester rise in the middle class they are moving out southwards and Kibworth with its excellent high school is now becoming sought after. (A sign of the times, perhaps: the old Rose and Crown on the A6 is now one of the best Indian restaurants in the region, and a favourite for wedding celebrations with the Indian community in the area.)

At the end of the first decade of the twenty-first century Kibworth reached what is perhaps the optimum size for a community, about 5,000 people (ten times its population in 1086). As it had in the nineteenth century, and during the Second World War, the village has a huge number of clubs, societies and institutions: in fact, more so than at any other time in its past. These many different groupings come together for spectacular events like the Relay for Life for Cancer Research, which raised £65,000. Of course, there have been huge changes in the last two centuries, but in some respects the village would still be recognizable to Woodford from the 1860s: it has football, bowls, golf and tennis clubs, and a very successful cricket club – founded 150 years ago, the club became national village champions in 2008. Music is still a very important aspect of village life, and there are many music and choral societies and two brass bands, one of which was established a century ago and became national village champions in 2006. The village has its own newspaper, the *Kibworth Chronicle*, which is published ten times a year, the layout done by hand in the village hall in the old-fashioned way for the simple reason that it involves more people. Kibworth also has a library, three dramatic societies, gardening clubs, three reading groups, Chinese and Indian takeaways and one of the finest Italian restaurants in England, set up by a charming Milanese, Lino Poli, who was drawn by love to Leicestershire, but 'just liked it in Kibworth'.

So going back to William Blake's aphorism with which this book began: one can always generalize about history; one can always tell it through the stories of kings and queens. But it is only by particularizing, by looking at it from the point of view of the ordinary people, that we begin to see the gradual development of society over time;

how our rights and duties evolved; how the people were actors in their own history from the earliest times. We can see, too, how waves of newcomers have changed us, and renewed us, in our gene pool and in our language and culture. Kibworth is an ordinary place, realistic and down to earth in its social life, but like thousands of other places in England it is a living testimony to the way our communities have crystallized over time; a pointer to the fact that deep-rooted ideas and habits can be transmitted over very long periods, persisting like a current just below the surface of history, unseen but still there none-theless, and still moving things along. Here the historian perhaps can only express a personal response to a year spent in one living and changing English community. There is at the moment an obsession with defining identity, with categorizing and even trying to measure it and teach it. But when we look at history from this perspective, through the eyes of one community over time, then what appears is obvious: that identity doesn't come from the top down at all, it is not genetic, it is not fixed, safe and secure, for it can be reshaped by his-tory and culture; so it is always in the making and never made; but it is the creation of the people themselves.

## 'For ever England'

Let us leave the last word to a villager. In late 1944 the editor of the *Kibworth Forces' Journal*, Leslie Clarke, was trying to catch up with the dramatic developments of the year for his news section: 'Christmas is fast approaching,' he wrote, 'what tricks of time the war plays on us all!' Clarke came from an old village family: by a strange chance, though he can scarcely have been aware of it, one of his ancestors in the seventeenth century had married a daughter of the Polles, who themselves after so many centuries in the village had finally run out of sons. So the story of the village ran in his veins far back in time, to the thirteenth century and beyond. He knew the face of war, having been wounded and captured in the Great War. Generous, public-spirited and self-effacing, he it was who had had the idea for the newspaper and the vision and energy to carry it through, 'trying always', as he put it, 'to convey the spirit of friendship and under-standing'. He had opened the letters page to the men and women on the front and had received comments from many of the three or four hundred young Kibworthians on active service, and from others who had read the paper as it was passed around, whether in Palestine, India or Africa. That winter of 1944, with the Allied march on Berlin now well under way, and victory all but certain, moved by what he read in their 'letters to the editor', his thoughts had turned to the future; about jobs for the young after the war; 'how youth is to be served when youth comes home', when a new, democratic and less class-ridden England would arise. But also, he wrote: 'it is as well for us at times to think backwards as well as to look forward', and he found himself reflecting on the history of the village:

During the past four and a half years I have gained such experience of the life of our village, but more important, I have found where the heart of the village lies. To me Kibworth has always been friendly, but that friendly spirit has never been more generously displayed than it is today . . . I walked through the three Parishes of Beauchamp, Harcourt and Smeeton the other evening. I looked upon them and thought of them. Yes, 'Our Village' (because we really should be one and united), with its houses tucked edge-ways and sideways, looked to me very homelike and very beautiful. For our village – which fought in Flanders, in Greece and Crete, at El Alamein, fought on the sea and under the sea, in the Battle of Britain, in North Africa and Italy, in Normandy and France . . . our grumbling, friendly, warm-hearted, gossip-loving village truly represents with ten thousand others of her kind, that free spirit – true and precious – which is, and will be, for ever England.

# Further Reading

One of the great pleasures of local history is the range of evidence involved, from manorial rolls to photos and diaries from our own time. A Second World War village newspaper or a landgirl's diary is just as informative and delightful as a builder's account from 1448 or a medieval butcher's letter. This bibliography makes no pretence of completeness. These are simply some of the books which I found helpful for both the big and the small pictures. I have not attempted to reference every source or quotation, but it will be obvious that this book is based on the work of many scholars and writers.

First, by way of introduction, an article about the historian whose work shadows this book, W. G. Hoskins: 'Hoskins' England' by Charles Phythian-Adams in the *Transactions of the Leicestershire Archaeological and Historical Society* (*TLAHS*), LXVI (1992); then a fascinating look at the culture of the English provinces: 'An Agenda for English Local History', in *Societies, Cultures and Kinship 1580–1850: Cultural Provinces and English Local History*, edited and with an introduction by Charles Phythian-Adams (1993), an overview of the wealth of English local history published between Lambarde's *Perambulation of Kent* and the present day. On the early searchers, Hoskins's 'Rediscovery of England', in *Provincial England* (1963), is still seminal. His pioneering *The Making of the English Landscape* (1955 and subsequent editions) is a broad introduction to landscape history, to which Francis Pryor's *The Making of the British Landscape* (2010) is a worthy successor. David Stocker, *The East Midlands* (2006), is a handsome and informative addition to the English Heritage England's Landscape series. The early travellers still offer much food for thought, especially Leland's *Itinerary*, ed. L. Toulmin Smith (5 vols., 1964). The great local history of Nichols (1795–1815) is described in my text; it is the predecessor of all later ones down to Hoskins's *Leicestershire* (1957) and Roy Millward's *A History of Leicestershire and Rutland* (1985). The Victoria County History

for Gartree Hundred is available in the British History online website –
an indispensable resource. The English Place Name Society volumes
for the shire, edited by Barrie Cox (4 vols., 1998–2009), came out just
in time to transform this book. I should also mention David Postles's
remarkable book on *The Surnames of Leicestershire and Rutland* (1998),
an invaluable social history of much wider import than the county
and the surnames, on which I have relied for my accounts of Sibil
and Scholastica in chapter 9, along with the stories of the 'brokers'.
G. Farnham's *Leicestershire Medieval Village Notes* (6 vols. 1929–33) provides invaluable transcriptions of key documents.

On village history – and on Kibworth – Hoskins was again the
modern pioneer. It was Frank Attenborough (the Anglo-Saxonist
father of the naturalist David) who brought the Devonian 'Bill'
Hoskins to Leicester University to found the Local History Unit, the
most important in Britain. A flurry of publications in the *TLAHS*
followed in the post-war period and several important books such as
*Essays in Leicestershire History* (1950), *Provincial England* (1963) and
Hoskins's famous study of Wigston, *The Midland Peasant* (1965). *Studies in Leicestershire Agrarian History* (edited by Hoskins in 1949) contains
a most important essay on Kibworth by an alumnus of my old school,
Manchester Grammar School: Rodney Hilton, 'Kibworth Harcourt,
a Merton Manor in the 13th and 14th centuries' (reprinted in his *Class,
Conflict and the Crisis of Feudalism* of 1985). This brilliant essay, following F. M. Maitland's lead but deploying Marxist principles, showed
how the local tale of one place could reveal the workings of great
movements in history. Since then other Merton manors have been
looked at (Paul Harvey on Cuxham, for example, in *A Medieval
Oxfordshire Village*, 1965), but it was Hilton's lead that led Cicely
Howell to write her pathbreaking book, the fundamental work in
this story, *Land, Family and Inheritance in Transition: Kibworth Harcourt
1280–1700*. Cicely Howell's work has been on my mind as a possible
film project almost since it came out in 1983.

Next it is appropriate to mention a few recent studies of medieval
life. One of the earliest and best, Ada Levett's *Studies in Manorial History*
(1938), inspired my film about a medieval villein, *Christina: A Medieval
Life* (2008). More recently there has been a huge amount of work on

medieval peasant society. Hoskins's current successor at Leicester, Christopher Dyer, for example, has produced a grand-sweep social history from 850 to 1520, *Making a Living in the Middle Ages* (2002), as well as *An Age of Transition?* (2005) and many other studies, including *Village, Hamlet and Field*, with C. Lewis and P. Fox (2001). An important aspect of all this is women's history: here I should mention Henrietta Leyser, *Medieval Women* (1995); Marjorie Keniston McIntosh, *Working Women in English Society 1300–1620* (2005); *Women in Medieval English Society,* ed. P. J. P. Goldberg (1997); Cordelia Beattie, *Medieval Single Women* (2007); and a pioneering life of one woman, Judith Bennett's *A Medieval Life* (1998).

The medieval sources for Kibworth are extraordinarily rich but how could one construct a narrative before that time? Here are a few pointers. On the pre-Conquest period in general, see my bibliography in *Domesday* (1986 and later editions). On DNA, see Stephen Oppenheimer, *The Origins of the British* (2006); David Miles, *The Tribes of Britain* (2005), is an amazing piece of synthesis. On the Roman period, a new introduction is David Mattingly, *An Imperial Possession: Britain in the Roman Empire* (2006). On the Anglo-Saxons, the best general guide is *The Blackwell Encyclopaedia of Anglo-Saxon England*, eds. Michael Lapidge and others (1999). On the coming of Christianity and attitudes to life, death and the afterlife, a new look is provided by Marilyn Dunn in *The Christianization of the Anglo-Saxons c.597–c.700* (2009).

Mercia is still poorly served, but for a good introduction see M. Brown and C. Farr, *Mercia: An Anglo-Saxon Kingdom in Europe* (2001). There are useful discussions of Mercian origins in *The Origins of Anglo-Saxon Kingdoms*, ed. S. R. Bassett (1989). The Staffordshire hoard has created a huge amount of discussion online but in print see the British Museum publication by Kevin Leahy and Roger Bland, *The Staffordshire Hoard* (2009).

On the Church, the fundamental introduction is John Blair, *The Church in Anglo-Saxon Society* (2005); on holy men and women, Graham Jones, *Saints in the Landscape* (2007). On early English law, there is Patrick Wormald's formidable *The Making of English Law* (1999). For the later Old English period see M. Lapidge and S. Keynes, *Alfred the Great* (1983), and *English Historical Documents*, ed. D. Whitelock (1979). On the Vikings, see D. Hadley, *The Vikings in England* (2006), and P. Stafford, *The East*

*Midlands in the Early Middle Ages* (1985). On the Kingdom of the English in the tenth century see my *In Search of England* (1999) and *Domesday* (1986). On the revolution of the 930s, see my recent essay in *Lay Intellectuals in the Carolingian World*, eds. Patrick Wormald and Janet L. Nelson (2007).

Domesday Book is available county by county in Phillimore editions; see also *The Norman Conquest of Leicestershire and Rutland*, ed. C. Phythian-Adams (1986). R. W. H. Erskine and Ann Williams (eds.), *The Story of Domesday Book* (2003), is a very useful guide; see also my *Domesday*. The Leicestershire Survey of 1130 has been edited by C. F. Slade (1956). For a masterly broad narrative of the period, see D. Carpenter, *The Struggle for Mastery* (2003). On the Barons' War, see J. R. Maddicott, *Simon de Montfort* (1994), and, specifically on the final battle, D. C. Cox, *The Battle of Evesham* (1988). On the Peatling Magna incident, see D. Carpenter, *The Reign of King Henry* III (1996), and my essay in *In Search of England* together with the references there. On the Hundred Rolls, see Sandra Raban, *A Second Domesday?* (2004); the manuscript of the lost Leicestershire Hundred Rolls is an eighteenth-century copy of Burton's notes: Bodleian Library, Rawlinson B 350. On English language and identity, see Thorlac Turville-Petre, *England the Nation* (1996). The fundamental book on literacy is M. Clanchy, *From Memory to Written Record* (1979 and later editions). On education, see Nicholas Orme, *Medieval Schools: From Roman Britain to Tudor England* (2006).

On Kibworth school and the school box, now being catalogued at Wigston, see Bernard Elliott, *A History of Kibworth Beauchamp Grammar School* (1957). For references to other early materials touching on Kibworth people's land grants, guild records, tallage lists and coroners' rolls, consult F. M. Stenton, *Documents Illustrative of the Social and Economic History of the Danelaw* (1920); *Borough Records of Leicester,* ed. M. Bateson (6 vols., 1899); and A. H. Thomson, *Calendar of Charters and Other Documents Belonging to the Hospital of William Wyggeston at Leicester* (1933). On the free peasantry generally in the East Midlands in the Norman period, see F. M. Stenton, *The Free Peasantry of the Northern Danelaw* (1969), and my *Domesday* (1986). On the famine, see W. C. Jordan, *The Great Famine* (1996), and Ian Kershaw, 'The Great Famine and Agrarian Crisis in England, 1315–22', in R. H. Hilton, *Peasants, Knights and Heretics* (1976). For overview essays of great value see *A Social History of England 1200–1500,* eds. R. Horrox and W. M. Ormrod (2006).

There are a number of sources for the manor and the open fields. See especially Mark Bailey's *The English Manor* (2002) and *Medieval Society and the Manor Court,* eds. Zvi Razi and Richard Smith (1996). For details on the open fields see C. S. and C. S. Orwin, *The Open Fields* (1938 and later editions but the earliest is best as it contains documents and maps); see too John Beckett, *A History of Laxton* (1989). On weather data I have used Derek Stern's book on one farm, *A Hertford Demesne of Westminster Abbey* (1999). Michelle Brown, *The World of the Luttrell Psalter* (2006), is a typically nuanced exploration. Roy Brigden, *Ploughs and Ploughing* (2003), is part of a very useful Shire publications series on rural labour. On ploughmen and their culture generally, see Michael Camille, *A Mirror in Parchment* (1998).

On medieval historical and political poetry, *Historical Poems of the XIVth and XVth Centuries,* ed. R. H. Robbins (1959), is still indispensable, as are Thomas Wright, *Political Songs of England,* ed. P. Coss (1996); R. T. Davies's anthology *Medieval English Lyrics* (1963); and *Early Middle English Texts,* eds. B. Dickins and R. M. Wilson (rev. edn 1956).

The best overview of the Black Death is Ole J. Benedictow, *The Black Death 1346–1353* (2004). John Hatcher, *The Black Death: An Intimate History* (2008), is a vivid account at grass-roots level. *The Peasants' Revolt of 1381,* ed. R. B. Dobson (2nd edn 1983), is the best collection of sources on the subject. The peasants' use of writing is a great issue in the pioneering study of Steven Justice, *Writing and Rebellion* (1994); two important recent studies on the subject are Wendy Scase, *Literature and Complaint in England, 1272–1553* (2007), and Andrew Cole, *Literature and Heresy in the Age of Chaucer* (2008).

An incredible wealth of material has emerged on the Lollards in the last fifty years. The Lollard Society is online, and classic older accounts have been superseded by Anne Hudson's *The Premature Reformation* (1988) and *Lollards and Their Books* (1985). Margaret Aston, 'Lollardy and Sedition', is an important essay in *Peasants, Knights and Heretics,* ed. R. H. Hilton (1976). J. Crompton, *Leicestershire Lollards,* in *TLAHS* (1968–9) is the key local study. For the Merton links I am indebted to Maureen Jurkowski, 'Heresy and Factionalism at Merton College in the Early Fifteenth Century', in the *Journal of Ecclesiastical History* (vol. 48, 1997), and to her many other articles. Richard Rex, *The Lollards* (2002), is a new look. For pointers towards the aftermath and possible continuities, see *The World of Rural Dissenters, 1520–1725*, ed. M. Spufford (1995).

Susan Brigden, *New Worlds, Lost Worlds* (2000), offers a general history of the Tudor period. Eamon Duffy, *The Stripping of the Altars* (1992), is a grand-sweep narrative of the Reformation. For a close-up view see his *The Voices of Morebath* (2001). On mentalities, see Keith Thomas, *Religion and the Decline of Magic* (1971), and *Man and the Natural World* (1983).

For Kibworth, Cicely Howell's book is rich on family histories through this period, but the history of the Reformation in the village is yet to be told, and I am conscious that my account is no more than a brief sketch. The Tudor wills cited in my text are all published here for the first time and were transcribed by Pat Grundy from original manuscripts in the Leicestershire Record Office in Wigston, and I must express my gratitude to Robin Jenkins for permitting their publication here. A catalogue of the astounding number of Tudor and Stuart wills from Leicestershire is available in Wigston. For interpretation of such data, the many books of David Cressy are a good start, for example *Birth, Marriage and Death: Ritual, Religion and the Life Cycle in Tudor and Stuart England* (1997). On the theory of the growth of capitalism see Alan Macfarlane, *Marriage and Love in England 1300–1840* (1986), and his classic *The Origins of English Individualism*. See also Lawrence Stone, *The Family, Sex and Marriage in England 1500–1800* (1977).

Among many books on the Civil War are Brian Manning, *The English People and the English Revolution* (1976); David Underdown, *Fire From Heaven* (1992) and *A Freeborn People* (1996); and D. E. Kennedy, *The English Revolution* (2000). On the radical movements out of which, for example, the Quakers came, see Christopher Hill's essay on George Fox in *The Experience of Defeat* (1984) and also *The World Turned Upside Down* (1972). *The Beginnings of Quakerism* is the classic account by William C. Braithwaite (rev. edn 1955); see too Adrian

Davies, *The Quakers in English Society 1655–1725* (2000). Nonconformity (so strong in Kibworth) is a very rich seam: see Michael Mullett, *Sources for the History of English Nonconformity 1660–1830* (1991), for the British Records Association. Also useful are the Society of Genealogists' guides, especially on religious groups such as Presbyterians, Baptists, Methodists and Jews in Britain. David Clifford, *My Ancestors were Congregationalists* (rev. edn 1997), is a very useful reference work on the local communities. Kibworth Methodist Church has published a useful booklet on the history of dissenting congregations in the area: Eileen Bromley, *Kibworth Methodist Church: A Celebration* (1996). Much anticipated is a forthcoming study of the Kibworth Academy by David Wykes, the curator of the Dr Williams Library in the Centre for Dissenting Studies, London.

In the Industrial Age we leave Cicely Howell's work behind. For a broad picture the classic is E. P. Thompson, *The Making of the English Working Class* (rev. edn 1968), which is very concerned with the textile industries of the East Midlands and framework knitting in Leicestershire. On this the old histories are by Felkin (1867) and Henson (1831); a modern guide is Marilyn Palmer, *Framework Knitting* (2002), but see too Richard Rutt, *A History of Hand Knitting* (1987). Jess Jenkins has written a vivid account of the knitters in the Kibworth area: *Honest Men But Destitute: The Plight of Leicestershire's Framework Knitters in the 1840s* (2005); see too D. Smith, *Industrial Archaeology of the East Midlands* (1965). On enclosure, see W. G. Hoskins, *Studies in Leicestershire Agrarian History* (1949), and on roads, Arthur Cossens, *The Turnpike Roads of Leicestershire and Rutland* (2003).

For the Victorian world, nineteenth-century Kibworth like most places in the UK has a very rich archive of standard government sources, censuses, Poor Laws, crime records, education Acts, and so on, some of which are being published by the Kibworth History Society, as are more recent memoirs such as those of G. Ringrose and Rose Holyoak which are quoted in this book. Jess Jenkins's work on local suffragettes, which I have gratefully used, is forthcoming in the *TLAHS*.

For both broad sweep and intimate detail on the modern period see Peter Hennessy, *Never Again: Britain 1945–51* (1992), and *Having It*

*So Good: Britain in the 1950s* (2006). David Kynaston, *Austerity Britain 1945–51* (2007), and Brian Harrison, *Finding a Role? The United Kingdom 1970–1990*, are models by great modern practitioners for how to write the history of our own times.

A brief word on the huge amount of information now on the internet. A very useful site for the local historian is A2A, which connects with the National Archives website: simply key in the name of your place and all catalogued documents in local and national archives will be listed. The National Archives itself is a great resource; from national censuses to military service records, a huge amount of raw data of our ancestors' lives is now available to the general researcher. The British Library also has a great online arm now. The PASE website references every named person who lived pre-Conquest in England; the Anglo-Saxon charters website has all pre-Conquest land documents with full bibliography and references to translations where available. Local archives and County Record Offices like Wigston all have their own websites, as do many villages. Kibworth's own website connects to the very useful *Kibworth Chronicle* site, which has many articles and features, including the autobiography of the redoubtable Edmund Knox.

Finally, a separate note is in order on the most important Merton manuscripts consulted here (and a special thanks here to Cicely Howell for her advice and for her transcripts of most of the key ones). Walter of Merton's purchase of the village is in MM 2877; Saer's debts to a Jewish moneylender – written in Hebrew – are in MM 2884; the first survey of c.1280 is in MM 6371; the statement of peasants' dues is in MM 6370; the eight acres of Richard the parson is in MM 2928; in MM 6368 is a bundle of materials including the field strips described *ex parte solis*; the Black Death 1349 roll is in MM 6405; the 1361 plague list is in MM 6372; John Pychard's letter is in MM 3344; the poor scholars of Kibworth are in e.g. MM 3622; the Polle family pedigrees are in MM 6365 and MM 6464; the building accounts for 'Brown's Place' are in MM 6324 and 6465; the 1447 Court of Recognition after the rent strike is in MM 6415.2, 6425.1; the inquiry into Nick Sibil's land and the succession of young John Sibil during the great famine is in MM 6219. For a list of other key manuscripts relating to families followed in this book, plus a full transcript of Pychard's letter, see Cicely Howell's book. On Merton and the Lollards, special thanks to Maureen Jurkowski: for Hulman going north on college business, see MM 3712; the activities of Gamalgay and associates are in MM 3720, MM 6278–80; taking monies from the village is in MM 6285; for Stoneham's visits to Kibworth (the friend of the lawyer Ralph Strode, Chaucer's friend), see MM 3718; on the link between Brown and the Dexters, see MM 6281; on the Gilberts, see MM 6276, 6277, 6280.

# Index